The Scope of Social Psychology

Social psychology attempts to understand, explain, predict, and, when needed, change people's thoughts, feelings, and behaviours. It is an awe-inspiring task; yet for a relatively young discipline it has made great strides. Although many of the major pioneers such as Lewin, Asch, Kelley, and Festinger worked in the period around the 1940s and 1950s, social psychology matured only at the end of the 1960s. Since then it has blossomed, both in investigating the basics of the discipline and in applying the insights from fundamental social psychology to different fields related to the area. This volume is devoted to the development of understanding in the field of social psychology over the last four decades, focusing on both basic and applied social psychology.

Contributions are gathered under five main areas: attitudes and attitude change; social cognition and emotion; interpersonal and group processes; health behaviour; and bereavement and coping. These five domains not only illustrate the scope of social psychology, but also pay tribute to one of the key figures in modern social psychology, Wolfgang Stroebe. He has, remarkably, made significant contributions across all five of these areas, and his research achievements exemplify the progress, prospects, and problems faced by modern social psychology over the last 40 years.

This volume includes contributions from some of the most distinguished names in the field, and all authors provide an overview or critical look at their specific area of expertise, tracing historical developments where appropriate. *The Scope of Social Psychology* provides a broad-ranging, illustrative review of the field of modern social psychology.

Miles Hewstone is Professor of Social Psychology and Fellow of New College, University of Oxford. He has published widely on the topics of attribution theory, social cognition, stereotyping, and intergroup relations. He is co-founding editor of the *European Review of Social Psychology*, and a former editor of the *British Journal of Social Psychology*.

Henk A. W. Schut is Assistant Professor in the Department of Clinical Psychology at Utrecht University, where he also earned his PhD. His research interests cover the processes of coping with loss, (the efficacy of) grief therapy, and the counselling of bereaved persons. He has co-authored several books and a large number of articles on grief and bereavement.

John B. F. de Wit is Associate Professor in Social Psychology of Health at Utrecht University. His past research focused on social-cognition models of health behaviour, and included work in attitude and behaviour change through the use of fear appeals and risk communication. His recent work is concerned with functional aspects of goal-setting and volitional processes in goal striving that are subsumed under a self-regulation perspective on health behaviour.

Kees van den Bos is Professor of Social Psychology at Utrecht University. His research interests focus on the psychology of fairness judgements and how people react to events they consider fair or unfair. His other research interests include uncertainty, social cognition, the psychology of religion and cultural worldviews, human decision making, and organisational behaviour.

Margaret S. Stroebe is Associate Professor in the Department of Clinical Psychology at Utrecht University. She received her PhD from the University of Bristol in cross-cultural psychology. Her major research interest is the study of reactions to interpersonal loss, particularly bereavement, focusing on theoretical approaches to grief and grieving, interactive patterns of coping, and the efficacy of bereavement intervention.

The Scope of Social Psychology
Theory and applications

Essays in honour of Wolfgang Stroebe

**Edited by Miles Hewstone,
Henk A. W. Schut, John B. F. de Wit,
Kees van den Bos, and Margaret S. Stroebe**

Psychology Press
Taylor & Francis Group
HOVE AND NEW YORK

First published 2007 by Psychology Press,
27 Church Road, Hove, East Sussex, BN3 2FA

Simultaneously published in the USA and Canada
by Psychology Press
270 Madison Avenue, New York, NY 10016

*Psychology Press is an imprint of the Taylor & Francis Group, an informa
business*

© 2007 Psychology Press.

Typeset in Times by RefineCatch Limited, Bungay, Suffolk
Printed and bound in Great Britain by
TJ International Ltd, Padstow, Cornwall
Cover design by Lisa Dynan

British Library Cataloguing in Publication Data
A catalogue record for this book is available from the British Library

Library of Congress Cataloging in Publication Data
A catalog record has been requested

ISBN10: 1–84169–645–5

ISBN13: 978–1–84169–645–4

Contents

Contributors

Georgios Abakoumkin, University of Thessaly, Volos, Greece

Icek Ajzen, University of Massachusetts—Amherst, USA

Arnold B. Bakker, Utrecht University, The Netherlands

Enny Das, Free University—Amsterdam, The Netherlands

Natascha de Hoog, Friedrich Schiller University, Jena, Germany

Evangelia Demerouti, Utrecht University, The Netherlands

John B. F. de Wit, Utrecht University, The Netherlands

Alice H. Eagly, Northwestern University, USA

J. Richard Eiser, University of Sheffield, UK

Martin C. Euwema, Utrecht University, The Netherlands

Susan Folkman, Osher Center for Integrative Medicine, University of California—San Francisco, USA

Kenneth Gergen, Swarthmore College, Swarthmore, PA, USA

Mary Gergen, Penn State University, Media, PA, USA

David L. Hamilton, University of California, Santa Barbara, USA

Robert Hansson, University of Tulsa, Tulsa, USA

Miles Hewstone, Oxford University, UK

Lizet Hoekert, Utrecht University, The Netherlands

Chester A. Insko, University of North Carolina, USA

Klaus Jonas, University of Zürich, Switzerland

Arie W. Kruglanski, University of Maryland, USA

John M. Levine, University of Pittsburgh, USA

Hein Lodewijkx, Open University, The Netherlands

Antony S. R. Manstead, Cardiff University, UK

Judith Tedlie Moskowitz, Osher Center for Integrative Medicine, University of California—San Francisco, USA

Bernard A. Nijstad, University of Amsterdam, The Netherlands

Karl-Dieter Opp, University of Leipzig, Germany

James W. Pennebaker, The University of Texas at Austin, USA

Jaap Rabbie, Utrecht University, The Netherlands

Bernard Rimé, University of Louvain, Louvain-la-Neuve, Belgium

Wilmar B. Schaufeli, Utrecht University, The Netherlands

Henk A. W. Schut, Utrecht University, The Netherlands

Norbert Schwarz, University of Michigan, USA

Gün Semin, Free University Amsterdam, The Netherlands

Russell Spears, Cardiff University, UK

Fritz Strack, Universität Würzburg, Germany

Lloyd H. Strickland, Carleton University, Ottawa, Canada

Katherine Stroebe, Leiden University, The Netherlands

Margaret S. Stroebe, Utrecht University, The Netherlands

Kees van den Bos, Utrecht University, The Netherlands

Rein van der Vegt, Utrecht University, The Netherlands

Robert S. Weiss, University of Massachusetts, Boston, USA

Scott T. Wolf, University of North Carolina, USA

Emmanuelle Zech, University of Louvain, Louvain-la-Neuve, Belgium

René Ziegler, University of Tübingen, Germany

Preface

Social psychology is the scientific study of how personal, situational, and societal factors influence the cognition, motivation, and behaviour of individuals and (members of) social groups. It ranges from intra-personal processes (e.g., attitudinal information processing), to interpersonal relations (e.g., close relationships), to intergroup relations (e.g., ethnic prejudice and stereotyping), and societal analyses (e.g., the beliefs shared by large numbers of people within a society). Alongside other disciplines, such as sociology, political science, and economics, social psychology has sculpted itself a unique perspective on and contribution to the behavioural sciences, the subjective view of the individual in a social context.

If the breadth of this approach were not ambitious enough, social psychology is above all theoretically driven; we refer with disdain to mere findings (in the absence of theory) as "dust-bowl empiricism". Social psychology strives to predict and explain, not merely detect and report. Increasingly, this theory building is supported by a range of ever more powerful methodological tools, including the methods used to study implicit, unconscious beliefs, and the powerful statistical techniques used to test theories (e.g., distinguishing mediation from moderation, structural equation modelling, and meta-analysis).

This volume highlights what we have learned in the four decades since the 1960s, a time when social psychology was maturing into an established science. It does so by focusing on both basic and applied social psychology, and to this end we have gathered together contributions under five main headings, three more basic, and two more applied: attitudes and attitude change; social cognition and emotion; interpersonal and group processes; health behaviour; and bereavement and coping. A final section places psychological theory and research in context.

We have chosen these five domains not only to elucidate basic and more applied processes, nor merely to illustrate "the scope of social psychology", but also because, with this volume, we wish to honour Wolfgang Stroebe, one of the key figures in modern social psychology. He has, remarkably, made significant contributions across *all five* of these areas. Such eclecticism is distinguished in itself, but so are his contributions; they have been characterised by theoretical innovation and clarity, and methodological rigour and sophistication. Wolfgang's research achievements exemplify the progress, prospects, and problems faced by modern social psychology in the last 40 years, and we dedicate this volume to him, in appreciation of the multitude and impact of his past contributions, and in the hope and expectation that he will continue to be involved in developments for many years to come.

One final note. Preparing this volume, in honour of a friend and colleague—and for one of us, at least, spouse—whom we hold in the greatest esteem has been no editorial labour in the usual sense. It has been, first, a pleasure, and second, the work of a team of equals. The only disagreement in editing this book has been with respect to the order of editors. And whereas members of some teams quarrel among themselves to get the individual selves placed higher, we could only agree on a final order of editors by the Utrecht majority oppressing the Oxford minority, who accepted strictly on the basis of *primus inter pares*. This volume is, then, very much the outcome of five equal labours. The editors wish to thank Professor Willem Koops, Dean of the Faculty of Social Sciences at Utrecht University for his enthusiastic support of this project.

Miles Hewstone
Henk A. W. Schut
John B. F. de Wit
Kees van den Bos
Margaret S. Stroebe

Wolfgang Stroebe

1 On the scope of social psychology

An introduction

Kees van den Bos
Utrecht University, The Netherlands

Miles Hewstone
Oxford University, UK

Henk A. W. Schut, John B. F. de Wit, and Margaret S. Stroebe
Utrecht University, The Netherlands

When you think about it for only a minute or so, you realise that trying to understand, explain, predict and, when needed, change people's thoughts, feelings, and behaviours is an awe-inspiring task. For example, we know that people often have little insight into their own thinking processes (e.g., Nisbett & Wilson, 1977), let alone the thoughts and cognitive processes of others (see also Nisbett & Ross, 1980). The same difficulties arise with people's affective feelings (e.g., Schwarz & Clore, 1983). Furthermore, and perhaps most difficult of all, explaining and predicting social behaviour may be among the most difficult things people can aspire to (e.g., Snyder & Cantor, 1998). Yet it is precisely the explanation and prediction of cognition, affect, and behaviour that social psychologists set out to achieve.

Since its founding days, the field of social psychology has flourished (for an overview, see, e.g., Jones, 1998). One well-known era that has been very important for our field was the period around the 1940s and 1950s, when people like Kurt Lewin (1935), Solomon Asch (1946, 1951), John Thibaut (1950; Thibaut & Kelley, 1959), and Leon Festinger (1954, 1957) formulated their groundbreaking theories and conducted their pioneering research studies. Yet, notwithstanding the crucial impact of this "golden" period, it could well be stated that social psychology matured only at the end of the 1960s. After all, it was around that time that social psychology moved into its next phase. Young people had been trained then by the pioneers of the field and went on to become key figures in what turned out to be the exciting modern science of social psychology. Meticulous theories and conceptual refinements were formulated and precise methodological tools were invented which could be used to test the hypotheses that followed from the theoretical models proposed.

As a result, since the end of the 1960s social psychology has blossomed, both in investigating the basics of the discipline and in applying the insights from fundamental social psychology to different fields related to the area. This book is devoted to what the field of social psychology has learned in the last four decades, focusing on both basic and applied social psychology. In doing so, we want to honour one of the key figures in modern social psychology: Wolfgang Stroebe.

The reason why we highlight Wolfgang Stroebe here is not so much his official retirement in May–June 2006. After all, knowing Wolfgang, and knowing his position as Fellow at the Utrecht University College, we are quite confident that he will remain very active as a researcher in both the basic and applied domains of our field. The main reasons why we emphasise Wolfgang's research are three-fold. First, his exceptional work is representative of the development of modern social psychology in the last 40 years. Second, he is one of those very rare individuals whose contributions have been made in the domains of both basic and applied social psychology. Third, in an era of ever-increasing specialisation (where academics are stereotyped as those who know "more and more, about less and less"), Wolfgang Stroebe's career contributions have been characterised by extraordinary eclecticism. He has contributed hugely to theory and research on attitudes and attitude change, social cognition and emotions, interpersonal and group processes, health behaviour and related changes, and bereavement and coping. Thus we have chosen these five areas as the constitutive sections of this volume. The scope of the chapters contained in this volume reflects Wolfgang's *and* social psychology's broad theoretical and research interests. As a result, the volume is designed to provide the reader a broad-ranging, illustrative review of the field of modern social psychology.

The chapters that make up this volume are written by experts in their fields. All authors provide an overview or critical look at their specific area of expertise, and they trace historical developments where appropriate. As the title of the book illustrates, the aim of the chapters taken together was to address the interface of theory and application. More specifically, three sections of the present volume focus on the basics of social psychology: Section 1 focuses on attitudes and attitude change, Section 2 on social cognition and emotion, and Section 3 on interpersonal and group processes. Chapters in these three sections focus on basic social-psychological processes and note important implications of the various lines of research reviewed. The next three sections also use basic social psychology as their starting point but then go on to focus more on applying the insights that follow from basic social psychology. Specifically, Section 4 focuses on health behaviour and conditions that lead to changes in health behaviour, Section 5 discusses theories and studies pertaining to bereavement and coping, and Section 6 places psychological theory and research in context. The book closes with an epilogue from various other observers of Wolfgang Stroebe's university activities. We now provide a brief overview of the various chapters in Sections 1–6, after which we will make some closing comments.

Section 1: Attitudes and attitude change

In the first chapter in the section on attitudes and attitude change, Richard Eiser reviews research on how individuals make evaluative judgements about objects, people, and events in ways that enable them to remain feeling generally positive about themselves and the decisions they make. This theme is examined in relation to the fields of attitudinal judgement, attitude maintenance, self-positivity, attitude learning, attitudes and decisions, and risk, trust, and social judgement.

In the next chapter, Klaus Jonas and René Ziegler focus on the issue of attitudinal ambivalence, which may result from evaluating attitude objects as both positive and negative simultaneously. The chapter discusses definitional aspects pertaining to ambivalence and different forms of attitudinal ambivalence as well as different ways of measuring the concept. The authors then review research on attitudinal ambivalence as a moderator of the attitude–behaviour relationship, showing the theoretical and applied implications of this work as well as the interrelationship between different moderating effects of ambivalence. The enhanced insight this gives into attitudes, attitude change, and the attitude–behaviour relationship is discussed, as well as additional facets of research on attitudinal ambivalence. The chapter ends by drawing conclusions and sketching lines of future research on attitudinal ambivalence.

Icek Ajzen and Antony Manstead use the theory of planned behaviour as an approach to change health-related behaviours. Introduced as an extension of the theory of reasoned action, this approach can not only predict intentions and behaviour quite accurately, it can also provide useful information about the behavioural, normative, and control considerations that influence adherence or non-adherence to recommended health practices. Many attempts to identify antecedents of health-related lifestyles focus on broad personal, demographic, and environmental factors. The theory of planned behaviour considers such factors as background variables that only influence health behaviour indirectly through their influence on more proximal factors that are directly linked to the behaviour of interest. The authors are also careful to note some important theoretical and applied limitations their approach may have, and specify the relevance of their model for health education campaigns and effective interventions.

Alice Eagly, in her chapter on the effects of defensive processing on attitudinal phenomena, comments on motivational analyses of attitudes and examines efforts to develop theory pertaining to defensive processes. Motivational themes have long been prominent in attitude theory and research. Among the most important and enduring of these themes is the idea that attitudes reflect motives to defend values and other positive states. This principle has emerged repeatedly in research on persuasion and attitudinal selectivity, and predictions based on it have enjoyed some success. After reflecting on these motivational analyses, Alice Eagly focuses on the concepts of value-relevant involvement as well as defence motivation as two important models of self-defensive processes. She also discusses applications of these concepts in research on attitudinal selectivity and persuasion.

Section 2: Social cognition and emotion

The section on social cognition and emotion begins with a chapter by David Hamilton and Miles Hewstone. These two authors review 35 years of theory and research on how people perceive groups. A noteworthy aspect of social psychology's long history of interest in group perception is that in the past three decades work on group perception has evolved and elaborated from a singular focus on the stereotypic associations for various groups into a multi-faceted analysis of various aspects of how groups are perceived. Similarly, conceptual understanding of intergroup relations, particularly the implications of intergroup contact for changing stereotypic beliefs and prejudicial attitudes, has advanced to more sophisticated analyses of how and why rather than simply when. In this chapter, the authors review these developments and highlight how this furthers insight into the dynamics of group perception and intergroup relations.

Arie Kruglanski and Gün Semin provide an original integration of two erstwhile separate domains, lay epistemology and the linguistic category model, to consider epistemic bases of interpersonal communication. Building on the notion that the essential function of communication is the exchange of some kind of knowledge, the chapter reviews evidence that the process of such conveyance is significantly influenced by communicators' epistemic motivations. That is, such motivations may determine the perspective that communicators may adopt, and may influence the level of linguistic abstraction at which communicators couch their messages. The chapter introduces the reader to the concept of epistemic motivations and reviews the specific theory and evidence that link such motivations to various communicative effects.

Norbert Schwarz and Fritz Strack, in their chapter on life satisfaction, consider what cognitive social psychology may contribute to a better understanding of the processes that cause people to think of themselves as happy or satisfied with their life in general. In doing so, these authors offer some tangible advice on how people should and should not think about their lives. Life-events play an important role in judgements of happiness and life-satisfaction. Yet their impact does not follow the simple assumption that good events will make people happy. Instead, the same event can increase as well as decrease life-satisfaction, depending on how people think about it. In their chapter, Schwarz and Strack consider the role of what comes to mind, how easily it comes to mind, and how it is used, as well as the impact of positive or negative feelings that a memory may elicit. The underlying processes are systematic and the reviewed results reliably replicable, provided that properly controlled experimental conditions channel how people think about their lives. In the absence of controlled conditions or controlled research methods, however, different people choose different judgement strategies, resulting in a wide variety of different outcomes.

Section 3: Interpersonal and group processes

Chester Insko and Scott Wolf open the section on interpersonal and group processes by discussing factors pertaining to the tendency for relations between groups to be more competitive and less cooperative than relations between individuals. The authors review findings of a meta-analysis, showing that this interindividual–intergroup discontinuity effect is descriptively large. As a result, understanding the circumstances in which this effect occurs is of obvious social significance. The chapter goes on to focus on three situational variables that impact the generality of the effect: (1) the correspondence of outcomes, (2) the joint control of outcomes, and (3) social support for the competitive choice. Findings are reviewed that show the importance of these variables as well as the need to be specific about the types of social situations and types of games in which these variables are studied.

In their chapter, Bernard Nijstad and John Levine argue that in order to understand group creativity, one needs to consider the different stages of creative problem solving. The authors discuss three stages of the creative process: (1) identifying and defining the problem, (2) generating solutions to the problem, and (3) choosing the best idea and then developing and implementing it. Group creativity, the authors propose, occurs if people collaborate in at least one of these stages and if the final product would not have been possible without that collaboration. One major conclusion to be drawn from the chapter's overview of the stages of creative group problem solving is that greater research effort should focus on the question of *when* it is useful to have input from other group members, rather than on the question of *whether* such input is useful. Furthermore, new group members can make useful contributions in all three stages of the creative process reviewed in this chapter.

Katherine Stroebe, Russell Spears, and Hein Lodewijkx contrast and integrate social identity and interdependence approaches as they pertain to intergroup discrimination in the minimal group paradigm. The authors argue that both approaches can help to explain intergroup discrimination in this paradigm and that it can be fruitful to consider them jointly. After reviewing the history of the social identity and interdependence approaches, studies are discussed that propose an integration of these approaches. Building on these integrative studies, a theoretical framework is proposed. This framework accounts for both social identity and interdependence processes, and determines factors that affect the relative strength of each process in a given context. In this way, the authors try to show that a joint approach may provide interesting theoretical avenues in future research on intergroup discrimination in the minimal group paradigm.

Section 4: Health behaviour and health behaviour change

This section begins with the chapter by Susan Folkman and Judith Moskowitz who make a strong case that positive affect occurs during stressful situations that are chronic, and that there is good reason to believe that the presence of positive affect over time can influence health, independent of negative affect. The authors review developments in psychologists' understanding of meaning-focused coping processes that play a major role in the regulation of positive affect, especially in chronically stressful situations where favourable outcomes are not readily available. Feedback loops are proposed through which both positive affect and meaning-focused coping can restore coping resources and motivate coping effort over the long term. In this way, this pioneering chapter tries to further work that will help elaborate insights into the role of positive emotions in enabling individuals to maintain well-being under highly stressful circumstances.

In the chapter by John de Wit, Enny Das, and Natascha de Hoog, the authors focus on the important role of beliefs regarding personal risk or vulnerability in understanding health-related behaviours and promoting change. In particular, the biased nature of these perceptions and subsequent information processing is addressed. Classic social-psychological theories of health and social behaviour have mostly been based on the assumption that health behaviour is guided by rational deliberation and cognitive processing of information. By contrast, more recent perspectives emphasise the interplay of affect and cognition in predicting persuasion. The complex dynamics between emotions and thoughts pertaining to health behaviour and health behaviour change constitute the main focus of this chapter. An important part of the chapter is devoted to theory and research regarding the efficacy of communication strategies to promote awareness and acceptance of a personal health threat. This overview features novel theoretical conceptualisations of health threat communication that see persuasion as resulting from the biased processing of information, and helps to synthesise extant theory and research.

Arnold Bakker, Wilmar Schaufeli, Evangelia Demerouti, and Martin Euwema present an organisational and social-psychological perspective on burnout and work engagement. After defining both burnout and work engagement, these authors discuss the central premises of their job demands–resources model, a psychological model that integrates previous organisational research on burnout and work engagement. The authors then argue that because burnout and work engagement affect employees in social contexts, it is important to study these phenomena using a social-psychological approach. In adopting such an approach, the authors argue that burnout and work engagement may transfer from employees to others in their social environment such as colleagues, supervisors, and intimate partners. The chapter closes with avenues for future research and a discussion of practical implications.

Section 5: Bereavement and coping

In the first chapter of this section, Robert Weiss reflects on a classic study in the literature on bereavement and coping, showing that while having supportive friends effectively ameliorates the distress associated with social isolation of widows and widowers, these factors do little to reduce the loneliness associated with marital loss (Stroebe, Stroebe, & Abakoumkin, 1996). Specifically, Weiss offers a theoretical and empirical context for these findings. The theoretical context stems from the work of Bowlby and includes an extension of this work to include a concern for community relationships and also a theory of loneliness. The empirical context includes efforts to establish that the emotional partnership of a marriage and the linkages to others that can be categorised under the heading of relationships of community make different provisions to individual well-being. It also includes efforts to establish that the loneliness that is associated with the absence of a marriage or similar relationship is different from the loneliness that is associated with the absence of relationships of community. Implications and future avenues for research are discussed.

The chapter by Georgios Abakoumkin, Kenneth Gergen, Mary Gergen, Robert Hansson, Henk Schut, and Margaret Stroebe has been inspired by work of Wolfgang Stroebe and his colleagues (e.g., Stroebe, Schut, & Stroebe, 2005). Building on this work, Abakoumkin et al. document the development of scientific research on bereavement across several decades. This review includes a description of how the bereavement research started and how the literature developed, and considers what future lines of research probably will be, or need to be. Fundamental questions asked are whether death of a loved one causes death of the remaining spouse; who participates in bereavement research; whether helping in the bereavement process really helps; and whether there is support for the notion that people have to do their grief work in order to come to terms with their loss. Within each main area of bereavement research, stringent empirical tests suggest that there is no sound empirical evidence that emotional disclosure facilitates adjustment to loss in *normal* bereavement (Stroebe et al., 2005). It simply takes time to heal from the loss of a loved one and precious little can be done to speed up the process. The implications of this conclusion for both bereavement researchers and popular media and counsellors are discussed.

The chapter by Emmanuelle Zech, Bernard Rimé, and Jamie Pennebaker closes the section on bereavement and coping. Following the Abakoumkin chapter, this chapter has been inspired by work of Wolfgang Stroebe and his colleagues—research that has debunked simple models of people's grief reactions and suggests that no interventions seem to work for most people in reducing the pain of bereavement (e.g., Stroebe et al., 2005). Zech et al. point out that these conclusions are both distressing and raise new challenges for the next generation of bereavement researchers. Furthermore, the strength of the research by Stroebe and colleagues has been in pointing to the shortcomings of many of the basic assumptions most of us hold about death and loss. Through carefully controlled real-world studies, they have repeatedly demonstrated the difficulty of modifying grief reactions. In short, Stroebe et al. highlighted the fact that understanding human reactions to bereavement is more complex than previously proposed: Specific sharing interactions should work for specific individuals at a precise point in time of their grieving process. The chapter by Zech et al. outlines potential moderators and mediators of the effects of emotional disclosure in coping with bereavement.

Section 6: Psychology in context

In this section, psychological research is put into context by pointing out the necessity of, and specific possibilities and opportunities for, starting interdisciplinary social-scientific research. Karl-Dieter Opp describes 30 years of interdisciplinary social-scientific research conducted by himself, Wolfgang Stroebe, and colleagues such as Hans Albert, Klaus Foppa, Bruno Frey, Wilhelm Meyer, Kurt Stapf, and Viktor Vanberg. The chapter describes how this group was founded and was able successfully to practise interdisciplinary work. In this way, this chapter may inspire and help scientists to look beyond the boundaries of their own scientific disciplines and start to conduct truly interdisciplinary scientific research.

Epilogue

This volume closes with an epilogue in four parts, written by Lloyd Strickland, Jaap Rabbie, Rein van der Vegt, and Lizet Hoekert. One of the things this epilogue describes is how to manage the other duties (such as administrative duties) one faces when aiming to be an active researcher. The epilogue may help social psychologists and other scientific researchers to get the maximum out of their research activities and other duties.

Closing comments

In closing this introductory chapter, we want to thank the people and organisations that have helped us to realise this project. These include Psychology Press—and especially Mike Forster—for their support for the enterprise, as well as the Department of Social and Organizational Psychology at Utrecht University, and the research school of Psychology and Health in the Netherlands. Furthermore, we thank all the authors involved here. As every social psychologist knows, the list of authors presented in this book is quite impressive, and if one realises how busy these famous social psychologists are, the list is even more striking. Thus, we wish to express our sincere gratitude to all of them for making space in their demanding schedules to contribute to this book. The reason why all the people and organisations involved were so willing to cooperate with this book, we think, was that all wanted to honour the exciting developments in the past four decades of the basic and applied domains of social psychology, and in doing so, wanted to show their deep scientific appreciation for the man who has played such an exemplary role in all these fields of active research and who still is such an active researcher in both basic and applied social psychology: Wolfgang Stroebe.

In a famous historical chapter on social psychology Gordon Allport (1968) remarked that "Today the outstanding mark of social psychology as a discipline is its sophistication in method and experimental design" (p. 67). But he also warned that "many contemporary studies seem to shed light on nothing more than a narrow phenomenon studied under specific conditions . . . some current investigations seem to end up in elegantly polished triviality—snippets of empiricism, but nothing more" (p. 68). Nothing could be further from the truth in the case of Wolfgang Stroebe's research contributions to social psychology—always elegantly polished; never trivial.

References

Allport, G. W. (1968). The historical background of modern social psychology. In G. Lindzey & E. Aronson (Eds.), *Handbook of social psychology* (2nd ed., Vol. 1, pp. 1–80). Reading, MA: Addison-Wesley.

Asch, S. E. (1946). Forming impressions of personality. *Journal of Abnormal and Social Psychology, 46*, 258–290.

Asch, S. E. (1951). Effects of group pressure upon the modification and distortion of judgments. In H. Guetzkow (Ed.), *Groups, leadership, and men* (pp. 177–190). Pittsburgh: Carnegie Press.

Festinger, L. (1954). A theory of social comparison processes. *Human Relations, 7*, 117–140.

Festinger, L. (1957). *A theory of cognitive dissonance*. Stanford, CA: Stanford University Press.

Jones, E. E. (1998). Major developments in five decades of social psychology. In D. Gilbert, S. T. Fiske, & G. Lindzey (Eds.), *The handbook of social psychology* (4th ed., Vol. 1, pp. 3–57). Boston, MA: McGraw-Hill.

Lewin, K. (1935). *A dynamic theory of personality: Selected papers*. New York: McGraw-Hill.

Nisbett, R. E., & Ross, L. (1980). *Human inference: Strategies and shortcomings of social judgment*. Englewood Cliffs, NJ: Prentice-Hall.

Nisbett, R. E., & Wilson, T. D. (1977). Telling more than we can know: Verbal reports on mental processes. *Psychological Review, 84*, 231–259.

Schwarz, N., & Clore, G. L. (1983). Mood, misattribution, and judgments of well-being: Informative and directive functions of affective states. *Journal of Personality and Social Psychology, 45*, 513–523.

Snyder, M., & Cantor, N. (1998). Understanding personality and social behavior: A functionalist strategy. In D. Gilbert, S. T. Fiske, & G. Lindzey (Eds.), *The handbook of social psychology* (4th ed., Vol. 1, pp. 635–679). Boston, MA: McGraw-Hill.

Stroebe, W., Schut, H., & Stroebe, M. S. (2005). Grief work, disclosure and counseling: Do they help the bereaved? *Clinical Psychology Review, 25*, 395–414.

Stroebe, W., Stroebe, M., & Abakoumkin, G. (1996). The role of loneliness and social support in adjustment to loss: A test of attachment versus stress theory. *Journal of Personality and Social Psychology, 70,* 1241–1249.

Thibaut, J. (1950). An experimental study of the cohesiveness of underprivileged groups. *Human Relations, 3,* 251–278.

Thibaut, J., & Kelley, H. H. (1959). *The social psychology of groups.* New York: Wiley.

Part 1

Attitudes and attitude change

2 Positive accentuation
Why a good product still needs an advertisement

J. Richard Eiser
University of Sheffield, UK

In the summer of 1970, when poorly paid British academics were driving clapped-out Minis (or worse), Wolfgang Stroebe's arrival in Bristol caused quite a stir. He swept into town in a brand new, brilliant white convertible Mercedes sports car. We tried to tell him that this was thoroughly impractical. Bristol was cursed by a total lack of car parking and chronic traffic jams. He'd be lucky ever to get out of second gear. But practicality was beside the point. It was all about image, and the message in the image was clear. Wolfgang, as events quickly proved, had no intention of staying single for very long. Even teasing him about it was less fun than it should have been, since he made no attempt to deny it. "N'Ja," he riposted when asked why he thought he needed such an extravagant prop to his manhood, "that's like saying that a good product needs no advertisement."

As it happens, I've never owned a sports car, and certainly not anything as flash as Wolfgang's Mercedes. You may think I'm jealous, but honestly, I don't really mind. It *would* have been horribly impractical, and dreadfully expensive to run, and I'd have felt terrible if I ever pranged it—which I'd have been sure to do. Cognitive dissonance is alive and well and living on a car dealer's forecourt. Over the years, my choice of cars has remained strictly average. But this doesn't make me unhappy. On the contrary, as far as car-ownership is concerned, if pressed I'd say I was happier than average. How come? A large part of the answer lies in how we selectively search for and interpret information from our environment and attach value to our experiences. This set of processes goes under the name of *social judgement*. One of the main characteristics of social judgement is a bias towards positive self-regard—a tendency to see ourselves as happier, more rational, intelligent, attractive, or simply *better* on any dimension you care to name, than a dispassionate observer might describe us. I refer to this bias as *positive accentuation*. This chapter will briefly examine the processes that give rise to this phenomenon, with illustrations from a number of different areas of research.

Attitudinal judgement

The focus of my early research and collaboration with Wolfgang Stroebe (Eiser & Stroebe, 1972) concerned the question of how individuals judge others' attitudes on a given issue. The specific context for this work was a methodological problem to do with the construction of attitude scales. Thurstone's Method of Equal-Appearing Intervals (Thurstone & Chave, 1929) involves presenting respondents (whose attitudes one wants to measure) with a series of attitude statements or "items" that express (i.e., are the kinds of statements that could be made by people with) a range of different opinions on a single issue. For example, respondents could be asked how much they agreed or disagreed with statements ranging from extreme opposition to extreme support for women's rights to abortion on demand. The logic of the method is quite simple: respondents who, on average, agree with more "pro-choice" statements can be said to hold a more "pro-choice" attitude themselves. The problem comes in using such patterns of agreement to calculate a *quantitative* measure of the extent to which a given individual supports or opposes abortion. For this to happen, we need a quantitative measure of the level of support or opposition expressed in the various statements with which any given respondent agrees. This is achieved, within Thurstone's method, by first having an independent group of participants, known as "judges", rate the statements in terms of the relative favourability or unfavourability towards the issue of the attitudes expressed in the statements. The average rating given by the judges to any given statement is then treated as its "scale value", i.e., a quantitative measure of where it falls along the attitude continuum. Note that these judges are rating how much each statement expresses support for, or opposition to, abortion, for example. They are *not* (as part of this task) saying whether they personally agree or disagree with the statements, and in fact are typically instructed to disregard their own opinion on the issue while making these ratings. Indeed, Thurstone and Chave (1929) stated explicitly that judges' ratings should be unaffected by their own position on the issue.

After three decades in which a huge number of attitude scales were constructed using this and similar derived techniques, Sherif and Hovland (1961) demonstrated that this assumption was incorrect. Judges whose own attitudes differed tended also to give different ratings of where they saw particular statements as falling along the continuum between the extremes of favourability and unfavourability. A debate then started over how best to explain the observed effects of judges' attitudes on their ratings. Our own contribution was to argue that many of these effects could be explained by an extension of Tajfel's accentuation theory (Tajfel & Wilkes, 1963). According to this theory, people tend to accentuate the perceived and/or judged differences between stimuli that fall into different classes in terms of some attribute. Tajfel's suggestion was that this could underlie processes of stereotyping and prejudice through leading, for example, to exaggerated perceptions of the differences between individuals of different race or gender. Such accentuation of differences can be produced experimentally by presenting stimuli along with labels (or "superimposed cues") that differentiate them into distinct classes, so that stimuli in one half of the range are labelled as belonging to one class, and stimuli in the other half of the range to another class. This was demonstrated for perceptual stimuli by Tajfel and Wilkes (1963) and for attitude statements by myself (Eiser, 1971).

Our argument was that, if judges *subjectively* categorise attitude statements into those they accept on the one hand, and those they reject on the other, they are also likely to accentuate the judged differences between these subjective categories of statements. Because individuals whose own positions lie at one extreme are more likely than those with more moderate or ambivalent positions to consistently prefer statements in their half of the range, individuals with more extreme positions should accentuate the differences between the two halves of the range, resulting in more polarised ratings. In other words, judges with more extreme opinions of their own should rate more statements as extremely unfavourable or extremely favourable. This prediction fits well with empirical findings presented by Sherif and Hovland (1961) and other authors.

Or almost. The trouble is that such accentuation or polarisation effects on some issues are asymmetrical. Specifically, in the largest corpus of relevant studies—those conducted in the US using the issue of attitudes to African Americans—judges with more committed pro-Black attitudes do indeed, as predicted, give more extreme or polarised ratings than more neutral judges of the degree of favourability or (especially) unfavourability towards Black people expressed by items drawn from established scales of racial attitude. Those with the most extreme anti-Black attitudes, however, do not show this pattern of increased polarisation. In fact, the trend is in the opposite direction. To account for this, we introduced a new principle. The effects depend on the implicit value of the language used to define the ends of the rating scale, and in particular on the ability of judges to describe items they accept in evaluatively positive terms, and those they reject in evaluatively negative terms. If judges are required to use a negatively valenced term to describe statements they agree with, they will tend to avoid using the more extreme response options on the rating scale, and hence show less polarisation. Perhaps this was what was happening in previous studies, where White participants endorsed expressions of racial prejudice that at the time were more culturally normative, but were reluctant to indentify these statements (or by implication, themselves) as anti-Black. This intuition was supported in subsequent experiments where participants were presented with judgement scales differing in implicit valence (Eiser & Mower White, 1974, 1975; Eiser & van der Pligt, 1982). The results are highly consistent. Judges with more extreme positions, whether pro or anti, polarise more only on those scales that allow them to describe their own position more positively. Accentuation, in other words, is not simply a device for achieving cognitive simplicity. It operates more selectively to enhance a *positive* view of oneself and the opinions one shares.

Attitude maintenance

Can this argument be extended beyond the somewhat technical problem of attitude scale construction? Might such patterns of judgement reflect a more general tendency to construe our social world so as to accentuate the positive aspects of people or things we approve of, while accentuating the negative aspects of people or things of which we disapprove? A clue that this is so is provided by the abundance of value-laden words in everyday language. For instance, Anderson (1968) presented ratings of the likeableness of 555 personality-trait words in the English language. Does this mean that we can identify 555 different personality traits? Clearly there is considerable redundancy, and one source of this is that language provides us with the flexibility not only to identify differences between things but also to communicate our feelings, or evaluative judgements, about them. These functions (technically referred to as denotation and connotation respectively) are frequently combined into single words, so the reason we have so many words is because we can have so many combinations of descriptions and evaluations. Thus, the same investment decision could be labelled as enterprising or foolhardy, the same spending pattern as thrifty or miserly, depending on the extent of our approval or disapproval. However, as a number of philosophers (e.g., Nowell-Smith, 1956; Stevenson, 1944; Walton, 2001) have pointed out, ordinary people are rarely alert to the distinct functions combined within single words. Propagandists and advocates thus make heavy use of such words in order to persuade others round to their point of view.

Another aspect of this can be noted when people use language, not just to persuade others, but to justify their own beliefs or behaviour to themselves. One of the most striking features of attitudes, but one that has received surprisingly little *direct* attention from researchers, is that different people can hold diametrically opposed views on a given issue (indeed, that is what makes something an issue) but yet be absolutely convinced, even to the death, that they are right and their opponents are wrong. From the perspective of most simple theories of social influence, this is strange. The more aware we are that at least some other people disagree with us, the *less* certain we should be of our own opinions. But this is often not the case. We can remain utterly convinced that we are right, even when we believe that the *majority* of other people disagree with us. Even stipulating that we should be more prepared to accept social influence from ingroup than outgroup members is only a partial answer, and arguably a circular one in many contexts: A main criterion for belonging to our ingroup could be sharing attitudes similar to our own. Somehow we can sustain certainty while still being aware that others hold different views with equal conviction. A large part of the answer to this familiar mystery has to be that we enhance the subjective worth of our own opinions and devalue those of our opponents.

One way of devaluing opponents' views is to brand them as "extremist"—or at least as more extreme than one's own. Dawes, Singer, and Lemons (1972) found that supporters and opponents of the Vietnam war each regarded the other side as more extreme than themselves. For example, when "doves" were asked to construct statements typical of what they thought "hawks" would say, these statements were rejected by hawks as too extreme. The same was true of the reactions of doves to statements made up by hawks to represent the anti-war position. The rationality, integrity, and motives of opponents can also be denigrated. In this respect, language plays a pivotal role.

Eiser and van der Pligt (1979) had nuclear industry employees and sympathisers on the one hand, and environmentalists opposed to nuclear power on the other, select adjectives that they thought best described the pro- and anti-nuclear activists. Pro-nuclear participants described their own side most frequently as "realistic", "rational", and "responsible", while seeing their opponents as "emotional", "alarmist", and "ill-informed". Anti-nuclear participants, however, described the pro-nuclear side as "materialistic", "complacent", and "elitist", while viewing their own side as "far-sighted", "humanitarian", and "responsible". Thus, each side chooses evaluatively positive terms to describe their own side and negative terms to describe their opponents. However, the terms used in this example and in persuasive definitions more generally are not mere synonyms of "good" or "bad". The kinds of words that work in such contexts are those that pick on some actual or perceived feature of the issue and give it a specific "spin". If (as the debate was constructed by many at the time) an economic cost–benefit analysis makes nuclear power worth considering, then the economic case for nuclear power can be regarded as "rational" by supporters, but "materialistic" by opponents who claim to be more "humanitarian". Likewise, downplaying the level of risk is either "realistic" or "complacent" depending on one's point of view, whereas bringing it onto the agenda is either "far-sighted" or "emotional" and "ill-informed".

What these findings, and many easily imagined examples from everyday life, show is that we will frequently deploy language (and other devices too) to defend our existing viewpoints rather than readily change our minds in the face of contradiction or conflicting evidence. Despite this, Eagly and Chaiken (1993, pp. 679–680) commented that "Relatively few attitude theories have resistance to change as their primary focus . . . From a motivational standpoint, people resist influence because change is threatening to the self or to one's personal freedom or merely to the stability of important, self-defining attitudes. From a cognitive standpoint, people resist influence when an attitude is linked to other attitudes and beliefs, and change in the attitude would destabilise a larger cognitive structure." But within both these interpretations there is a prior assumption that one's self and one's existing attitudes have intrinsic value, and hence are worth defending.

Self-positivity

A similar message comes from another large area of research in which individuals assess their own characteristics, ability, or vulnerability to risks in comparison to those of other people. A frequently observed effect is that termed relative or "unrealistic" optimism. According to Weinstein (1980, p. 807), "People believe that negative events are less likely to happen to them than to others, and they believe that positive events are more likely to happen to them than to others." Such optimism is often termed "unrealistic" since, when asked to compare themselves with an "average" person, participants tend *on average* to say that their chances of, say, contracting skin cancer (Eiser & Arnold, 1999) or AIDS (Van der Velde, van der Pligt, & Hooykaas, 1994) are *less than average* for their reference group. This is despite the fact that, in both these cases, individual differences in self-ratings of vulnerability partly reflect differences in levels of exposure. Closely related is a tendency for individuals to rate themselves, on average, as "above average" (Dunning, Meyerowitz, & Holzberg, 1989) or "better than average" (Alicke, Klotz, Breitenbecher, Yurak, & Vredenburg, 1995) in terms of ability or personal traits. In all such cases, although some individuals may indeed be less at risk or better than the average for their group, the group as a whole cannot be better than its own average, so there must be some kind of bias operating.

How much does such a bias matter? The idea that individuals may underestimate their vulnerability to health risks, at first sight, looks worrying from the perspective of preventive health. If smokers tend to downplay the link between smoking and cancer, for instance, this might lead them to be less motivated to quit. In fact, smokers generally admit that they are more at risk of cancer than non-smokers, but not by as much as the medical statistics show (Eiser, Reicher, & Podpadec, 1995). However, interpreting associations between risk perceptions and risk behaviour is not always straightforward. Some individuals may engage in risk behaviour because they estimate their own risk as low (implying an inverse relationship), whereas others may estimate their own risk as high because they admit that they are taking risks (Weinstein & Nicolich, 1993; Weinstein, Rothman, & Nicolich, 1998). Other research also points to the benefits of such positive beliefs, even if they are illusory, for feelings of well-being and self-efficacy (Armor & Taylor, 1998; Taylor & Brown, 1988, 1994).

Although this bias towards self-positivity or relative optimism may be functional motivationally, there are still important questions about its more cognitive underpinning and its relationship to how we process information about ourselves and others. In a series of studies (Eiser, Pahl, & Prins, 2001; Pahl & Eiser, in press) we have demonstrated that the extent of such relative optimism is highly dependent on the format of question to which participants respond. In the standard procedure, participants are asked questions of the general form "Compared with the average student, what are your chances of X?" or "Compared with the average student, how X are you?" with response categories ranging from, for example, "A lot worse than average" to "A lot better than average". However, if the format is reversed so that participants compare others with the self (e.g. "Compared with you, how X is the average student?") relative optimism or positivity for the self is greatly reduced or eliminated.

One interpretation, consistent with other research (Klar & Giladi, 1999), is that, under the first ("self–other focus") condition, participants do not really construct a clear representation of the comparison standard, especially when it is defined in vague and impersonal terms (e.g., "the average student"). In other words, what looks like a comparative rating is effectively an absolute one. Indeed, when participants provide both self–other comparisons and absolute (i.e., separate) ratings of the self and other, their comparative ratings correlate highly with their self-ratings, but not with their ratings of the other. By contrast, under the second ("other–self focus") condition, both self-ratings and ratings of the other predict the comparative rating to comparable extents. This may be because the other–self format requires participants to think more carefully about the characteristics of the other.

The implications of these findings pull in opposite directions. One reading could be that much of the claimed generality for relative optimism is arte-factual—a product of the particular way in which the question is asked. But even if this is so, the artefact (if that is what it is) depends on two implicit assumptions: first, that representations of the self and one's own experiences are "chronically accessible" (Higgins, 1996) or at least more so than represen-tations of other people, and second that self-representations tend to be pre-dominantly positive. Our findings with regard to manipulating comparison focus in no way undermine this latter assumption; in fact, their interpretation depends on it.

So we are still left with the question of why we tend to think positively about ourselves. Is it just that we tend to interpret our experiences in a posi-tive light? Or might it be that, for most of us most of the time, our experiences tend to fall on the positive side of some subjective neutral point? The idea that we judge objects and events in comparison to a subjective neutral point or adaptation level has a long tradition in judgement theory (Eiser & Stroebe, 1972; Helson, 1964). It could well be that, when participants rate themselves as better, luckier, happier or safer "than average", they are not really comparing themselves with some vague *external* standard, but rather with an *internal* subjective standard derived from their own experience. So then the question shifts to how individuals derive subjective standards from their own experience. But here there is a new problem. In the original formu-lation of adaptation-level theory (Helson, 1964), individuals are said to derive their adaptation level or subjective neutral point, from the (weighted) *average* of their experiences within a given stimulus domain. If this is so, how, on average, can individuals rate themselves as better than average?

An ingenious answer to this problem has been suggested by Parducci (1984), based on his theory of "range–frequency compromise" (Parducci,

1963). This theory proposes that adaptation level is best predicted from a combination of the mid-point and median of any set of stimulus experiences. Now, if these experiences are distributed symmetrically around the mean, as in a standard normal distribution, the mid-point, median, and mean will all coincide. However, if the distribution is skewed, the mid-point and median will be pulled apart. So how, Parducci asks, can we explain the widespread phenomenon that people tend to rate themselves as happy rather than unhappy? Perhaps, he suggests, because most people's experiences are skewed towards the happy end. In other words, we may have a few, perhaps extremely, negative experiences but most of our experiences will be somewhat positive. Because of this skew, the mid-point of our distribution of happy and unhappy experiences will be lower than the median of this distribution. Hence, if we set our subjective neutral point to be somewhere between the mid-point and median, most of our experiences will fall on the positive side of this neutral point. The result—happiness! Or more generally, positive self-esteem and a feeling of being "better than average". But to cash in this intriguing speculation, we need to assume other processes that lead both to negative experiences, even if infrequent, having a strong effect on judgements, and to our generally having a distribution of experiences that is skewed towards the positive.

Attitude learning

It is a commonplace assumption in attitude theory that attitudes in some way guide or direct our behaviour (e.g., Allport, 1935; Eagly & Chaiken, 1993; Fazio, 1990). The crisis of confidence resulting from early research showing low attitude–behaviour correlations (e.g., Wicker, 1969) has long been resolved as a product of poor matching of behavioural and attitudinal indicators (Ajzen & Fishbein, 1977). Nonetheless, many classic and contemporary perspectives leave the full dynamics of the interrelationships between attitudes and behaviour underspecified. By "dynamics" I refer not merely to the idea that attitudes have a motivational influence, but rather that our attitudes, behaviour, and experienced environment together form a dynamical system (Eiser, 1994) and mutually influence one another. Attitudes guide behaviour, but this isn't the end of the story. Our behaviour has consequences that we experience, and these consequences in turn shape both our attitudes and our subsequent behaviour.

Recently, Russell Fazio and I have developed a paradigm to directly investigate these dynamics. This involves learners being provided with the opportunity to acquire information about the valence of novel objects that are associated with either positive (gain) or negative (loss) consequences. The critical element is that such consequences are only experienced if the learner decides to approach or explore the object in question. If the learner avoids the object, no feedback about the object's valence is provided. In other words, learning requires the learner to approach the objects, but approach carries the possibility of either gain or loss. Following familiar principles of reinforcement learning (Sutton & Barto, 1998), this should lead the learner to continue to approach "good" objects associated with previous gain, but to avoid "bad" objects expected to lead to loss.

I use the term "learner" because there are two strands to this programme of work—human experimentation and computer simulation. In the experimental work (Fazio, Eiser, & Shook, 2004), participants play a computer game ("Beanfest") in which they imagine they are in a virtual world where their survival depends on their learning to distinguish between different kinds of visually presented "beans", varying in terms of shape and speckledness, some of which are good or nutritious and provide energy, and others of which are bad or poisonous and lead to a loss of energy. However, in order to discover whether a bean is good or bad, participants have to "eat", that is, approach it. So information gain carries a risk.

The main findings of these experiments are as follows. First, there is a clear "learning asymmetry", as assessed at the end of learning. Typically, participants learn to identify more of the bad than the good beans. (In fact, there are equal numbers of good and bad beans, but participants are not told this.) This asymmetry involves participants incorrectly judging some of the good beans as bad, so avoiding them and so never discovering that their negative judgements were incorrect. Second, there is a "generalisation asymmetry", based on data from when participants estimate the valence of novel beans that are similar but not identical to those presented during the training phase (i.e., the game proper). There is stronger generalisation from bad than good beans, and more novel beans are predicted to be bad. Third, when participants are given prior but misleading information (supposedly from a previous player of the game) about the valence of the beans, they will learn to disregard advice to approach certain beans that turn out to be bad, but will be less likely to correct false information or "prejudice" that some beans (that are actually good) are bad and should be avoided.

The computer simulations (Eiser, Fazio, Stafford, & Prescott, 2003) involve training a feed-forward neural network to differentiate between input patterns in a two-dimensional array formally equivalent to the stimulus array used in the human experiments. The familiar *backpropagation of error* training procedure (Rumelhart, Hinton, & Williams, 1986) is adapted so that the network only receives feedback (i.e., an error signal leading to updating of the connection weights) if the network selects an action or output corresponding to approaching (or "eating") the stimulus. As in the human experiments, these simulations demonstrate less complete learning of the positive than negative stimuli (i.e., a learning asymmetry), generalisation of this learning to novel stimuli, which are more likely to be predicted to be negative, and more difficulty in overcoming early biases towards excessive avoidance rather than excessive approach. Various manipulations indicate that the learning asymmetry can be reduced the more the network is set occasionally to approach or "eat" stimuli it has categorised as somewhat bad.

The two sets of findings taken together strongly support the following general principle. In a learning environment where feedback is contingent on learners exploring rather than avoiding objects in their environment, and where the major factor determining whether the learners will explore or avoid is the anticipated valence of the object presented, learning of good objects may be incomplete, whereas objects correctly *or* incorrectly believed to be bad will be consistently avoided. This has a non-obvious consequence. Provided individuals have sufficient freedom that they can avoid enough experiences they believe would be damaging, *most of their experiences will be positive*, even if the potential benefits in the environment are not fully exploited. And what of the rarer negative experiences, when a bad object is incorrectly approached? Although such actions are less likely to be repeated, the associated negative beliefs appear particularly resistant to change, echoing classic findings on avoidance learning in animals (Solomon & Wynne, 1954). Furthermore, such negative experiences appear, particularly in the human generalisation data, to have a disproportionately strong influence on evaluations of novel objects that resemble the training stimuli, fitting in with the broader literature on the importance of negative information in impression formation and social cognition (Baumeister, Bratslavsky, Finkenauer, & Vohs, 2001; Rozin & Royzman, 2001). Thus, Parducci's (1984) speculations on the origins of happiness seem consistent with the distribution of outcomes that individuals experience under conditions of reasonably free choice, but limited information.

Attitudes and decisions

What does this dynamic relationship between attitudes, behaviour, and its consequences imply for the quality of people's decision making under conditions of uncertainty? Quality in this context is an ambiguous term. If it means making decisions that, on balance, lead to positive consequences for the decision maker, there is no doubt that the process just described will lead to quality decisions. Indeed, it would be amazing if something as engrained into our psychological evolution as reinforcement learning failed to convey an advantage. But advantage is not always the same thing as accuracy, another possible definition of quality. The learning asymmetry observed in the Beanfest experiments is also an asymmetry in the types of errors participants make. By the end of training, the typical participant will make very few false-positive errors (i.e., treating a bad bean as good) but many more false-negative errors (i.e., treating a good bean as bad). As recognised long ago by Signal Detection Theory (Swets, 1973), different kinds of errors can be associated with different costs, and where this is so, this can lead to a response bias in the direction of either greater risk acceptance, or greater risk aversion or caution. The constraints of the Beanfest paradigm are such that false positive errors are more costly than false negative ones, and as a consequence participants can obtain adequate returns by finding a number of good beans, continuing to "eat" these whenever they are presented, but avoiding all other beans as though they are bad.

But is this bias merely a feature of our experimental constraints, or can it be found in other contexts where individuals are called upon to make risky decisions? According to Kahneman and Tversky (1979), there is a consistent tendency towards risk aversion whenever individuals choose between beneficial prospects of similar or equivalent expected value. That is, "sure thing" gains of $10 with 100% certainty tend to be regularly preferred to riskier prospects of a 10% chance of winning $100—or even slightly more: individuals require a premium in terms of expected value before they are indifferent between more and less certain outcomes. This looks like persuasive evidence of the generality of the bias we have described, but it should be noted that the paradigms are rather different. In this paradigm, and typically also in other similar experimental gambles and tests of economic decision making, participants are informed about the probabilities and values of the alternative options in advance. Hertwig, Barron, Weber, and Erev (2004) refer to this kind of task as eliciting "decisions from description", in contrast to "decisions from experience" where, as in more everyday situations, individuals have to discover these probabilities and outcomes for themselves over time.

Arguably, a bias that emerges from the manner in which we selectively process feedback from our own exploratory behaviour is likely to have wider generality than one that depends, less plausibly, on decision makers having full prior knowledge of the probabilities and values they are asked to compare. Our Beanfest studies involve exposing individuals to an environment in which they (were they to explore it fully) would find that the probabilities of good and bad outcomes happen to be equal. Our participants exhibit risk aversion by repeatedly approaching objects they believe confidently to be good, and avoiding those they believe to be bad or are less confident about. The acquisition of such habits and expectancies is a direct consequence of their learning from experience. But the same reinforcement learning principles can account for risk aversion in choices more similar to those considered by Kahneman and Tversky (1979), that is, choices between more and less probable prospects of the same expected value (such as a 100% chance of $10 vs a 10% chance of $100), in so far as one can assume such preferences develop over time. As argued by March (1996), choices that produce highly certain positive outcomes will tend to be consistently reinforced, and hence repeated, even if the absolute size of the reward on any given trial is modest. By contrast, the chance of receiving the less frequent (albeit higher) reward on any given trial is lower, by definition. In other words, on most trials the riskier option will produce a worse outcome than the cautious option, and so will not be reinforced. Thus, even if there is a large jackpot out there to be won, it may never be discovered. Even if one is lucky enough to hit the jackpot on an early trial, its reinforcement effects are likely to extinguish fairly rapidly on subsequent non-reinforced trials.

So does this mean that risk taking is a "bad thing"? Not necessarily. In many circumstances innovation and exploration, even dangerous exploration, are essential for survival. The environment can change. Previous secure sources of food or other positive reinforcements can become depleted, and competition from rivals or dangers from predators can become more intense. We are currently introducing variations to our experimental paradigm to investigate the effects of such changes.

Risk, trust, and social judgement

If our decision-making capacities are adaptive to our survival in a risky world, what are the kinds of risks that confront us? As we contemplate the death toll from recent natural disasters such as earthquakes, tsunamis, and hurricanes, it is easy to think of human beings as powerless victims of huge forces beyond their control. And of course, the physical forces involved in such disasters are huge on any reasonable definition. Yet what determines the scale of such disasters—the number of fatalities, for instance—is not the strength of the physical events alone, but also human decision making. Poor decision making exacerbates risk. Good decision making can help prevent hazards turning into disasters, and can help ameliorate their consequences. Whereas much experimental work has looked at how individuals accept or reject risks for themselves, in real life we affect each other by the quality of our decisions. We are interdependent. Risk is in large part a social product, and hence assessment of risk is a form of social judgement.

One of the main contexts where this matters is when we depend on other people—so-called "experts"—to make decisions on our behalf and/or to inform and advise us what to do. Not only are we unable personally to control many of the things that put us at risk, we are often unable to estimate the extent of risk without the advice of experts. But are the "experts" really expert? Yes, if they know what they're talking about. No, if they don't. This amounts to a judgement about competence, and if the "experts" lack competence, they aren't experts at all and we shouldn't rely on what they say. But competence by itself is not a sufficient condition for trust. We can ask not just "Do they know what they're talking about?" but also "And would they tell us, even if they do?". How eager would a food manufacturer be to warn customers about possible side-effects of certain additives, even if they had preliminary indications of a problem? What credence can be put in assertions by tobacco manufacturers that conclusions about the health-damaging and addictive properties of cigarettes have been exaggerated? In many contexts, we take what people say with a pinch of salt because we infer that their claims or denials reflect, not the evidence they actually have or what they personally believe, but what they *want* us to believe, for their own self-interest. Formally, this intuition reflects the principle that response bias reflects perceived costs and benefits, independently of actual knowledge or discrimination ability.

All this implies that much of the reason why the world is a risky place is that we can anticipate that other people act in their own interest much or most of the time, and sometimes their interest will be inconsistent with our own. So distinguishing friend from foe, those who would help us from those who would do us down, has to be one of the most important social skills. In keeping with research on the salience of negative information (Baumeister et al., 2001; Rozin & Royzman, 2001), it has been suggested that trust can be easily lost through exceptional acts of betrayal, and once lost, is difficult to regain (e.g., Slovic, 1993). To the extent that attitudes of trust and distrust are acquired over time, this fits in with our work on attitudinal learning. Negative attitudes (in this case, distrust) may persist, even on the basis of little, or at least infrequently experienced, evidence because they lead to avoidance of both the distrusted person and exposure to information that might correct such negative impressions.

But how long does it take to build up a picture of someone as trustworthy or untrustworthy? An intelligence officer may take ages to decide if a political defector is a spy, a double agent, or an innocent refugee. But many decisions—including life-changing and life-saving decisions—are made and need to be made far more quickly.

Slovic, Finucane, Peters, and MacGregor (2002) use the term "affect heuristic" to describe how positive and negative affective feelings, occurring immediately and often without conscious deliberation, can guide more calculative judgements and decisions about risks and benefits. In the context of judgements about decision makers as opposed to physical hazards, this implies that immediate intuitive feelings about whether someone is for us or against us can lead us in the direction of greater or lesser trust and dependence, and steer the course of our interactions with them. And where this is so, it is not only the other's expertise that we are choosing to trust (or not), but our own intuitive ability to discern the other's character and the extent of their good will towards us.

Advertising goodness

Which brings us back to where we started. We can only do so much in one life. Every choice taken is also an alternative opportunity lost. Selectivity is not only adaptive but inevitable. So it matters that we make good choices. But it matters just as much that we feel good about the choices we have made. Both in terms of the experiences we seek out and how we represent such experiences during and after the event, accentuating the positive enables us to trust our own judgement as well as that of others. At the same time, feeling good about ourselves is no mere subjective self-appraisal. It guides our exploration of our social environment and the formation of new friendships. It is shaped hugely by how we believe others feel about us and appraise our attributes. Our interdependence makes us all both judges and judged. And for this reason, we need to transmit social signals as well as receive them. We need to do enough to be noticed, since as William James (1890, p. 292) put it eloquently, "No more fiendish punishment could be devised, were such a thing physically possible, than that one should be turned loose in society and remain absolutely unnoticed by all the members thereof."

So in hindsight, I'm convinced that Wolfgang Stroebe was right. Good products still need advertising. But whether he thought he needed a Mercedes to advertise himself, or whether he simply thought he was advertising the Mercedes, I'm no longer altogether sure.

References

Ajzen, I., & Fishbein, M. (1977). Attitude–behavior relations: A theoretical analysis and review of empirical research. *Psychological Bulletin, 84*, 888–918.

Alicke, M. D., Klotz, M. L., Breitenbecher, D. L., Yurak, T. J., & Vredenburg, D. S. (1995). Personal contact, individuation, and the better-than-average effect. *Journal of Personality and Social Psychology, 68*, 804–825.

Allport, G. W. (1935). Attitudes. In C. Murchison (Ed.), *Handbook of social psychology* (pp. 798–844). Worcester, MA: Clark University Press.

Anderson, N. H. (1968). Likeableness ratings of 555 personality-trait words. *Journal of Personality and Social Psychology, 9*, 272–279.

Armor, D. A., & Taylor, S. E. (1998). Situated optimism: Specific outcome expectancies and self-regulation. In M. P. Zanna (Ed.), *Advances in experimental social psychology* (Vol. 30, pp. 309–379). San Diego, CA: Academic Press.

Baumeister, R. F., Bratslavsky, E., Finkenauer, C., & Vohs, K. D. (2001). Bad is stronger than good. *Review of General Psychology, 5*, 323–370.

Dawes, R. M., Singer, D., & Lemons, F. (1972). An experimental analysis of the contrast effect and its implications for intergroup communication and the indirect assessment of attitude. *Journal of Personality and Social Psychology, 37*, 1364–1376.

Dunning, D., Meyerowitz, J. A., & Holzberg, A. D. (1989). Ambiguity and self-evaluation: The role of idiosyncratic trait definitions in self-serving assessments of ability. *Journal of Personality and Social Psychology, 57*, 1082–1090.

Eagly, A. H., & Chaiken, S. (1993). *The psychology of attitudes.* Fort Worth, TX: Harcourt Brace Jovanovich.

Eiser, J. R. (1971). Enhancement of contrast in the absolute judgment of attitude statements. *Journal of Personality and Social Psychology, 17*, 1–10.

Eiser, J. R. (1994). *Attitudes, chaos and the connectionist mind.* Oxford, UK: Blackwell.

Eiser, J. R., & Arnold, B. W. A. (1999). Out in the midday sun: Risk behaviour and optimistic beliefs among residents and visitors on Tenerife. *Psychology and Health, 14*, 529–544.

Eiser, J. R., Fazio, R. H., Stafford, T., & Prescott, T. J. (2003). Connectionist simulation of attitude learning: Asymmetries in the acquisition of positive and negative evaluations. *Personality and Social Psychology Bulletin, 29*, 1221–1235.

Eiser, J. R., & Mower White, C. J. (1974). Evaluative consistency and social judgment. *Journal of Personality and Social Psychology, 30*, 349–359.

Eiser, J. R., & Mower White, C. J. (1975). Categorization and congruity in attitudinal judgment. *Journal of Personality and Social Psychology, 31*, 769–775.

Eiser, J. R., Pahl, S., & Prins, Y. R. A. (2001). Optimism, pessimism and the direction of self–other comparisons. *Journal of Experimental Social Psychology, 37*, 77–84.

Eiser, J. R., Reicher, S. D., & Podpadec, T. J. (1995). Smokers' and non-smokers' estimates of their personal risk of cancer and of the incremental risk attributable to cigarette smoking. *Addiction Research, 3,* 221–229.

Eiser, J. R., & Stroebe, W. (1972). *Categorization and social judgement.* London: Academic Press.

Eiser, J. R., & van der Pligt, J. (1979). Beliefs and values in the nuclear debate. *Journal of Applied Social Psychology, 9,* 524–536.

Eiser, J. R., & van der Pligt, J. (1982). Accentuation and perspective in attitudinal judgment. *Journal of Personality and Social Psychology, 42,* 224–238

Fazio, R. H. (1990). Multiple processes by which attitudes guide behavior: The MODE model as an integrative framework. In M. P. Zanna (Ed.), *Advances in experimental social psychology* (Vol. 23, pp. 75–109). San Diego, CA: Academic Press.

Fazio, R. H., Eiser, J. R., & Shook, N. J. (2004). Attitude formation through exploration: Valence asymmetries. *Journal of Personality and Social Psychology, 87,* 293–311.

Helson, H. (1964). *Adaptation-level theory.* New York: Harper & Row.

Hertwig, R., Barron, G., Weber, E. U., & Erev, I. (2004). Decisions from experience and the effect of rare events in risky choice. *Psychological Science, 15,* 534–539.

Higgins, E. T. (1996). Knowledge activation: Accessibility, applicability, and salience. In E. T. Higgins & A. W. Kruglanski (Eds.), *Social psychology: Handbook of basic principles* (pp. 133–168). New York: Guilford Press.

James, W. (1890). *Principles of psychology.* New York: Henry Holt.

Kahneman, D., & Tversky, A. (1979). Prospect theory: An analysis of decision under risk. *Econometrics, 47,* 263–291.

Klar, Y., & Giladi, E. E. (1999). Are most people happier than their peers, or are they just happy? *Personality and Social Psychology Bulletin, 25,* 585–594.

March, J. G. (1996). Learning to be risk averse. *Psychological Review, 103,* 309–319.

Nowell-Smith, P. H. (1956). *Ethics.* Harmondsworth, UK: Penguin.

Pahl, S., & Eiser, J. R. (in press). The focus effect and self-positivity in ratings of self–other similarity and difference. *British Journal of Social Psychology.*

Parducci, A. (1963). Range–frequency compromise in judgment. *Psychological Monographs, 77*(2, Whole No. 565).

Parducci, A. (1984). Value judgments: Toward a relational theory of happiness. In J. R. Eiser (Ed.), *Attitudinal judgment* (pp. 3–21). New York: Springer.

Rozin, P., & Royzman, E. B. (2001). Negativity bias, negativity dominance, and contagion. *Personality and Social Psychology Review, 5,* 296–320.

Rumelhart, D. E., Hinton, G. E., & Williams, R. J. (1986). Learning internal representations by error propagation. In D. E. Rumelhart, J. L. McClelland, & the PDP research group (Eds.), *Parallel distributed processing: Explorations in the microstructure of cognition* (pp. 318–362). Cambridge, MA: MIT Press.

Sherif, M., & Hovland, C. I. (1961). *Social judgment: Assimilation and contrast effects in communication and attitude change.* New Haven, CT: Yale University Press.

Slovic, P. (1993). Perceived risk, trust, and democracy. *Risk Analysis, 13*(6), 675–682.

Slovic, P., Finucane, M., Peters, E., & MacGregor, D. G. (2002). The affect heuristic. In T. Gilovich, D. Griffin, & D. Kahneman (Eds.), *Heuristics and biases: The psychology of intuitive judgment* (pp. 397–420). New York: Cambridge University Press.

Solomon, R. L., & Wynne, L. C. (1954). Traumatic avoidance learning: The principles of anxiety conservation and partial irreversibility. *Psychological Review, 61,* 353–385.

Stevenson, C. L. (1944). *Ethics and language*. New Haven, CT: Yale University Press.

Sutton, R. S., & Barto, A. G. (1998). *Reinforcement learning: An introduction*. Cambridge, MA: MIT Press.

Swets, J. A. (1973). The receiver operating characteristic in psychology. *Science, 182*, 990–1000.

Tajfel, H., & Wilkes, A. L. (1963). Classification and quantitative judgment. *British Journal of Psychology, 54*, 101–114.

Taylor, S. E., & Brown, J. D. (1988). Illusion and well-being: A social psychological perspective on mental health. *Psychological Bulletin, 103*, 193–210.

Taylor, S. E., & Brown, J. D. (1994). Positive illusions and well-being revisited: Separating fact from fiction. *Psychological Bulletin, 116*, 21–27.

Thurstone, L. L., & Chave, E. J. (1929). *The measurement of attitude*. Chicago: University of Chicago Press.

Van der Velde, F. W., van der Pligt, J., & Hooykaas, C. (1994). Perceiving AIDS-related risk: Accuracy as a function of differences in actual risk. *Health Psychology, 13*, 25–33.

Walton, D. (2001). Persuasive definitions and public policy arguments. *Argumentation and Advocacy, 37*, 117–132.

Weinstein, N. D. (1980). Unrealistic optimism about future life events. *Journal of Personality and Social Psychology, 39*, 806–820.

Weinstein, N. D., & Nicolich, M. (1993). Correct and incorrect interpretations of correlations between risk perceptions and risk behaviors. *Health Psychology, 12*, 235–245.

Weinstein, N. D., Rothman, A. J., & Nicolich, M. (1998). Use of correlational data to examine the effects of risk perceptions on precautionary behavior. *Psychology and Health, 13*, 479–501.

Wicker, A. W. (1969). Attitudes versus actions: The relationships of overt and behavioral responses to attitude objects. *Journal of Social Issues, 25*, 41–78.

3 Attitudinal ambivalence

Klaus Jonas
University of Zürich, Switzerland

René Ziegler
University of Tübingen, Germany

Most attitude researchers agree in defining attitudes as tendencies to impute a certain degree of positive or negative evaluation to a given attitude object (e.g., Ajzen, 2001; Eagly & Chaiken, 1998; Petty & Wegener, 1998). Attitudes have been shown to be important predictors of behaviour (e.g., Ajzen, 2001) and to have an impact on information processing (e.g., Hassin, Uleman, & Bargh, 2005). Implicit in the definition of attitudes as tendencies to evaluate an attitude object is the assumption that this evaluation is unidimensional. Thus, attitude objects are assumed to be evaluated as positive or negative or neutral, but not as both positive and negative simultaneously.

However, this may not adequately represent cases in which the attitude holder likes or dislikes the same object at the same time as it occurs—for example, when an individual finds shutting down certain industries a positive choice because this may reduce air pollution, but also regards this measure negatively because it may cause more unemployment (e.g., Costarelli & Colloca, 2004). Attitude researchers label such cases of evaluative inconsistency within the attitude structure as attitudinal ambivalence (e.g., Kaplan, 1972; Newby-Clark, McGregor, & Zanna, 2002; Thompson, Zanna, & Griffin, 1995). This inconsistency may exist within a class of evaluative responding (e.g., cognitive, affective) or across classes (between cognitions and affect; e.g., Hodson, Maio, & Esses, 2001).

It should be noted that ambivalent attitudes are different from truly neutral attitudes (Klopfer & Madden, 1980): The evaluation implied by a neutral attitude is midway between a positive and a negative evaluation. Neutral attitudes are not associated with evaluative inconsistency.

Algebraic attitude theories such as the theory of reasoned action (Fishbein & Ajzen, 1975) or the information integration theory (Anderson, 1981) do take attitudes that are based on evaluatively inconsistent beliefs into consideration. However, they conceptualise attitudes merely as an arithmetical combination of the evaluative implications of underlying beliefs. Thus, the resulting attitude score predicted by these theories is the same, be it derived from, for example, six beliefs with neutral evaluations, or from three beliefs with positive evaluations and three beliefs with negative evaluations. However, such differences regarding the evaluative consistency of the beliefs that underlie a certain attitude deserve more attention, because—as a number of studies show—they have important consequences with respect to the relationship between the pertinent attitudes and the relevant behaviours and other phenomena involving attitudes (e.g., Armitage & Conner, 2000; Conner, Povey, Sparks, James, & Shepherd, 2003; see in more detail below).

The term "ambivalence" (German: *Ambivalenz*) was introduced into psychology and psychiatry by the Swiss psychiatrist Eugen Bleuler (1911). By *Ambivalenz* he meant the simultaneous occurrence of incompatible emotions, cognitions, or intentions within one person. Bleuler regarded ambivalence as the primary symptom of schizophrenia, but assumed that ambivalence may also occur among normal persons. Freud (1912/1943) adopted the term ambivalence into his psychoanalytic theory. According to Freud, ambivalence refers mainly to inconsistencies between emotions, such as love and hate.

In developmental psychology, the ambivalence concept is considered relevant for patterns of attachment (e.g., Ainsworth, 1989; Bowlby, 1982; see also Maio, Fincham, & Lycett, 2000). According to Ainsworth, Blehar, Waters, and Wall (1978) an anxious–ambivalent attachment style is associated with the simultaneous occurrence of approach and avoidance tendencies of a child in response to attachment-relevant events (e.g., a separation from the primary caregiver) and is assumed to result from inconsistent reactions of the primary caregiver to the child's needs.

Katz (1981) proposed a theory of the process underlying ambivalent reactions towards a broad range of socially stigmatised others. In particular, according to his *racial ambivalence* theory (Katz & Hass, 1988) the attitudes of most Whites towards Blacks tend to include both favourable and unfavourable beliefs due to a conflict between the two core values of egalitarianism (emphasising equality, justice, and fairness) and individualism (emphasising freedom, self-reliance, devotion to work, and achievement).

Sexist ambivalence refers to men's attitude towards women as a group. Men who are ambivalent towards women are assumed to hold simultaneously two sets of related sexist beliefs of opposite valence (Glick & Fiske, 1996). Sexist (i.e., ambivalent) men may have genuinely positive attitudes towards women who embrace traditional roles or show prototypical behaviour (e.g., helping) as well as hostile attitudes towards women who threaten their paternalistic, gender-identified needs and desires as a consequence of non-stereotypical behaviour (e.g., striving for a career).

Ambivalence over emotional expression (King, 1998; King & Emmons, 1990) is a different concept from the foregoing. Individuals who are ambivalent over their emotional expression may be inexpressive because they inhibit their desire to express emotions, or they may express emotions but regret their expression.

Whereas the above ambivalence concepts have played a certain role in their respective fields, the focus of the present chapter is on *attitudinal ambivalence*; that is, an aspect of the attitude structure that is assumed to moderate the relationship between attitudes and behaviours as well as between attitudes and information processing. Attitudinal ambivalence may be held towards behaviours, goals, events, or states of affairs (cf. Conner, Sparks, Povey, James, Shepherd, & Armitage, 2002). In particular, ambivalence can be expected to be a rather frequent event associated with personal behaviours or goals (cf. Conner et al., 2002).

Whereas attitude research began in the 1920s (e.g., Thurstone & Chave, 1929), the ambivalence concept was introduced into attitude research relatively late, by Scott (e.g., 1966, 1969). However, the upsurge of ambivalence research began more recently, in the 1990s (e.g., Priester & Petty, 1996; Thompson et al., 1995). Several researchers (e.g., Thompson et al., 1995) trace the previous neglect of ambivalence in attitude research back to the strong influence of consistency approaches in attitude research (e.g., Abelson, Aronson, McGuire, Newcomb, Rosenberg, & Tannenbaum, 1968). Consistency theories regard ambivalence as a relatively short-lived state that will soon result in a state in which existing inconsistencies are resolved. However, ambivalence as such is more compatible with the social cognition approach that has become dominant in social psychology since the 1970s. Social cognition researchers do not assume that the cognitions underlying or associated with a certain attitude are consistent all the time. In addition, not all cognitive elements that are relevant to a certain attitude have to be accessible according to the social cognition approach.

Similar to ambivalence, cognitive dissonance involves "inconsistency" in a general sense. Dissonance is an unpleasant state that occurs when a person's behaviour is inconsistent with his or her beliefs or self-concept. Common to traditional and more recent approaches to explain dissonance phenomena (Aronson, 1969; Cooper & Fazio, 1984; Stone, Aronson, Craine, Winslow, & Fried, 1994) is the assumption that dissonance is the result of an inconsistency between one's cognitions and (cognitions about) one's own behaviour. In comparison, an individual may be ambivalent without having performed a certain behaviour (or being committed to it) merely because of evaluatively conflicting cognitions and/or affects.

Definition and measurement of attitudinal ambivalence

Attitudinal ambivalence is the simultaneous existence of positive and negative beliefs or emotions with regard to the same object in an individual's attitude base. Attitude researchers commonly distinguish three types of ambivalence (cf. Thompson et al., 1995). The first can be called *cognitive ambivalence* ("mixed beliefs") since it consists in having beliefs about an object that are associated with inconsistent evaluations. An example would be when a person believes that a certain brand of car is fuel efficient (positive belief) but also expensive to buy (negative belief). The second type, *affective ambivalence* ("torn feelings"), exists when positive and negative emotions such as, for example, love and hate are experienced at the same time. The third type, *affective-cognitive ambivalence* ("heart vs mind conflict") consists of positive cognitions combined with negative affect, or vice versa, such as, for example, when a person likes to smoke but also knows that smoking is associated with health risks (e.g., Lipkus, Pollak, McBride, Schwartz-Bloom, Lyna, & Bloom, 2005).

There is currently no consensus among attitude researchers on how to measure ambivalence. Mainly two different approaches of measuring ambivalence can be found in ambivalence research. The oldest and most common approach consists in instructing individuals to provide separate ratings of their positive and negative reactions towards the attitude object (e.g., Kaplan, 1972). These positive and negative reactions are then combined according to a mathematical formula (see below). This type of measure has been called "objective ambivalence", "formula-based ambivalence" (e.g., Jonas, Brömer, & Diehl, 2000), "indirect measure of ambivalence" (Conner et al., 2002), or "potential ambivalence" (e.g., Newby-Clark et al., 2002), the latter term implying that providing participants with a separate opportunity to express their positive and negative evaluation maps the potential ambivalence associated with a certain attitude object, which may not be tantamount to the subjective feeling of ambivalence that is experienced at a certain moment in time.

One of the most frequently used indexes for assessing potential ambivalence is arguably the so-called "Griffin index" (Thompson et al., 1995). The Griffin index captures the intensity of the positive and negative evaluations as well as the level of similarity between the two evaluations, thus:

$$\text{Ambivalence} = (\text{positive} + \text{negative})/2 - |\text{positive} - \text{negative}|. \quad (1)$$

This formula indicates maximal ambivalence when the positive and the negative evaluations are both intense and similar (see Breckler, 1994; for other indexes of measuring ambivalence see Jonas et al., 2000).

The second approach of measuring ambivalence has been termed "experienced ambivalence" (e.g., Jonas et al., 2000), "felt ambivalence" (e.g., Newby-Clark et al., 2002), or "direct measurement of ambivalence" (Conner et al., 2002). For example, Lipkus et al. (2005) asked their participants to express their agreement or disagreement, respectively, on several items such as, for example, "You find yourself feeling torn between wanting and not wanting to smoke". Cacioppo, Gardner, and Berntson (1997) requested their respondents to describe their reactions towards the attitude object using adjectives such as "divided", "tense", and "contradictory", rated on a scale ranging from 1 (very slightly or not at all) to 5 (extremely).

The relation between potential and felt ambivalence

The two types of indexes, that is, potential and felt ambivalence, have often been shown to be only moderately correlated (e.g., Priester & Petty, 1996;

Thompson et al., 1995; cf. Newby-Clark et al., 2002). Thus, they cannot be regarded as interchangeable. The less than maximal correlation between the two measures has evoked at least two (interrelated) questions: (1) Which of the two measures is to be preferred? and (2) How can the rather low correlation be explained? Regarding the first question, each of the two measures has found its implicit or explicit supporters. For example, Armitage and Conner (2000) rely on a measure of potential ambivalence. Potential ambivalence is also the preferred measure of Thompson et al. (1995) who use felt ambivalence only for validational purposes, that is, to establish construct validity. In contrast, Lipkus et al. (2005) use a measure of felt ambivalence only, whereas Costarelli and Colloca (2004) employ both types of measures.

A convincing answer to the question of which of the two types of measures is to be preferred seems to depend on finding an answer to the second question; that is, why the intercorrelation between the diverse measures is often so low. Several explanations have been proposed to explain this result; common to these explanations is the assumption that the two types of measures have different determinants. For example, Priester and Petty (2001) argue that felt ambivalence is partly determined by interpersonal discrepancy; that is, the perception of the attitude holder that, although he dislikes (likes) a certain attitude object, important others do (not) like it. Obviously, this assumption is based on notions from Heider's balance theory (Heider, 1958). Thus, according to this approach, the correlation between formula-based measures of ambivalence and measures of felt ambivalence is inevitably less than perfect, since formula-based measures do not capture the perceived attitudes of significant others, whereas measures of felt ambivalence do (to the extent that the individual's experience of ambivalence takes into account the attitudes of others with respect to the particular attitude object).

Other researchers (Newby-Clark et al., 2002) assume that the low intercorrelation between felt ambivalence and formula-based measures is due to the fact that formula-based measures map the "potential ambivalence" and that felt ambivalence reflects only those aspects of the potential ambivalence that are salient at a given time. According to this approach, the rather moderate correlation between the two types of measures that is often observed is due to the circumstance that only a limited aspect of the underlying attitude structure is salient at a given point in time; that is, the actual degree of ambivalence experienced may be less than the potential degree.

Thus, no general answer can be provided to the question of whether a measure of felt ambivalence or a measure of potential ambivalence should be employed. The answer depends on the assumptions underlying the particular investigation. For example, if a researcher undertakes a longitudinal study investigating the moderating role of attitudinal ambivalence in the relationship between a particular attitude and the pertinent behaviour, a measure of potential ambivalence may be more adequate than a measure of felt ambivalence. Only potential ambivalence captures the diverse aspects of the attitude structure which may be activated in the different situational contexts lying ahead, whereas felt ambivalence is restricted to the aspects that are salient in the momentary situation.

Attitudinal ambivalence as a moderator of the attitude–behaviour relationship

Even before the concentrated onset of research on the antecedents and consequences of attitudinal ambivalence, several attitude researchers hypothesised that ambivalence should weaken the relationship between attitudes and behaviour (e.g., Eagly & Chaiken, 1993).

Conner et al. (2002), for example, conducted two prospective studies on the moderating effect of ambivalence on the attitude–behaviour relationship. For two kinds of dietary behaviour (eating a low-fat diet and eating five portions of fruit and vegetables per day), high ambivalence was found to be associated with a weaker attitude–behaviour relationship than low ambivalence (the authors used a formula based/indirect measure). With respect to the first dieting behaviour, the interaction of ambivalence and attitudes even held when past dieting behaviour was controlled for.

Ambivalence is a measure of attitude strength, and stronger attitudes should be better predictors of behaviour (see Petty & Krosnick, 1995); this could be due to the greater stability of stronger attitudes across time (but see Armitage & Conner, 2000) or due to the fact that stronger attitudes are more accessible at any moment in time (for an overview concerning these and related explanations see Conner et al., 2002, 2003). Also related to these properties of ambivalent attitudes may be a presumed greater context dependency of ambivalent attitudes (Jonas et al., 2000): Ambivalence of an attitude indicates that the cognitions and/or emotions underlying the attitude are evaluatively mixed. For example, an ambivalent attitude towards avoiding drugs or practising safe sex means that the individual possesses not only cognitions implying the avoidance of drugs or practising safe sex, but also cognitions implying the opposite behaviour (see Priester, 2002). Thus, dependent on the situational context (e.g., a risk-taking or a responsible sexual partner) different behavioural implications may be evoked that guide the actual behaviour.

Ambivalent attitudes may therefore have a basis (i.e., their underlying cognitions or emotions) that is not completely salient at every moment in time. As a result, even the experience of ambivalence may vary across time, depending on the degree to which the individual senses the extent to which his or her relevant cognitions or emotions are inconsistent or contradictory. Corroborating these assumptions, Newby-Clark et al. (2002) found that the relationship between potential and felt ambivalence was strongest for those participants whose contradictory evaluations of the pertinent issues (capital punishment and abortion) were relatively high in simultaneous accessibility; interestingly, this relationship was even stronger for participants with high preference for consistency.

Maio, Bell, and Esses (1996) have argued that as felt ambivalence is an unpleasant experience it may motivate more elaborate thinking or more elaborate message processing, since (message) elaboration helps to cope with discomfort and to render a more clear-cut favourable or unfavourable evaluation. Consistent with this assumption, Maio et al. (1996) and Jonas, Diehl, and Brömer (1997) have shown that ambivalence is indeed associated with a higher level of systematic processing. Also consistent with the idea of ambivalence as an unpleasant psychological state that induces cognitive elaboration to resolve it are the predictions postulated by Hodson et al. (2001). According to these authors, attitudinal ambivalence may motivate the search for information that could be useful in resolving conflict between the incompatible evaluations. Consistent with this notion, Hodson et al. (2001) found that ambivalent individuals were more susceptible to consensus information of their supposed peers.

These two moderating effects of ambivalence, the moderation of the relationship between attitudes and behaviour and the moderation of the likelihood or depth of elaboration, appear to be interrelated, rather than separate phenomena. As shown by Jonas et al. (1997), the increased systematic processing accompanying states of ambivalence leads to an increase in the relationship between attitudes and intentions. In a mediational analysis, these authors showed that the relation between attitudes and intentions is indeed mediated by the amount of elaboration. This finding is consistent with the results of other studies indicating that elaboration tends to increase the strength of attitudes.

The concept of attitudinal ambivalence as a moderator of the consistency between attitudes and behaviour fits in nicely with well-established relevant theories such as the theory of planned behaviour (TPB; Ajzen & Fishbein, 2000) and the transtheoretical model (TTM), a model well supported in health psychology (e.g., Prochaska & DiClemente, 1983; see also Armitage, Povey, & Arden, 2003). According to the TPB, an intention is the proximal determinant of the pertinent behaviour and intentions are determined by attitudes towards the behaviour, the subjective norm, and perceived behavioural control. The concept of attitudinal ambivalence can be integrated easily here; the "most natural" link concerned is obviously the link between attitudes and intentions (although Conner et al., 2003, speculate about influences of ambivalence on other TPB links, e.g., the link between intentions and behaviour). An ambivalent attitude may weaken the attitude–intention relationship due to one or more of the processes explained above, for example, because of the presumed stronger context dependency or due to the process hypothesised by Conner et al. (2003). These authors argue that the capacity of an attitude to predict behaviour may be partly dependent on the attitude's ability to bias perceptions of the attitude object and the context in which the behaviour is performed. Thus, strong attitudes such as those characterised by low ambivalence can be assumed to be more readily accessible and therefore be expected to produce these biasing effects with a higher likelihood.

In fact, Conner et al. (2003) conducted a prospective study in which participants (at time 1) answered measures of the TPB in relation to 20 components of healthy dieting, a measure of ambivalence towards healthy dieting in general, and (1 week later) self-reported behaviour. Analyses showed that the relation between attitude and behaviour as well the relation between perceived behavioural control and behaviour was stronger for participants with low (vs high) attitudinal ambivalence (these authors used a formula based/indirect measure for dividing participants into the high vs low groups).

Likewise, attitudinal ambivalence is a welcome supplement to the transtheoretical model. As compared to the TPB, the most notable feature of the TTM is the incorporation of a longitudinal aspect. The model describes the process of achieving a particular health goal (such as giving up smoking) as a sequence of five stages that have to be traversed successfully (cf. Armitage et al., 2003). In the precontemplation stage individuals do not even consider changing their problematic behaviour (e.g., smoking, alcohol abuse). When they reach the contemplation stage they are thinking about their problematic behaviour and its possible adverse consequences. The third stage—the preparation stage—consists in mental preparation of a behaviour change; that is, the formulation of intentions and action plans. The fourth stage, the action stage, is characterised by open attempts to change or abandon the problematic behaviour, although in this stage relapses are frequent. The fifth stage, maintenance, consists in maintaining the changed behaviour successfully over a relatively long period of time (often operationalised as a 6-month period without relapse).

The TTM assumes that two important psychological variables accompany the (successful) transition from stage to stage. The first is self-efficacy (Bandura, 2001); that is, an individual's perception that he or she is able to carry out the pertinent behaviour (e.g., stop smoking). The second variable, which is more important in the present context, is the so-called decisional balance, a concept borrowed from the decision theory of Janis and Mann (1977). Decisional balance deals with the consideration of the positive and the negative consequences (pros and cons) of a particular (negative health) behaviour such as smoking. According to the TTM the pros and cons are polarised at the precontemplation and at the maintenance stage, but tend to be more or less equally strong during the three stages in between. It is evident from this description that a rather close correspondence between decisional balance and (cognitive) ambivalence can be expected or even that the two concepts refer to an identical construct (admittedly, however, the decisional balance construct neglects the affective aspect that is included in the ambivalence construct). Therefore, the TTM allows us to derive the prediction that potential as well as felt ambivalence should show a curvilinear relationship across the five stages, being maximal during the contemplation, preparation, or action stages, and assuming very low values during the precontemplation and maintenance stage. In fact, this kind of discontinuity pattern was found by Armitage et al. (2003) with respect to attitudinal ambivalence (towards the consumption of five portions of fruit and vegetables per day and towards eating a low-fat diet).

The TTM enriches the existing ambivalence research by at least three interesting theoretical notions, the first being the decision-theoretical assumption that a certain degree of conflict between pros and cons is a necessary concomitant of certain behaviour changes. The second is the assumption that ambivalence is not at all a stable characteristic of an attitude but more a transitional stage. The third notable aspect inherent in the TTM is the implication that measures of potential and of felt ambivalence tend to reflect the underlying decisional balance more in the way of a mirror variable, rather than being a causal variable per se.

Additional facets of research on attitudinal ambivalence

An interesting application of attitudinal ambivalence with respect to children's attachment style was presented by Maio et al. (2000). These authors investigated whether ambivalence towards parents in boys and girls between 12 and 14 years of age was related to these children's general attachment styles (cf. Bartholomew & Horowitz, 1991; Bowlby, 1982). In two studies it was found that ambivalence towards the father was related negatively to security in attachment to others (results were similar though weaker for ambivalence towards the mother). This relation held even when each of a number of other attitude properties (valence, extremity, commitment, inconsistency, and embeddedness) was controlled for. Furthermore, mediational analyses were consistent with the hypothesis that the relation between children's ambivalence towards their father and their general secure attachment was mediated by their secure attachment to the father.

Kachadourian, Fincham, and Davila (2005) were interested in the role of attitudinal ambivalence towards the partner with respect to forgiveness of a partner transgression. Specifically, they reasoned that a partner transgression is likely to prime the negative component of their ambivalence. As a consequence, ambivalent individuals were predicted to be less forgiving. Further, however, ruminating about a transgression was assumed to chronically prime the negative component of an individual's partner-related ambivalence. Together, this led to the prediction of an interaction of ambivalence and rumination regarding forgiveness. Controlling for transgression severity, marital satisfaction, and current depressive symptoms, a study involving married couples showed, in fact, that for both husbands and wives high (but not low) in rumination, higher attitudinal ambivalence towards the partner was related negatively to forgiveness regarding a transgression of the partner.

Riketta and Ziegler (2005a, 2005b) studied the role of ambivalence with respect to the self. According to a widely accepted definition, self-esteem is an attitude towards the self as a whole (Baumeister, 1998; Rosenberg, 1965). Much research on self-esteem is focused on the valence dimension of this attitude by distinguishing between high (i.e., relatively positive) and low (i.e., relatively negative) self-esteem (see Baumeister, Campbell, Krueger, & Vohs, 2003). Usually, researchers define low self-esteem people as those whose scores on a (self-report) self-esteem measure are lower than those of most of the others in a given sample. Actually, however, most people classified this way as having low self-esteem have scores around, or even slightly above, the scale midpoint. More important, this suggests two alternative interpretations concerning the nature of low self-esteem. First, these scores may reflect indifference, or a neutral attitude towards the self. In this case, low self-esteem in its common operationalisation would denote "the absence of positive views of self rather than ... the presence of negative views" (Baumeister, 1993, p. 204). Second, those moderate self-ratings may reflect self-ambivalence, or a conflicted attitude towards the self. In this case, low self-esteem would denote the co-existence of positive and negative self-views.

In fact, in four studies it was found that self-esteem correlates negatively with self-ambivalence (Riketta & Ziegler, 2005b). The average (cross-sectional, n-weighted) correlations across the studies of potential and felt self-ambivalence with self-esteem were $-.40$ and $-.65$, respectively. Thus, at least some people with low self-esteem are characterised by (a) the co-presence of positive and negative self-views (potential self-ambivalence) and (b) the experience of mixed feelings and contradictory beliefs with regard to the self (felt self-ambivalence). Further, it was shown that both felt and potential ambivalence remained fairly stable over a 4-week period.

Riketta and Ziegler (2005a) tested the role of self-ambivalence with respect to individuals' reactions to success versus failure by manipulating the difficulty of a cognitive task that participants had to perform (cf. Brown & Dutton, 1995). Drawing on the ambivalence-amplification hypothesis (Katz, 1981), it was expected, and found, that the effects of the feedback on self-evaluations (i.e., state self-esteem and appraisal of one's ability in the domain of the task) would be stronger among people high versus low in self-ambivalence. Importantly, these moderating effects were found to be independent of trait self-esteem.

Conclusions

Research on attitudinal ambivalence has enhanced our understanding of the nature of the attitude–behaviour relationship. Several studies have shown that attitudinal ambivalence moderates the relation between attitudes and behaviour (e.g., Conner et al., 2002, 2003), with higher ambivalence leading to lower correlations between the two. Thinking about attitudinal ambivalence as an aspect of the underlying attitude structure helps to clarify some of the possible reasons: Attitudes with a lower degree of ambivalence tend to be stronger; thus, they tend to be more salient at any point in time and therefore more influential in directing relevant behaviours (and possibly tend to bias the perception of the pertinent attitude objects; e.g., Conner et al., 2003). In addition, ambivalent attitudes are connected with a more contradictory attitude structure, an aspect that makes them more susceptible to influences of the situational context, rendering the positive or the negative consequences of a certain behaviour more or less salient. In addition, theorising about attitudinal ambivalence has helped to integrate several theoretical traditions that have coexisted without a very close interrelationship, such as the TPB and the TTM. The TPB profits from the TTM perspective, which is more longitudinal and more process oriented than the TPB, and the construct of attitudinal ambivalence is an additional theoretical link to bridge the gap between the two: The degree of ambivalence may be seen as a mark to indicate the point reached by an individual in the process that the individual undergoes in a decision for a certain (health-related) behaviour. Seen in this perspective, the underlying decisional balance, rather than ambivalence as such, is the relevant moderator of the attitude–behaviour relationship.

Admittedly, several aspects of this theorising still have to be regarded as speculative since the existing research on the attitude–behaviour relationship lacks experimental studies that could be designed to clarify the underlying processes in more detail. This is an obvious task for the next generation of ambivalence studies. Besides clarifying in more detail the consequences of ambivalence for processing information, these studies should also attempt to integrate the additional facets of ambivalence research carried out so far. Thus, they should try to take into consideration the interesting theoretical and empirical developments that have been observed in the research on ambivalence with respect to important complex attitude objects such as one's own self (e.g., Riketta & Ziegler, 2005a, 2005b) and significant others (e.g., Kachadourian et al., 2005; Maio et al., 2000). Whereas previous ambivalence research has focused mainly on rather "simple" attitude objects such as eating a low-fat diet or eating fruit, it remains to be shown whether the existing theorising about the determinants and consequences of ambivalence, as well as its moderating effects, can be transferred to more complex attitude objects such as one's own self.

References

Abelson, R. P., Aronson, E., McGuire, W. J., Newcomb, T. M., Rosenberg, M. J., & Tannenbaum, P. H. (Eds.). (1968). *Theories of cognitive consistency: A sourcebook.* Chicago: Rand McNally.

Ainsworth, M. D. S. (1989). Attachment beyond infancy. *American Psychologist, 44,* 709–716.

Ainsworth, M. D. S., Blehar, M. C., Waters, E., & Wall, S. (1978). *Patterns of attachment.* Hillsdale, NJ: Lawrence Erlbaum Associates Inc.

Ajzen, I. (2001). Nature and operation of attitudes. *Annual Review of Psychology, 52,* 27–58.

Ajzen, I., & Fishbein, M. (2000). Attitudes and the attitude–behavior relation: Reasoned and automatic processes. In W. Stroebe & M. Hewstone (Eds.), *European review of social psychology* (Vol. 11, pp. 1–33). Chichester, UK: Wiley.

Anderson, N. H. (1981). *Foundations of information integration theory*. San Diego, CA: Academic Press.

Armitage, C. J., & Conner, M. (2000). Attitudinal ambivalence: A test of three key hypotheses. *Personality and Social Psychology Bulletin, 26*, 1421–1432.

Armitage, C. J., Povey, R., & Arden, M. A. (2003). Evidence for discontinuity patterns across the stages of change: A role for attitudinal ambivalence. *Psychology and Health, 18*, 373–386.

Aronson, E. (1969). The theory of cognitive dissonance: A current perspective. In L. Berkowitz (Ed.), *Advances in experimental social psychology* (Vol. 4, pp. 1–34). San Diego, CA: Academic Press.

Bandura, A. (2001). Social cognitive theory: An agentic perspective. *Annual Review of Psychology, 52*, 1–26.

Bartholomew, K., & Horowitz, L. M. (1991). Attachment styles among young adults: A test of a four category model. *Journal of Personality and Social Psychology, 61*, 226–244.

Baumeister, R. F. (1993). Understanding the inner nature of low self-esteem: Uncertain, fragile, protective, and conflicted. In R. F. Baumeister (Ed.), *Self-esteem: The puzzle of low self-regard* (pp. 201–218). New York: Plenum.

Baumeister, R. F. (1998). The self. In D. T. Gilbert, S. T. Fiske, & G. Lindzey (Eds.), *Handbook of social psychology* (4th ed., pp. 680–740). New York: McGraw-Hill.

Baumeister, R. F., Campbell, J. D., Krueger, J. I., & Vohs, K. D. (2003). Does high self-esteem cause better performance, interpersonal success, happiness or healthier lifestyles? *Psychological Science in the Public Interest, 4*, 1–44.

Bleuler, E. (1911). Vortrag über Ambivalenz [Lecture on ambivalence]. *Zentralblatt für Psychoanalyse, 1*, 266–268.

Bowlby, J. (1982). *Attachment and loss (Vol. 1). Attachment* (2nd ed.). New York: Basic Books.

Breckler, S. J. (1994). A comparison of numerical indexes for measuring attitude ambivalence, *Educational and Psychological Measurement, 54*, 350–365.

Brown, J. D., & Dutton, K. A. (1995). The thrill of victory, the complexity of defeat: Self-esteem and people's emotional reactions to success and failure. *Journal of Personality and Social Psychology, 68*, 712–722.

Cacioppo, J. T., Gardner, W. L., & Berntson, G. G. (1997). Beyond bipolar conceptualizations and measures: The case of attitudes and evaluative space. *Personality and Social Psychology Review, 1*, 3–25.

Conner, M., Povey, R., Sparks, P., James, R., & Shepherd, R. (2003). Moderating role of attitudinal ambivalence within the theory of planned behavior. *British Journal of Social Psychology, 42*, 75–94.

Conner, P., Sparks, P., Povey, R., James, R., Shepherd, R., & Armitage, C. J. (2002). Moderator effects of attitudinal ambivalence on attitude–behaviour relationships. *European Journal of Social Psychology, 32*, 705–718.

Cooper, J., & Fazio, R. H. (1984). A new look at dissonance theory. In L. Berkowitz (Ed.), *Advances in experimental social psychology* (Vol.17, pp. 229–266). San Diego, CA: Academic Press.

Costarelli, S., & Colloca, P. (2004). The effects of attitudinal ambivalence on pro-environmental behavioural intentions. *Journal of Environmental Psychology, 24*, 279–288.

Eagly, A. H., & Chaiken, S. (1993). *The psychology of attitudes*. Forth Worth, TX: Harcourt Brace Jovanovich.

Eagly, A. H., & Chaiken, S. (1998). Attitude structure and function. In D.T. Gilbert, S.T. Fiske, & G. Lindzey (Eds.), *Handbook of social psychology* (4th ed., Vol. 2, pp. 269–322). Boston, MA: McGraw-Hill.

Fishbein, M., & Ajzen, I. (1975). *Belief, attitude, intention, and behavior: An introduction to theory and research.* Reading, MA: Addison-Wesley.

Freud, S. (1943). Zur Dynamik der Übertragung. In S. Freud, *Gesammelte Werke chronologisch geordnet* [Collected works chronologically arranged] (pp. 364–374). London: Imago (original work published 1912).

Glick, P., & Fiske, S.T. (1996). The ambivalent sexism inventory: Differentiating hostile and benevolent sexism. *Journal of Personality and Social Psychology, 70,* 491–512.

Hassin, R., Uleman, J. S., & Bargh, J. A (Eds.). (2005). *The new unconscious.* New York: Oxford University Press.

Heider, F. (1958). *The psychology of interpersonal relations.* New York: Wiley.

Hodson, G., Maio, G. R., & Esses, V. M. (2001). The role of attitudinal ambivalence in susceptibility to consensus information. *Basic and Applied Social Psychology, 23,* 197–205.

Janis, I. L., & Mann, L. (1977). *Decision making: A psychological analysis of conflict, choice and commitment.* New York: The Free Press.

Jonas, K., Brömer, P., & Diehl, M. (2000). Attitudinal ambivalence. In W. Stroebe & M. Hewstone (Eds.), *European review of social psychology* (Vol. 11, pp. 35–74). Chichester, UK: Wiley.

Jonas, K., Diehl, M., & Brömer, P. (1997). Effects of attitudinal ambivalence on information processing and attitude–intention consistency. *Journal of Experimental Social Psychology, 33,* 190–210.

Kachadourian, L. K., Fincham, F., & Davila, J. (2005). Attitudinal ambivalence, rumination, and forgiveness of partner transgressions in marriage. *Personality and Social Psychology Bulletin, 31,* 334–342.

Kaplan, K. J. (1972). On the ambivalence–indifference problem in attitude theory and measurement. A suggested modification on the semantic differential technique. *Psychological Bulletin, 77,* 361–372.

Katz, I. (1981). *Stigma: A social psychological analysis.* Hillsdale, NJ: Lawrence Erlbaum Associates Inc.

Katz, I., & Hass, R. G. (1988). Racial ambivalence and American value conflict: Correlational and priming studies of dual cognitive structures. *Journal of Personality and Social Psychology, 55,* 893–905.

King, L. A. (1998). Ambivalence over emotional expression and reading emotions in situations and faces. *Journal of Personality and Social Psychology, 74,* 753–762.

King, L. A., & Emmons, R. A. (1990). Conflict over emotional expression: Psychological and physiological correlates. *Journal of Personality and Social Psychology, 58,* 864–877.

Klopfer, F. J., & Madden, T. M. (1980). The middlemost choice on attitude items: Ambivalence, neutrality, or uncertainty? *Personality and Social Psychology Bulletin, 6,* 97–101.

Lipkus, I. M., Pollak, K. I., McBride, C. M., Schwartz-Bloom, R., Lyna, P., & Bloom, P. N. (2005). Assessing attitudinal ambivalence towards smoking and its association with desire to quit among teen smokers. *Psychology and Health, 20,* 373–387.

Maio, G. R., Bell, D. W., & Esses, V. M. (1996). Ambivalence and persuasion: The processing of messages about immigrant groups. *Journal of Experimental Social Psychology*, *32*, 513–536.

Maio, G. R., Fincham, F. D., & Lycett, E. J. (2000). Attitudinal ambivalence toward parents and attachment style. *Personality and Social Psychology Bulletin*, *26*, 1451–1464.

Newby-Clark, I. R., McGregor, I., & Zanna, M. P. (2002). Thinking and caring about cognitive inconsistency: When and for whom does attitudinal ambivalence feel uncomfortable? *Journal of Personality and Social Psychology*, *82*, 157–166.

Petty, R. E., & Krosnick, J. A. (Eds.). (1995). *Attitude strength: Antecedents and consequences*. Mahwah, NJ: Lawrence Erlbaum Associates Inc.

Petty, R. E., & Wegener, D. T. (1998). Attitude change: Multiple roles for persuasion variables. In D. T. Gilbert, S. T. Fiske, & G. Lindzey (Eds.), *Handbook of social psychology* (4th ed., Vol. 1, pp. 323–390). Boston, MA: McGraw-Hill.

Priester, J. R. (2002). Sex, drugs, and attitudinal ambivalence: How feelings of evaluative tension influence alcohol use and safe sex behaviors. In W. Crano & M. Burgoon (Eds.), *Mass media and drug prevention: Classic and contemporary theories and research* (pp. 145–162). Mawah, NJ: Lawrence Erlbaum Associates Inc.

Priester, J. R., & Petty, R. E. (1996). The gradual threshold model of ambivalence: Relating the positive and negative bases of attitudes to subjective ambivalence. *Journal of Personality and Social Psychology*, *71*, 431–449.

Priester, J. R., & Petty, R. E. (2001). Extending the bases of subjective attitudinal ambivalence: Interpersonal and intrapersonal antecedents of evaluative tension. *Journal of Personality and Social Psychology*, *80*, 19–34.

Prochaska, J., & DiClemente, C. (1983). Stages of processes of self-change of smoking: Towards an integrative model of change. *Journal of Consulting and Clinical Psychology*, *51*, 390–395.

Riketta, M., & Ziegler, R. (2005a). *Self-ambivalence and reactions to success versus failure*. Unpublished manuscript, University of Tübingen, Germany.

Riketta, M., & Ziegler, R. (2005b). *Self-ambivalence and self-esteem*. Unpublished manuscript, University of Tübingen, Germany.

Rosenberg, M. (1965). *Society and the adolescent self-image*. Princeton, NJ: Princeton University Press.

Scott, W. A. (1966). Measures of cognitive structure. *Multivariate Behavioral Research*, *1*, 391–395.

Scott, W. A. (1969). Structure of natural cognitions. *Journal of Personality and Social Psychology*, *4*, 261–278.

Stone, J., Aronson, E., Craine, A. L., Winslow, M. P., & Fried, C. B. (1994). Inducing hypocrisy as a means of encouraging young adults to use condoms. *Personality and Social Psychology Bulletin*, *20*, 116–128.

Thompson, M. M., Zanna, M. P., & Griffin, D. W. (1995). Let's not be indifferent about (attitudinal) ambivalence. In R. E. Petty & J. A. Krosnick (Eds.), *Attitude strength: Antecedents and consequences* (pp. 361–386). Mahwah, NJ: Lawrence Erlbaum Associates Inc.

Thurstone, L. L., & Chave, E. J. (1929). *The measurement of attitude*. Chicago, IL: University of Chicago Press.

4 Changing health-related behaviours

An approach based on the theory of planned behaviour

Icek Ajzen
University of Massachusetts—Amherst, USA

Antony S. R. Manstead
Cardiff University, UK

Human behavior is at the centre of much research in the health domain because of its potential contribution to the myriad of medical conditions that afflict people every day. The detrimental health effects of cigarette smoking, alcohol and drug abuse, lack of exercise, poor nutrition, and so forth are well documented (see Stroebe, 2000). These lifestyle behaviours increase, among other things, the risk for various types of cancer, emphysema, coronary heart disease, diabetes, osteoporosis, and sleep disorders. Besides raising morbidity, these behaviours can also have a generally detrimental impact on quality of life. In the first part of this chapter we use a reasoned action approach, the theory of planned behaviour (Ajzen, 1988, 1991), to examine the causal antecedents of health-related behaviours, asking why people perform, or fail to perform, recommended health practices. A good understanding of these antecedents is of interest in its own right but, equally important, it is essential for designing effective intervention programmes, a topic we address in the second part of this chapter. We illustrate the potential utility of the theory of planned behaviour in this regard and then focus on one particular problem faced by any reasoned action approach, the question of behavioural routines, habits, and addictions.

Explaining health-related behaviours

Compliance with recommended health practices can be difficult due to changing health recommendations occasioned by new scientific discoveries, or contradictory advice coming from investigators and journalists who over-interpret or misinterpret the research findings (Friedman, 2003). With respect to most lifestyle behaviours, however, there is good agreement in the medical community, and—at least in developed countries—advice regarding recommended practices is widely disseminated. Thus, most people in these countries know that smoking, excessive drinking, use of hard drugs, and lack of exercise are detrimental to health; and that a healthy diet should be low in fat and include a balance of different food groups, in particular, a sufficient amount of fruit and vegetables. Nevertheless, many people exhibit a lifestyle that fails to follow the recommended practices.

Prevailing research efforts

Most current attempts to understand the antecedents of health-related lifestyles tend to focus on a variety of environmental, demographic, and personal factors. Environmental factors such as peer and parental pressure as well as media exposure can influence health-related lifestyles (He, Kramer, Houser, Chomitz, & Hacker, 2004), and diagnosis of an illness such as cancer or heart disease can prompt lifestyle changes (Blanchard et al., 2003). Relatively little, however, is known about the psychological mechanisms that mediate these effects. Lifestyles are also often found to differ across demographic segments of the population that vary in social class, income, education, age, and sex (e.g., He et al., 2004; Karvonen, West, Sweeting, Rahkonen, & Young, 2001; Vereecken, Maes, & De Bacquer, 2004). However, a relation between these factors and particular lifestyle behaviours is not always observed, results are inconsistent across studies, and the amount of variance in lifestyle behaviours accounted for by demographic characteristics tends to be relatively low. Most importantly, demographic characteristics can point towards potentially relevant factors to be considered, but by themselves they do not provide an explanation for observed differences in health-related behaviours.

Many studies have attempted to identify general personality or individual difference variables relevant for health-related lifestyles. Personal factors of this kind would appear to hold out the greatest promise of providing a psychologically interesting explanation of health-related behaviour. Alas, attempts to identify important personal factors have met with relatively little success. For example, among the personal factors studied, self-esteem stands out as a potentially important determinant of health-related lifestyles. Generally speaking, low self-esteem would be expected to predispose such detrimental health behaviours as smoking, drug and alcohol abuse, and unsafe sex. However, a recent review of the literature (Baumeister, Campbell, Krueger, & Vohs, 2003, p. 35) found little evidence for these expectations:

> Most studies on self-esteem and smoking have failed to find any significant relationship, even with very large samples and the correspondingly high statistical power . . . Large, longitudinal investigations have tended to yield no relationship between self-esteem and either drinking in general or heavy, problem drinking in particular . . . Self-esteem does not appear to prevent early sexual activity or teen pregnancy.

Similarly disappointing results are found in research on other types of psychological factors. For example, very weak correlations were reported between basic human values and food-related lifestyles (Brunso, Scholderer, & Grunert, 2004); health locus of control had no effect on the ability to cut down on fatty food or smoking, to exercise regularly, or to lose weight (de Valle & Norman, 1992); and very low correlations were found between perceived health status and a measure of health-promoting lifestyle that included physical activity, nutrition, and stress management (Pullen, Walker, & Fiandt, 2001).

In sum, the search for explanations of lifestyle behaviours in terms of environmental, demographic, and personal factors has met with very limited success. All we know is that certain environmental factors can affect lifestyles and prompt lifestyle changes, that demographic characteristics are sometimes associated with different lifestyles, and that general psychological factors such as self-esteem, life values, and health consciousness tend to be of little relevance. This approach has clearly failed to provide a useful overarching framework for understanding health-related lifestyle behaviours.

An alternative paradigm: The theory of planned behaviour

Perhaps the most popular conceptual framework to date for thinking about the determinants of particular behaviours is provided by the theory of planned behaviour (Ajzen, 1991). This theory has been used successfully in attempts to provide a better understanding of such diverse health-related behaviours as exercising, donating blood, adhering to a low-fat diet, using condoms for AIDS prevention, using illegal drugs, and wearing a safety helmet, among many more (for recent reviews, see Ajzen & Fishbein, 2005; Armitage & Conner, 2001; Blue, 1995; Hagger, Chatzisarantis, & Biddle, 2002; Sutton, 1998).

Briefly, according to the theory of planned behaviour, human action is influenced by three major factors: a favourable or unfavourable evaluation of the behaviour (attitude towards the behaviour), perceived social pressure to perform or not perform the behaviour (subjective norm), and perceived capability to perform the behaviour (perceived behavioural control). In combination, attitude towards the behaviour, subjective norm, and perception of behavioural control lead to the formation of a behavioural intention. As a general rule, the more favourable the attitude and subjective norm, and the greater the perceived behavioural control, the stronger should be the person's intention to perform the behaviour in question. Finally, given a sufficient degree of actual control over the behaviour, people are expected to carry out their intentions when the opportunity arises. Intention is thus assumed to be an immediate antecedent of behaviour. However, because many behaviours pose difficulties of execution that may limit volitional control, it is useful to consider perceived behavioural control in addition to intention. To the extent that people are realistic in their judgements of a behaviour's difficulty, a measure of perceived behavioural control can serve as a proxy for actual control and contribute to the prediction of the behaviour in question. A schematic representation of the theory is shown in Figure 4.1.

When applied to a health-related behaviour, such as eating a low-fat diet, the theory of planned behaviour suggests that intentions, together with perceived behavioural control, predict the likelihood that a person will actually perform this behaviour. Intentions to eat a low-fat diet, in turn, are determined by attitudes towards eating a low-fat diet, by perceived social pressure to do so (subjective norm), and by perceptions of control over this behaviour.

The three major determinants in the theory of planned behaviour—attitudes towards the behaviour, subjective norms, and perceptions of behavioural control—are traced to corresponding sets of behaviour-related beliefs. Consistent with an expectancy-value model (Fishbein, 1963; Fishbein & Ajzen, 1975), attitude towards eating a low-fat diet is assumed to be determined by beliefs about the consequences of this behaviour, each belief weighted by the subjective value of the outcome in question. A similar logic applies to the relation between normative beliefs and subjective norm, and the relation between control beliefs and perceived behavioural control. Normative beliefs refer to the perceived behavioural expectations of important referent individuals or groups such as the person's family, friends, co-workers, and health professionals. These normative beliefs—in combination with the motivation to comply with the different referents—determine the prevailing subjective norm regarding the behaviour. Finally, control beliefs have to do with the perceived presence of factors that can facilitate or impede performance of a behaviour. It is assumed that the perceived power of each control factor to impede or facilitate performing the behaviour contributes to

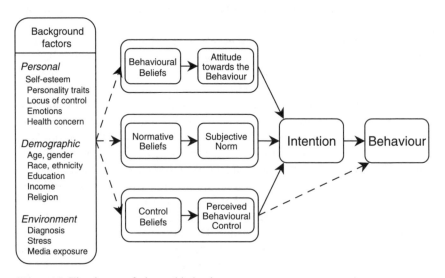

Figure 4.1 The theory of planned behaviour.

perceived control in direct proportion to the person's subjective probability that the control factor is present.

In focusing on these subjective psychological determinants, the theory does not deny the importance of demographic, environmental, and personal characteristics. However, as can be seen in Figure 4.1, in the theory of planned behaviours these kinds of factors are considered background variables that can influence behaviour indirectly by affecting behavioural, normative, and control beliefs.

Illustrations

A large number of studies have applied the theory of planned behaviour to examine the psychological antecedents of specific health-related behaviours, and more recently attempts have also been made to use the theory as a framework for behavioural interventions. It is beyond the scope of the present chapter to review this large body of research (for summaries, see Albarracin, Johnson, Fishbein, & Muellerleile, 2001; Godin & Kok, 1996; Hausenblas, Carron, & Mack, 1997). Overall, the theory has been well supported. With regard to the prediction of behaviour, many studies have substantiated the predictive validity of behavioural intentions. Meta-analyses of studies dealing with specific health behaviours, such as condom use and exercise, have revealed mean intention–behaviour correlations ranging from .44 to .56 (Albarracin et al., 2001; Godin & Kok, 1996; Hausenblas et al., 1997; Sheeran & Orbell, 1998). Moreover, it has been found that the addition of perceived behavioural control can improve prediction of behaviour considerably, especially when performance of the behaviour is difficult. For example, in a sample of smokers, a measure of perceived behavioural control accounted for an additional 12% of the variance in smoking behaviour over and above intentions (Godin, Valois, Lepage, & Desharnais, 1992).

Regarding the antecedents of intentions, Table 4.1 summarises the results of a few recent studies that attempted to predict behavioural intentions in the health domain. It can be seen that the theory of planned behaviour accounted for appreciable variance in people's intentions to perform a diverse set of behaviours: physical exercise, using illicit drugs, eating a low-fat diet, consuming diary products, and performing breast self-examinations. Indeed, several meta-analyses of the empirical literature have provided strong evidence to show that intentions to perform health-related behaviours can be predicted with considerable accuracy from measures of attitudes towards the behaviour, subjective norms, and perceived behavioural control or self-efficacy (Albarracin et al., 2001; Godin & Kok, 1996; Hagger et al., 2002; Sheeran & Taylor, 1999).

Substantive information about the considerations that guide the decision to perform a given behaviour is obtained by examining the behavioural, normative, and control beliefs that provide the basis for attitudes, subjective norms, and perceptions of behavioural control. The role of behavioural and

Table 4.1 Prediction of intentions from attitude towards the behaviour (A_B), subjective norm (SN), and perceived behavioural control (PBC)

Intention	Correlation coefficients			Regression coefficients			
	A_B	SN	PBC	A_B	SN	PBC	R
Physical exercise (Courneya, 1995)	.51	.47	.48	.22	.17	.18	.62
Using cannabis (Conner & McMillan, 1999)	.70	.55	.69	.42	.11	.43	.81
Eating a low-fat diet (Armitage & Conner, 1999)	.68	.43	.59	.36	.16	.33	.78
Consuming dairy products (Kim, Reicks, & Sjoberg, 2003)	.42	.33	.48	.38	.11*	.30	.65
Breast self-examination (Norman & Hoyle (2004)	.56	.52	.80	.26	.03*	.70	.85

* Not significant; all other coefficients $p < .05$.

Table 4.2 Mean behavioural belief strength and outcome evaluations for people intending and not intending to eat a low-fat diet

Outcome	Belief strength		Outcome evaluation	
	Intenders	Non-intenders	Intenders	Non-intenders
Feel good about myself	1.53	−0.24*	2.59	2.40
Eat boring foods	−0.87	−0.01*	−2.14	−2.27
Reduce risk of heart disease	2.29	2.12	2.77	2.63
Eat bad-tasting food	−1.08	−0.39*	−2.07	−2.51*
Feel healthier	1.95	0.59*	2.61	2.43
Reduce enjoyment of food	−0.59	0.21*	−2.21	−2.48
Maintain lower weight	1.93	1.27*	1.88	0.67*
Make me not feel guilty	0.24	0.24	1.97	2.07

From Armitage and Conner (1999). Behavioural belief strength and outcome evaluations scored −3 to +3.
* Difference between intenders and non-intenders $p < .05$.

control beliefs is illustrated in a study on adherence to a low-fat diet among college students (Armitage & Conner, 1999). As can be seen in Table 4.2, participants who intended to adhere to a low-fat diet differed significantly from participants who did not intend to do so in their assessment of this behaviour's likely outcomes, as well as in their evaluations of some of the anticipated outcomes. Specifically, they were more likely to believe that adhering to a low-fat diet makes them feel good about themselves, makes them feel healthier, and helps them to maintain lower weight; and they were less likely to believe that it means eating boring or bad-tasting food, or that it would reduce their enjoyment from eating. Moreover, in comparison to participants who did not intend to adhere to a low-fat diet, those who intended to do so placed greater value on maintaining lower body weight and were somewhat less concerned about the poor taste of a low-fat diet.

Similar comparisons reveal interesting differences in control beliefs, as can be seen in Table 4.3. Participants who intended to adhere to a low-fat diet were less likely to believe that such a diet is expensive or that they lack the requisite knowledge of the fat content in foods. In addition, they realised more strongly the potential difficulties posed by temptation of high-fat foods, by the motivation required to maintain a low-fat diet, and by lack of information about fat content in foods.

Finally, an example of the role that normative beliefs can play in influencing health-related behaviour is provided by a study on mothers' choice of breast vs bottle feeding their newborn babies (Manstead, Proffitt, & Smart, 1983). Examination of the differences between mothers who breast fed their babies and mothers who used the bottle showed first that there was little difference in their motivation to comply with their important normative referents. Most of the women were highly motivated to comply with the expectations of the baby's father and somewhat less so in relation to the expectations of their mothers, close female friends, and medical advisers. However, there were considerable differences in their normative beliefs regarding the two methods, as can also be seen in Table 4.4. Inspection of the normative beliefs for mothers who used the breast-feeding method reveals that, in their opinions, important referents strongly supported this method over the alternative bottle-feeding method. In contrast, women who believed that their referents

Table 4.3 Mean control belief strength and power of control factors for people intending and not intending to eat a low-fat diet

Control factors	Belief strength		Facilitating power	
	Intenders	Non-intenders	Intenders	Non-intenders
Time-consuming	3.44	3.67	3.78	3.48
Expensive	3.73	4.19*	3.73	3.54
Temptation of high-fat foods	4.53	4.88	3.50	2.85*
Requires strong motivation	4.86	5.20	4.53	3.85*
Inconvenient	5.22	5.38	3.36	3.01
Lack of knowledge of fat content	3.30	4.05*	4.80	3.74*
Low availability	4.67	5.04	3.40	3.36

From Armitage and Conner (1999). Control belief strength and power scored 1 to 7.
* Difference between intenders and non-intenders $p < .05$.

Table 4.4 Mean normative beliefs about breast and bottle feeding

Normative beliefs	Mothers who breast fed	Mothers who bottle fed
About breast feeding		
Baby's father	6.15	4.45
Own mother	5.57	4.45
Closest female friend	5.39	4.47
Medical adviser	6.20	5.25
About bottle feeding		
Baby's father	2.89	4.16
Own mother	3.24	3.99
Closest female friend	3.43	3.98
Medical adviser	2.96	3.55

From Manstead et al. (1983). Normative beliefs scored from 1 to 7. All differences between breast-feeding and bottle-feeding mothers are statistically significant ($p < .05$).

had no strong preferences for either method were more likely to feed their babies by means of a bottle.

Behavioural interventions

Although to date, most research with the theory of planned behaviour has been concerned with predicting and explaining various behaviours, the theory has also been used to design behavioural interventions (see Hardeman Johnston, Johnston, Bonetti, Wareham, & Kinmonth, 2002 for a review). For example, Parker, Manstead, and Stradling (1996) built on previous theory of planned behaviour (TPB) studies in which they had identified the beliefs and values that predict intention to commit driving violations, such as speeding. Four short videos were developed in order to assess the effectiveness of interventions to reduce speeding that were grounded in the TPB. Three of the videos featured the major constructs of the TPB model—that is, behavioural beliefs, normative beliefs, and perceived behavioural control— and were specifically designed to influence beliefs that earlier research had found to differentiate those who intended to speed from those who did not. The fourth video featured anticipated regret; that is, the expectation that one might experience negative affect after having performed a behaviour. This construct had previously been shown to add significantly to the predictive performance of the TPB model in relation to driving violations (Parker, Manstead, & Stradling, 1995). The beliefs about and attitudes towards speeding of participants who viewed one of the four experimental videos were compared with those of control subjects who saw a video irrelevant to speeding. Between 45 and 50 members of the general public saw each video twice. Results indicated that two of the videos, namely those featuring normative beliefs and anticipated regret, brought about significant belief changes with respect to scores on TPB items, and significant changes in general attitudes to speeding. However, there was no significant change on a measure of intentions to speed, perhaps reflecting the brevity of the intervention and the resistance to change of certain health-related behaviours.

The results of other intervention studies offer scope for greater optimism. For example, Brubaker and Fowler (1990) evaluated an intervention to encourage men to perform testicular self-examinations (TSE) in order to enhance the chances of early detection of testicular cancer. In addition to testing the effectiveness of the intervention, this study also provided information about changes in some of the underlying beliefs about the behaviour. Male college students were exposed to a 10-minute tape-recorded message designed to change their beliefs about the consequences of performing TSE. Participants in a second condition of the experiment were exposed to a message of equal length that provided general information about testicular cancer, and participants in a control condition received no message at all. About 4 weeks later, all participants completed a theory of planned behaviour questionnaire and reported whether they had performed TSE in the interim.

The results of the study showed the effectiveness of a theory-based intervention. In the no-message control group, about 19% of the participants reported having performed TSE at the end of the 4-week period. This compares with about 44% in the general information group and fully 71% in the theory-based message condition. A structural equation analysis showed that exposure to the messages influenced beliefs with respect to performing TSE; that these changes in beliefs affected attitudes towards the behaviour, subjective norms, and perceptions of behavioural control; and that changes in these three factors raised intentions to perform TSE which, in turn, led to the observed increase in reported TSE.

Even where an intervention is not successful, application of the TPB can shed light on *why* it is not successful. Consider, for example, a study by De Wit, Kok, Timmermans, and Wijnsma (1990) in which they evaluated the effectiveness of a health education programme designed to promote condom use that had been developed by Dutch Educational Television. Secondary-school students completed questionnaires at two time-points. In the intervening period half the students were exposed to the AIDS health education programme, and the other half were not. Condom use intentions were significantly predicted by attitudes towards condom use, perceived norms concerning condom use, and the perceived effectiveness of using condoms. However, although exposure to the programme increased knowledge about AIDS, it had little effect on these antecedents of intentions or on the intentions themselves. Such findings are consistent with the TPB in the sense that there is no reason to believe the mere provision of information about a behaviour will affect intentions or behaviour unless the underlying behavioural, normative or control beliefs about the behaviour are changed.

A considerable strength of the TPB as a tool for designing effective interventions is the fact that—provided the necessary preliminary research has been carried out—it enables health educators to devise focused interventions.

By this we mean that the intervention can be tailored to address those beliefs that have been shown to differ significantly between intenders and non-intenders (or performers and non-performers) of the behaviour in question. It does not make psychological or economic sense to design interventions that address beliefs that are held equally by intenders and non-intenders. For example, based on the research reported by Armitage and Conner (1999), summarised in Table 4.2 above, it would not make sense to focus an intervention intended to increase the consumption of low-fat food on trying to persuade consumers that a low-fat diet reduces the risk of heart disease, because those who intended to eat low-fat food did not differ from their non-intending counterparts with respect to this belief. In fact, all participants strongly agreed that a low-fat diet reduces the risk of heart disease. Rather, it would be more effective to focus intervention efforts on addressing beliefs that eating a low-fat diet makes you feel good, helps you to control your weight, and need not lead to eating bad-tasting or boring food.

A limitation of the TPB with respect to interventions is that it is silent with respect to *how* the beliefs underlying a given behaviour should be changed. However, the model was never intended to serve as a theory of belief change, and there are of course several theories of attitude change available that can be used to design effective interventions. Most obviously, dual-process models such as the Elaboration Likelihood Model (ELM; Petty & Cacioppo, 1986) or the Heuristic Systematic Model (HSM; Chaiken, 1980) can be used for this purpose. A shared assumption of these models is that lasting belief change depends to an important degree on the mental engagement of the audience, in the sense that those exposed to an intervention need to process the information it contains in a systematic way, thinking about its implications for them. The fact that this is a tough set of conditions to fulfil in the context of health education tells us a lot about the difficulty of changing health-related behaviours. If the audience is unmotivated or unable to process the content of an intervention carefully, the intervention is unlikely to be effective.

A final set of considerations relating to interventions anticipates the issues of habit and addiction, which are addressed more fully in the following section. A potential barrier to the effectiveness of an intervention is the habitual or addictive nature of the behaviour that is to be changed. People who engage in a behaviour may be motivated to change it for something healthier, but precisely because of the habitual or addictive nature of the behaviour in question they may find it difficult to act on their good intentions. It is under these conditions that another approach to interventions may be useful. This approach stems from the work of Heckhausen (1991) and Gollwitzer (1993) on the roles of motivation and volition in action. These authors distinguish between a motivational or deliberative stage, which results in the formation of an intention to perform a behaviour, and a volitional or implemental stage, which involves the translation of the intention into behaviour. So whereas the interventions considered above focused on the antecedents of intention, with a view to shaping intentions and thereby behaviour, a different but complementary approach to health interventions focuses on the "intention–behaviour gap". The favoured technique for helping individuals to act on their healthy intentions is to get them to form *implementation intentions*, which differ from ordinary intentions in that they specify where and when the behaviour in question will be enacted. The idea is that acting in accordance with one's intentions becomes easier because some of the responsibility for doing so is transferred from the individual to the external or internal cues.

An example of an intervention using this approach is provided by Armitage (2004), who compared an implementation intention intervention to reduce dietary fat intake with a control condition in which there was no instruction to form implementation intentions. Participants were members of the general public who were randomly allocated to one of these two conditions. A validated food frequency measure was administered before and after the intervention to assess fat intake. The implementation intention manipulation was very simple, consisting only of the instruction "We want you to plan to eat a low-fat diet during the next month. You are free to say how you will do this, but we want you to formulate your plans in as much detail as possible. Please pay particular attention to the situation in which you will implement these plans" (Armitage, 2004, p. 320). Fat intake did not differ between the two groups at baseline; however, it decreased significantly between baseline and a 1-month follow-up in the experimental group (but not in the control group) and it also differed significantly between the two groups at follow-up.

These findings, together with those of others studies (see Gollwitzer & Sheeran, in press; Sheeran, 2002), demonstrate that there are conditions under which an intervention focused on implementation intentions can be effective. Prime among these conditions, of course, is that the persons targeted by the intervention must have the intention to perform the behaviour in question. If they do not have the intention to begin with, planning when and where to implement the intention makes no sense.

Habits and addictions

Like other theoretical frameworks (e.g., Bandura, 1997; Triandis, 1977), the theory of planned behaviour emphasises the reasoned, deliberative aspects of human behaviour. This is revealed in the important role accorded to intentions and to beliefs as the fundamental determinants of intentions and behaviour. Behavioural, normative, and control beliefs represent the information people have about a behaviour, and it is ultimately on the basis of this information that they are said to make their decisions. This aspect of the theory of planned behaviour and of its predecessor, the theory of reasoned action (Ajzen & Fishbein, 1980), has been a matter of debate almost since the theory's inception (see, e.g., Bagozzi, 1981; Bentler & Speckart, 1979; Fredricks & Dossett, 1983); and it has continued to occupy investigators (e.g., Aarts, Verplanken, & van Knippenberg, 1998; Ouellette & Wood, 1998). A common element of these critiques has to do with the role of prior behaviour as an antecedent of later behaviour. Specifically, the assumption is usually made that repeated performance of a behaviour results in the establishment of a *habit*; and that behaviour at a later time occurs at least in part habitually, without the mediation of beliefs, attitudes, or intentions. Once a habit has been established, initiation of the behaviour is said to come under the direct control of external or internal stimulus cues. In the presence of these discriminative stimuli, the behaviour is assumed to be automatically activated (see Bargh & Chartrand, 1999; Bargh, Gollwitzer, Lee-Chai, Barndollar, & Troetschel, 2001; Ouellette & Wood, 1998).

Bentler and Speckart (1979) submitted aspects of this analysis to an empirical test. Using structural equation techniques, they showed that a model with a direct path from prior behaviour to later behaviour provided a significantly better fit to the data than did the theory of reasoned action in which the effects of prior behaviour are mediated by attitudes, subjective norms, and intentions. A number of investigators have later reported similar results, showing that the relation between prior and later behaviour is often not fully mediated by the predictors in the theories of reasoned action or planned behaviour (e.g., Albarracin et al., 2001; Bagozzi, 1981; Fredricks & Dossett, 1983; Norman & Smith, 1995; for reviews, see Conner & Armitage, 1998; Ouellette & Wood, 1998).

Triandis (1977) was perhaps the first theorist explicitly to include habit in a reasoned action model of social behaviour. According to Triandis, the probability of an act is directly proportional to the weighted sum of intention and habit strength. The effect of the weighted sum on behaviour is further moderated by the presence or absence of facilitating factors (ability, knowledge, situational constraints, etc.). This model is expressed symbolically in Equation 1:

$$P_a = (w_1 I + w_2 H)\, F \tag{1}$$

In this equation, P_a is the probability of an act, I and H are intention and habit strength, respectively, each assigned an empirical weight, and F represents facilitating conditions. According to Triandis, the more frequently a behaviour has been performed, the stronger the habit that has been established. More recently, this view has been qualified to suggest that formation of a habit requires not only repeated opportunities to perform the behaviour but also a stable context (Ouellette & Wood, 1998).

The view that repeated behaviour becomes automatic and is directly activated by stimulus cues implies that intentions become increasingly irrelevant as a behaviour habituates. In other words, a measure of intention should be a good predictor of relatively novel or unpractised behaviours, but it should lose its predictive validity when it comes to routine or habitual responses in familiar situations. Empirical findings lend little support to this prediction. In fact, we are aware of only one published study (Verplanken, Aarts, van

Knippenberg, & Moonen, 1998) that reported data consistent with the habit hypothesis; other available evidence largely contradicts it. Ouellette and Wood (1998) performed a meta-analysis on 15 data sets from studies that reported intention–behaviour correlations. They classified each data set as dealing with a behaviour that can be performed frequently (e.g., seat belt use, coffee drinking, class attendance) or infrequently (e.g., flu shots, blood donation, nuclear protest). Contrary to the habit hypothesis, prediction of behaviour from intentions was found to be quite accurate for both types of behaviour (mean r = .59 and r = .67 for high- and low-opportunity behaviours, respectively). The difference between these two correlations is not statistically significant. The same conclusion arose from a similar meta-analysis based on 51 data sets (Sheeran & Sutton, unpublished data).[1] The mean intention–behaviour correlation was .51 for behaviours that could be performed infrequently (once or twice a year), and it was .53 for high-opportunity behaviours that could be performed daily or once a week.

Addictions

The theory of planned behaviour is often misinterpreted as implying that people form a conscious intention prior to carrying out each and every behaviour. In reality, the theory assumes that, after repeated opportunities for performance of a given behaviour, deliberation is no longer required because the intention to perform (or not perform) the behaviour is activated spontaneously in a behaviour-relevant situation (see Ajzen & Fishbein, 2000). In other words, the behaviour has become so routine that it is initiated with minimal conscious effort or attention. Many behaviours in everyday life are of this kind: We brush our teeth, leave the house for work, put on a seat belt, walk up stairs, and so forth without first forming conscious intentions to enact these behaviours. There is no need to assume that such behaviours are activated automatically or unconsciously, without prior intentions; only that the intentions are activated spontaneously without much conscious effort.

Some investigators, however, have challenged this approach more broadly, questioning the basic assumption that human behaviour can be described as reasoned. According to this critique, the theories of reasoned action and planned behaviour are too rational, failing to take into account emotions, compulsions, and other non-cognitive or irrational determinants of human behaviour (e.g., Armitage, Conner, & Norman, 1999; Gibbons, Gerrard, Blanton, & Russell, 1998; Ingham, 1994; Morojele & Stephenson, 1994; van der Pligt & de Vries, 1998). Perhaps the best examples in the health domain are such behaviours as smoking, drinking, and drug use, behaviours that may be at least in part under the control of strong physiological addictions. Such behaviours may be performed despite conscious intentions to the contrary, and they can be highly resistant to change.

This is not to say, however, that performance of addictive behaviours cannot be explained or predicted in the context of the theory of planned behaviour.

On the contrary, addictive behaviours have been studied quite successfully within this theoretical framework. Consider, for example, use of illicit drugs and alcohol consumption. In a study of these behaviours among college students (Armitage, Conner, Loach, & Willetts, 1999), self-reported frequency of cannabis use and of alcohol consumption were well predicted from intentions assessed 1 week earlier. The study also provided evidence to show that these intentions could be predicted from attitudes, subjective norms, and perceptions of behavioural control which, in turn, could be explained by examining the underlying behavioural, normative, and control beliefs. Interestingly, Bentler and Speckart (1979) found that even when past behaviour (as an indicator of habit strength) was added to the prediction equation, intentions continued to exert strong effects on alcohol, marijuana, and hard drug use among college students. In this study, past behaviour improved prediction of future behaviour over and above intentions, but intentions continued to account for a large proportion of the behavioural variance.

Nevertheless, some behaviours can involve strong dependencies that are beyond a person's control such that neither intentions nor perceived behavioural control are good predictors of future behaviour. Some evidence for this can be found in a recent study on binge drinking. Lambert and Manstead (2005) asked students to complete measures of TPB constructs, plus measures of frequency of past behaviour, in relation to drinking more than 10 units of alcohol in a single session during the coming 2 weeks. At the end of the 2-week period participants reported how often they had engaged in this behaviour during the previous 2 weeks. The standard TPB constructs predicted both intentions quite well ($R^2 = .48$, with attitudes and perceived behavioural control as significant predictors) and self-reported behaviour ($R^2 = .50$, with intention being the sole significant predictor), although prediction of both intentions and behaviour was significantly enhanced by the addition of past behaviour as a predictor. Especially relevant in the present context is the fact that past behaviour significantly moderated the intention–behaviour relation. This reflected the fact that the behaviour of participants who reported being relatively infrequent binge drinkers (one or fewer occasions in the past 2 weeks as assessed at time 1) was significantly predicted by their intentions, whereas the behaviour of those who reported being relatively frequent binge drinkers (two or more occasions in the past 2 weeks as assessed at time 1) was not.

The research on habitual behaviour reviewed above suggests that, as a general rule, people behave in accordance with their intentions even in the case of addictive behaviours, except in the case of overwhelming dependencies. However, problems are often encountered when people try to change their addictive behaviours; that is, when they try to cease smoking, to stop using drugs, or to reduce alcohol consumption. Even highly motivated individuals, and even with the aid of cessation programmes, often find it very difficult to change their behaviour. Data collected in the framework of the theory of planned behaviour can help illuminate the difficulties of behavioural change and direct intervention efforts, but the success of such efforts is by no means assured.

Consider, for example, the case of smoking cessation. A study by Norman, Conner, and Bell (1999) illustrates the potential utility of the theory of planned behaviour in this domain, as well as its limitations. Smokers who attended a health promotion clinic were given information on the benefits of quitting and were advised to quit smoking. At that time, they also completed a theory of planned behaviour questionnaire formulated with respect to not smoking over the next 6 months. The participants completed a second questionnaire 6 months later in which they reported whether they had attempted to quit smoking in the past 6 months and, if so, for how long they had managed to abstain. Of the 84 participants in the study, 53 (63%) reported having made an attempt to quit smoking, and the average period of abstention for these individuals was 10.24 weeks. In a demonstration of the difficulty of smoking cessation, only 13 (24.5%) of those who had made an attempt to quit reported that they had not resumed smoking after 6 months.

Regarding the theory of planned behaviour, it was found that intentions could be predicted quite accurately from the theory's three components ($R = .70$), and that this predictive validity was largely due to the effect of perceived behavioural control. However, prediction of actual smoking cessation was more problematic. Although intentions predicted attempts to quit reasonably well ($r = .49$), they had a correlation of only .28 with length of abstinence; nor did perceived behaviour control fare any better ($r = .22$ and .32, respectively). Together, intentions and perceptions of control predicted length of abstinence with a multiple correlation of .28, accounting for only 8% of the variance. These findings have important implications for interventions designed to reduce cigarette smoking. Given the strong impact of perceived behavioural control on intentions, it can be suggested that interventions should focus on raising participants' sense of behavioural control in an effort to strengthen quitting intentions. It is also clear, however, that focusing on intentions is not enough. Strengthening intentions to cease smoking can produce attempts to quit but these attempts do not necessarily translate into long-term abstinence. Solutions to this problem go beyond the theory of planned behaviour. This theoretical framework can help to identify the problem and focus attention on the stage at which the behavioural change must be reinforced, but it offers little guidance as to how this can be done. Interventions designed to overcome resistance to long-term change will have to supplement the theory of planned behaviour with considerations based on other theoretical frameworks or on practical experience with smoking cessation programmes.

Conclusions

Many attempts to identify antecedents of health-related lifestyles focus on broad personal, demographic, and environmental factors. By and large, this approach has proven to be of very limited value. In the context of the theory of planned behaviour, such factors are considered background variables that only influence health behaviour indirectly through their impact on more proximal factors that are directly linked to the behaviour of interest. A great number of studies have demonstrated the utility of the theory of planned behaviour in the health domain. We saw that data collected in the framework of this theory can not only predict intentions and behaviour quite accurately, but can also provide useful information about the behavioural, normative, and control considerations that influence adherence or non-adherence to recommended health practices.

Despite its overall success, the theory of planned behaviour is not without limitations. A vexing issue for the theory continues to be the question of volitional control. The theory was introduced as an extension of the theory of reasoned action (Ajzen & Fishbein, 1980) in an attempt to expand its range of application to habitual, addictive, and other behaviours over which people have limited control. It was assumed that a measure of perceived behavioural control can serve as a proxy for actual control, to the extent that people's perceptions of control are reasonably accurate. Empirical research has supported this assumption in a variety of domains, showing that a consideration of perceived behavioural control can improve prediction of intentions and behaviour. This research has also shown that intentions do not lose their predictive validity for frequently performed behaviours, or even for such addictive behaviours as smoking and drinking. However, there is a limit to how far the application of this theory can be pushed. Recent data support the common-sense expectation that addictions can progress to a point beyond volitional control. In these instances, intentions will predict behaviour only to the extent that people are cognisant of the fact that the behaviour is beyond their control, report their lack of control truthfully, and take it into account as they form their intentions.

The theory of planned behaviour also has important implications for interventions designed to produce changes in intentions and behaviour. By identifying some of the important determinants of a behaviour, the theory permits us to design behavioural interventions and to trace the effects of such interventions from beliefs to attitudes, subjective norms, and perceptions of control, through intentions to behaviour. In this fashion, it is possible to determine where the intervention had its strongest impact and, if it failed to influence behaviour, how it could be improved.

In the final chapter of his book *Social psychology and health*, Stroebe (2000, p. 267) argues that there are three "limits to persuasion" in the domain of health education. Specifically, he notes that "It is difficult to convince people that they are vulnerable to a health risk", and that "Even if we do convince them that they are vulnerable, this may not be sufficient to motivate them to change." Finally, he argues that "Even if individuals are persuaded to change health-impairing behaviors, they often find it difficult to act on these intentions." We would not take serious issue with any of these points, but we do want to suggest that carefully considered use of the theory of planned behaviour should attenuate the influence of the first two factors. If one first identifies those considerations that distinguish people who have adopted a recommended health practice from those who have not, one should be in a stronger position to persuade the latter group to change their behaviour in a healthy direction. Note that some of the belief differences between adopters and non-adopters may have little or nothing to do with perceived vulnerability to a health risk. For example, if a health behaviour such as smoking is negatively valued by the majority of the population, it may be more effective to focus interventions on these negative normative beliefs than on the health-damaging consequences of smoking. Where the risk to any given individual of illness or death resulting from an unhealthy practice is perceived to be low, it may be especially beneficial to focus an intervention on other beliefs and values associated with the behaviour. Stroebe's third barrier to persuasion, which relates to the difficulty of getting people to act on healthy intentions, is one that could be overcome at least to some degree by devising interventions that make use of implementation intentions or other means to keep people focused on the task, prevent procrastination, and help them carry out their intentions.

Stroebe (2000) goes on to argue that some of the problems arising from the limits to persuasion that he identifies could be overcome by altering the incentive structure associated with health-related behaviours. By this he means changing the cost of engaging in behaviours, making unhealthy behaviours more expensive than healthy alternatives, and/or changing the legal status of behaviours, such that unhealthy options attract legal penalties. There is no doubt that such an approach can be effective; where a persuasion-based approach is unlikely to be effective, as in the case of addictive behaviours, an incentive-based measure constitutes a good alternative. Note that, in the context of the theory of planned behaviour, this amounts to changing beliefs about the likely consequences of the behaviour; that is, behavioural beliefs. In addition, or alternatively, educational campaigns can focus on normative expectations. As Stroebe (2000, pp. 270–271) notes, increases in taxes on cigarettes in the USA were made possible by health education campaigns that changed subjective norms with respect to smoking, and one might add that the criminalisation of driving while drunk in the USA and much of the rest of the world has been made possible by health education campaigns that changed the climate of public opinion concerning this behaviour. So even where the ultimately effective intervention is one that relies on changing the incentive structure associated with a given behaviour, the effectiveness of such an intervention depends on changing behavioural, normative, or control beliefs; constructs central to the theory of planned behaviour.

Note

1 We are grateful to Paschal Sheeran for providing us with the results of these meta-analyses.

References

Aarts, H., Verplanken, B., & van Knippenberg, A. (1998). Predicting behavior from actions in the past: Repeated decision making or a matter of habit? *Journal of Applied Social Psychology*, *28*, 1355–1374.

Ajzen, I. (1988). *Attitudes, personality, and behavior*. Chicago: Dorsey Press.

Ajzen, I. (1991). The theory of planned behavior. *Organizational Behavior and Human Decision Processes*, *50*, 179–211.

Ajzen, I., & Fishbein, M. (1980). *Understanding attitudes and predicting social behavior*. Englewood-Cliffs, NJ: Prentice-Hall.

Ajzen, I., & Fishbein, M. (2000). Attitudes and the attitude–behavior relation: Reasoned and automatic processes. In W. Stroebe & M. Hewstone (Eds.), *European review of social psychology* (Vol. 11, pp. 1–33). Chichester, UK: Wiley.

Ajzen, I., & Fishbein, M. (2005). The influence of attitudes on behavior. In D. Albarracín, B. T. Johnson, & M. P. Zanna (Eds.), *Handbook of attitudes and attitude change: Basic principles* (pp. 173–221). Mahwah, NJ: Lawrence Erlbaum Associates Inc.

Albarracin, D., Johnson, B. T., Fishbein, M., & Muellerleile, P. A. (2001). Theories of reasoned action and planned behavior as models of condom use: A meta-analysis. *Psychological Bulletin*, *127*, 142–161.

Armitage, C. J. (2004). Evidence that implementation intentions reduce dietary fat intake: A randomized trial. *Health Psychology*, *23*, 319–323.

Armitage, C. J., & Conner, M. (1999). Distinguishing perceptions of control from self-efficacy: Predicting consumption of a low-fat diet using the theory of planned behavior. *Journal of Applied Social Psychology*, *29*, 72–90.

Armitage, C. J., & Conner, M. (2001). Efficacy of the theory of planned behavior: A meta-analytic review. *British Journal of Social Psychology*, *40*, 471–499.

Armitage, C. J., Conner, M., Loach, J., & Willetts, D. (1999). Different perceptions of control: Applying an extended theory of planned behavior to legal and illegal drug use. *Basic and Applied Social Psychology*, *21*, 301–316.

Armitage, C. J., Conner, M., & Norman, P. (1999). Differential effects of mood on information processing: Evidence from the theories of reasoned action and planned behaviour. *European Journal of Social Psychology*, *29*, 419–433.

Bagozzi, R. P. (1981). Attitudes, intentions, and behavior: A test of some key hypotheses. *Journal of Personality and Social Psychology*, *41*, 607–627.

Bandura, A. (1997). *Self-efficacy: The exercise of control*. New York: Freeman.

Bargh, J. A., & Chartrand, T. L. (1999). The unbearable automaticity of being. *American Psychologist*, *54*, 462–479.

Bargh, J. A., Gollwitzer, P. M., Lee-Chai, A., Barndollar, K., & Troetschel, R. (2001). The automated will: Nonconscious activation and pursuit of behavioral goals. *Journal of Personality and Social Psychology*, *81*, 1014–1027.

Baumeister, R. F., Campbell, J. D., Krueger, J. I., & Vohs, K. D. (2003). Does high self-esteem cause better performance, interpersonal success, happiness, or healthier lifestyles? *Psychological Science in the Public Interest*, *4*, 1–44.

Bentler, P. M., & Speckart, G. (1979). Models of attitude–behavior relations. *Psychological Review*, *86*, 452–464.

Blanchard, C. M., Denniston, M. M., Baker, F., Ainsworth, S. R., Courneya, K. S., Hann, D. M. et al. (2003). Do adults change their lifestyle behaviors after a cancer diagnosis? *American Journal of Health Behavior*, *27*, 246–256.

Blue, C. L. (1995). The predictive capacity of the Theory of Reasoned Action and the Theory of Planned Behavior in exercise research: An integrated literature review. *Research in Nursing and Health*, *18*, 105–121.

Brubaker, R. G., & Fowler, C. (1990). Encouraging college males to perform testicular self-examination: Evaluation of a persuasive message based on the revised theory of reasoned action. *Journal of Applied Social Psychology*, *20*, 1411–1422.

Brunso, K., Scholderer, J., & Grunert, K. G. (2004). Testing relationships between values and food-related lifestyle: Results from two European countries. *Appetite*, *43*, 195–205.

Chaiken, S. (1980). Heuristic versus systematic information processing and the use of source versus message cues in persuasion. *Journal of Personality and Social Psychology*, *39*, 752–766.

Conner, M., & Armitage, C. J. (1998). Extending the theory of planned behavior: A review and avenues for further research. *Journal of Applied Social Psychology*, *28*, 1429–1464.

Conner, M., & McMillan, B. (1999). Interaction effects in the theory of planned behavior: Studying cannabis use. *British Journal of Social Psychology*, *38*, 195–222.

Courneya, K. S. (1995). Understanding readiness for regular physical activity in older individuals: An application of the theory of planned behavior. *Health Psychology*, *14*, 80–87.

De Valle, M. N., & Norman, P. (1992). Causal attributions, health locus of control beliefs and lifestyle changes among pre-operative coronary patients. *Psychology and Health*, *7*, 201–211.

De Wit, J. B. F., Kok, G. J., Timmermans, C. A. M., & Wijnsma, P. (1990). Determinanten van veilig vrijen en condoomgebruik bij jongeren [Determinants of practising safe sex and using condoms in young people]. *Gedrag en Gezondheid*, *18*, 121–133.

Fishbein, M. (1963). An investigation of the relationships between beliefs about an object and the attitude toward that object. *Human Relations*, *16*, 233–240.

Fishbein, M., & Ajzen, I. (1975). *Belief, attitude, intention, and behavior: An introduction to theory and research*. Reading, MA: Addison-Wesley.

Fredricks, A. J., & Dossett, D. L. (1983). Attitude–behavior relations: A comparison of the Fishbein–Ajzen and the Bentler–Speckart models. *Journal of Personality and Social Psychology*, *45*, 501–512.

Friedman, H. S. (2003). Healthy life-style across the life-span: The heck with the surgeon general! In J. Sulls & K. A. Wallston (Eds.), *Social psychological foundations of health and illness* (pp. 3–21). Oxford, UK: Blackwell.

Gibbons, F. X., Gerrard, M., Blanton, H., & Russell, D. W. (1998). Reasoned action and social reaction: Willingness and intention as independent predictors of health risk. *Journal of Personality and Social Psychology*, *74*, 1164–1180.

Godin, G., & Kok, G. (1996). The theory of planned behavior: A review of its applications to health-related behaviors. *American Journal of Health Promotion*, *11*, 87–98.

Godin, G., Valois, P., Lepage, L., & Desharnais, R. (1992). Predictors of smoking behaviour: An application of Ajzen's theory of planned behaviour. *British Journal of Addiction, 87,* 1335–1343.

Gollwitzer, P. M. (1993). Goal achievement: The role of intentions. In W. Stroebe & M. Hewstone (Eds.), *European review of social psychology* (Vol. 4, pp. 141–185). Chichester, UK: Wiley.

Gollwitzer, P. M., & Sheeran, P. (in press). Implementation intentions and goal achievement: A meta-analysis of effects and processes. *Advances in Experimental Social Psychology.*

Hagger, M. S., Chatzisarantis, N. L. D., & Biddle, S. J. H. (2002). A meta-analytic review of the theories of reasoned action and planned behavior in physical activity: Predictive validity and the contribution of additional variables. *Journal of Sport and Exercise Psychology, 24,* 3–32.

Hardeman, W., Johnston, M., Johnston, D. W., Bonetti, D., Wareham, N. J., & Kinmonth, A. L. (2002). Application of the Theory of Planned Behaviour in behaviour change interventions: A systematic review. *Psychology and Health, 17,* 123–158.

Hausenblas, H. A., Carron, A. V., & Mack, D. E. (1997). Application of the theories of reasoned action and planned behavior to exercise behavior: A meta-analysis. *Journal of Sport and Exercise Psychology, 19,* 36–51.

He, K., Kramer, E., Houser, R. F., Chomitz, V. R., & Hacker, K. A. (2004). Defining and understanding healthy lifestyles choices for adolescents. *Journal of Adolescent Health, 35,* 26–33.

Heckhausen, H. (1991). *Motivation and action.* New York: Springer.

Ingham, R. (1994). Some speculations on the concept of rationality. *Advances in Medical Sociology, 4,* 89–111.

Karvonen, S., West, P., Sweeting, H., Rahkonen, O., & Young, R. (2001). Lifestyle, social class and health-related behaviour: A cross-cultural comparison of 15 year olds in Glasgow and Helsinki. *Journal of Youth Studies, 4,* 393–413.

Kim, K., Reicks, M., & Sjoberg, S. (2003). Applying the theory of planned behavior to predict dairy product consumption by older adults. *Journal of Nutrition Education and Behavior, 35,* 294–301.

Lambert, D. S., & Manstead, A. S. R. (2005). *"Falaraki nights": An analysis of binge drinking in young British adults using the theory of planned behavior.* Manuscript submitted for publication.

Manstead, A. S. R., Proffitt, C., & Smart, J. (1983). Predicting and understanding mothers' infant-feeding intentions and behavior: Testing the theory of reasoned action. *Journal of Personality and Social Psychology, 44,* 657–671.

Morojele, N. K., & Stephenson, G. M. (1994). Addictive behaviours: Predictors of abstinence intentions and expectations in the Theory of Planned Behaviour. In D. R. Rutter & L. Quine (Eds.), *Social psychology and health: European perspectives* (pp. 47–70). Aldershot, UK: Avebury/Ashgate.

Norman, P., Conner, M., & Bell, R. (1999). The theory of planned behavior and smoking cessation. *Health Psychology, 18,* 89–94.

Norman, P., & Hoyle, S. (2004). The theory of planned behavior and breast self-examination: Distinguishing between perceived control and self-efficacy. *Journal of Applied Social Psychology, 34,* 694–708.

Norman, P., & Smith, L. (1995). The theory of planned behaviour and exercise: An investigation into the role of prior behaviour, behavioural intentions and attitude variability. *European Journal of Social Psychology, 25,* 403–415.

Ouellette, J. A., & Wood, W. (1998). Habit and intention in everyday life: The multiple processes by which past behavior predicts future behavior. *Psychological Bulletin*, *124*, 54–74.

Parker, D., Manstead, A. S. R., & Stradling, S. G. (1995). Extending the theory of planned behaviour: The role of personal norm. *British Journal of Social Psychology*, *34*, 127–137.

Parker, D., Manstead, A. S. R., & Stradling, S. G. (1996). Modifying beliefs and attitudes to exceeding the speed limit: An intervention study based on the theory of planned behavior. *Journal of Applied Social Psychology*, *26*, 1–19.

Petty, R. E., & Cacioppo, J. T. (1986). *Communication and persuasion: Central and peripheral routes to attitude change*. New York: Springer.

Pullen, C., Walker, S. N., & Fiandt, K. (2001). Determinants of health-promoting lifestyle behaviors in rural older women. *Family and Community Health*, *24*, 49–72.

Sheeran, P. (2002). Intention–behavior relations: A conceptual and empirical review. In W. Stroebe & M. Hewstone (Eds.), *European review of social psychology* (Vol. 12, pp. 1–36). Chichester, UK: Wiley.

Sheeran, P., & Orbell, S. (1998). Do intentions predict condom use? Meta-analysis and examination of six moderator variables. *British Journal of Social Psychology*, *37*, 231–250.

Sheeran, P., & Taylor, S. (1999). Predicting intentions to use condoms: A meta-analysis and comparison of the theories of reasoned action and planned behavior. *Journal of Applied Social Psychology*, *29*, 1624–1675.

Stroebe, W. (2000). *Social psychology and health* (2nd ed.). Buckingham, UK: Open University Press.

Sutton, S. (1998). Predicting and explaining intentions and behavior: How well are we doing? *Journal of Applied Social Psychology*, *28*, 1317–1338.

Triandis, H. C. (1977). *Interpersonal behavior*. Monterey, CA: Brooks/Cole.

van der Pligt, J., & de Vries, N. K. (1998). Expectancy-value models of health behavior: The role of salience and anticipated regret. *Psychology and Health*, *13*, 289–305.

Vereecken, C. A., Maes, L., & De Bacquer, D. (2004). The influence of parental occupation and the pupils' educational level on lifestyle behaviors among adolescents in Belgium. *Journal of Adolescent Health*, *34*, 330–338.

Verplanken, B., Aarts, H., van Knippenberg, A., & Moonen, A. (1998). Habit versus planned behavior: A field experiment. *British Journal of Social Psychology*, *37*, 111–128.

5　In defence of ourselves

The effects of defensive processing on attitudinal phenomena

Alice H. Eagly
Northwestern University, USA

Motivational themes have long been prominent in attitude theory and research. Among the most important and enduring of these themes is the idea that attitudes reflect motives to defend values and other positive states. This principle has emerged repeatedly in research on persuasion and attitudinal selectivity, and predictions based on it have enjoyed some success. In this chapter, I first comment briefly on motivational analyses of attitudes and then examine two efforts to develop theory pertaining to defensive processes: the concepts of value-relevant involvement (Johnson & Eagly, 1989) and defence motivation (Chaiken, Liberman, & Eagly, 1989). Finally, some of the applications of these concepts in research on attitudinal selectivity and persuasion are considered.

Motivation in attitude theory and research

Despite some ebb and flow in attention to motivation, there are few attitudinal phenomena that can be adequately analysed without taking individuals' motives into account. It is not surprising that the insights of early attitude theorists were heavily laced with motivational constructs. Examples include incentive and drive-reduction theories of persuasion, cognitive consistency theories (particularly dissonance theory), and functional theories of attitudes (see Eagly & Chaiken, 1993).

With the cognitive revolution of the 1970s, attitude theorists, like other psychologists, turned their attention away from motivation and towards detailed issues of cognitive processing. Many efforts in this period attempted to show that phenomena that had been given motivational interpretations could be reframed in nonmotivational, cognitive terms (e.g., Miller & Ross, 1975). However, during the past 20 years, the balance between motivation and cognition has been restored. Motivational issues again have a high profile, and attitude theorists attempt to blend their knowledge of cognitive and motivational processes to produce more general theories. The approaches discussed in this chapter facilitate joining motivational and cognitive principles in broader theories.

Many analyses of the motives most relevant to attitudes, including those that I consider in this chapter, contrast a motive to hold attitudes that accurately portray reality with motives to hold attitudes that favour certain other positive states of oneself. These positive states that can be linked to attitudes include positive self-regard, cognitive consistency, ideological coherence, social approval, wealth, and good health.

In general, motives to achieve accurate attitudes and to arrive at particular self-serving or self-supportive attitudes are somewhat in conflict, with accuracy motives restraining self-serving motives. Despite this restraint by reality, preferences for attitudes that support one's preferred states bias exposure to information, thinking about and processing information, and memory (Eagly & Chaiken, 1993, 1998). Development of the insight that such motives can prevail, despite the presence of pressures towards accuracy, requires understanding of the mechanisms through which motivational biases exert their effects and of the principles that regulate the strength of these effects. In this chapter, I explore this theme, especially in relation to people's defence of their existing attitudinal positions.

Motivation as types of involvement

Ego involvement and issue involvement

Involvement, a concept with a long history, has contributed to the understanding of motivational effects on attitudes. This construct emerged in attitude research in the writings of M. Sherif and Cantril (1947), who proposed a construct of *ego involvement*, which they defined in the following terms: "All attitudes that define a person's status or that give him some relative role with respect to other individuals, groups, or institutions are ego-involved" (p. 96). Because these theorists used the term *ego* similarly to the way that the term *self* came to be used by later theorists, this seminal work implicated the self-concept as embedded in attitudinal processes. This insight was evident in empirical research on the effects of ego involvement (e.g., C. W. Sherif & Sherif, 1967; C. W. Sherif, Sherif, & Nebergall, 1965; M. Sherif & Hovland, 1961).

The involvement concept declined in popularity in the late 1960s and subsequently rose again in research that Petty and Cacioppo and their colleagues (e.g., Petty & Cacioppo, 1979a, 1979b) carried out in the context of their tests of their elaboration likelihood model of persuasion (Petty & Cacioppo, 1981, 1986). Like earlier theorists, Petty and Cacioppo (1979b, p. 1915) proposed a very broad definition of involvement, specifically as "the extent to which the attitudinal issue under consideration is of personal importance".

The older and newer treatments of involvement were quite different in their implications for attitude change. Drawing on their proposition that the attitudinal continuum is divided into latitudes of acceptance, rejection, and noncomitment, M. Sherif, C. W. Sherif, and their colleagues (e.g., C. W. Sherif et al., 1965) predicted that, to the extent that recipients are highly involved in the issue discussed in a counterattitudinal message, they have a relatively large latitude of rejection—that is, they find issue positions unacceptable if they deviate from their favoured position. Therefore, as involvement increases, the possibility increases that positions are regarded as objectionable and therefore are unpersuasive. That involvement increases resistance to attitude change was thus the main attitudinal prediction from the Sherifs' perspective.

In subsequent research, Petty and Cacioppo (e.g., 1979a, 1979b) proposed involvement (initially often labelled "issue involvement" and later "personal relevance") as a state that motivates message recipients to process messages carefully and systematically. Therefore, the effects of involvement on persuasion depend on other variables, especially on the quality of the arguments contained in the message. With strong arguments, involvement facilitates attitude change, but with weak arguments, it inhibits attitude change. The more careful processing motivated by high involvement reveals the strengths of strong arguments and the weaknesses of weak arguments. These predictions were consistent with Petty and Cacioppo's (1981, 1986) then emerging dual-process elaboration likelihood theory. In this theory, in which involvement serves as a motivational variable, recipients were assumed to process messages in greater depth to the extent that they have both the capability and motivation to do so. The resulting contingent prediction that the persuasion induced by involvement depends on argument strength was thus different from the Sherif prediction that involvement induces general resistance to change.

Given this disparity of predictions, it appeared that these two sets of researchers had studied different forms of involvement, which warranted distinctive definitions. This insight emerged from studying how involvement had been operationalised in the two traditions. In the Sherif tradition (e.g., M. Sherif & Hovland, 1961), high-involvement participants belonged to groups supporting a particular stand on an issue, whereas low-involvement participants did not. Other approaches included self-reports of involvement or the importance of issues, assessments of the width of the latitude of acceptance, and the selection of issues that varied in how controversial they were (see Johnson & Eagly, 1989). In contrast, the experiments by Petty and Cacioppo and their colleagues (e.g., Petty, Cacioppo, & Goldman, 1981) manipulated involvement by informing student participants that the recommendation advocated by a message (e.g., that comprehensive exams be instituted) would potentially take effect at the participants' own university versus a distant university, or that the recommended change take effect soon versus in the distant future.

Despite the obvious differences in involvement manipulations typical of these two traditions, engagement of the self was inherent in both methods of producing high involvement. In the Sherif tradition, the presentation of persuasive messages discrepant with high-involvement participants' attitudes (e.g., on the morality of the war in Vietnam) threatened their self-defining values. In contrast, in the elaboration likelihood tradition, the presentation of messages discrepant with high-involvement participants' attitudes raised the possibility that they might personally experience favourable or unfavourable consequences from a proposed change—typically, the introduction of comprehensive exams into the university curriculum.

Defining types of involvement

This insight about the differing implications of persuasive messages for the self in these two traditions led to the proposal of two types of involvement: (a) *Value-relevant involvement* (i.e., ego involvement) refers to the motivational state created by an association between an activated attitude and one's central and important values, and (b) *outcome-relevant involvement* (i.e., issue involvement or personal relevance) refers to the motivational state created by an association between an activated attitude and one's ability to attain desirable outcomes. Outcomes refer to explicit personal goals that one expects to obtain relatively soon, mainly by one's own efforts, and that may affect aspects of one's behaviour. Both types of involvement would potentially threaten the self, but in different ways. Value relevance would threaten to disrupt self-defining values and thus arouse defensive responding, whereas outcome relevance would raise questions about possible hindrance or facilitation of progress towards important goals and thus arouse reality-seeking responding.

Although it is the contrast between value relevance and outcome relevance that is of most interest in this essay, Blair Johnson and I (1989) also proposed a third category—*impression-relevant involvement*. This addition recognised involvement manipulations that had established a concern with holding an opinion that is socially acceptable to potential evaluators. Such experiments manipulated involvement by stressing the self-presentational consequences of the attitude that participants anticipated they would express to others after they received a communicator's viewpoint. In studies of this type, first conducted by Zimbardo (1960), involvement threatens the social self—that is, the image that one presents to others. The likely response would be to adopt a flexible, moderate position, as long as the anticipated audience is not known to prefer a polarised position (see Cialdini & Petty, 1981; Leippe & Elkin, 1987). Because flexible and nonpolarised positions generally offer self-presentational advantages, recipients should be reluctant to allow themselves to be greatly influenced, even by appeals based on strong, cogent arguments, or to fully reject appeals based on weak, specious arguments.

Our resulting three-part conceptual scheme brought these disparate motivational concepts together under a common umbrella, while delineating the important differences between them. The commonality in the three approaches was their focus on the implications of persuasive appeals for the self. Johnson and Eagly (1989) therefore defined an overarching involvement construct as the motivational state induced by an association between an activated attitude and some aspect of the self-concept and delineated the three types in terms of the particular aspects of the self-concept implicated (Johnson & Eagly, 1989, pp. 293–294):

> For value-relevant involvement, the pertinent aspect of the self is one's enduring values: The persuasive message activates an attitude that was linked to one's values prior to the experiment or that became linked during the experiment. For impression-relevant involvement, the pertinent aspect of the self is the public self or the impression one makes on others: The issue on which one expects to express an attitude after receiving a persuasive message is linked to the public self by the anticipation that this attitude will be known to an evaluative audience. For outcome-relevant involvement, the pertinent aspect of the self is one's ability to attain desirable outcomes: The information that the persuasive message provides and the attitude one forms on the basis of this information are made to appear relevant to the attainment of these outcomes.

Evidence supporting the involvement analysis

The initial evidence for this tripartite framework came from a meta-analysis of the persuasion literature that encompassed studies in each of the three traditions of involvement research (Johnson & Eagly, 1989). The findings of this meta-analysis were largely consistent with the predictions inherent in this typology, which in turn were consistent with the predictions of most of the researchers who had worked within each of these traditions. Specifically, with value-relevant involvement, the anticipated resistance effect emerged: High-involvement participants were less persuaded than low-involvement participants. With outcome-relevant involvement, high-involvement participants were more persuaded than low-involvement participants by strong arguments and less persuaded by weak arguments. And with impression-relevant involvement, high-involvement participants were slightly less persuaded than low-involvement participants. As predicted, argument strength acted as a strong moderator of persuasion effects for the outcome-relevant studies. In addition, argument strength acted as a weak moderator for the value-relevant studies and yielded no moderation for the impression-relevant studies. These results thus confirmed the view that the effects of involvement on attitude change cannot be adequately described without using a label that denotes the aspect of the self-concept from which involvement derives.[1]

Evidence has mounted that value-relevant involvement induces resistance to influence and the processes that mediate resistance (Johnson, Lin, Symons, Campbell, & Ekstein, 1995; Zuwerink & Devine, 1996; see overview by Levin, Nichols, & Johnson, 2000). For example, Maio and Olson (1995) manipulated the extent to which participants experienced value-relevant or outcome-relevant involvement. The participants exposed to the condition that elicited value-relevant involvement did not show argument-strength effects but instead were generally resistant to persuasion. However, these findings emerged only among participants who considered outcomes or values to be important.

A different approach to validating the distinction between the three types of involvement consists of establishing measures that assess each type. Cho and Boster (2005) developed sets of items designed to distinguish between the three types of involvement. They instantiated these items for three social issues (abortion, death penalty, and marijuana) and two consumer products (jeans, toothpaste). Examples of value-relevant items are "The values that are the most important to me are what determine my stand on [issue]" and "My position on [issue] reflects who I am". Examples of outcome-relevant items are "It is easy for me to think of ways that [issue] affects my life" and "Changes in laws for and against [issue] will have little effect on me [reverse-scored]". Examples of impression-relevant items are "The impressions that others have of me are very much affected when I talk with them about my position on [issue]" and "If I express the right kind of opinion on [issue] people will find me more attractive". As expected, the items loaded on three separate factors for all five issues, reflecting the three types of involvement. To establish the construct validity of the three types of involvement, Cho and Boster related involvement to other measures. As expected, impression-relevant involvement was correlated with the personality variable of other-directedness (Dillard & Hunter, 1989), and outcome-relevant involvement with the tendency to seek information on the specific issue.

Reformulation of the processing instigated by outcome-relevant involvement

Research and theory in recent years have raised questions about Johnson and Eagly's (1989) reasoning about the processing of messages by recipients who are involved on an outcome-relevant basis. Consistent with the assumptions of dual-process persuasion theories of the 1980s (e.g., Chaiken & Stangor, 1987; Petty & Cacioppo, 1986), Johnson and Eagly argued that outcome-relevant involvement instigated relatively "unbiased and open-minded" message processing (p. 310), whereas value-relevant involvement led to biased processing that served to defend existing value-linked attitudes. In their involvement typology, Johnson and Eagly thus distinguished between relatively open-minded and closed-minded message processing.

In contrast to this reasoning, Darke and Chaiken (2005) presented evidence that the effects of outcome relevance (i.e., personal relevance) are consistent with biased processing driven by self-interest. In agreement with Johnson and Eagly's (1989) assumptions, the attitudinal effects of outcome relevance appear to reflect message recipients' analysis of personal costs and benefits. However, by engaging in "a self-interested analysis of issue-related costs and argument-specified benefits" (Darke & Chaiken, 2005, p. xx), recipients are not open-minded but biased in favour of ensuring themselves the most favourable outcomes. From this perspective, outcome-relevant involvement would function to defend positive states of the self, just as value-relevant involvement would.

Motivation as the multiple motives of the heuristic-systematic model

The tripartite involvement analysis was published in the same year as the tripartite motivational analysis put forth by Chaiken et al. (1989). Even though I was part of both projects, the similarity of these analyses did not derive from my own partitions of attitude research. As is inherent in producing an integrative review of research on a particular domain, the distinctions about types of involvement were in large part empirically driven by the content of the then existing research literature on involvement. In contrast, the distinctions about motives were theoretically driven in the context of the earlier functional analyses of attitudes.

The chapter by Chaiken and her colleagues (1989) proposed a multiple-motive version of Chaiken's (1980) heuristic-systematic model of persuasion, which was initially developed to apply to persuasion settings in which people's primary motivational concern is to attain accurate attitudes consistent with the relevant facts (Chaiken, 1980, 1987). Recognising the limitations of this framework, Chaiken et al. proposed that *accuracy motivation*, a desire to align one's attitudes with the facts, is only one possible motivational orientation that message recipients might adopt in a situation of potential social influence. Two additional motives may be prepotent: *defence motivation*, the desire to form or to defend particular attitudinal positions, and *impression motivation*, the desire to express attitudes that are socially acceptable or that, more generally, facilitate self-presentation (see also Chaiken, Giner-Sorolla, & Chen, 1996; Chen & Chaiken, 1999).

Defence motivation, the desire to form or defend particular attitudinal positions, has considerable scope because it can arise for attitudes that are linked to a variety of important self-defining concepts, including ethnic or gender identity, political or religious ideologies, and personal attributes such as intelligence, honesty, sociability, and healthfulness. From this view, attitudes on particular issues can be linked to a variety of more abstract attitudes in a hierarchical interattitudinal structure (see Eagly & Chaiken, 1995, for discussion). For example, I might be motivated to defend my attitude towards women's reproductive freedom because it is linked to my positive attitude towards myself as a woman, but defend my attitude towards exercise because it is linked to my positive attitude towards myself as a healthy person. In contrast, impression motivation, or the desire to express socially acceptable attitudes, arises in situations that have important interpersonal consequences that affect one's well-being or reputation. This motive links to theories of impression management and self-presentation that emphasise the importance of the public self (e.g., Jones, 1990; Schlenker, 1982).

The close alignment of the three types of involvement and the three motives meant that Johnson and Eagly (1989) might have adopted the three-motive terminology by exchanging accuracy motivation for outcome-relevant involvement, defence motivation for value-relevant involvement, and impression motivation for impression-relevant involvement. However, this translation was not appropriate for the meta-analysis because the involvement trilogy arose to classify studies that had invoked the involvement construct, albeit in three different ways. This project therefore called for three types of involvement with motivational implications rather than three motives. Moreover, defence motivation is framed more broadly than value-relevant involvement. Although people may defend their attitudes because they are linked to important self-defining values, they may also defend their attitudes to protect many other positive aspects of the self-concept including, for example, one's view of oneself as healthy or intelligent.

Does it matter that these overlapping functional constructs are defined as motives or forms of involvement? In this context, motives refer to rather broadly formulated goals that are linked to attitudes on specific issues. The forms of involvement refer to the motivational state induced by the linking of an attitude on an issue with an aspect of the self. Therefore, the presentation of a message challenging one's attitude on an important and self-defining political issue would arouse a motive to defend one's attitude in Chaiken et al.'s (1989) terms, and would activate one's enduring self-defining values in Johnson and Eagly's (1989) terms, a state that would induce a motive to defend the threatened attitude. Thus analysed, the distinction between involvement and motives seems minor.

Despite this similarity, the involvement framework is more limited than the motive framework because it specifically connotes attitude research framed in terms of involvement, whereas the motive framework is relevant to that research and many other attitudinal and judgemental phenomena. Although the three forms of involvement and three motives are conceptual first cousins, motives thus provide a more general analysis than do types of involvement. The three motives also gain substantially from their embedding in the broader dual-process heuristic-systematic model (see discussion below), whereas the involvement distinctions arose in a context in which consideration of mediating processes was secondary to the prediction of attitudes.

The greater scope of the three motives is validated by a comparison of the popularity of the two seminal papers—the Johnson and Eagly (1989) involvement meta-analysis and the Chaiken et al. (1989) chapter introducing the multiple-motive heuristic-systematic model. *Web of Science* lists a very respectable 204 citations of the Johnson and Eagly article but an extremely impressive 526 citations of the Chaiken et al. chapter.

How many motives?

Both the three motives and the three types of involvement have roots in the grand tradition of functional theories of attitudes proposed by Katz (1960) and Smith, Bruner, and White (1956). In these earlier analyses, attitudes were held to serve various functions in the personality and thus to have different motivational bases. In particular, the construct of value-relevant involvement corresponded to Katz's value-expressive function, which recognised that people are motivated to maintain their self-defining values. The construct of outcome-relevant involvement corresponded to Katz's instrumental or utilitarian function, which recognised that people are motivated to attain goals they regard as rewarding. The construct of impression-relevant involvement corresponded most closely to Smith et al.'s social-adjustive function, which recognised that people are motivated to maintain positive relationships with other people. The trio of motives has similar roots, although the greater breadth of defence motivation than value-relevant involvement suggests its commonality with Katz's ego-defensive function as well as his value-expressive function. Also, accuracy motivation encompasses Katz's knowledge function as well as his utilitarian function. Other functional precursors can be found in Kelman's (1958, 1961) three processes of social influence and French and Raven's (1959) theorising about six bases of social power (see Eagly & Chaiken, 1993, 1998 for discussion).

The plethora of functions proposed by early functional theorists suggested that it would be helpful to streamline these typologies to a critical number of the most useful and general-purpose functional ideas that provide guidance for research on attitudes and social influence. The partial overlap of the tripartite involvement and motive frameworks suggests that three functions have considerable scope. Other investigators have similarly recognised three or four functions.

Among these other efforts is Briñol and Petty's (2005) motivational framing of research on individual differences in attitude change. They organised individual difference variables that have proven to be useful in attitude research in terms of four motives that they argued govern thinking and action: the needs (a) to know, (b) to achieve consistency or internal coherence of one's explanatory system, (c) to develop and maintain a positive self-concept, and (d) to obtain social inclusion and approval. This organisation is largely consistent with the multiple-motive heuristic-systematic model—that is, defence motivation coincides with the self-concept category and impression motivation with the social inclusion category. New in this framework is the addition of the consistency and internal coherence category, which could be folded into the "to know" category that coincides with accuracy motivation.

Also notable is Boninger, Krosnick, and Berent's (1995) effort to understand the determinants of attitudes' importance, which could as well be regarded as proposing three types of importance. Based on multiple methods, this project derived three determinants of importance: self-interest, social identification with reference groups or individuals, and cherished values. The kinship with outcome-relevant involvement, impression-relevant involvement, and value-relevant involvement is especially close in this scheme.

Finally, three motives have also emerged in the social influence literature. In a review of this extensive tradition, Prislin and Wood (2005) framed social influence phenomena in terms of three fundamental social motives: the needs (a) to understand reality, (b) to relate to other people and convey an appropriate impression to them, and (c) to achieve a positive and coherent self-concept. The first and second of these motives were prominent in classic theorising about informational and normative motives that govern conformity in group settings. Especially well known is Deutsch and Gerard's (1955) definition of informational influence as "influence to accept information obtained from another as *evidence* about reality" and normative influence as "influence to conform with the positive expectations of another" (p. 629). In Prislin and Wood's scheme, preferences for self-serving attitudes emerge from the need to achieve a positive and coherent self-concept as well as the need to relate to others and convey an appropriate impression to them.

Implementing motives through cognitive processes

To predict attitudinal effects, it is not enough to know what motive or need is aroused or what form of involvement is prepotent. Without further specification, predictions from motives to attitudinal processes can be less than straightforward because there is no necessary relation between the motives that are activated and the mode in which people process messages. Motives specify processing goals but not processing modes and therefore may be served by a wide range of specific processes. In particular, within the dual-process tradition of persuasion theories, a motive may be served by a thoughtful, systematic analysis of the content of a persuasive message or by a more superficial analysis that relies on heuristics—that is, simple decision rules such as "experts can be trusted" (Chaiken et al., 1989; Chen & Chaiken, 1999). To serve a particular motive, perceivers can call on heuristic or systematic processing or, for that matter, on both modes of processing. When defence motivation is prepotent, people apply systematic or heuristic processes in a biased manner that favours their existing attitude; when impression motivation is prepotent, people are also biased but apply these processes to favour cementing social bonds or achieving a positive self-presentation.

Despite these complexities, several overarching principles link motives with attitudinal processes. A basic principle is that people select and prefer information that promotes their goals and find it persuasive, whereas they select against and dislike information that threatens their goals and find it unpersuasive. Such effects thus differ depending on the particular goal that is prepotent. An auxiliary principle is that stronger motives tend to favour more thoughtful, or systematic, processing, regardless of their accuracy, defence, or impression basis. This generalisation follows from the well-accepted proposition that systematic or elaborative processes require both the motivation to process information and the capacity to process it (Chaiken et al., 1989; Petty & Cacioppo, 1986). Given adequate capacity, motivation is crucial to thoughtful, elaborative processing. Moreover, this more systematic processing generally offers advantages because it yields greater judgemental confidence than more superficial processing.

A related principle is that processing strategies that demand less cognitive effort are applied before those that require more effort (Abelson, 1968; Chaiken, 1987; Chaiken et al., 1989; Chen & Chaiken, 1999). Because people desire both to minimise effort and to achieve adequate judgemental confidence, they are likely to first process messages more simply or heuristically and, if this approach does not yield adequate confidence, then invoke more effortful, systematic processing. In the more formal terms of Chaiken's *sufficiency principle*, people's actual level of confidence in confronting persuasive information is often lower than their desired level of confidence. High levels of motivation—regardless of their source in accuracy, defence, or impression motives—raise the desired level of confidence and thus typically increase the gap between actual and desired levels of confidence. When confidence is less than desired, people will attempt to bring their confidence to the desired level. If low-effort processes do not close the confidence gap, high-effort, systematic processing is more likely to occur. With higher motivation and typically larger confidence gaps, systematic processing tends to dominate, although heuristic processing may continue to occur.

Defensive processes in attitudinal selectivity

The goal of defending positive states of the self should affect attitudinal selectivity—that is, the selection and processing of information that is relevant to one's attitudes. It had long been assumed that the result of this defence should be that people select in favour of attitudinally agreeable information and against attitudinally disagreeable information. Consistent with this reasoning, this research area had been dominated by one overarching principle, which is now generally labelled the *congeniality hypothesis*. This hypothesis states that attitudes bias information processing in favour of attitudinally congenial, or congruent, material—that is, in favour of information that supports one's attitudes and against information that challenges one's attitudes (see Eagly, 1992; Eagly & Chaiken, 1993, 1998). This bias could occur at various stages of information processing: People might not expose themselves to uncongenial information at all; if exposed to it, they might not pay attention to it; they could distort it perceptually in a way that blunts its persuasive impact; they could evaluate it unfavourably; and they could fail to remember it. The overall theme in much early theory about the effects of attitudes on information processing was that people are closed-minded in the sense that they are reluctant to encode or remember information that challenges their attitudes.

However reasonable the congeniality hypothesis might have seemed, it does not necessarily follow that the goal of defending one's attitudes would be prepotent. Also, even if attitudinal defence is a principal goal, it does not necessarily follow that congeniality effects would prevail. In fact, in so far as the empirical history of congeniality effects is concerned, findings have been far less consistent than would have been expected in terms of early treatments of attitudinal selectivity (e.g., Festinger, 1957; Levine & Murphy, 1943). It has been difficult to come to a clear theoretical understanding of how attitudes affect information processing, and it has been difficult to document expected phenomena empirically (see Eagly & Chaiken, 1993, 1998).

Notwithstanding these difficulties, some of the advances that psychologists have made in understanding motivation have illuminated the phenomena of attitudinal selectivity. Research on memory for attitude-relevant information illustrates this progress. Researchers' traditional expectation was for a congeniality bias whereby people have better memory for attitudinally congenial than uncongenial information. Despite some early confirmations of the congeniality hypothesis in memory experiments (e.g., Levine & Murphy, 1943), much of the early research suffered from methodological weaknesses, and congeniality effects have been inconsistently obtained in subsequent years (e.g., Greenwald & Sakumura, 1967).

It is reasonable to assume that defence motivation was often active in attitude memory studies because they were usually implemented with highly controversial social issues, with participants selected on the basis of polarised pro or con attitudes. People with polarised attitudes on important social issues should be motivated to resist changing their attitudes because the attitudes are linked to their values and important reference groups (e.g., Eagly & Chaiken, 1995; Johnson & Eagly, 1989; Zuwerink & Devine, 1996).

Despite the plausibility of early researchers' perspectives about attitudinal selectivity, there were two central flaws in their reasoning. One flaw is the failure to take the competing influence of accuracy motivation (or outcome-relevant involvement) into account. Accuracy-oriented processing should dampen the selectivity that follows from defence motivation and thus should lessen tendencies towards congeniality in information processing.

The second flaw in early theorists' reasoning was their assumption that motivation to defend attitudes necessarily proceeds through passive processes that allow message recipients to avoid the challenging implications of the information. Instead, given sufficient motivation and capability in persuasion contexts, people are likely to mount an active defence involving systematic processing, which would be biased towards negative thoughts but still enhance memory for counterattitudinal information (e.g., Eagly & Chaiken, 1995; K. Edwards & Smith, 1996; Liberman & Chaiken, 1992). Similarly, in research on motivated reasoning, information inconsistent with preferences has produced a greater quantity of processing than information consistent with preferences (Ditto, 1998; Ditto & Lopez, 1992; see also Kunda, 1990).

With these considerations in mind, Eagly, Chen, Chaiken, and Shaw Barnes (1999) conducted a meta-analysis of research on memory for attitude-relevant information. They found limited overall evidence of congeniality in experiments using memory measures that are relatively unlikely to produce artefacts. Nonetheless, consistent with a motivational analysis, studies that had presented recipients with issues higher in value relevance produced stronger congeniality effects, and studies with issues higher in outcome relevance produced weaker congeniality effects. The relative balance between defence motivation and accuracy motivation thus affected the extent to which researchers had obtained a congeniality bias in memory.

The idea that, even in the presence of defence motivation, active defensive processes frequently quash congeniality effects on memory was confirmed in experiments by Eagly, Kulesa, Brannon, Shaw-Barnes, and Hutson-Comeaux (2000; see also Eagly, Chen, Kulesa, & Chaiken, 2001). In experiments that presented attitudinally polarised participants with communications on highly value-relevant topics, congeniality effects were absent: Congenial and uncongenial messages proved to be equally memorable. More important, the processes by which the messages became memorable differed, depending on messages' congeniality with recipients' own attitudes. Attitude-consistent information appeared to be remembered by a fairly superficial process by which message recipients matched the information to their existing attitudes, whereas attitude-inconsistent information was remembered by active and sceptical scrutiny of its content. This systematic defensive processing was revealed by the message recipients' active, refutational thoughts, which correlated positively with memory for the counterattitudinal information.

In general, stored beliefs supportive of attitudes enable people not only to remember congenial arguments but also to refute challenging information (Biek, Wood, & Chaiken, 1996; Eagly & Chaiken, 1993, 1995, 1998; Wood, Rhodes, & Biek, 1995). Moreover, familiarity with arguments opposed to one's own attitude may further enable refutational elaboration of uncongenial information. Such active refutational processes would reflect an attitudinal bias against uncongenial information but may enhance rather than reduce memory for such information because the processes entail careful scrutiny of this information. Research on memory for attitude-relevant information thus illustrates the inadequacy of the simple congeniality bias hypothesis for understanding memory effects and shows that memory for persuasive information can be achieved through differing processes.

Finally, research on attitudinal selectivity consistent with tripartite motivational analyses has emerged in the social influence literature. Specifically, Lundgren and Prislin (1998, Study 1) experimentally observed effects on selective exposure and attitudes (see also related research by Chen, Shechter, & Chaiken, 1996; Nienhuis, Manstead, & Spears, 2001). Participants in this study expected to discuss an attitude issue with another participant. Some participants were initially informed that the study provided an opportunity to defend their own position on the topic. When given the opportunity to select reading material, they chose material that supported their own view, and they indicated relatively polarised attitudes. Other participants, who were told that the study concerned accuracy of understanding about issues, selected material to read on both sides of the issue and indicated relatively neutral attitudes. Finally, other participants, who were sensitised to their relations with others, selected material that was congruent with the view ostensibly held by their partner and indicated attitudes relatively congenial with their partner's views. It thus appeared that the participants implemented selective exposure to meet whatever goal was salient.

Defensive processes in reactions to health-relevant appeals

Defence motivation has proven to be a useful concept in persuasion research in general (see Chaiken, Wood, & Eagly, 1996) and particularly useful for understanding reactions to health-relevant communications. Suggestive of defensive processing of such communications, it is difficult to change people's behaviour to induce them to engage in practices that protect their health (see Stroebe, 2000). For example, despite the warnings about unfavourable health consequences of smoking that appear on cigarette packs and in anti-smoking media campaigns, smoking remains a widespread practice. Similarly, despite much media attention to exercise and weight control, the proportion of people who are obese continues to increase in many industrial-ised nations. Such facts have induced researchers to direct their attention to the processing of health-relevant messages to discover what factors impede acceptance of the advice given in these communications. It is in this context that motivational analyses of persuasion, especially the concept of defence motivation, have proven to be especially valuable.

In general, messages portraying serious health threats tend to evoke nega-tive affect, which motivates the rejection of the message and can interfere with thinking about changing behaviour that would reduce such threats (Leventhal, 1970; Witte, 1992). People are generally critical of such messages (e.g., Liberman & Chaiken, 1992; Reed & Aspinwall, 1998). However, recent research on fear appeals has revealed the advantages of taking a more detailed look at defensive processing in such contexts. In a series of experiments on fear appeals, De Hoog, Stroebe, and their colleagues have shown that respondents who are vulnerable to a severe health risk generally engage in biased system-atic processing rather than less effortful, avoidant reactions (Das, de Wit, & Stroebe, 2003; De Hoog, 2005; De Hoog, Stroebe, & de Wit, 2005).

It is the details of this systematic processing that proved especially interest-ing in this research. Specifically, the negative affect that vulnerable respond-ents experienced from health-threatening communications induced thoughts that minimised the severity of the consequences described in the message as well as their own vulnerability to the threat. However, a different picture emerged in relation to the processing of information about recommended protective actions. In relation to such information, respondents' vulnerability induced positively biased systematic processing. This processing took the form of favourably biased thoughts, which resulted in stronger intentions to change behaviour, regardless of the quality of the arguments that were presented or the credibility of the source of the information. It thus appeared that vulnerable people find information about a threat to their health to be unwelcome, but information about possible protective measures to be welcome. Processing of both of these aspects of health-relevant information was systematic but different in direction—negatively biased in relation to the threat itself but positively biased in relation to the potential remedy. This subtle understanding of the effects of fear appeals sheds light on the ways in which motives affect information processing as well as on links of health-relevant attitudes to intentions and behaviour.

Conclusion

Attention to motivated processing of attitude-relevant information continues to grow in scope and sophistication. Having restored the balance between motivation and cognition, social psychologists and other behavioural scientists have probed a range of motivational conceptions that are relevant to attitudes. Although motivational typologies abound, they have produced some consensus on three motives that are especially relevant in contexts of attitudes and social influence. Whether these are framed as motives or types of involvement, the realisation that a motivation towards accuracy competes with motives towards other goals is an extremely important insight, but only a beginning towards understanding how information processing is affected by motivation. The other critical theoretical insight is that motives may be served by a range of specific processes. Process distinctions are thus also crucially important and have been framed in terms of more effortful systematic processes and more superficial heuristic processing and also in terms of more active and more passive processes. These insights warrant further development in relation to both attitudinal selectivity and persuasion.

Note

1 This meta-analysis also uncovered a research group effect that clouded to some extent the results within the outcome-relevant set of studies. The effects of outcome-relevant involvement were strong and consistent for some researchers (loosely categorised as those associated with the social psychology programme at Ohio State University) but much weaker, especially in the weak-argument conditions, among other researchers who had used manipulations that were procedurally highly similar. For a critique of the Johnson and Eagly (1989) article that discusses this issue and alternative explanations of the differing effects of the three types of involvement, see Petty and Cacioppo (1990). For a response to this critique, see Johnson and Eagly (1990).

References

Abelson, R. P. (1968). Psychological implication. In R. P. Abelson, E. Aronson, W. J. McGuire, T. M. Newcomb, M. J. Rosenberg, & P. H. Tannenbaum (Eds.), *Theories of cognitive consistency: A sourcebook* (pp. 112–139). Chicago: Rand McNally.

Biek, M., Wood, W., & Chaiken, S. (1996). Working knowledge, cognitive processing, and attitudes: On the determinants of bias. *Personality and Social Psychology Bulletin, 22*, 547–556.

Boninger, D. S., Krosnick, J. A., & Berent, M. K. (1995). Origins of attitude importance: Self-interest, social identification, and value relevance. *Journal of Personality and Social Psychology, 68*, 61–80.

Briñol, P., & Petty, R. E. (2005). Individual differences in attitude change. In D. Albarracin, B. T. Johnson, & M. P. Zanna (Eds.), *Handbook of attitudes and attitude change* (pp. 575–616). Mahwah, NJ: Lawrence Erlbaum Associates Inc.

Chaiken, S. (1980). Heuristic versus systematic information processing and the use of source versus message cues in persuasion. *Journal of Personality and Social Psychology, 39*, 752–766.

Chaiken, S. (1987). The heuristic model of persuasion. In M. P. Zanna, J. M. Olson, & C. P. Herman (Eds.), *Social influence: The Ontario Symposium* (Vol. 5, pp. 3–39). Hillsdale, NJ: Lawrence Erlbaum Associates Inc.

Chaiken, S., Giner-Sorolla, R., & Chen, S. (1996). Beyond accuracy: Defense and impression motives in heuristic and systematic information processing. In P. M. Gollwitzer & J. A. Bargh (Eds.), *The psychology of action: Linking cognition and motivation to behavior* (pp. 553–578). New York: Guilford Press.

Chaiken, S., Liberman, A., & Eagly, A. H. (1989). Heuristic and systematic processing within and beyond the persuasion context. In J. S. Uleman & J. A. Bargh (Eds.), *Unintended thought* (pp. 212–252). New York: Guilford Press.

Chaiken, S., & Stangor, C. (1987). Attitudes and attitude change. *Annual Review of Psychology, 38*, 575–630.

Chaiken, S., Wood, W. L., & Eagly, A. H. (1996). Principles of persuasion. In E. T. Higgins & A. Kruglanski (Eds.), *Social psychology: Handbook of basic principles* (pp. 702–742). New York: Guilford Press.

Chen, S., & Chaiken, S. (1999). The heuristic-systematic model in its broader context. In S. Chaiken & Y. Trope (Eds.), *Dual-process theories in social psychology* (pp. 73–96). New York: Guilford Press.

Chen, S., Shechter, D., & Chaiken, S. (1996). Getting at the truth or getting along: Accuracy versus impression motivated heuristic and systematic processing. *Journal of Personality and Social Psychology, 71*, 262–275.

Cho, H., & Boster, F. J. (2005). Development and validation of value-, outcome-, and impression-relevant involvement scales. *Communication Research, 32*, 235–264.

Cialdini, R. B., & Petty, R. E. (1981). Anticipatory opinion effects. In R. E. Petty, T. M. Ostrom, & T. C. Brock (Eds.), *Cognitive responses in persuasion* (pp. 217–235). Hillsdale, NJ: Lawrence Erlbaum Associates Inc.

Darke, P. R., & Chaiken, S. (2005). The pursuit of self-interest: Self-interest bias in attitude judgment and persuasion. *Journal of Personality and Social Psychology, 89*, 864–883.

Das, E. H. H. J., de Wit, J. B. F., & Stroebe, W. (2003). Fear appeals motivate acceptance of action recommendations: Evidence for a positive bias in the processing of persuasive messages. *Personality and Social Psychology Bulletin, 29*, 650–664.

De Hoog, N. (2005). *Fear-arousing communications and persuasion: The impact of vulnerability on processing and accepting fear appeals.* Unpublished doctoral dissertation, Utrecht University, The Netherlands.

De Hoog, N., Stroebe, W., & de Wit, J. B. F. (2005). The impact of fear appeals on the processing and acceptance of action recommendations. *Personality and Social Psychology Bulletin, 31,* 24–33.

Deutsch, M., & Gerard, H. B. (1955). A study of normative and informational social influences upon individual judgment. *Journal of Abnormal and Social Psychology, 51,* 629–636.

Dillard, J. P., & Hunter, J. E. (1989). On the use and interpretation of the Emotional Empathy Scale, the Self-Consciousness Scales, and the Self-Monitoring Scale. *Communication Research, 16,* 104–129.

Ditto, P. H. (1998). Motivated sensitivity to preference-inconsistent information. *Journal of Personality and Social Psychology, 75,* 53–69.

Ditto, P. H., & Lopez, D. L. (1992). Motivated skepticism: Use of differential decision criteria for preferred and nonpreferred conclusions. *Journal of Personality and Social Psychology, 63,* 568–584.

Eagly, A. H. (1992). Uneven progress: Social psychology and the study of attitudes. *Journal of Personality and Social Psychology, 63,* 693–710.

Eagly, A. H., & Chaiken, S. (1993). *The psychology of attitudes.* Orlando, FL: Harcourt Brace.

Eagly, A. H., & Chaiken, S. (1995). Attitude strength, attitude structure, and resistance to change. In R. E. Petty & J. A. Krosnick (Eds.), *Attitude strength: Antecedents and consequences* (pp. 413–432). Hillsdale, NJ: Lawrence Erlbaum Associates Inc.

Eagly, A. H., & Chaiken, S. (1998). Attitude structure and function. In D. Gilbert, S. Fiske, & G. Lindzey (Eds.), *The handbook of social psychology* (4th ed., pp. 269–322). New York: McGraw-Hill.

Eagly, A. H., Chen, S., Chaiken, S., & Shaw-Barnes, K. (1999). The impact of attitudes on memory: An affair to remember. *Psychological Bulletin, 125,* 64–89.

Eagly, A. H., Chen, S., Kulesa, P., & Chaiken, S. (2001). Do attitudes affect memory? Tests of the congeniality hypothesis. *Current Directions in Psychological Science, 10,* 5–9.

Eagly, A. H., Kulesa, P., Brannon, L. A., Shaw-Barnes, K., & Hutson-Comeaux, S. (2000). Why counterattitudinal messages are as memorable as proattitudinal messages: The importance of active defense against attack. *Personality and Social Psychology Bulletin, 26,* 1392–1408.

Edwards, K., & Smith, E. E. (1996). A disconfirmation bias in the evaluation of arguments. *Journal of Personality and Social Psychology, 71,* 5–24.

Festinger, L. (1957). *A theory of cognitive dissonance.* Stanford, CA: Stanford University Press.

French, J. R. P. Jr., & Raven, B. (1959). The bases of social power. In D. Cartwright (Ed.), *Studies in social power* (pp. 150–167). Ann Arbor: University of Michigan.

Greenwald, A. G., & Sakumura, J. S. (1967). Attitude and selective learning: Where are the phenomena of yesteryear? *Journal of Personality and Social Psychology, 7,* 387–397.

Johnson, B. T., & Eagly, A. H. (1989). Effects of involvement on persuasion: A meta-analysis. *Psychological Bulletin, 106,* 290–314.

Johnson, B. T., & Eagly, A. H. (1990). Involvement and persuasion: Types, traditions, and the evidence. *Psychological Bulletin, 107*, 375–384.

Johnson, B. T., Lin, H. Y., Symons, C. S., Campbell, L. A., & Ekstein, F. (1995). Initial beliefs and attitudinal latitudes as factors in persuasion. *Personality and Social Psychology Bulletin, 21*, 502–511.

Jones, E. E. (1990). *Interpersonal perception.* New York: W. H. Freeman.

Katz, D. (1960). The functional approach to the study of attitudes. *Public Opinion Quarterly, 24*, 163–204.

Kelman, H. C. (1958). Compliance, identification, and internalization: Three processes of attitude change. *Journal of Conflict Resolution, 2*, 51–60.

Kelman, H. C. (1961). Processes of attitude change. *Public Opinion Quarterly, 25*, 57–78.

Kunda, Z. (1990). The case for motivated reasoning. *Psychological Bulletin, 108*, 480–498.

Leippe, M. R., & Elkin, R. A. (1987). When motives clash: Issue involvement and response involvement as determinants of persuasion. *Journal of Personality and Social Psychology, 52*, 269–278.

Leventhal, H. (1970). Findings and theory in the study of fear communications. In L. Berkowitz (Ed.), *Advances in experimental social psychology* (Vol. 5, pp. 119–186). New York: Academic Press.

Levin, K. D., Nichols, D. R., & Johnson, B. T. (2000). Involvement and persuasion: Attitude functions for the motivated processor. In G. R. Maio & J. M. Olson (Eds.), *Why we evaluate: Functions of attitudes* (pp. 163–194). Mahwah, NJ: Lawrence Erlbaum Associates Inc.

Levine, J. M., & Murphy, G. (1943). The learning and forgetting of controversial material. *Journal of Abnormal and Social Psychology, 38*, 507–517.

Liberman, A., & Chaiken, S. (1992). Defensive processing of personally relevant health messages. *Personality and Social Psychology Bulletin, 18*, 669–679.

Lundgren, S. R., & Prislin, R. (1998). Motivated cognitive processing and attitude change. *Personality and Social Psychology Bulletin, 24*, 715–726.

Maio, G. R., & Olson, J. M. (1995). Involvement and persuasion: Evidence for different types of involvement. *Canadian Journal of Behavioural Science, 27*, 64–78.

Miller, D. T., & Ross, M. (1975). Self-serving biases in the attribution of causality: Fact or fiction? *Psychological Bulletin, 82*, 213–225.

Nienhuis, A. E., Manstead, A. S. R., & Spears, R. (2001). Multiple motives and persuasive communication: Creative elaboration as a result of impression motivation and accuracy motivation. *Personality and Social Psychology Bulletin, 27*, 118–132.

Petty, R. E., & Cacioppo, J. T. (1979a). Effects of forewarning of persuasive intent and involvement on cognitive responses and persuasion. *Personality and Social Psychology Bulletin, 5*, 173–176.

Petty, R. E., & Cacioppo, J. T. (1979b). Issue involvement can increase or decrease persuasion by enhancing message-relevant cognitive responses. *Journal of Personality and Social Psychology, 37*, 1915–1926.

Petty, R. E., & Cacioppo, J. T. (1981). *Attitudes and persuasion: Classic and contemporary approaches.* Dubuque, IA: Brown.

Petty, R. E., & Cacioppo, J. T. (1986). The elaboration likelihood model of persuasion. In L. Berkowitz (Ed.), *Advances in experimental social psychology* (Vol. 19, pp. 123–205). San Diego, CA: Academic Press.

Petty, R. E., & Cacioppo, J. T. (1990). Involvement and persuasion: Tradition versus integration. *Psychological Bulletin, 107*, 367–374.

Petty, R. E., Cacioppo, J. T., & Goldman, R. (1981). Personal involvement as a determinant of argument-based persuasion. *Journal of Personality and Social Psychology, 41*, 847–855.

Prislin, R., & Wood, W. (2005). Social influence in attitudes and attitude change. In D. Albarracin, B. T. Johnson, & M. P. Zanna (Eds.), *Handbook of attitudes and attitude change* (pp. 671–706). Mahwah, NJ: Lawrence Erlbaum Associates Inc.

Reed, M. B., & Aspinwall, L. G. (1998). Self-affirmation reduces biased processing of health-risk information. *Motivation and Emotion, 22*, 99–132.

Schlenker, B. R. (1982). Translating actions into attitudes: An identity-analytic approach to the explanation of social conduct. In L. Berkowitz (Ed.), *Advances in experimental social psychology* (Vol. 15, pp. 193–247). New York: Academic Press.

Sherif, C. W., & Sherif, M. (Eds.). (1967). *Attitude, ego-involvement, and change.* New York: Wiley.

Sherif, C. W., Sherif, M., & Nebergall, R. E. (1965). *Attitude and attitude change.* Philadelphia: Saunders.

Sherif, M., & Cantril, H. (1947). *The psychology of ego-involvements: Social attitudes and identifications.* New York: Wiley.

Sherif, M., & Hovland, C. I. (1961). *Social judgment: Assimilation and contrast effects in communication and attitude change.* New Haven, CT: Yale University Press.

Smith, M. B., Bruner, J. S., & White, R. W. (1956). *Opinions and personality.* New York: Wiley.

Stroebe, W. (2000). *Social psychology and health* (2nd ed.). Buckingham, UK: Open University Press.

Witte, K. (1992). Putting the fear back into fear appeals: The extended parallel process model. *Communication Monographs, 59*, 329–349.

Wood, W., Rhodes, N., & Biek, M. (1995). Working knowledge and attitude strength: An information-processing analysis. In R. E. Petty & J. A. Krosnick (Eds.), *Attitude strength: Antecedents and consequences* (pp. 283–313). Hillsdale, NJ: Lawrence Erlbaum Associates Inc.

Zimbardo, P. G. (1960). Involvement and communication discrepancy as determinants of opinion conformity. *Journal of Abnormal and Social Psychology, 60*, 86–94.

Zuwerink, J. R., & Devine, P. G. (1996). Attitude importance and resistance to persuasion: It's not just the thought that counts. *Journal of Personality and Social Psychology, 70*, 931–944.

Part 2

Social cognition and emotion

6 Conceptualising group perception

A 35-year evolution

David L. Hamilton
University of California, Santa Barbara, USA

Miles Hewstone
Oxford University, UK

Social psychology's long history of interest in group perception has, in the past three decades, progressed and developed in several new and important directions. Work on group perception has evolved and elaborated from a singular focus on the stereotypic associations for various groups into a multifaceted analysis of various aspects of how groups are perceived. Similarly, conceptual understanding of the implications of intergroup contact for changing stereotypic beliefs and prejudicial attitudes has advanced to more sophisticated analyses of how and why rather than simply when. In this chapter we review these developments and highlight their contributions to understanding the dynamics of group perception and intergroup relations.

Understanding group perception

The study of stereotypes has a long history, being among the earliest topics to be studied empirically in the newly emerging discipline of social psychology (Katz & Braly, 1933). For many years this research was almost exclusively concerned with measuring the content of various racial, religious, and national stereotypes. This work, while useful, had serious constraints on the questions it could address (see Brigham, 1971; Hamilton, Stroessner, & Driscoll, 1994). After several decades of this singular focus, the period of time covered by this chapter has witnessed numerous advances in understanding not only stereotypes but also several other basic elements of group perception.

Stereotypes

The modern era in stereotype research began in the early 1970s, as a result of two quite independent developments, both of which had a definite cognitive "ring" to them, that led, at least in some important ways, in the same direction. These two new thrusts were social identity theory and social cognition.

The first of those developments was inspired by the work of Henri Tajfel, who posed new questions and provided new answers to long-standing problems. In 1969 he published an article entitled "Cognitive Aspects of Prejudice" that had enormous impact and in fact has been cited as the "single publication that marks the birth of the cognitive revolution in the intergroup area" (Rothbart & Lewis, 1994, p. 363). Tajfel's approach, and the research he and his students generated, dramatically and convincingly highlighted the role of categorisation and its centrality for understanding intergroup perception (Tajfel, 1970). Although Allport (1954) had earlier discussed the implications of categorisation for stereotyping and prejudice (see Fiske, 2005), it was Tajfel's emphasis on the ingroup/outgroup distinction and his demonstrations using the minimal group paradigm that gave empirical flesh to the conceptual skeleton Allport had offered (for reviews, see Brewer, 1979; Diehl, 1990).

Prior to Tajfel's groundbreaking work (see Tajfel, 1969, 1970), the primary conceptual frameworks guiding research on and interpretations of intergroup behaviour saw stereotypes and prejudice in terms of either sociocultural or personal causes (see Stroebe & Insko, 1989, for a thoughtful overview using this framework). *Sociocultural* accounts included conflict theories such as realistic conflict theory (Campbell, 1965; Sherif, 1966) and relative deprivation theory (e.g., Berkowitz, 1972; see Billig, 1976). Both of these approaches, valuable as they were, rested heavily on the origins of intergroup conflict having their roots in *actual* intergroup differences. One of the startling, and fascinating, elements of Tajfel's work was that he and his colleagues demonstrated that differential intergroup perception, as well as actual intergroup discrimination, could arise as a result of simple intergroup differentiation. The mere categorisation of individuals into two groups, an ingroup and an outgroup, was sufficient to shape both perception and behaviour. The result was a laboratory demonstration of a means by which both evaluative bias (prejudice) and preferential treatment (discrimination) could develop in the absence of any history of intergroup conflict over, for example, scarce resources or differential distribution of resources.

In contrast, psychodynamic theories saw stereotypes and prejudice in terms of *personal* causes (e.g., Adorno, Frenkel-Brunswik, Levinson, & Sanford, 1950). These approaches view prejudice as "a sign of some intrapersonal conflict or maladjustment" (Stroebe & Insko, 1989, p. 17), as in scapegoat theory (e.g., Miller & Bugelski, 1948), whereby prejudice or outgroup-directed hostility is the result of displaced aggression from a powerful frustrating source to a powerless minority group. Although the psychodynamic approach to intergroup relations is now largely discredited (see Billig, 1976), the cognitive approach (discussed below) has shown the importance of under-standing the *individual* cognitive system in order to understand *intergroup* prejudice and stereotyping.

Tajfel's (1969) pioneering work on social identity inspired several related theoretical developments, including two that focused further on cognitive determinants and two that highlighted motivational variables. The first cognitive development came in research on *accentuation* effects, which identi-fied processes of intercategory contrast and intracategory assimilation (see Doise, 1978; Eiser & Stroebe, 1972; McGarty, 1999). This work paved the way for later understanding of ingroup–outgroup differences in per-ceived homogeneity (see below). The cognitive emphasis was also central in self-categorisation theory (Turner, 1981; Turner, Hogg, Oakes, Reicher, & Wetherell, 1987), which clearly specified a cognitive category differentiation component of social identity theory. In this view, self-categorisation as an ingroup member entails assimilation of the self to the ingroup category prototype and enhanced similarity to other ingroup members (see Turner & Reynolds, 2001). Self-categorisation theory emphasises that we all belong to several social categories and therefore may have a series of social identifica-tions. The intergroup differentiation that is salient at the time determines one's momentary self-identification. Thus self-categorisation theory addresses self as well as other stereotyping, ingroup and outgroup stereotyping, and emphasises that individuals ascribe to themselves characteristics associated with their ingroup.

Two other theoretical developments recognise the important contribution of motivational processes. Optimal distinctiveness theory (Brewer, 1991) pro-poses that social identity involves a compromise between two opposing needs: the need for assimilation and the need for differentiation. People are motivated to identify with groups that provide an optimal balance between these two needs. Finally, Hogg's (2000) subjective uncertainty reduction the-ory proposes that people are motivated to reduce subjective uncertainty. One way to reduce such uncertainty is to identify with social groups that provide clear normative prescriptions for behaviour.

SOCIAL COGNITION: EMPHASIS ON STRUCTURE AND PROCESS

The second major development that challenged traditional perspectives on group perception was the emergence of social cognition as a new approach to analysing social phenomena. This approach soon provided a new perspec-tive on intergroup perception which emphasised the importance of stereo-types as cognitive structures that guide information processing in ways that had direct bearing on the perception of groups and their members (Hamilton, 1981). No longer were stereotypes viewed as *necessarily* rooted in and driven by unresolved internal conflicts that resulted in projecting unwanted qualities in the self onto outgroups. No longer were stereotypes viewed as *necessarily* based on the social learning and social reinforcement of prevailing intergroup attitudes. Rather, an impressive series of empirical findings reported during the 1970s and 1980s demonstrated that aspects of normal cognitive functioning can be the basis of both the formation and maintenance of stereotypes.

For example, the differential frequencies of exposure to certain groups, along with the differential frequency of certain types of behaviour, can result in the differential perception of the groups, even though the information provided about those groups was evaluatively equivalent (Hamilton & Gifford, 1976). Certain persons or groups that are salient, based solely on the social context, can be perceived as different from others and viewed in more stereotypic ways, compared to when those same persons are not contextually salient (Taylor, Fiske, Etcoff, & Ruderman, 1978). Stereotypes, as cognitive structures that contain the perceiver's expectancies about a group, can guide one's attention to and greater encoding of information that is consistent with those expectancies (Bodenhausen, 1988), can influence how information is construed or interpreted (Darley & Gross, 1983; Sagar & Schofield, 1980), can result in overestimation of the frequency of stereotype-consistent behaviours (Hamilton & Rose, 1980), and when interacting with members of stereotyped groups, can influence how those people behave such that the perceiver's stereotypic expectancy is fulfilled (Snyder, Tanke, & Berscheid, 1977; Word, Zanna, & Cooper, 1974). All of these findings (and many more in an ever-accumulating literature) document the central role of basic cognitive mechanisms in stereotyping (see Fiske, 1998).

Together, these two developments—the social identity orientation and social cognition—changed the landscape of the stereotype literature. Prior to the advent of these new directions, the study of group perception had been almost exclusively focused on stereotypes of the large ethnic, religious, national, and gender categories. Moreover, that work had been focused almost exclusively on the *content* of those stereotypes. Little research had been devoted to trying to understand (a) what stereotypes look like, (b) how they develop, or (c) how they function. The social identity literature, with its emphasis on the categorisation process in intergroup perception, and the social cognition approach, with its emphasis on stereotypes as cognitive structures that guide information processing, have revised and expanded our understanding of group perception. They have transformed this literature from the study of *stereotypes* to the study of *stereotyping*, and with it, a change from a focus on *content* to a focus on *structure and process*.

Although research on stereotypes and stereotyping continues to be one of the most prominent and active areas of research in all of social psychology, it is not (unlike the pre-1970 era) the only focus of research on group perception. Research on several other aspects of group perception has developed during this period, enlightening us about some fundamental questions, such as how we perceive groups, how we perceive group members, and even how we perceive an assortment of people to be a group. We now highlight two of these more recent topic areas.

Perceived group variability

As we noted above, one of the consequences of categorisation is the perceived assimilation of category members (Tajfel & Wilkes, 1963)—members of the same category are perceived to be similar to each other. This pervasive outcome of the categorisation process is manifested in intergroup perception in an interesting way, one that follows directly from Tajfel's emphasis on the ingroup/outgroup differentiation. Specifically, outgroup members are perceived as being more similar to each other than are ingroup members—the well-known, highly robust *outgroup homogeneity effect* (for a review, see Ostrom & Sedikides, 1992; for exceptions, see Simon, 1992). Understanding when, how, and why people perceive variability among the members of a group, and the bases for the differential perception of ingroup and outgroup in this regard, has been the focus of an enormous amount of research during the last 20 years (see Yzerbyt, Judd, & Corneille, 2004). Various explanations have been offered for the outgroup homogeneity effect, and this has been a matter of dispute in the literature (for discussions, see Devos, Comby, & Deschamps, 1996; Doosje, Spears, Ellemers, & Koomen, 1999; Judd & Park, 1988; Linville & Fischer, 1993; Linville, Fischer, & Salovey, 1989; Park, Judd, & Ryan, 1991).

One reason for the interest in perceived variability is its direct implications for the topic we have just discussed, namely, stereotyping. As first pointed out in Allport's (1954) seminal analysis of intergroup perception, one of the hallmarks of stereotyping is overgeneralisation. Stereotyping inherently involves ascribing the same attributes and qualities to all members of a target group; that is, seeing a group as homogeneous and making them, for the perceiver, functionally equivalent. Therefore, conditions that promote the perception of homogeneity in groups would make it easier to generalise about all group members; that is, to stereotype them. The fact that people are more likely to see homogeneity in outgroups thereby inclines them to stereotype more about those outgroups. This is, then, another instance in which basic cognitive processing mechanisms generate a condition (homogeneity) that quite naturally leads to generalisation (stereotyping) about the attributes of group members, and this is more likely to happen for outgroups than for groups to which one belongs.

Perceived entitativity

Stereotypes are cognitive structures that contain a perceiver's knowledge, beliefs, and expectancies about a social group. The social groups of interest in stereotyping are typically large categories of people defined by gender, nationality, race, religion, or some other defining characteristic. Yet these are not the only groups we as perceivers encounter in the social world. Indeed, our lives are constantly invested in perceiving, interacting in, reacting to, and even imagining the groups that have meaning to us—family, friends, social clubs, employment groups, the city council, sports teams, unions, an orchestra, people living in the neighbourhood, and so on. All of these entities are groups in some way and for some purpose. These groups also differ in many ways, but they are not the broad social categories about which we develop stereotypes. Nevertheless, they may play important, even central, roles in our lives. How do we perceive such groups? Do we have cognitive structures representing them? What kinds of distinctions do we make among these various groups? What differences follow from those perceptions?

These are important questions that address some basic aspects of how people perceive the numerous and varied groups they encounter in their daily lives. Yet it is only within the last decade that research has begun empirically to explore these questions and to pursue their ramifications. Campbell (1958) coined the term *entitativity* to refer to the extent to which the group has the quality of being an entity; that is, entitativity refers to the perceived "group-ness" of groups. The sampling of groups cited above varies considerably in this respect. The family is clearly high in entitativity; it is close-knit, bonded together through extensive interaction, caring, and sharing in outcomes. The city council meets regularly to plan and implement policies that affect a considerable number of people. Nevertheless, the group members' inter-actions are more constrained, their investment in the group less crucial to them, and even their membership in the group will someday end. The social club meets only periodically, provides enjoyable experiences, but is not central in the lives of most of its members. These differences reflect variations in the entitativity of the groups.

Research in the last decade has shed considerable light on these issues. Following Campbell's (1958) conceptual analysis, Lickel, Hamilton, Wiec-zorkowska, Lewis, Sherman, and Uhles (2000) showed that several variables predict the perceived entitativity of groups, including interaction among group members, importance of the group, shared goals and outcomes, and similarity among members. Groups for which these descriptions would be true are perceived as high in entitativity—they are groups possessing the quality of being an entity. Moreover, perceivers differentiate perceptually and cognitively among several distinct types of groups (Lickel et al., 2000; Sherman, Castelli, & Hamilton, 2002) that are perceived as meeting different social needs (Johnson et al., in press). Intimacy groups (family, close friends, support group) are small, highly interactive groups that are very important to their members, and they are seen as meeting attachment needs of the participants. Task groups (committee, jury, work group) are also small and interactive, but less important to members, and share common goals. Such groups are perceived as functional because they help members meet achievement needs. Social categories (women, Germans, Schwabians, African-Americans, Presbyterians) are large groups with low levels of interaction, and a moderate degree of interaction, but they have a long history of existence and are perceived as meeting members' identity needs. Importantly, these group types also differ in their perceived entitativity, with intimacy groups being most entitative, followed by task groups and then social categories. Interestingly, the type of groups about whom stereotypes are so prominent are not among the most entitative of groups.

Research has also shown that several consequences follow from perceiving a group as high in entitativity. Most generally, people engage in more integrative processing about entitative than nonentitative groups. That is, when learning about a group perceived as high in entitativity, people are likely to make on-line judgements, recall more of the information presented, process persuasive communications more systematically, perceive enhanced similarity among members, make more extreme, polarised judgements about the group, identify with the group more, and generalise attributes of one group member to other members of the group. None of these processes occurs as readily for groups perceived as low in entitativity (Crawford et al., 2002; McConnell, Sherman, & Hamilton, 1997; Pickett, 2001; Rydell & McConnell, 2005; Susskind, Maurer, Thakkar, Hamilton, & Sherman, 1999; Yzerbyt, Corneille, & Estrada, 2001; for reviews of this literature, see Hamilton, Sherman, & Castelli, 2002; Hamilton, Sherman, & Rodgers, 2004; Sherman, Hamilton, & Lewis, 1999).

Implicit aspects of group perception

The preceding subsections discuss different foci of research that have emerged as the study of group perception has evolved in recent decades. There is one additional topic that is of equal importance in understanding changes in this literature, but one that is qualitatively different from the others. It differs because (a) it is not concerned with one particular aspect of group perception and (b) it permeates, to some degree, all aspects of group perception. It is the focus on automatic or implicit processes and their role in intergroup perception.

Prior to the mid-1980s the question of automaticity in information processing and judgement simply had not been directly raised and confronted. Early stereotype research was primarily focused on measuring stereotypes, using tasks (e.g., questionnaires) that explicitly and directly engaged the respondent's conscious, deliberative thoughts about various target groups. Those thoughts were also highly susceptible to social desirability biases, and researchers were well aware of the need to address these concerns (see Brigham, 1971).

The possibility that stereotypes are automatically activated when perceivers are confronted with outgroup stimuli was first raised in a now classic article by Devine (1989). Devine argued that people have two cognitive structures related to stereotyping; one representing the cultural (widely held and shared) stereotype of the target group and the other being the individual's personal beliefs about the group. The degree of correspondence between the two structures was said to vary according to the prejudice level of the individual (Devine, 1989). Devine argued that, because people have shared a common history within a society, the cultural stereotype is well known to everyone in that society and has been frequently activated during one's life in that society. As a consequence, that culturally held stereotype is automatically activated in all persons (regardless of prejudice level), but may be overridden by deliberate use of the personal belief system. Thus, activation of one cognitive component is automatic, whereas use of the other requires intention and controlled processes.

Although specific aspects of Devine's conceptual argument have been challenged by other researchers (e.g., Fazio, Jackson, Dunton, & Williams, 1995; Lepore & Brown, 1997), the importance of automaticity in stereotyping and intergroup perception has been repeatedly documented in varied ways and contexts. This blossoming literature has changed the research landscape in at least two ways. First, the use of implicit tasks and measures (e.g., priming techniques; the Implicit Association Test, IAT) for studying information processing outside of conscious awareness and not under intentional control has (at least in part) addressed the need to circumvent social desirability and self-presentational biases that plagued research in this area in earlier eras. Second, and perhaps even more important, this research has revealed the ease with which stereotypes can be automatically activated and the extent to which unconscious processing, driven in part by pre-existing stereotypes, permeates numerous aspects of intergroup perception (Hassim, Uleman, & Bargh, 2005).

Understanding changes in group perceptions

In this second part of the chapter we explore the impact of changes in how we conceptualise group perception for our understanding of *change* in such perceptions. We begin by reviewing research on the "contact hypothesis", which has focused on intergroup attitudes, and found a weaker impact of contact on stereotypes than on attitudes. We then explore the importance of perceptions of group variability and entitativity, and how these can be used as either outcome measures or moderator variables. Finally, we review the limited evidence for contact-induced changes in implicit aspects of group perception, and ask what this evidence means.

Intergroup contact

It is just over 50 years since Allport (1954) proposed his famous "contact hypothesis", the idea that prejudice could be reduced by bringing together members of different groups to meet on an equal status footing, to pursue common goals through cooperative interaction, in such a way as to allow the development of close relationships with members of the outgroup, and with the support of institutional authorities. The assessment of this hypothesis has undergone a remarkable transformation (cf. Dovidio, Glick, & Rudman, 2005).

When Amir (1969) published his authoritative review of the area, there was an air of pessimism about the efficacy of contact as a social intervention to improve intergroup relations. Scholars expressed concerns about inconsistent results, the failure to generalise, difficulties of fulfilling an increasingly long list of apparently necessary conditions, and the seeming lack of real-world impact of intergroup contact (see Forbes, 1997; Hewstone & Brown, 1986; Stephan, 1987). Yet today there is little doubt that the core propositions of the contact hypothesis have received substantial empirical support. Greatest credit for this reversal is due to Pettigrew and Tropp (in press). Their meta-analysis of over 500 separate contact studies, conducted in a wide range of contexts and involving over 250,000 participants of various nationalities, delievers an unequivocal empirical assessment. Across all these studies, contact per se had beneficial effects in reducing prejudice: the overall relationship between contact and prejudice was significant, though modest in size (Pearson's r of just above $-.20$). However, this effect was substantially stronger ($r = -.287$) in those contexts that Allport identified as "optimal" conditions for intergroup contact to have beneficial effects.

A crucial development in our understanding of processes involved in intergroup contact is the focus on moderating and mediating processes (Baron & Kenny, 1986; Brown & Hewstone, 2005; Kenworthy, Turner, Hewstone, & Voci, 2005). Moderator variables address "when" questions (e.g., *when* does contact between members of different groups lead to an improvement in outgroup attitudes?), whereas mediator variables address "how" or "why" questions (e.g., *how* or *why* does contact improve attitudes?). Both moderation and mediation effects involve more than two variables; that is, they both deal with what happens when a third variable comes into play. But they do so in very different ways. Moderation implies that the *level* of the third variable can change the relationship between the other two variables, whereas mediation implies that the relationship between the two variables can actually be created by the third variable.

Hewstone and Brown (1986; see modification by Hewstone, 1996; Vivian, Hewstone, & Brown, 1997) sought to identify the conditions that would allow the generalisation of attitudes and behaviour change beyond the specific context in which the contact occurs. They hypothesised that group salience—broadly speaking, the extent to which group memberships are psychologically "present" during contact—would play a key role in encouraging such generalisation, essentially suggesting that salience *moderates* the effects of contact on prejudice reduction. Recently Brown and Hewstone (2005) reported extensive support for this moderational hypothesis.

With regard to mediating processes, more recent research has sought to identify the underlying processes by which contact improves intergroup attitudes. Although Allport (1954) extensively discussed the conditions under which intergroup contact would prove beneficial (the "when" question), he devoted less attention to "how" or "why" contact works effectively. His original formulation focused on contact working by improving *knowledge* about the outgroup. However, enthusiasm for this variable has dwindled in the light of its rather meagre effects (see Pettigrew & Tropp, in press; Stephan & Stephan, 1984).

A key change in this literature during the last 20 years has been the acknowledgement that intergroup contact cannot be considered only in terms of its cognitive processes (Pettigrew, 1998), but also requires recognition of the role of affective processes (Fiske, Cuddy, Glick, & Xu, 2002; Mackie, Devos, & Smith, 2000). Consistent with this view, Brown and Hewstone (2005) reported extensive evidence for mediation of contact effects on attitudes by affective factors. These include reducing negative intergroup affect such as intergroup anxiety (e.g., Islam & Hewstone, 1993; Paolini, Hewstone, Cairns, & Voci, 2004; Voci & Hewstone, 2003) and realistic and symbolic threats (Tausch, Hewstone, Kenworthy, Cairns, & Christ, in press), as well as promoting positive emotions (such as empathy, perspective taking, and accompanying reciprocal self-disclosure; see Harwood, Hewstone, Paolini, & Voci, 2005; Tam, Hewstone, Harwood, Voci, & Kenworthy, in press).

Notwithstanding these achievements of theory and research on intergroup contact, one remaining source of frustration is that contact is much less effective for changing stereotypes than for changing intergroup attitudes. In addressing this question, three lines of enquiry may be potentially fruitful: types of contact situations, affective processes in stereotype change, and whether moderation is necessary for stereotype change.

First, Rothbart and John's (1985) perceptive analysis of stereotype change noted that characteristics of the contact situation are correlated with the observation of particular types of behaviours (e.g., one is more likely to observe extraverted behaviours in informal than formal settings). Thus future research should study whether stereotype change may be relatively more constrained than attitude change by the restricted range and nature of settings in which intergroup contact actually occurs.

Second, research on stereotype change (see Hewstone, 1996) has been almost exclusively cognitive, and has neglected affective processes. If affect is stored with schemas, then contact might need to target these "affective tags" (Fiske, 1982) and not simply cognitive, information-based components of stereotypes. Moreover, the relative weight of the affective component of people's reactions to groups may vary not only across individuals (Stangor, Sullivan, & Ford, 1991), but across intergroup contexts (Haddock, Zanna, & Esses, 1993). Thus future research should undertake a more systematic analysis of individual differences in affect and stereotyping across a range of settings (Paolini, Hewstone, Voci, Harwood, & Cairns, in press).

Third, Wolsko et al. (2000) have argued that stereotypes, especially, are moderated by group salience. If this is the case, then perhaps meta-analytic results will be different once there are sufficient studies of the effect of contact on stereotypes which have also measured category salience during contact.

Changes in perceived group variability and entitativity: Outcome and/or moderator?

If there are relatively few studies of intergroup contact using stereotypes as an outcome measure, there are even fewer using measures of perceived outgroup variability (most studies have measured only the central-tendency component of stereotypes, and not dispersion). However, the available studies have shown that contact is associated with greater perceived outgroup variability. Thus Islam and Hewstone (1993) found that positive intergroup contact between Hindus and Muslims in Bangladesh not only improved outgroup attitudes, but also was associated with a more complex and differentiated view of the outgroup; moreover, this relationship was mediated by decreased intergroup anxiety.

Paolini et al. (2004) reported similar results from two surveys of Catholics and Protestants in Northern Ireland. Both studies showed that having cross-group friends, whether these were direct friends or indirect friends (i.e., having a friend in the ingroup who had an outgroup friend; see Wright, Aron, McLaughlin-Volpe, & Ropp, 1997), was associated with reduced prejudice towards the religious outgroup and increased perceived outgroup variability; both effects were mediated, in part at least, by intergroup anxiety.

Finally, Stangor, Jonas, Stroebe, and Hewstone (1996) studied contact longitudinally in a group of American students before and after they had spent a year studying in Europe (either in Tuebingen, Germany or Bristol, England). Interestingly, they found that attitudes and central-tendency measures of stereotypes shared at least one predictor, as did both central tendency and perceived variability measures of stereotypes; but there was no overlap in the predictors of attitudes and variability.

Most of the available studies also show poorer explained variance in outcome measures for perceived variability than for attitudes (e.g., Paolini et al., 2004; Voci & Hewstone, 2003). This may reflect difficulties experienced by some respondents when completing variability measures (e.g., marking the range; see Judd & Park, 1988), as well as shared method variance between rating-scale measures of contact and attitudes, but not contact and perceived variability.

A further complexity surrounding measures of perceived variability is whether they should be conceived, and used, as outcome measures, or as moderating variables. We noted above that conditions that promote the perception of homogeneity in groups would make it easier to generalise about all group members; that is, to stereotype them. Somewhat paradoxically, this should mean that some degree of perceived homogeneity of the outgroup would also facilitate generalisation of *positive* change brought about by contact. This prediction has been borne out by both experimental and correlational-survey research.

In experimental research on stereotype change, a laboratory analogue of some of the processes involved in intergroup contact, the typical finding is that the same amount of disconfirming information has more impact when it is "dispersed" across several group members (each of whom is seen as typical of the group) than when it is "concentrated" in one or two group members (who are seen as atypical; see Hewstone, 1994, for a review). The impact of the dispersed vs concentrated pattern of disconfirming information is, however, moderated by the perceived variability of the target group (Hewstone & Hamberger, 2000). For a group presented as being low in variability (i.e., most members are alike), there was more stereotyping under concentrated than dispersed information. But when the group was presented as being high in variability (i.e., group members are different from one another), then there was no difference in the impact of the two patterns of disconfirming information. Relatedly, recent survey research on intergroup trust among Catholics and Protestants in Northern Ireland (Hewstone et al., 2006) found that positive outgroup contact was more strongly associated with some types of trust towards the outgroup for respondents who viewed the outgroup as "high" versus "low" on homogeneity.

Overall, these findings confirm the view that measures of perceived variability complement more general measures of group perception. They can be used as outcome measures, and revealing that the outgroup is viewed in a more differentiated way can be an important effect of social interventions such as intergroup contact—indeed, it targets the outgroup homogeneity effect we mentioned earlier. But measures of perceived variability can also function as moderators, having similar effects on the contact–outcome relationship to measures of group salience; but the exact effect depends on the precise nature of the outcome measure.

As far as we are aware, there has been no published research relating measures of intergroup contact and measures of entitativity. If we define perceived outgroup entitativity as the degree to which participants view the outgroup as being a cohesive social unit, whose members perceive group membership to be important, and who are similar in terms of their goals and outcomes (see Brewer & Harasty, 1996), this view appears to be less derogatory (indeed not necessarily derogatory at all) than the view that they are homogeneous ("they are all alike"). It is not therefore apparent that entitativity should be treated as an outcome measure. It may, however, function as a moderator, in just the same way as perceived variabiliy. Hewstone et al. (2006) explored this idea in a recent survey of Catholics and Protestants in Northern Ireland. They tested the relationship between quality of contact and different types of outgroup trust. Quality of contact was associated with outgroup trust, and the effect was stronger for those respondents who perceived the outgroup to have high versus low perceived entitativity.

Can contact bring about changes in implicit measures of group perception?

Although there has been a remarkable burgeoning of research using implicit measures of intergroup bias (see Hewstone, Rubin, & Willis, 2002), these have only just begun to have an impact on research on intergroup contact (Pettigrew & Tropp's, in press, meta-analysis retrieved no such studies). However, a small of number of recent studies have begun to collect such data.

A series of studies (Aberson & Haag, in press; Tam et al., in press; Turner, Hewstone & Voci, 2004), using different target groups, investigated the association between measures of contact, mediators, and implicit bias, assessed by the Implicit Association Test (IAT; Greenwald, McGhee, & Schwartz, 1998). They found that various measures of "contact" (including opportunity for contact, cross-group friends, and measures of quantity and quality of contact) are associated with implicit bias. Moreover, these studies found that the effect of contact on implicit bias, in contrast to its effect on explicit measures of group perception, is a direct effect, unmediated by a range of measured potential mediators.

Implicit measures of intergroup bias, because they do not require participants to report their attitudes directly, are less likely to be influenced by social desirability than are explicit measures. Implicit measures are also important because they may better predict spontaneous behaviour than do explicit measures (Dovidio, Kawakami, Johnson, Johnson, & Howard, 1997). It is interesting to note that the effects detected thus far were direct, unmediated effects. In other words, it seems as though respondents who were more familiar with outgroup members held more positive (or less negative) implicit associations with them. Thus Karpinski and Hilton (2001) have argued that the IAT is a measure of environmental associations, rather than bias per se.

Implicit measures of bias are evaluations and beliefs that are automatically activated by the mere presence of the attitude object; because they tap unintentional bias, of which well-intentioned and would-be unprejudiced people are largely unaware, they should constitute important and useful outcomes measures for research on contact. We hope that they will receive more research attention in the future.

Conclusions: Retrospect and prospect

In this chapter we have reviewed developments and changes in how social psychology has conceived and implemented the study of group perception over the last 35 years. We have noted the change from a narrow focus on the stereotypic associations for various groups to a more multifaceted analysis of how groups are perceived. We have pointed to two key theoretical developments in this era: the nascence of social identity theory, with its emphasis on the categorisation process in intergroup perception, and the maturity of the social cognition approach, with its emphasis on stereotypes as cognitive structures that guide information processing. These two theoretical develop-ments have ushered in a transformation in this literature, from the study of stereotypes to the study of stereotyping, and from a focus on content to a concern with structure and process. In particular, we have highlighted the new understanding of these phenomena gleaned by the more modern concepts of perceived group variability, perceived entitativity, and implicit measures of group perception.

In the second part of the chapter we reported on how these conceptual changes (allied to parallel increases in methodological sophistication) have increased our understanding of the implications of intergroup contact for changing stereotypic beliefs and prejudicial attitudes. Specifically, we demon-strated how the field has moved on from questions of whether and when intergroup contact can effect changes in group perception (focused on atti-tudes), to the pursuit of how and why it can do so, as well as when it is most successful in instigating generalised change in group perceptions and evaluations.

We believe that the progress has been impressive. There have been huge strides in our understanding of underlying processes, and contemporary models of group perception and intergroup contact are infinitely more sophis-ticated than those of yesteryear. Thus the last 35 years have deepened our understanding of the phenomena of group perception and intergroup con-tact, and marshalled the conceptual and empirical tools of social psychology to mount a concerted attack on the pernicious social problems posed by stereotyping and prejudice.

Note

Preparation of this chapter was supported in part by NIMH Grant MH-40058 to the first author, and grants from the Russell Sage Foundation and the Community Relations Unit (Northern Ireland) to the second author.

References

Aberson, C. L., & Haag, S. C. (in press). Contact, perspective taking, and anxiety as predictors of stereotype endorsement, explicit attitudes, and implicit attitudes. *Group Processes and Intergroup Relations*.

Adorno, T. W., Frenkel-Brunswik, E., Levinson, D. J., & Sanford, R. N. (1950). *The authoritarian personality*. New York: Harper & Row.

Allport, G. W. (1954). *The nature of prejudice*. Garden City, NY: Doubleday/Anchor.

Amir, Y. (1969). Contact hypothesis in ethnic relations. *Psychological Bulletin, 71*, 319–342.

Baron, R. M., & Kenny, D. A. (1986). The moderator–mediator distinction in social psychological research: Conceptual, strategic, and statistical considerations. *Journal of Personality and Social Psychology, 51*, 1173–1182.

Berkowitz, L. (1972). Frustrations, comparisons, and other sources of emotional arousal as contributors to social unrest. *Journal of Social Issues, 28*, 77–91.

Billig, M. (1976). *Social psychology and intergroup relations*. London: Academic Press.

Bodenhausen, G. V. (1988). Stereotypic biases in social decision making and memory: Testing process models of stereotype use. *Journal of Personality and Social Psychology, 55*, 726–737.

Brewer, M. B. (1979). In-group bias in the minimal intergroup situation: A cognitive-motivational analysis. *Psychological Bulletin, 86*, 307–324.

Brewer, M. B. (1991). The social self: On being the same and different at the same time. *Personality and Social Psychology Bulletin, 17*, 475–482.

Brewer, M. B., & Harasty, A. S. (1996). Seeing groups as entities: The role of perceiver motivation. In R. Sorrentino & E. T. Higgins (Eds.), *Handbook of motivation and cognition* (Vol. 3, pp. 347–370). New York: Guilford Press.

Brigham, J. C. (1971). Ethnic stereotypes. *Psychological Bulletin, 76*, 15–33.

Brown, R., & Hewstone, M. (2005). An integrative theory of intergroup contact. In M. Zanna (Ed.), *Advances in experimental social psychology* (Vol. 37, pp. 255–343). San Diego, CA: Academic Press.

Campbell, D. T. (1958). Common fate, similarity and other indices of the status of aggregate persons as social entities. *Behavioral Science, 3*, 14–25.

Campbell, D. T. (1965). Ethnocentrism and other altruistic motives. In D. Levine (Ed.), *Nebraska symposium on motivation* (Vol. 13, pp. 283–311). Lincoln, NE: University of Nebraska Press.

Crawford, M. T., Sherman, S. J., & Hamilton, D. L. (2002). Perceived entitativity, stereotype formation, and the interchangeability of group members. *Journal of Personality and Social Psychology, 83*, 1076–1094.

Darley, J. M., & Gross, P. H. (1983). A hypothesis-confirming bias in labeling effects. *Journal of Personality and Social Psychology, 44*, 20–33.

Devine, P. G. (1989). Stereotypes and prejudice: Their automatic and controlled components. *Journal of Personality and Social Psychology, 56*, 5–18.

Devos, T., Comby, L., & Deschamps, J. (1996). Asymmetries in judgements of ingroup and outgroup variability. In W. Stroebe & M. Hewstone (Eds.), *European review of social psychology* (Vol. 7, pp. 95–144). Chichester, UK: Wiley.

Diehl, M. (1990). The minimal group paradigm: Theoretical explanation and empirical findings. In W. Stroebe & M. Hewstone (Eds.), *European review of social psychology* (Vol. 1, pp. 263–392). Chichester, UK: Wiley.

Doise, W. (1978). *Groups and individuals: Explanations in social psychology*. Cambridge, UK: Cambridge University Press.

Doosje, B., Spears, R., Ellemers, N., & Koomen, W. (1999). Perceived group variability in intergroup relations: The distinctive role of social identity. In W. Stroebe & M. Hewstone (Eds.), *European review of social psychology* (Vol. 10, pp. 41–73). Chichester, UK: Wiley.

Dovidio, J., Glick, P., & Rudman, L. (Eds.). (2005). *On the nature of prejudice: Fifty years after Allport*. Malden, MA & Oxford, UK: Blackwell.

Dovidio, J., Kawakami, K., Johnson, C., Johnson, B., & Howard, A. (1997). The nature of prejudice: Automatic and controlled processes. *Journal of Experimental Social Psychology, 33*, 510–540.

Eiser, J. R., & Stroebe, W. (1972). *Categorization and social judgment*. London: Academic Press.

Fazio, R. H., Jackson, J. R., Dunton, B. C., & Williams, C. J. (1995). Variability in automatic activation as an unobtrusive measure of racial attitudes: A bona fide pipeline. *Journal of Personality and Social Psychology, 69*, 1013–1027.

Fiske, S. T. (1982). Schema-triggered affect: Applications to social perception. In M. S. Clark & S. T. Fiske (Eds.), *Affect and cognition: The 17th Annual Carnegie Symposium* (pp. 55–77). Hillsdale, NJ: Lawrence Erlbaum Associates Inc.

Fiske, S. T. (1998). Stereotyping, prejudice, and discrimination. In D. T. Gilbert, S. T. Fiske, & G. Lindzey (Eds.), *The handbook of social psychology* (4th ed., Vol. 2, pp. 357–411). Boston, MA: McGraw-Hill.

Fiske, S. T. (2005). Social cognition and the normality of prejudgment. In J. F. Dovidio, P. Glick, & L. A. Rudman (Eds.), *On the nature of prejudice: Fifty years after Allport* (pp. 36–53). Malden, MA & Oxford, UK: Blackwell.

Fiske, S. T., Cuddy, A. J., Glick, P., & Xu, J. (2002). A model of (often mixed) stereotype content: Competence and warmth respectively follow from perceived status and competition. *Journal of Personality and Social Psychology, 82*, 878–902.

Forbes, H. D. (1997). *Ethnic conflict: Commerce, culture, and the contact hypothesis.* New Haven, CT: Yale University Press.

Greenwald, A. G., McGhee, D. E., & Schwartz, J. L. K. (1998). Measuring individual differences in implicit cognition: The Implicit Association Test. *Journal of Personality and Social Psychology, 74*, 1464–1480.

Haddock, G., Zanna, M. P., & Esses, V. M. (1993). Assessing the structure of predicial attitudes: The case of attitudes toward homosexuals. *Journal of Personality and Social Psychology, 65*, 1105–1118.

Hamilton, D. L. (Ed.). (1981). *Cognitive processes in stereotyping and intergroup behavior.* Hillsdale, NJ: Lawrence Erlbaum Associates Inc.

Hamilton, D. L., & Gifford, R. K. (1976). Illusory correlation in interpersonal perception: A cognitive basis of stereotypic judgments. *Journal of Experimental Social Psychology, 12*, 392–407.

Hamilton, D. L., & Rose, T. (1980). Illusory correlation and the maintenance of stereotypic beliefs. *Journal of Personality and Social Psychology, 39*, 832–845.

Hamilton, D. L., Sherman, S. J., & Castelli, L. (2002). A group by any other name— The role of entitativity in group perception. In W. Stroebe & M. Hewstone (Eds.), *European review of social psychology* (Vol. 12, pp. 139–166). Chichester, UK: Wiley.

Hamilton, D. L., Sherman, S. J., & Rodgers, J. (2004). Perceiving the groupness of groups: Entitativity, homogeneity, essentialism, and stereotypes. In V. Yzerbyt, C. M. Judd, & O. Corneille (Eds.), *The psychology of group perception: Perceived variability, entitativity and essentialism* (pp. 39–60). Philadelphia, PA: Psychology Press.

Hamilton, D. L., Stroessner, S. J., & Driscoll, D. M. (1994). Social cognition and the study of stereotyping. In P. G. Devine, D. L. Hamilton, & T. M. Ostrom (Eds.), *Social cognition: Impact on social psychology* (pp. 291–321). San Diego, CA: Academic Press.

Harwood, J., Hewstone, M., Paolini, S., & Voci, A. (2005). Grandparent–grandchild contact and attitudes towards older adults: Moderator and mediator effects. *Personality and Social Psychology Bulletin, 31*, 393–406.

Hassim, R., Uleman, J. S., & Bargh, J. A. (Eds.) (2005). *The new unconscious.* New York: Oxford University Press.

Hewstone, M. (1994). Revision and change of stereotypic beliefs: In search of the elusive subtyping model. In W. Stroebe & M. Hewstone (Eds.), *European review of social psychology* (Vol. 5, pp. 69–109). Chichester, UK, Wiley.

Hewstone, M. (1996). Contact and categorization: Social psychological interventions to change intergroup relations. In N. Macrae, C. Stangor, & M. Hewstone (Eds.), *Stereotypes and stereotyping* (pp. 323–368). New York: Guilford Press.

Hewstone, M., & Brown, R. (1986). Contact is not enough: An intergroup perspective on the "Contact Hypothesis". In M. Hewstone & R. Brown (Eds.), *Contact and conflict in intergroup encounters* (pp. 1–44). Oxford, UK: Blackwell.

Hewstone, M., Cairns, E., Kenworthy, J., Hughes, J., Tausch, N., Voci, A. et al. (2006). Stepping stones to reconciliation in Northern Ireland: Intergroup contact, forgiveness and trust. In A. Nadler, T. E. Malloy, & J. D. Fisher (Eds.), *The social psychology of intergroup reconciliation*. New York: Oxford University Press.

Hewstone, M., & Hamberger, J. (2000). Perceived variability and stereotype change. *Journal of Experimental Social Psychology, 36*, 103–124.

Hewstone, M., Rubin, M., & Willis, H. (2002). Intergroup bias. *Annual Review of Psychology, 53*, 575–604.

Hogg, M. A. (2000). Subjective uncertainty reduction through self-categorization: A motivational theory of social identity processes and group phenomena. In W. Stroebe, & M. Hewstone (Eds.), *European review of social psychology* (Vol. 11, pp. 223–55). Chichester, UK: Wiley.

Islam, M. R., & Hewstone, M. (1993). Dimensions of contact as predictors of intergroup anxiety, perceived out-group variability, and out-group attitude: An integrative model. *Personality and Social Psychology Bulletin, 19*, 700–710.

Johnson, A. L., Crawford, M. T., Sherman, S. J., Rutchick, A. M., Hamilton, D. L., Ferreira, M. et al. (in press). A functional perspective on group memberships: Differential need fulfillment in a group typology. *Journal of Experimental Social Psychology*.

Judd, C. M., & Park, B. (1988). Out-group homogeneity: Judgments of variability at the individual and group levels. *Journal of Personality and Social Psychology, 54*, 778–788.

Karpinski, A., & Hilton, J. L. (2001). Attitudes and the Implicit Association Test. *Journal of Personality and Social Psychology, 81*, 774–788.

Katz, D., & Braly, K. (1933). Racial stereotypes in one hundred college students. *Journal of Abnormal and Social Psychology, 28*, 280–290.

Kenworthy, J., Turner, R., Hewstone, M., & Voci, A. (2005). Intergroup contact: When does it work, and why? In J. Dovidio, P. Glick, & L. Rudman (Eds.), *On the nature of prejudice: Fifty years after Allport* (pp. 278–292). Malden, MA & Oxford, UK: Blackwell.

Lepore, L., & Brown, R. (1997). Category and stereotype activation: Is prejudice inevitable? *Journal of Personality and Social Psychology, 72*, 275–287.

Lickel, B., Hamilton, D. L., Wieczorkowska, G., Lewis, A., Sherman, S. J., & Uhles, A. N. (2000). Varieties of groups and the perception of group entitativity. *Journal of Personality and Social Psychology, 78*, 223–246.

Linville, P. W., & Fischer, G. W. (1993). Exemplar and abstraction models of perceived group variability and stereotypicality. *Social Cognition, 11*, 92–125.

Linville, P. W., Fischer, G. W., & Salovey, P. (1989). Perceived distributions of the characteristics of in-group and out-group members: Empirical evidence and a computer simulation. *Journal of Personality and Social Psychology, 57*, 165–188.

Mackie, D. M., Devos, T., & Smith, E. R. (2000). Intergroup emotions: Explaining offensive action tendencies in an intergroup context. *Journal of Personality and Social Psychology, 79*, 602–616.

McConnell, A. R., Sherman, S. J., & Hamilton, D. L. (1997). Target entitativity:

Implications for information processing about individual and group targets. *Journal of Personality and Social Psychology, 72*, 750–762.

McGarty, C. (1999). *Categorization in social psychology*. London: Sage.

Miller, N. E., & Bugelski, R. (1948). Minor studies in aggression: The influence of frustrations imposed by the ingroup on attitudes toward outgroups. *Journal of Psychology, 25*, 437–442.

Ostrom, T. M., & Sedikides, C. (1992). Out-group homogeneity effects in natural and minimal groups. *Psychological Bulletin, 112*, 536–552.

Paolini, S., Hewstone, M., Cairns, E., & Voci, A. (2004). Effects of direct and indirect cross-group friendships on judgments of Catholics and Protestants in Northern Ireland: The mediating role of an anxiety-reduction mechanism. *Personality and Social Psychology Bulletin, 30*, 770–786.

Paolini, S., Hewstone, M., Voci, A., Harwood, J., & Cairns, E. (in press). Intergroup contact and the promotion of intergroup harmony: The influence of intergroup emotions. In R. Brown & D. Capozza (Eds.), *Social identities: Motivational, emotional, cultural influences*. Hove, UK: Psychology Press.

Park, B., Judd, C. M., & Ryan, C. S. (1991). Social categorization and the representation of variability information. In W. Stroebe & M. Hewstone (Eds.), *European review of social psychology* (Vol. 2, pp. 211–245). Chichester, UK: Wiley.

Pettigrew, T. F. (1998). Intergroup contact theory. *Annual Review of Psychology, 49*, 65–85.

Pettigrew, T. F., & Tropp, L. R. (in press). A meta-analytic test and reformulation of intergroup contact theory. *Journal of Personality and Social Psychology*.

Pickett, C. L. (2001). The effects of entitativity beliefs on implicit comparisons among group members. *Personality and Social Psychology Bulletin, 27*, 515–525.

Rothbart, M., & John, O. P. (1985). Social categorization and behavioural episodes: A cognitive analysis of the effects of intergroup contact. *Journal of Social Issues, 41*, 81–104.

Rothbart, M., & Lewis, S. (1994). Cognitive processes and intergroup relations: A historical perspective. In P. G. Devine, D. L. Hamilton, & T. M. Ostrom (Eds.), *Social cognition: Impact on social psychology* (pp. 347–378). San Diego, CA: Academic Press.

Rydell, R. J., & McConnell, A. R. (2005). Perceptions of entitativity and attitude change. *Personality and Social Psychology Bulletin, 31*, 99–110.

Sagar, H. A., & Schofield, J. W. (1980). Racial and behavioral cues in black and white children's perceptions of ambiguously aggressive acts. *Journal of Personality and Social Psychology, 39*, 590–598.

Sherif, M. (1966). *Group conflict and cooperation*. London: Routledge & Kegan Paul.

Sherman, S. J., Castelli, L., & Hamilton, D. L. (2002). The spontaneous use of a group typology as an organizing principle in memory. *Journal of Personality and Social Psychology, 82*, 328–342.

Sherman, S. J., Hamilton, D. L., & Lewis, A. C. (1999). Perceived entitativity and the social identity value of group memberships. In D. Abrams & M. A. Hogg (Eds.), *Social identity and social cognition* (pp. 80–110). Oxford, UK: Blackwell.

Simon, B. (1992). The perception of ingroup and outgroup homogeneity: Reintroducing the social context. In W. Stroebe & M. Hewstone (Eds.), *European review of social psychology* (Vol. 3, pp. 1–30). Chichester, UK: Wiley.

Snyder, M., Tanke, E. D., & Berscheid, E. (1977). Social perception and interpersonal behavior: On the self-fulfilling nature of social stereotypes. *Journal of Personality and Social Psychology, 35*, 656–666.

Stangor, C., Jonas, K., Stroebe, W., & Hewstone, M. (1996). Influence of student exchange on national stereotypes, attitudes and perceived variability. *European Journal of Social Psychology, 26*, 663–657.

Stangor, C., Sullivan, L. A., & Ford, T. E. (1991). Affective and cognitive determinants of prejudice. *Social Cognition, 9*, 359–380.

Stephan, W. G. (1987). The contact hypothesis in intergroup relations. In C. Hendrick (Ed.), *Group processes and intergroup relations: Review of personality and social psychology* (Vol. 9, pp. 13–40). Newbury Park, CA: Sage.

Stephan, W. G., & Stephan, C. W. (1984). The role of ignorance in intergroup relations. In N. Miller & M. B. Brewer (Eds.), *Groups in contact: The psychology of desegregation* (pp. 229–255). Orlando, FL: Academic Press.

Stroebe, W., & Insko, C. A. (1989). Stereotype, prejudice, and discrimination: Changing conceptions in theory and research. In D. Bar-Tal, C. F. Graumann, A. W. Kruglanski, & W. Stroebe (Eds.), *Stereotyping and prejudice: Changing conceptions* (pp. 3–34). New York: Springer-Verlag.

Susskind, J., Maurer, K., Thakkar, V., Hamilton, D. L., & Sherman, J. W. (1999). Perceiving individuals and groups: Expectancies, dispositional inferences, and causal attributions. *Journal of Personality and Social Psychology, 76*, 181–191.

Tajfel, H. (1969). Cognitive aspects of prejudice. *Journal of Social Issues, 25*, 79–97.

Tajfel, H. (1970). Experiments in intergroup discrimination. *Scientific American, 223*, 96–102.

Tajfel, H. (1978). Interindividual behaviour and intergroup behaviour. In H. Tajfel (Ed.), *Differentiation between social groups: Studies in the social psychology of intergroup relations* (pp. 27–60). London: Academic Press.

Tajfel, H., & Wilkes, A. L. (1963). Classification and quantitative judgment. *British Journal of Psychology, 54*, 101–114.

Tam, T., Hewstone, M., Harwood, J., Voci, A., & Kenworthy, J. (in press). Intergroup contact and grandparent–grandchild communication: The effects of self-disclosure on implicit and explicit biases against older people. *Group Processes and Intergroup Relations*.

Tausch, N., Hewstone, M., Kenworthy, J., Cairns, E., & Christ, O. (in press). Cross-community contact, perceived status differences and intergroup attitudes in Northern Ireland: The mediating roles of individual-level vs. group-level threats and the moderating role of social identification. *Political Psychology*.

Taylor, S. E., Fiske, S. T., Etcoff, N. L., & Ruderman, A. J. (1978). Categorical and contextual bases of person memory and stereotyping. *Journal of Personality and Social Psychology, 36*, 778–793.

Turner, J. C. (1981). The experimental social psychology of intergroup behavior. In J. C. Turner & H. Giles (Eds.), *Intergroup behaviour* (pp. 1–32). Oxford, UK: Basil Blackwell.

Turner, J. C., Hogg, M. A., Oakes, P. J., Reicher, S. D., & Wetherell, M. S. (1987). *Rediscovering the social group: A self-categorization theory*. Oxford, UK: Blackwell.

Turner, J. C., & Reynolds, K. J. (2001). The social identity perspective in intergroup relations: Theories, themes, and controversies. In R. Brown & S. L. Gaertner (Eds.), *Blackwell handbook of social psychology: Intergroup processes* (pp. 133–52). Oxford, UK: Blackwell.

Turner, R. N., Hewstone, M., & Voci, A. (2004). *The impact of cross-group friendship on explicit and implicit prejudice in children.* Manuscript submitted for publication.

Vivian, J. E., Hewstone, M., & Brown, R. J. (1997). Intergroup contact: Theoretical and empirical developments. In R. Ben-Ari & Y. Rich (Eds.), *Enhancing education in heterogeneous schools* (pp. 13–46). Tel Aviv: University Press.

Voci, A., & Hewstone, M. (2003). Intergroup contact and prejudice towards immigrants in Italy: The mediational role of anxiety and the moderational role of group salience. *Group Processes and Intergroup Relations, 6,* 37–54.

Wolsko, C., Park, B., Judd, C., & Wittenbrink, B. (2000). Framing interethnic ideology: Effects of multicultural and color-blind perspectives on judgments of groups and individuals. *Journal of Personality and Social Psychology, 78,* 635–654.

Word, C. O., Zanna, M. P., & Cooper, J. (1974). The nonverbal mediation of self-fulfilling prophecies in interracial interaction. *Journal of Experimental Social Psychology, 10,* 109–120.

Wright, S. C., Aron, A., McLaughlin-Volpe, T., & Ropp, S. A. (1997). The extended contact effect: Knowledge of cross-group friendships and prejudice. *Journal of Personality and Social Psychology, 73,* 73–90.

Yzerbyt, V. Y., Judd, C. M., & Corneille, O. (Eds.) (2004). *The psychology of group perception: Perceived variability, entitativity, and essentialism.* London: Psychology Press.

Yzerbyt, V. Y., Corneille, O., & Estrada, C. (2001). The interplay of naive theories and entitativity from the outsider and the insider perspectives. *Personality and Social Psychology Review, 5,* 141–155.

7 The epistemic bases of interpersonal communication

Arie W. Kruglanski
University of Maryland, USA

Gün Semin
*Free University Amsterdam,
The Netherlands*

The essential function of communication is the exchange of some kind of knowledge. This chapter reviews evidence that the process of such convey- ance is significantly affected by a communicator's epistemic motivations. Specifically, such motivations may determine (1) the perspective communica- tors may adopt in addressing a recipient, and (2) the level of linguistic abstraction at which they will couch their messages.

To discuss these phenomena we first introduce the concept of epistemic motivations, and then review the specific theory and evidence that link such motivations to various communicative effects.

Epistemic motivations and their antecedents

Individuals' knowledge-formation activities are to a large extent propelled by their epistemic motivations; that is, by the (implicit or explicit) goals one possesses with respect to knowledge. It is possible to distinguish (Kruglanski, 1989, 2004) between four types of such motivations classifiable on two orthogonal dimensions; the first, closure seeking versus avoidance and the second, specificity versus nonspecificity. The first distinction asks whether the individual's goal is to *approach* or *avoid closure*. The second distinction asks whether the closure one is seeking or avoiding is of a *specific* or *nonspecific kind*, namely whether any closure or absence of closure would do.

The four motivational types yielded by the foregoing classification can be thought of as quadrants defined by two conceptual continua. One con- tinuum relates to the motivation towards nonspecific closure and ranges from a strong desire to possess or approach it (i.e., a strong need *for* nonspecific closure) to a strong desire to avoid it (i.e., a strong need *to avoid* nonspecific closure). The second continuum relates to the motivation towards a given or specific closure and it too ranges from a strong desire to possess it (i.e., a strong need *for* this specific closure), to a strong desire to avoid it (i.e., a strong need *to avoid* this specific closure). In what follows we briefly characterise these four motivational types in turn.

The need for nonspecific closure may be defined as the individual's desire for a firm answer to a question, any firm answer as compared to confusion and/or ambiguity. The need to avoid nonspecific closure pertains to situations where definite knowledge is eschewed and *judgemental noncommitment* is valued and desired. A need for a specific closure represents a preference for a particular answer to a question that may be flattering, reassuring, or otherwise desirable. Finally, the need to avoid a specific closure may represent the tendency away from a specific unpleasant answer to one's question. We assume that the needs for nonspecific or specific closure are elevated by the perceived benefits of possessing such closures and/or the costs of lacking them (Kruglanski, 2004; Kruglanski & Webster, 1996; Kruglanski, Pierro, Mannetti, & DeGrada, 2006; Webster & Kruglanski, 1998). Likewise, the needs to avoid nonspecific or specific closures are elevated by the perceived benefits of lacking and the costs of possessing such closures. Such a conceptualisation asserts the *functional equivalence* of a wide variety of possible cost and benefit factors assumed to impact the needs for nonspecific and specific closure, and in so doing makes strong assumptions about a common dynamic that numerous, and in some ways quite different, states, characterised by different types of costs and benefits, may share.

Consequences of epistemic motivations: "Seizing" and "freezing" processes

Given that an individual's need for closure has been heightened, two fundamental consequences may ensue. First, the person may experience a sense of urgency about reaching closure. Second, once an initial closure has been formulated the individual may adhere to it come what may and treat it as relatively permanent. The sense of urgency may prompt the tendency to "seize" quickly on any notion that promises closure. The craving for permanence may induce the tendency to "freeze" upon an extant closure, but also to prefer a potentially lasting closure over a transient, context-specific closure. Space considerations prevent us from a more extensive exposition of need for closure theory (for more extensive treatments the reader is referred to Kruglanski, 2004, and Kruglanski et al., 2006). In what follows we focus on our common interest in the processes of interpersonal communication and their interface with epistemic motivation.

Interpersonal communication and need for closure

A fundamental presumption of communication theory is that in conveying messages to others, speakers take the listeners' perspective into account, and refer their utterances to the social reality they both share. From this perspective, speakers tailor their messages according to their own and their listeners' shared beliefs and assumptions so that their communications reach the audience and are interpreted accurately.

A significant issue in this context is that different audiences may differ in the knowledge they share with the communicator. It is therefore necessary to pitch one's communications appropriately in order to take these differences into account. As Clark and Murphy (1982) noted, "in ordinary conversation we tailor what we say to the particular people we are talking to" (p. 287). They label this process as "audience design" and state that "an essential part of (such) design . . . is the use of the speaker's and addressee's mutual knowledge, beliefs, and suppositions, or common ground (p. 288). Indeed, the notion of *common ground* has been a mainstay of the communication literature, and even though its origins, development, and properties have been discussed in different ways (e.g., Danks, 1970; Fussell & Krauss, 1991; Horton & Keysar, 1996; Krauss & Fussell, 1991), its ubiquitous presence in interpersonal communication has been treated as a given.

The discussions of audience-design phenomena in the communication literature often have a functionalist flavour in deriving the existence of such effects from their role in making the communication process efficient. Yet not all communications are in fact efficient, and there may exist a corresponding variability in the success of imposing adequate "audience designs" on one's communications. After all, taking the perspective of another and determining what is and what is not part of a common ground may require fairly advanced reasoning skills, involved in appreciating the potential differences in perspective between oneself and one's interlocutor in given communicative circumstances.

An important task for communication theory is therefore to specify conditions under which extensive efforts at audience design will be undertaken and to characterise the cognitive activities they may involve. Krauss and Fussell (1991, p. 4) argued in this connection that assumptions about what others know may be thought of as tentative "hypotheses that participants continuously modify and reformulate on the basis of additional evidence", such as verbal and nonverbal feedback (see also Powell & O'Neal, 1976). The realisation that an important aspect of communication entails a hypothesis-testing process suggests that the discovery of a valid common ground may not be taken for granted. As with other hypothesis-testing endeavours, the search for common ground may vary in depth and directionality, and ultimately in the degree to which it yields an accurate perception.

Intriguing questions concerning the hypothesis-testing process in audience design concern (1) its point of departure, that is, the hypothesis about the other's perspective that first comes to mind, (2) its depth or extent, that is, the degree to which it deviates from the early hypotheses and adjusts them in light of additional processing of information. With regard to the first question, extant evidence indicates that the point of origin is often the communicator's own knowledge projected onto the listener (Fussell & Krauss, 1991; Horton & Keysar, 1996; Nickerson, Baddeley, & Freeman, 1987; Ross, Greene, & House, 1977). Indeed, Horton and Keysar (1996) found that while in the absence of time pressure speakers did incorporate common ground into their communications, common ground was not used when the speaker was under time pressure. They concluded that this finding supported their "monitoring and adjustment" model, whereby a speaker's initial hypothesis in formulating an utterance is based on his own knowledge and on information that is salient to him. Given sufficient time, however, the individual will modify or adjust that hypothesis to incorporate the common ground shared with the listener. Of course, the presence or absence of subjectively sufficient time—that is, time pressure—has constituted one of the major ways in which the need for (nonspecific) cognitive closure has been operationalised in past research (Kruglanski & Freund, 1983; Shah, Kruglanski, & Thompson, 1998). It is thus possible that a high level of this need may reduce the amount of effort communicators invest in their search for common ground. As a consequence, communications by high need for closure individuals may be excessively biased in the direction of the communicator's own perspective, which might reduce their comprehensibility to the listeners. Richter and Kruglanski (1997) recently investigated this hypothesis using the Fussel and Krauss (1989) two-stage referential task paradigm.

In that paradigm, participants are provided with a set of abstract figures and are asked to write descriptions of those figures so that they them-selves (the Nonsocial condition) or another person (the Social condition) could match the descriptions to the figures on a subsequent occasion. In our experiment, this task was performed by participants with high or low disposi-tional need for nonspecific closure (Webster & Kruglanski, 1994). In the study by Fussell and Krauss (1989) participants in the Social condition exhib-ited attempts at creating common ground with their audience. They provided lengthier, as well as more verbal, descriptions and used more literal (less figurative) language in their communications; that is, language less idiosyn-cratically comprehensible to themselves but not to others. We expected to replicate this result and to find in addition that high (vs low) need for closure individuals would produce shorter and more figurative messages, a difference expected to be particularly pronounced in the Social condition.

Participants, introductory psychology students at the University of Maryland, were scheduled to appear in the laboratory for two sessions, corresponding to two separate research phases. In the *description phase*, par-ticipants wrote descriptions of each of 30 figures after having received either *social* or *nonsocial* encoding instructions. In the *identification phase*, carried out 3 to 5 weeks later, participants attempted to match a series of 90 descrip-tions written by themselves and others to their respective 30 figures presented on a poster board.

The results confirmed our predictions. First, we replicated the findings of Fussell and Krauss (1989) that communications in the Social condition were significantly lengthier as well as more literal (or less figurative) than those in the Nonsocial condition. Of greater present interest, the need for closure variable produced the expected effects: Participants with high (vs low) need for closure used significantly fewer words in their descriptions, and they produced significantly more figurative (or less literal) descriptions. Furthermore, the predicted interaction between encoding condition (Social vs Nonsocial) and need for closure was significant for message length, though not for literalness. The average number of words used by participants with low need for closure was more than double in the Social versus the Nonsocial condition. This difference was much less pronounced and nonsignificant for participants with a high need for closure.

Do these need for closure driven differences matter to communicative efficacy? Apparently so. First, replicating again the Fussell and Krauss (1989) research, we found that in decoding descriptions by other people the rate of successful matching was significantly higher if those descriptions were encoded in the Social versus the Nonsocial condition. More importantly from the present perspective, significantly more descriptions encoded by low need for closure communicators were correctly matched to the appropriate figures than descriptions encoded by high need for closure communicators.

Specific closure effects

If our theoretical analysis is correct, needs for specific closure should also have significant impact on communicators' ability to impose effective "audience designs" on their messages. Specifically, the ability to impose such designs should depend on the relative "pleasantness" to the communicator of her own versus the interlocutor's perspective. If the communicator's perspective is subjectively rather pleasing whereas the interlocutor's is rather undesirable (to the communicator), her audience design may be relatively poor. Marie Antoinette's famous alleged message to the hungry Parisians that in the absence of bread they should eat cakes represents a prototypical case of such failed communication based on the "freezing" on one's own pleasing perspective that all is basically well with the world, and the motivated reluctance to attune oneself to the audience's desperate conviction that things cannot go on in the "business as usual" manner. The case where one's own perspective is much more pleasing than that of one's interlocutor is, in fact, prototypical of severe conflicts of various types (on interpersonal, intergroup or international levels) resulting in severe communication failures and misperceptions (cf. Jervis, 1976; Vertzberger, 1990) that may undermine the parties' ability to reach satisfactory resolution of their conflicts. The institution of third-party mediation (e.g., in marriage counselling) aims precisely at improving each party's ability to appreciate the other's perspective and hopefully increase their success in taking that perspective into account while designing their communications to the other party.

To the contrary, if the communicator's perspective is much less pleasing to him than the interlocutor's perspective, he may rather readily alter his perspective to that of the interlocutor and adjust his messages accordingly. Indeed, research on cognitive tuning (Zajonc, 1960) and the "communication game" (Higgins, McCann, & Fondacaro, 1982) attests to communicators' tendency to modify their communications so as to suit their audience's putative preferences. In this particular case, the communicator's initial perspective might be less pleasing or desirable to himself than the audience's perspective, as adhering to the former might bring about a cool reaction from the audience. By the same token, adopting the audience's perspective is desirable or pleasing, as its adoption promises a warm audience response that speakers typically desire.

The language of interpersonal discourse

If need for closure induces the tendency to seek permanent knowledge and avoid the recurrence of ambiguity, it should foster a bias towards general, *trans-situationally stable* knowledge. Accordingly, people under a heightened need for closure should prefer abstract descriptions and category labels over concrete, situationally specific depictions. Consistent with these assumptions, Mikulincer, Yinon, and Kabili (1991) found that persons with high (vs low) "need for structure" (an alternate term used to denote the need for closure) tended more to attribute failure to stable and global (hence, general and abstract) causes as assessed by the Attributional Style Questionnaire (Seligman, Abramson, Semmel, & Von Baeyer, 1979). In the same research, high (vs low) need for structure individuals who worked on unsolvable problems were more likely to attribute failure to global causes and exhibited impaired performance on a subsequent task.

In a different paradigm, Boudreau, Baron, and Oliver (1992) asked participants to communicate their impressions of a target to an individual either more or less generally knowledgeable than themselves. Boudreau et al. assumed that the task of communicating to a knowledgeable other would increase concerns about judgemental validity and lower the need for closure, whereas communication to a less knowledgeable other would reduce concerns about validity, thus enhancing the need for closure. Consistent with this expectation, their results revealed that participants expecting to communicate their impressions to a non-knowledgeable other increased the preponderance of global trait labels in their descriptions, whereas participants expecting to communicate to a knowledgeable other used a lower proportion of global trait labels. The abstraction bias manifest under a heightened need for closure is relevant to a body of work on linguistic abstraction, guided by the Linguistic Category Model (Semin & Fiedler, 1988). We now review the basic premises of this model and subsequently tie it to the theme of epistemic motivations.

The Linguistic Category Model

The Linguistic Category Model (LCM; Semin, 2000; Semin & Fiedler, 1988, 1991) is a classificatory approach to the domain of interpersonal language which consists of interpersonal (transitive) verbs that are tools used to describe *actions* (help, punch, cheat, surprise) or psychological *states* (love, hate, abhor) and *adjectives* and *nouns* that are employed to characterise persons (e.g., extroverted, helpful, religious).

This model of interpersonal language furnishes the means by which it is possible to identify the nuances of how people use interpersonal terms, and thus is informative about how verbal behaviour is driven strategically by psychological processes and communication constraints. This is made possible by providing a systematic model of the meanings that are peculiar to the linguistic terms (verbs, adjectives, and nouns) that we use in communicating about social events and their actors.

In this model a distinction is made between five different categories of interpersonal terms, namely Descriptive Action Verbs (DAVs), Interpretative Action Verbs (IAVs), State Action Verbs (SAVs), State Verbs (SVs), and Adjectives (ADJs) (see Semin & Fiedler, 1991). The distinction between the categories is obtained on the basis of a number of conventional grammatical tests and semantic contrasts (cf. Bendix, 1966; Brown & Fish, 1983; Miller & Johnson-Laird, 1976).

DAVs are the most concrete terms and are used to convey a description of a single, observable event and preserve perceptual features of the event (e.g., "A punches B" whereby punching is always achieved by means of a fist). Similarly, the second category (IAVs) describes specific observable events. However, these verbs are more abstract in that they refer to a general class of behaviours and do not preserve the perceptual features of an action (e.g., "A hurts B").

The distinction between DAVs and IAVs from the next two categories, namely SAVs and SVs, is self-evident. SAVs and SVs refer to psychological states while DAVs and IAVs do not. Finally, DAVs are distinct from IAVs. DAVs refer to an invariant physical feature of action, as in the case of kick, kiss, *inter alia*. In contrast, IAVs serve as frames for a variety of actions that can be described by the same verb. Thus, the verb "to help" may refer to a great variety of distinct and different actions, ranging from mouth to mouth resuscitation to aiding an old lady to cross the street. SAVs refer to the affective consequences of actions that are not specified any further (to amaze, surprise, bore, thrill, etc.) but can be supplied when asked (e.g., "Why was she surprised?").

The next category (SVs) typically describes an unobservable emotional state and not a specific event (e.g., "A hates B"). One can distinguish between SVs and the three action verbs (DAV, IAV, SAV) on the basis of two separate criteria. It is difficult to use the imperative unrestrictively in the case of SVs (e.g., "Please admire me!" or "Need money!"). Additionally, SVs resist taking the progressive form (e.g., "John is liking Mary"). Whereas both SVs and SAVs refer to psychological states in contrast to IAVs and DAVs, it is possible to distinguish between SAVs and SVs by means of the "but" test (cf. Bendix, 1966; Johnson-Laird & Oatley, 1989, p. 98 ff.). SAVs refer to states that are caused by the observable action of an agent, and describe the "emotional

consequences" of this action upon a patient (surprise, bore, thrill). The latter, SVs, refer to unobservable states (love, hate, despise). Whereas one can say "I like Mary, but I do not know why", it is awkward to say "Mary entertained me, but I do not know why". The reason is mainly because SAVs "signify a feeling that has a cause known to the individual experiencing it" (Johnson-Laird & Oatley, 1989, p. 99).

Finally, adjectives (e.g., "A is aggressive") constitute the last and most abstract category. These generalise across specific events and objects and describe only the subject. They show a low contextual dependence and a high conceptual interdependence in their use. In other words, the use of adjectives is governed by abstract, semantic relations rather than by the contingencies of contextual factors. The opposite is true for action verbs (e.g., Semin & Fiedler, 1988; Semin & Greenslade, 1985). The most concrete terms retain a reference to the contextual and situated features of an event.

This dimension of abstractness–concreteness of interpersonal predicates has been operationalised in terms of a number of different inferential features or properties. Some of these inferential properties are: (1) how enduring the characteristic is of the sentence subject; (2) the ease and difficulty of confirming and disconfirming statements constructed with these predicates; (3) the temporal duration of an interpersonal event depicted by these terms; (4) how informative the sentence is about situational pressures or circumstances; (5) the likelihood of an event recurring at a future point in time (Maass, Salvi, Arcuri, & Semin, 1989; Semin & Fiedler, 1988; Semin & Greenslade, 1985; Semin & Marsman, 1994). These variables have been shown to form a concrete–abstract dimension on which the four categories of the Linguistic Category Model (Semin & Fiedler, 1988) are ordered systematically. Descriptive Action Verbs (hit, kiss) constitute the most concrete category. Interpretative Action Verbs (help, cheat) are more abstract. State Verbs (like, abhor) follow, and Adjectives (friendly, helpful) are the most abstract predicates. Thus, one can determine how abstractly or concretely people represent an event in conversation. For example, the very same event can be described as somebody *hitting* a person, *hurting* a person (actions), *hating* a person (state), or simply as being *aggressive* (adjective).

It is important to note that the properties by which abstractness–concreteness has been operationalised are *generic to the entire predicate classes* represented in the LCM. The types of meanings or implications as defined by the distinctive inferential properties of the LCM are different from the more conventional study of meaning, namely semantics. The more conventional approaches in linguistics are the study of meaning in terms of *semantic fields*, *semantic relations*, or the analysis of lexical items in terms of *semantic features* to investigate the semantic component of a grammar's organisation. While semantic fields are concerned with how vocabulary is organised into domains or areas within which lexical items interrelate, semantic or sense relations address relationships such as synonymity (e.g., affable, amiable, friendly) and antonymity (e.g., friendly vs unfriendly, good vs bad).

The inferential properties identified by the LCM are not domain specific, nor are they expressed in terms of interrelationships between the surface properties of terms. One may refer to the meaning domain identified by the LCM as meta-semantic, since the inferential properties apply across semantic fields and are also distinctive in that they escape conscious access (Franco & Maass, 1996, 1999; Von Hippel, Sekaquaptewa, & Vargas, 1997).

Linguistic categories and epistemic motivations

Assuming the existence of an abstraction bias under heightened need for closure, how might it affect the use of language in interpersonal discourse, and what effects might it have on interpersonal rapport? Rubini and Kruglanski (1997) set out to investigate these issues in a question and answer paradigm. This particular paradigm simulates the situation wherein we acquire knowledge by formulating questions and directing them at others capable of providing informative answers. Research by Semin, Rubini, and Fiedler (1995) indicates that the abstractness level of questions influences the locus of causal origin for answers. Specifically, questions formulated with action verbs (e.g., "to help", "to write") cue the logical *subject* of a question as the causal origin of answers. Questions formulated with state verbs (e.g., "to love" or "to like") cue the logical *object* of a question as the causal origin for answers. Thus, if asked such a simple and mundane question as "Why do you *own* a dog?" (using an interpretative action verb), persons are prompted to respond by referring to themselves (the subject of the question) as the causal agent in the answer, e.g., by stating "Because *I* enjoy the companionship that dogs provide". If one is asked "Why do you *like* dogs?", however, one is prompted to respond by referring to the object itself, e.g., "Because *dogs* are good companions" (Semin & de Poot, 1997).

One interesting implication of this effect is that individuals might feel that they disclose more about themselves when asked questions formulated with action verbs as opposed to state verbs, or more generally speaking, questions formulated at a lower (vs higher) level of abstractness. As a consequence, respondents asked questions at a low level of abstractness might feel closer and friendlier towards the interviewer, which may elicit reciprocal friendliness on their part. By contrast, respondents asked questions at a higher level of abstractness may feel more distant and less friendly towards the interviewer, again inviting a response in kind.

Semin et al. (1995) also found that the abstractness level of the questions tends to be matched by the abstractness of the answers. Thus, the more abstractly formulated questions tend also to elicit the more abstract answers. Such a drift towards abstraction might increase the felt interpersonal distance and feelings of estrangement in and of itself, apart from any possible effects due to implicit causality. After all, abstractness connotes generality and deindividuation, hence it may well depersonalise the interaction and render it more distant and less friendly.

In their first experiment designed to investigate these issues, Rubini and Kruglanski (1997) had participants under high (vs low) need for closure (operationalised via ambient noise) rank order questions out of a list in terms of their likelihood of using them in a real interview. The list included 32 questions, 8 questions on each of four different topics. It was found that participants under noise (versus no noise) assigned higher ranks to questions characterised by higher (versus lower) level of abstractness. In a follow-up study, questions selected by participants under high (vs low) need for closure were found to elicit more abstract answers from respondents, and ones focused more on the logical *object* (vs *subject*) of the question. In addition, respondents reported that they felt less friendly towards the interviewer whose questions were more (vs less) abstract. Finally, in a third study the results of the previous two experiments were replicated in a free-interaction context. Interviewers with high (vs low) need for closure asked more abstract questions, which in turn elicited more abstract answers and ones focused more on the logical *object* (vs *subject*) of the question, and elicited lesser friendliness from the interviewee. These results suggest that the permanence tendency induced by the need for nonspecific closure may affect the level of linguistic abstractness, and in so doing may permeate the nascent social relations among conversation partners.

Specific closure effects

The inclination towards (linguistic or conceptual) abstractness, and its inter-personal consequences should be affected by needs for specific (as well as nonspecific) closure. That should depend on whether and to what degree abstractness or concreteness was congruent with the desired closure. Abstract-ness signifies that the characteristic in question transcends the specific situ-ation and hence that it implies generality, stability, or globality. If such a characteristic was desirable and pleasing one might well want to perpetuate its applicability and hence manifest an "abstraction bias". By contrast, if the characteristic in question was negative or undesirable, one might wish to minimise its implications and restrict them to the specific context by concretising the way one thinks or talks about this particular feature.

Research on the *linguistic intergroup bias* (LIB) (Maass & Arcuri, 1992; Maass et al., 1989; Maass & Stahlberg, 1993; Maass, Milesi, Zabbini, & Stahlberg, 1995) is consistent with these notions. The LIB involves a tendency for individuals to describe positive ingroup and negative outgroup behaviours in relatively abstract terms, implying that the behaviour is attributable intern-ally, to the actor's stable characteristics. Conversely, negative ingroup and positive outgroup behaviours are typically described in relatively concrete terms, implying situational specificity, and hence an external attribution of the behaviour. One possible mechanism of the LIB could be motivational (Maass & Stahlberg, 1993), having to do with the fact that abstract descrip-tions of positive ingroup behaviours and of negative outgroup behaviours portray the ingroup in favourable and the outgroup in unfavourable terms, implying that these behaviours are due to enduring characteristics. Similarly, concrete depictions of negative ingroup behaviours minimise their significance as evidence for corresponding group characteristics, as do concrete depictions of positive outgroup behaviours. In other words, those linguistic (and conceptual) tendencies serve to protect the perception that the ingroup is superior to the outgroup.

It appears then that the "seizing and freezing" tendencies prompted by the need for cognitive closure are not restricted to *intrapersonal* effects on social perception and cognition, but impact such important *interpersonal* phenomena as communication. As may be expected, these tendencies may often have a detrimental effect on our capacity to interact with others: They may diminish our ability to appreciate our interlocutors' unique vantage point, hence reducing our ability to interact effectively with those individuals.

Conclusions

In this chapter we reviewed evidence showing that the central function of communication, namely exchanging knowledge, is driven by a communicator's epistemic motivations. In particular, such motivations have been shown to determine the type of perspective communicators may adopt in addressing a recipient, and the level of linguistic abstraction as manifested in their strategic language use in the formulation of their messages. We then extended this theme from individual differences that drive strategic language use in a number of diverse contexts such as question–answer situations, and the description of positive and negative behaviours of ingroups and outgroups. These research fields show the same phenomena with regard to language use. The epistemic motivations of a communicator drive the manner in which language is strategically used to describe the behaviours of others (e.g., as a function of group membership) or the types of goals people attempt to maximise in communication. The advantage of examining strategic language use in relation to chronic or situated differences in epistemic motivation is that its systematic examination reveals commonalities across diverse phenomena.

References

Bendix, E. H. (1966). *Componential analysis of general vocabulary: The semantic structure of a set of verbs in English, Hindu and Japanese*. The Hague: Mouton.

Boudreau, L. A., Baron, R., & Oliver, P. V. (1992). Effects of expected communication target expertise and timing of set on trait use in person description. *Personality and Social Psychology Bulletin, 18*, 447–452.

Brown, R., & Fish, D. (1983). The psychological causality implicit in language. *Cognition, 14*, 237–273.

Clark, H. H., & Murphy, G. L. (1982). Audience design in meaning and reference. In

J. F. LeNy & W. Kintsch (Eds.), *Language and comprehension* (pp. 287–299). New York: North Holland.

Danks, J. H. (1970). Encoding of novel figures for communication and memory. *Cognitive Psychology, 1*, 179–191.

Franco, F. M., & Maass, A. (1996). Implicit versus explicit strategies of out-group discrimination: The role of intentional control in biased language use and reward allocation. *Journal of Language and Social Psychology, 15*, 335–359.

Franco, F. M., & Maass, A. (1999). Intentional control over prejudice: When the choice of the measure matters. *European Journal of Social Psychology, 29*, 469–477.

Fussell, S. R., & Krauss, R. N. (1989). The effects of intended audience design on message production and comprehension: Reference in a common ground framework. *Journal of Experimental Social Psychology, 25*, 203–219.

Fussell, S. R., & Krauss, R. N. (1991). Accuracy and bias in estimates of others' knowledge. *European Journal of Social Psychology, 21*, 445–454.

Higgins, E. T., McCann, C. D., & Fondacaro, R. (1982). The "communication game": Goal directed encoding and cognitive consequences. *Social Cognition, 1*, 21–37.

Horton, W. S., & Keysar, B. (1996). When do speakers take into account common ground? *Cognition, 59*, 91–17.

Jervis, R. (1976). *Perception and misperception in international politics*. Princeton, NJ: Princeton University Press.

Johnson-Laird, P. N., & Oatley, K. (1989). The language of emotions: An analysis of the semantic field. *Cognition and Emotion, 3*, 81–123.

Krauss, R. M., & Fussell, S. R. (1991). Perspective taking in communication: Representations of others' knowledge in reference. *Social Cognition, 9*, 2–24.

Kruglanski, A. W. (1989). *Lay epistemics and human knowledge: Cognitive and motivational bases*. New York: Plenum.

Kruglanski, A. W. (2004). *The psychology of closed mindedness*. New York: Psychology Press.

Kruglanski, A. W. (in press). The nature of fit and the origins of "feeling right": A goal systemic analysis. *Journal of Marketing Research*.

Kruglanski, A. W., & Freund, T. (1983). The freezing and unfreezing of lay inferences: Effects on impressional primacy, ethnic stereotyping and numerical anchoring. *Journal of Experimental Social Psychology, 19*, 448–468.

Kruglanski, A. W., Pierro, A., Mannetti, L., & DeGrada, E. (2006). Groups as epistemic providers: Need for closure and the unfolding of group centrism. *Psychological Review, 113*, 1–17.

Kruglanski, A. W., & Webster, D. M. (1996). Motivated closing of the mind: "Seizing" and "Freezing". *Psychological Review, 103*(2), 263–283.

Maass, A., & Arcuri, L. (1992). The role of language in the persistence of stereotypes. In G. Semin & K. Fiedler (Eds.), *Language, interaction and social cognition* (pp. 129–43). Newbury Park, CA: Sage.

Maass, A., Milesi, A., Zabbini, S., & Stahlberg, D. (1995). The linguistic intergroup bias: Differential expectancies or in-group protection? *Journal of Personality and Social Psychology, 68*, 116–126.

Maass, A., Salvi, D., Arcuri, L., & Semin, G. (1989). Language use in intergroup contexts: The linguistic intergroup bias. *Journal of Personality and Social Psychology, 57*, 981–93.

Maass, A., & Stahlberg, D. (1993). *The linguistic intergroup bias: The role of differential expectancies and in-group protective motivation*. Paper presented at the conference of EAESP, Lisbon, September.

Mikulincer, M., Yinon, A., & Kabili, D. (1991). Epistemic needs and learned helplessness. *European Journal of Personality, 5,* 249–258.

Miller, G. A., & Johnson-Laird, P. (1976). *Language and perception*. Cambridge, UK: Cambridge University Press.

Nickerson, R. S., Baddeley, A., & Freeman, B. (1987). Are people's estimates of what other people know influenced by what they themselves know? *Acta Psychologica, 64,* 245–259.

Powell, R. S., & O'Neal, E. C. (1976). Communication feedback and duration as determinants of accuracy, confidence, and differentiation in interpersonal perception. *Journal of Personality and Social Psychology, 34,* 746–756.

Richter, L., & Kruglanski, A. W. (1997). The accuracy of social perception and cognition: Situationally contingent and process-based. *The Swiss Journal of Psychology, 56,* 62–81.

Ross, L., Greene, D., & House, P. (1977). The false consensus phenomenon: An attribution bias in self-perception and social perception processes. *Journal of Experimental Social Psychology, 13,* 279–301.

Rubini, M., & Kruglanski, A. W. (1997). Brief encounters ending in estrangement: Motivated language use and interpersonal rapport in the question–answer paradigm. *Journal of Personality and Social Psychology, 72,* 1047–1060.

Seligman, M. E. P., Abramson, L. Y., Semmel, A., & von Baeyer, C. (1979). Depressive attributional style. *Journal of Abnormal Psychology, 88,* 242–247.

Semin, G. R. (2000). Language as a cognitive and behavioral structuring resource: Question–answer exchanges. In W. Stroebe & M. Hewstone (Eds.), *European review of social psychology* (pp. 75–104). Chichester, UK: Wiley.

Semin, G. R., & De Poot, C. J. (1997). The question–answer paradigm: You might regret not noticing how a question is worded. *Journal of Personality and Social Psychology, 73,* 472–480.

Semin, G. R., & Fiedler, K. (1988). The cognitive functions of linguistic categories in describing persons: Social cognition and language. *Journal of Personality and Social Psychology, 54,* 558–568.

Semin, G. R., & Fiedler, K. (1991). The linguistic category model, its bases, applications and range. In W. Stroebe & M. Hewstone (Eds.), *European review of social psychology* (Vol. 2., pp. 1–30). Chichester, UK: Wiley.

Semin, G. R., & Greenslade, L. (1985). Differential contributions of linguistic factors to memory based ratings: Systematizing the systematic distortion hypothesis. *Journal of Personality and Social Psychology, 49,* 1713–1723.

Semin, G. R., & Marsman, G. (1994). On the information mediated by interpersonal verbs: Event precipitation, dispositional inference and implicit causality. *Journal of Personality and Social Psychology, 67,* 836–849.

Semin, G. R., Rubini, M., & Fiedler, K. (1995). The answer is in the question: The effect of verb causality on locus of explanation. *Personality and Social Psychology Bulletin, 21,* 834–841.

Shah, J. Y., Kruglanski, A. W., & Thompson, E. P. (1998). Membership has its (epistemic) rewards: Need for closure effects on ingroup bias. *Journal of Personality and Social Psychology, 75,* 383–393.

Vertzberger, Y. Y. I. (1990). *The world in their minds*. Stanford, CA: Stanford University Press.

Von Hippel, W., Sekaquaptewa, D., & Vargas, P. (1997). The linguistic intergroup bias as an implicit indicator of prejudice. *Journal of Experimental Social Psychology*, *33*, 490–509.

Webster, D. M., & Kruglanski, A. W. (1994). Individual differences in need for cognitive closure. *Journal of Personality and Social Psychology*, *67*, 1049–1062.

Webster, D. M., & Kruglanski, A. W. (1998). Cognitive and social consequences of the motivation for closure. In W. Stroebe & M. Hewstone (Eds.), *European review of social psychology* (Vol. 8, pp. 133–174). New York: John Wiley & Sons, Inc.

Zajonc, R. B. (1960). The process of cognitive tuning and communication. *Journal of Abnormal and Social Psychology*, *61*, 159–167.

8 Thinking about your life

Healthy lessons from social cognition

Norbert Schwarz
University of Michigan, USA

Fritz Strack
Universität Würzburg, Germany

There is hardly another branch of psychology that has made stronger contributions to the analysis of applied problems than social psychology. This is particularly obvious for the case of psychological aspects of health, which have been predominantly studied from a social-psychological vantage point (Stroebe, 2000, 2002).

While critical live events were acknowledged as important determinants of health, their actual influence was found to depend on a variety of psychological variables (see Stroebe & Jonas, 2001). A similar state of affairs exists in the study of subjective well-being that has recently been praised as "positive psychology" (Snyder & Lopez, 2002). Although objective circumstances certainly influence people's sense of well-being, their impact is much weaker than one might expect. Instead, psychological mechanisms play an important role in how people feel about their lives.

In this chapter we would like to show that social psychology, in this case *cognitive* social psychology, may contribute to a better understanding of the processes that cause people to think of themselves as happy or satisfied. Along the way, we will also offer some tangible advice on how you should (or should not) think about your life. The advice will be derived from our judgement model of subjective well-being that identifies and describes the mental mechanisms that contribute to judgements of happiness and satisfaction (see Schwarz & Strack, 1991). These include the accessibility of information, the determinants of its use, the role of affect, and the different ways of thinking about one's past.

Information accessibility

Most studies of well-being ask respondents for a global evaluation of their lives, for example, "Taking all things together, how would you say things are these days? Would you say you are very happy, pretty happy, not too happy?" Unfortunately, "taking all things together" is a difficult mental task. In fact, as an instruction to think about all aspects of one's life, it requests something impossible from the respondent. How can a person conduct a complete review of "things these days", particularly in a survey interview in which the average time to answer a question is frequently less than one minute (Groves & Kahn, 1979)? Therefore, the person will certainly not think about all aspects but probably about some of them. The question is: which ones?

What happens to come to mind

One of the central principles in social cognition research predicts that it is the most accessible information that enters into the judgement. Individuals rarely retrieve all the information that potentially bears on a judgement, but truncate the search process as soon as enough information has come to mind to form the judgement with a reasonable degree of subjective certainty (for reviews see Bodenhausen & Wyer, 1987; Higgins, 1996). Accordingly, the judgement reflects the implications of the information that comes to mind most easily. One determinant of the accessibility of information is the frequency and recency with which it is used. Applied to judgements of subjective well-being, prior use of relevant information may increase the likelihood that this information enters into the happiness judgement.

To test this assumption, we asked participants to write down three events that were either particularly positive and pleasant or particularly negative and unpleasant (Strack, Schwarz, & Gschneidinger, 1985, Exp. 1). This was done under the pretext of collecting life events for a life-event inventory, and the dependent variables, among them "happiness" and "satisfaction", were said to be assessed in order to "find the best response scales" for that instrument. As predicted, participants who had been induced to think about positive aspects of their present life described themselves as happier and more satisfied with their lives as a whole than participants who had been induced to think about negative aspects.

In a related study (Strack, Martin, & Schwarz, 1988), participants were led to think about a relevant life domain simply by asking a specific question before they had to report their general happiness. Generating an answer should render this specific information more accessible for subsequent use and therefore influence the judgement. Specifically, we asked American students how frequently they went out for a date, and how happy they were with their lives as a whole, varying the order in which the two questions were presented. When the general happiness question preceded the dating frequency question, both measures correlated $r = -.12$, a correlation that is not significantly different from zero. Based on this correlation, we would conclude that dating frequency contributes little, if anything, to students' life satisfaction. Yet reversing the question order increased the correlation to $r = .66$. In this case, we would conclude that dating frequency is a major determinant of students' overall happiness and life satisfaction. Similarly, we observed that marital satisfaction and general life satisfaction correlated $r = .32$ when the life-satisfaction question preceded the marital-satisfaction question, but $r = .67$ when the question order was reversed (Schwarz, Strack, & Mai, 1991). This question-order effect could also be observed in respondents' mean reports. Those who were happily married reported higher general life satisfaction when they first thought about their marriage than when they did not. Conversely, those who were unhappily married reported lower general life satisfaction under this condition.

In combination, these and related findings indicate that judgements of life satisfaction are not based on the myriad of positive and negative aspects that characterise one's life. Instead, they are based on a small subset of these aspects, namely the ones that happen to come to mind at the time of judgement. Some of these aspects are "chronically" accessible and likely to come to mind under most circumstances. A person suffering from a severe illness, or currently going through a painful divorce, may consider this aspect of her life under most circumstances. Other aspects, however, are only "temporarily" accessible and may simply come to mind because our attention was recently drawn to them. In general, chronically accessible information lends some stability to our judgements, whereas temporarily accessible information is the source of context effects of the type discussed above (Schwarz & Bless, 1992). These context effects raise considerable problems for empirical research into the conditions that make for a happy life, as the above findings illustrate. In general, we will overestimate the influence of circumstances that are brought to mind by the research instrument, at the expense of circumstances that are not brought to mind (see Schwarz & Strack, 1999, for a more detailed discussion of methodological implications).

ADVICE

In light of these findings, our first piece of advice will not come as a surprise: Thinking about positive aspects of your life is good for you! But before you try to count your blessings, we urge you to read on—or else the outcome may not be what you hope for.

How easily it comes to mind

In the study summarised above, Strack et al.'s (1985) participants reported higher life satisfaction after they had to recall three positive rather than three negative events that recently happened to them. Suppose, however, that we had asked them to recall 12 events. Chances are that at least some participants would have found it difficult to do so. In this case, they may have concluded that there weren't many positive (negative) events in their lives—or else recalling them would not be so difficult.

Consistent with this conjecture, we observed in several studies that the implications of *what* comes to mind are qualified by *how easily* it can be brought to mind (for a review see Schwarz, 1998). For example, we asked American students to list either four or twelve things they liked or disliked about their date. As expected, those who had to list four positive aspects subsequently reported higher relationship satisfaction than those who had to list four negative aspects. This pattern, however, reversed for participants who had to list 12 aspects. Finding it difficult to think of 12 unique positive aspects of their date, they concluded that their date wasn't that wonderful after all, resulting in decreased relationship satisfaction. Conversely, those who found it difficult to think of 12 negative aspects of their date reported very high satisfaction, despite the numerous negative aspects rendered accessible by the recall task.

As these findings illustrate, the ease or difficulty with which information can be brought to mind is informative in its own right. People assume that frequent events are easier to recall than rare events. Accordingly, ease of recall suggests that there are many similar events, whereas difficulty of recall suggests that the recalled event is relatively rare (Tversky & Kahneman, 1973). As a result, our judgements are only consistent with the implications of *what* comes to mind when it comes to mind easily, but are opposite to the implications of recalled content when recall is experienced as difficult (for a review see Schwarz, 1998). This influence of the subjective accessibility experience is eliminated when the informational value of the experience is called into question. When participants believe, for example, that the recall task is only so difficult because they are distracted by background music played to them, they discount the experienced difficulty and rely on the recalled content, even when it is difficult to bring to mind (e.g., Schwarz, Bless, Strack, Klumpp, Rittenauer-Schatka, & Simons, 1991).

ADVICE

Thinking of a few good things is good for you—but don't try too hard! The more blessings you try to count, the more likely it is that you'll find it difficult to come up with them, leaving you with the bleak inference that there aren't enough blessings in your life. Instead, enjoy the few you can easily think of—there must surely be many of them if a few come to mind so easily!

Conversely, when a few bad things spring to mind, don't stop there! Are there really that many bad things? Trying to enumerate as many as you can will eventually make the task difficult, hopefully convincing you that your life isn't as bad as you may have feared.

How is accessible information used? Assimilation and contrast

To predict how a given piece of accessible information influences a judgement, we further need to understand how it is used. In general, any evaluative judgement requires two mental representations, namely a representation of the target of judgement ("my life") and a representation of a standard, against which the target is evaluated (Schwarz & Bless, 1992). Both representations are constructed on the spot, based on the information that comes to mind at the time of judgement. When a given piece of information (say, "my wonderful vacation" or "my surgery") is included in the representation formed of the target ("my life"), it results in an assimilation effect. In this case, we are more satisfied with our lives as a whole when we think of a positive (vacation) rather than negative (surgery) aspect. Under some conditions, however, the accessible information may instead be used in constructing a standard of comparison against which we evaluate our lives in general, resulting in a contrast effect. Thus, we would be less satisfied when we evaluate our lives relative to a positive standard (vacation) rather than a negative one (surgery). As this example illustrates, the *same* information can have a positive or a negative influence on our judgements, depending on how it is used. We now turn to a selective review of some variables that determine information use (for a more detailed theoretical discussion see Schwarz & Bless, 1992; Schwarz & Strack, 1999).

Temporal distance

In the Strack et al. (1985) studies, discussed above, we not only varied the hedonic quality of the life event that participants had to recall, but also the time perspective. Some participants had to think about a recent event, others about an event that had occurred several years ago. When the event was recent, participants reported higher general life satisfaction after recalling a positive rather than a negative event, as already seen. Not so, however, when the event was several years in the past. In this case, participants who had to recall a past positive event reported *lower* current life satisfaction than participants who had to recall a past negative event.

These and related findings (see Schwarz & Strack, 1999) indicate that highly accessible information will influence the judgement in the direction of its hedonic quality, resulting in assimilation effects, if it pertains directly to one's present living conditions. If the accessible information bears on one's previous living conditions, on the other hand, it will serve as a salient standard of comparison, resulting in contrast effects. These experimental results are further supported by correlational data (Elder, 1974) indicating, for senior citizens in the US, that the "children of the great depression" are more likely to report high subjective well-being the more they had to suffer under adverse economic conditions when they were adolescents. The cumulation of negative experiences during childhood and adolescence apparently established a baseline against which all subsequent events could only be seen as an improvement. Portraying the other side of the coin, Runyan (1980) found that the upwardly mobile recollected their childhood as less satisfying than did the downwardly mobile, presumably because they used their current situation in evaluating their past.

Salient category boundaries

While the above findings bear on the impact of the temporal distance of the event per se, subsequent research demonstrated that it is not temporal distance by itself that moderates the use of accessible information, but rather the subjective perception of whether the event one thinks about pertains to one's current conditions of living or to a different episode of one's life. In one study (Strack, Schwarz, & Nebel, 1987), we asked students to describe either a positive or a negative event that they expected to occur in "five years from now". For half of the sample, we emphasised a major role transition that would occur in the meantime, namely leaving university and entering the job market. Theoretically, this should increase the probability that respondents would assign the expected event to a "different" phase of their life, and would therefore use it as a standard of comparison. The results supported this reasoning. When the role transition was *not* emphasised, participants reported higher happiness and life satisfaction when they had to describe positive rather than negative expectations. When the role transition *was* emphasised, this pattern was reversed, and participants reported higher well-being after thinking about negative rather than positive future expectations. Thus, a positive future can make us unhappy when it serves as a standard of comparison, relative to which our current life looks bleak. Conversely, a negative future may help us appreciate the current situation.

Implications

Note that findings of this type have important methodological implications: Any given positive (or negative) life event may have a positive or a negative influence on judgements of happiness and life satisfaction, depending on whether the event is used in constructing a mental representation of the target ("my life") or a mental representation of the standard. It is therefore not surprising that the empirical relationship between the objective occurrence of an event and individuals' subjective evaluations of their lives is weak. Knowing that a person experienced event X does not allow us to predict the impact of X on the person's life satisfaction. Instead, we need to know whether the event comes to mind at the time of judgement and how the person uses the event in constructing the respective mental representations. Both of these aspects are, in part, a function of the research instrument used, giving rise to a host of complex methodological issues (see Schwarz & Strack, 1999).

ADVICE

As our findings illustrate, today's misery can be source of tomorrow's happiness—if you play it right. Thus, when a negative life event comes to mind, make sure you assign it to its proper place in your life. Surely, whatever happened in the past is not representative of what your life is like now, a full week, if not more, later. And relative to this past moment of misery, life now looks pretty good, doesn't it?

Conversely, if a positive life event comes to mind, frolic in the endless stream of life that knows no boundaries. Who says that it isn't part of your current life, just because it occurred a few years in the past? It's your one and only life, after all, from the cradle to the grave. Seeing it any differently only turns yesterday's pleasure into today's source of misery.

The role of feelings

So far, we considered how information about our own lives influences our judgements of happiness and life satisfaction. These judgements, however, are not only a function of what we think about, but also of how we feel at the time of judgement. As we are all aware, there are days when life seems just great and others when life seems rather dreadful, even though nothing of any obvious importance has changed in the meantime. Rather, it seems that minor events which may affect our moods may greatly influence how we evaluate our lives. Not surprisingly, experimental data confirm these experiences. Thus, we reported that finding a dime on a copy machine greatly increased respondents' reported happiness with their lives as a whole (Schwarz, 1987), as did receiving a chocolate bar (Münkel, Strack, & Schwarz, 1987), spending time in a pleasant rather than an unpleasant room (Schwarz, Strack, Kommer, & Wagner, 1987, Exp. 2), or watching the German soccer team win rather than lose a championship game (Schwarz et al., 1987, Exp. 1). We first address the processes underlying these mood effects and subsequently explore how the feelings elicited by recalled life events qualify the advice we provided so far.

Mood-congruent recall or mood as information?

What are the mental processes underlying the observed impact of moods on judgements of life satisfaction? Two possible processes deserve particular attention. On the one hand, it has been shown that moods increase the accessibility of mood-congruent information in memory (for reviews see Blaney, 1986; Bower, 1981; Schwarz & Clore, 1996). That is, individuals in a good mood are more likely to recall positive information from memory, whereas individuals in a bad mood are more likely to recall negative information. Thus, thinking about one's life while being in a good mood may result in a selective retrieval of positive aspects of one's life, and therefore in a more positive evaluation.

On the other hand, the impact of moods may be more direct. People may assume that their momentary well-being at the time of judgement is a reasonable and parsimonious indicator of their well-being in general. Thus, they may base their evaluation of their life as a whole on their feelings at the time of judgement and may evaluate their well-being more favourably when they feel good rather than bad. In doing so, lay people may follow the same logic as psychologists who assume that one's mood represents the global overall state of the organism (e.g., Ewert, 1983) and reflects all the countless experiences one goes through in life (e.g., Bollnow, 1956). According to this perspective, which has a long tradition in European phenomenological psychology, our moods are an integrative function of all our experiences. If people share this perspective, they may evaluate their life on the basis of their mood at the time of judgement, a strategy that would greatly reduce the complexity of the judgemental task.

In fact, when people are asked how they decide whether they are happy or not, most of them are likely to refer explicitly to their current affect state, saying, for example, "Well, I feel good." Accordingly, Ross, Eyman, and Kishchuk (1986) report that explicit references to one's affective state accounted for 41% to 53% of the reasons that various samples of adult Canadians provided for their reported well-being, followed by future expectations (22% to 40%), past events (5% to 20%), and social comparisons (5% to 13%).

We conducted a number of laboratory and field experiments to explore the judgemental processes that underlie the impact of respondents' current mood on reported well-being: Is the impact of moods mediated by mood-congruent recall from memory, or by the use of one's mood itself as an informational basis? In one of these studies (Schwarz & Clore, 1983, Exp. 2), we called respondents on sunny or rainy days and assessed their happiness and life satisfaction in telephone interviews. As expected, respondents reported being in a better mood, and being happier and more satisfied with their lives as a whole, on sunny than on rainy days.

To test the hypothesis that the impact of mood on reported well-being is due to respondents' use of their perceived mood as a piece of information, some respondents were induced to attribute their current mood to a transient external source which was irrelevant to the evaluation of one's life. If respondents attribute their current feelings to transient external factors, they should be less likely to use them as an informational basis for evaluating their lives in general and the impact of participants' current mood should be greatly reduced. In the weather study, this was accomplished by directing respondents' attention to the weather. In one condition, the interviewers pretended to call from out of town and asked, "By the way, how's the weather down there?." With this manipulation, we wanted to suggest to respondents that their mood may be due to the weather and may therefore not be diagnostic for the overall quality of their lives.

The results confirmed our predictions. Whereas good or bad weather resulted in a pronounced difference in reported life satisfaction when the weather was *not* mentioned, this difference was eliminated when respondents' attention was directed to the weather as an irrelevant external source of their current mood. In addition, a measure of current mood, assessed at the end of the interview, was not affected by the attention manipulation, which indicates that the manipulation did not affect respondents' current mood itself but only their inferences based on it. Accordingly, the mood measure was more strongly correlated with reported happiness and life satisfaction when the weather was not mentioned than when it was mentioned.

In summary, these results and related ones (see Schwarz, 1987) demonstrate that respondents use their affective state at the time of judgement as a parsimonious indicator of their well-being in general, unless the informational value of their current mood is called into question. Moreover, the attributional effects obtained in the present study, as well as in our follow-ups, rule out an alternative explanation based on mood-congruent retrieval. According to this hypothesis, respondents may recall more negative information about their life when in a bad rather than a good mood, and may therefore base their evaluation on a selective sample of data. Note, however, that the impact of a selective database should be independent of respondents' attributions for their current mood. Attributing one's current mood to the weather only discredits the informational value of one's current mood itself, but not the evaluative implications of any positive or negative events one may recall. Inferences based on selective recall should therefore be unaffected by salient explanations for one's current feelings. Accordingly, the present findings demonstrate that moods themselves may serve informative functions. This hypothesis has meanwhile received considerable support in different domains of judgement and has provided a coherent framework for conceptualising the impact of affective states on cognitive processes (for a review see Schwarz & Clore, 1996).

ADVICE

As the weather experiment illustrates, you do *not* want to know the source of your momentary mood when you feel good. You may only find out that your upbeat feelings are merely due to the weather or to finding a coin that a benign experimenter left for you. Instead, enjoy your good feelings and ask yourself how you *feel* about your life. After all, things must be going fine if you feel well.

If you feel bad, however, you're well advised to find a transient source. You surely don't want a rainy day to spoil an otherwise enjoyable life? And besides, there must be more relevant information to evaluate your life than your momentary feelings. Who wants to be at the mercy of one's mood, anyway?

Fortunately, chances are that you will do so spontaneously. As a large body of research indicates, individuals in a sad mood are likely to search for causal explanations and engage in systematic judgement strategies, with considerable attention to the details at hand. In contrast, individuals in a happy mood are likely to use simplifying judgement strategies, such as the "How-do-I-feel-about-this?" heuristic (for reviews see Schwarz, in press; Schwarz & Clore, 1996). Accordingly, people are usually more likely to look for external sources for their sad than for their happy moods, with beneficial effects for their desire to see their lives in a positive light.

When do people rely on their mood rather than other information?

So far, we have seen that individuals may evaluate their lives on the basis of comparison processes or on the basis of their affective state at the time of judgement. This raises the question of the conditions under which they will rely on one rather than the other source of information. On theoretical grounds, we may assume that people are more likely to use the simplifying strategy of consulting their affective state the more burdensome the judgement would be to make on the basis of comparison information. After all, humans have frequently been shown to be "cognitive misers" (Taylor, 1981) who prefer simple strategies to more complex ones whenever they are available. In this regard, it is important to note a basic difference between judgements of happiness and satisfaction with one's life as a whole vs judgements of specific life domains. Evaluations of general life satisfaction pose an extremely complex task that requires a large number of comparisons along many dimensions with ill-defined criteria and the subsequent integration of the results of these comparisons into one composite judgement. As noted earlier, one may evaluate one's current situation by comparing it with what one expected, with what others have, with what one had earlier, and so on. And which domains is one to select for these comparisons? Health, income, family life, the quality of your environment, and what else? And after making all these comparisons how should one integrate their results? How much weight should be attached to each outcome? Facing this complex task, people may rarely engage in it. Rather, they may base their judgement on their perceived mood at that time, unless the informational value of their current mood is discredited.

Evaluations of specific life domains, on the other hand, are often less complex. In contrast to judgements of general life satisfaction, comparison information is usually available for judgements of specific life domains and criteria for evaluation are well defined. An attempt to compare one's income or one's "life as a whole" with that of colleagues aptly illustrates the difference. Moreover, one's affective state is not considered relevant information in evaluating many domains. Therefore, judgements of domain satisfaction are more likely to be based on comparison strategies than on the heuristic use of one's affective state at the time of judgement. In line with this reasoning, we found that the outcome of the games played by the German national soccer team during the 1982 World Cup affected respondents' general life satisfaction but not their satisfaction with work and income (Schwarz et al., 1987, Exp. 1).

The hypothesis that judgements of general life satisfaction are based on respondents' affective state, while judgements of domain satisfaction are based on comparison processes, raises the intriguing possibility that the *same* event may influence evaluations of one's life as a whole and evaluations of specific domains in opposite directions. For example, an extremely positive event in domain X may induce good mood, resulting in reports of increased general life satisfaction. However, the same event may also increase the standard of comparison used in evaluating domain *X*, resulting in judgements of decreased satisfaction with this particular domain. Such a differential impact of the same objective event may in part account for the weak relationships that global evaluations were found to have with specific evaluations as well as with measures of objective circumstances, which was a frequent concern of sociological researchers in the tradition of subjective social indicators (Campbell, 1981; Glatzer & Zapf, 1984).

We explored this possibility by testing participants in either a pleasant or an unpleasant room, namely a friendly office or a small, dirty laboratory that was overheated and noisy, with flickering lights and a bad smell (Schwarz et al., 1987, Exp. 2). As expected, participants were in a better mood, and reported higher happiness and satisfaction with their lives as a whole, in the pleasant rather than the unpleasant room. This replicates the mood effects observed in other studies (Schwarz, 1987). Yet, participants' housing satisfaction did not benefit from their good mood. To the contrary, participants reported higher housing satisfaction when they were tested in the unpleasant rather than the pleasant room, indicating that the room served as a relevant standard of comparison. After all, even a regular dorm room looked like a palace compared to our dirty laboratory.

In combination, these findings highlight that a given extreme event may have *opposite* effects on judgements of general life satisfaction and judgements of domain satisfaction. If the event puts us in a good (bad) mood, it will increase (decrease) our general life satisfaction. At the same time, however, the event may serve as a standard of comparison, resulting in contrast effects on evaluations of the life domain to which the event is relevant. Note that these *diverging* influences imply that judgements of overall life satisfaction are not simply an "average" of one's satisfaction in different domains. Instead, evaluations of one's life as a whole and of specific domains are often based on different inputs and different evaluative strategies, as the present findings illustrate.

Recalled life events: Content versus feeling

We now return to our discussion of the role of recalled life events in judgements of life satisfaction. In the first part of this chapter, we took a purely cognitive perspective and highlighted that our judgements depend on *what* comes to mind, how *easily* it comes to mind, and how we *use* the information that comes to mind. The interplay of these factors is further complicated by the fact that recalling a life event may also change our feelings. This is particularly likely when we recall the event in vivid detail, reliving it in our mind's eye. In that case, positive events elicit a positive mood, and negative events elicit a negative mood, with important consequences for subsequent judgements.

Recall that Strack et al. (1985, Exp. 1) observed contrast effects when participants were induced to think about past positive or negative events. That is, their participants were more satisfied with their current lives when they evaluated them against a memory of past misery rather than a memory of past pleasure. Importantly, this result was obtained under conditions that discouraged the "reliving" of the past event. Specifically, we provided participants with only a couple of lines on which to report the event, thus discouraging detailed elaborations. In subsequent experiments, we manipulated the extent to which the recall task was emotionally involving. In one study (Strack et al., 1985, Exp. 2), some participants were again asked simply to list an event on two lines, whereas others were asked to describe an event in considerable detail and were given a full page to do so. In a related study (Strack et al., 1985, Exp. 3), some participants were asked to explain "why" the event occurred, whereas others were asked to relive the event in their mind's eye and to describe "how" it unfolded. As expected, detailed recall and "how" descriptions induced a temporary happy or sad mood. In contrast, merely naming the event or analysing "why" it occurred did not affect participants' mood.

In the latter case, participants' judgements of life satisfaction replicated the contrast effects we observed earlier. Participants who merely listed the event, or who provided pallid "why" descriptions, reported *lower* current life satisfaction after thinking about a past positive rather than a past negative event. Not so, however, when describing the event in great detail, or providing a vivid "how" description, elicited a current happy or sad mood. In that case, participants who felt happy due to elaborating on a past positive event reported *higher* current life satisfaction than participants who felt sad due to elaborating on a past negative event. This replicates the mood effects discussed above (for related findings see Clark & Collins, 1993; Clark, Collins, & Henry, 1994).

In combination, these results indicate that individuals draw on their current feelings as a source of information when they are in a pronounced mood state, but use other accessible information about their life in the absence of pronounced mood states. Accordingly, the impact of a past life event on judgements of overall life satisfaction depends crucially on whether the memory does, or does not, elicit a corresponding mood. When recalling a past event does *not* put us into a corresponding mood, it serves as a standard of comparison, resulting in a contrast effect. When it *does* elicit a corresponding mood, the affective influence overrides the otherwise observed contrast effect.

ADVICE

When a positive past event comes to mind, you are well advised to flesh it out in detail. Revel in the good memories and enjoy the warm feelings they elicit. Those feelings will brighten your life. But remember that the art of reminiscing requires detailed memories that allow you to "relive" the good feelings.

If that positive past event remains pallid, it may only serve as a standard of comparison for your current life.

Conversely, when a past negative event comes to mind, by all means keep it pallid. Reliving this event in your mind's eye will only make you feel bad, clouding your whole life. But if you can keep it pallid, your past misery makes for a great standard of comparison, relative to which you can enjoy how much better your life is now.

Conclusions

As our selective review indicates, life events play an important role in judgements of happiness and life satisfaction. Yet their impact does not follow the simple assumption that good events will make us happy. Instead, the *same* event can increase as well as decrease life satisfaction, depending on how we think about it. In the present chapter, we considered the role of what comes to mind, how easily it comes to mind, and how it is used, as well as the role of positive or negative feelings a memory may elicit. The underlying processes are systematic and the reviewed results reliably replicable, provided that properly controlled experimental conditions channel how people think about their lives. In the absence of controlled conditions, however, different people choose different judgement strategies, resulting in a wide variety of different outcomes. Accordingly, it comes as no surprise that surveys of well-being observed only weak relationships between objective characteristics of life and their subjective evaluation, as noted in the introduction—we can't predict a person's life satisfaction without taking his or her judgemental processes into account. In fact, the actual picture is more complex than the current chapter conveys because judgements of well-being are further influenced by comparisons with others and a host of additional variables, which are beyond the scope of the present chapter (for a comprehensive review see Schwarz & Strack, 1999). In our assessment, global questions about life satisfaction are more likely to teach us about the dynamics of human judgement than about the conditions of a happy life. To learn about the latter, it is probably more promising to assess how people feel on a moment-to-moment basis as they go through their lives (see Kahneman, 1999, for a conceptual discussion). At present, research using such a "momentary" approach is still in its infancy and the future will show whether it can uncover more systematic relationships between the objective conditions of life and subjective well-being (see Kahneman, Krueger, Schkade, Schwarz, & Stone, 2004).

In closing, let us return to the advice we provided, admittedly tongue-in-cheek. Can you really "think yourself happy" by following our recommendations? Yes, if a benign experimenter presents a task that structures your thought processes, as we did in the reviewed experiments. In this case, you are unlikely to become aware of the underlying processes and simply experience your thoughts and feelings as your "natural" response to what you are thinking about (see Higgins, 1998). Unfortunately, you are less likely to be successful when you are aware of what you are doing. When we ask you, for example, to list 12 terrible things about your job, you may notice with some relief that they are difficult to bring to mind, concluding that your job can't be that bad after all. Yet the same trick is less likely to work to your satisfaction when two bad aspects of your job come to mind and you tell yourself, "I'll list another 10 to make this difficult." Similarly, finding a dime may brighten your life—but looking for a dime to brighten it is unlikely to work. Unfortunately, the mind's benevolent magic works best when left unobserved.

By the same token, however, following our advice is likely to limit negative inferences. Knowing about the role of ease of recall may protect you against the inference that there are many negative aspects to your job, simply because two happen to come to mind easily. Similarly, knowing about the pervasive influence of moods may protect you against the inference that your whole life is lacking enjoyment simply because you feel bad on a rainy day. Thus, although you may not be able to think yourself happy, you may at least be able to limit inferences of unhappiness. And this certainly seems to be a healthy thing.

References

Blaney, P. H. (1986). Affect and memory: A review. *Psychological Bulletin, 99*, 229–246.

Bodenhausen, G. V., & Wyer, R. S. (1987). Social cognition and social reality: Information acquisition and use in the laboratory and the real world. In H. J. Hippler, N. Schwarz, & S. Sudman (Eds.), *Social information processing and survey methodology* (pp. 6–41). New York: Springer Verlag.

Bollnow, O. F. (1956). *Das Wesen der Stimmungen*. Frankfurt: Klostermann.

Bower, G. H. (1981). Mood and memory. *American Psychologist, 36*, 129–148.

Campbell, A. (1981). *The sense of well-being in America*. New York: McGraw-Hill.

Clark, L. F., & Collins, J. E. (1993). Remembering old flames: How the past affects assessments of the present. *Personality and Social Psychology Bulletin, 19*, 399–408.

Clark, L. F., Collins, J. E., & Henry, S. M. (1994). Biasing effects of retrospective reports on current self-assessments. In N. Schwarz & S. Sudman (Eds.), *Autobiographical memory and the validity of retrospective reports* (pp. 291–304). New York: Springer Verlag.

Elder, G. H. (1974). *Children of the Great Depression*. Chicago: University Press.

Ewert, O. (1983). Ergebnisse und Probleme der Emotionsforschung. In H. Thomae (Ed.), *Theorien und Formen der Motivation. Enzyklopädie der Psychologie* (C, IV, Vol. 1, pp. 398–452). Goettingen: Hogrefe.

Glatzer, W., & Zapf, W. (1984). Lebensqualität in der Bundesrepublik. In W. Glatzer & W. Zapf (Eds.), *Lebensqualität in der Bundesrepublik*. Frankfurt: Campus.

Groves, R. M., & Kahn, R. L. (1979). *Surveys by telephone*. New York: Academic Press.

Higgins, E. T. (1996). Knowledge: Accessibility, applicability, and salience. In E. T. Higgins & A. Kruglanski (Eds.), *Social psychology: Handbook of basic principles* (pp. 133–168). New York: Guilford Press.

Higgins, E. T. (1998). The aboutness principle: A pervasive influence on human inference. *Social Cognition, 16*, 173–198.

Kahneman, D. (1999). Objective happiness. In D. Keman, E. Diener, & N. Schwarz (Eds.), *Well-being: The foundations of hedonic psychology* (pp. 3–25). New York: Russell Sage Foundation.

Kahneman, D., Krueger, A. B., Schkade, D. A., Schwarz, N., & Stone, A. A. (2004). A survey method for characterizing daily life experience: The day reconstruction method. *Science, 306*, 1776–1780.

Münkel, T., Strack, F., & Schwarz, N. (1987, April). *Der Einfluss der experimentellen Honorierung auf Stimmung und Wohlbefinden: Macht Schokolade glücklich?* 29th Tagung Experimentell Arbeitender Psychologen, Aachen, Germany.

Ross, M., Eyman, A., & Kishchuck, N. (1986). Determinants of subjective well-being. In J. M. Olson, C. P. Herman, & M. Zanna (Eds.), *Relative deprivation and social comparison* (pp. 79–93). Hillsdale, NJ: Lawrence Erlbaum Associates Inc.

Runyan, W. M. (1980). The life satisfaction chart: Perceptions of the course of subjective experience. *International Journal of Aging and Human Development, 11*, 45–64.

Schwarz, N. (1987). *Stimmung als Information: Untersuchungen zum Einfluß von Stimmungen auf die Bewertung des eigenen Lebens.* Heidelberg: Springer Verlag.

Schwarz, N. (1998). Accessible content and accessibility experiences: The interplay of declarative and experiential information in judgment. *Personality and Social Psychology Review, 2*, 87–99.

Schwarz, N. (in press). Feelings, fit, and "funny effects": A situated cognition perspective. *Journal of Marketing Research.*

Schwarz, N., & Bless, H. (1992). Constructing reality and its alternatives: Assimilation and contrast effects in social judgment. In L. L. Martin & A. Tesser (Eds.), *The construction of social judgment* (pp. 217–245). Hillsdale, NJ: Lawrence Erlbaum Associates Inc.

Schwarz, N., Bless, H., Strack, F., Klumpp, G., Rittenauer-Schatka, H., & Simons, A. (1991). Ease of retrieval as information: Another look at the availability heuristic. *Journal of Personality and Social Psychology, 61*, 195–202.

Schwarz, N., & Clore, G. L. (1983). Mood, misattribution, and judgments of well-being: Informative and directive functions of affective states. *Journal of Personality and Social Psychology, 45*, 513–523.

Schwarz, N., & Clore, G. L. (1996). Feelings and phenomenal experiences. In E. T. Higgins & A. Kruglanski (Eds.), *Social psychology: A handbook of basic principles* (pp. 433–465). New York: Guilford Press.

Schwarz, N., & Strack, F. (1991). Evaluating one's life: A judgement model of subjective well-being. In F. Strack, M. Argyle, & N. Schwarz (Eds.), *Subjective well-being* (pp. 27–47). Oxford, UK: Pergamon.

Schwarz, N., & Strack, F. (1999). Reports of subjective well-being: Judgmental processes and their methodological implications. In D. Kahneman, E. Diener, & N. Schwarz (Eds.), *Well-being: The foundations of hedonic psychology* (pp. 61–84). New York: Russell Sage Foundation.

Schwarz, N., Strack, F., Kommer, D., & Wagner, D. (1987). Soccer, rooms and the quality of your life: Mood effects on judgments of satisfaction with life in general and with specific life-domains. *European Journal of Social Psychology, 17*, 69–79.

Schwarz, N., Strack, F., & Mai, H. P. (1991). Assimilation and contrast effects in part–whole question sequences: A conversational-logic analysis. *Public Opinion Quarterly, 55*, 3–23.

Snyder, C. R., & Lopez, S. J. (Eds.). (2002). *Handbook of positive psychology.* London: Oxford University Press.

Strack, F., Martin, L. L., & Schwarz, N. (1988). Priming and communication: Social determinants of information use in judgments of life satisfaction. *European Journal of Social Psychology, 18*, 429–442.

Strack, F., Schwarz, N., & Gschneidinger, E. (1985). Happiness and reminiscing: The role of time perspective, mood, and mode of thinking. *Journal of Personality and Social Psychology, 49*, 1460–1469.

Strack, F., Schwarz, N., & Nebel, A. (1987, March). *Thinking about your life: Affective and evaluative consequences.* Conference on "Ruminations, Self-Relevant Cognitions, and Stress", Memphis State University, Memphis, TN.

Stroebe, W. (2000). *Social psychology and health.* Buckingham, UK: Open University Press.

Stroebe, W. (2002). Social psychology and health. *British Journal of Health Psychology, 7*, 495.

Stroebe, W., & Jonas, K. (2001). Social psychology and health. In M. Hewstone & W. Stroebe (Eds.), *Introduction to social psychology* (3rd ed., pp. 519–557). Oxford, UK: Blackwell.

Taylor, S. E. (1981). The interface of cognitive and social psychology. In J. Harvey (Ed.), *Cognition, social behavior, and the environment* (pp. 189–211). Hillsdale, NJ: Lawrence Erlbaum Associates Inc.

Tversky, A., & Kahneman, D. (1973). Availability: A heuristic for judging frequency and probability. *Cognitive Psychology, 5*, 207–232.

Part 3

Interpersonal and group processes

9 Situational variance in intergroup conflict

Matrix correlations, matrix interactions, and social support

Chester A. Insko and Scott T. Wolf
University of North Carolina, USA

> Isolated he may be a cultivated individual; in a crowd he is a barbarian—that is a creature acting by instinct.
>
> LeBon (1895/1896, p. 13)

Historical background

Although concern with the consequences of group formation can be traced back to Plato's *Republic*, it was not until the waning years of the 19th century that this issue began to receive the attention of prominent social scientists (Durkheim, 1898; LeBon, 1895) that would continue into the next century (Allport, 1924; Freud, 1922; McDougall, 1920). The central question pertained to why decent people, when banded together, behave indecently.

LeBon's (1895) general answer was to claim that group formation created a group mind. The group mind was conceived of as an unconscious, ancestral heritage, which was common for all humans, and which contained primitive, uncivilised instincts. LeBon argued that when under the influence of the group mind, group members are highly suggestible and prone to violence.

Among American social scientists, Floyd Allport (1924) is well known for having rejected the concept of a group mind. Allport's polemic played an important role in removing the group mind from the lexicon of acceptable social science terms. He did, however, share with LeBon an uncritical acceptance of a poorly phrased issue. As can be seen in the introductory LeBon quotation, the contrasting behaviours that required explanation pitted people in groups against the individual alone or in isolation. This phrasing of the issue was repeated many years later when Floyd Allport discussed the "group versus individual agency" under the general rubric of "the master problem of social psychology" (1962, p. 3). One can appreciate Allport's recognition of the overwhelming importance of LeBon's issue, but the problem is that individuals who are alone cannot by definition engage in interpersonal behaviours including, of course, the competing and aggressing behaviours of interest to LeBon and others. The most interesting behaviour of waking individuals who are alone involves work on tasks, and this is what Allport's (1920, 1924) early, influential studies of social facilitation addressed. Furthermore, it is clear from Allport's later (1962) discussion that he saw these studies as relevant to the set of issues suggested by LeBon's concept of a group or crowd mind (see, for example, 1962, p. 3).

In order to address interpersonal behaviours directly, the minimal social unit must be the dyad and the basic comparison must be between dyadic behaviour and intergroup behaviour. The absence of a systematic set of studies involving such a contrast was noted by Gordon Allport (1985). In a comprehensive review of issues surrounding the group mind Allport notes that, with the exception of Sighele, a contemporary of LeBon, "no other social psychologist seems to have focused his work at the basic level of the dyad, and then tested his views in relation to progressively larger groupings" (p. 23). Although Gordon Allport does not directly mention his brother Floyd, one can interpret this statement as an implied criticism.

We should, however, clarify that we do believe that an understanding of the within-group processes contributing to the greater or lesser task accomplishment of groups than individuals is important, and we suspect that Gordon Allport would agree. In fact, one can point to what could be characterised as a "grand tradition" of studies comparing the task-relevant behaviour of groups and individuals. In addition to studies of social facilitation, we have, for example, studies of individual versus group problem solving (Shaw, 1932), social loafing (Latané, Williams, & Harkins, 1979), bystander intervention (Latané & Darley, 1970), and brain storming (Diehl & Stroebe, 1991).

Significance of the topic

The importance of intergroup relations and conflict was highlighted by a series of articles in the August 1998 *APA Monitor*. One article written by Patrick A. McGuire (1998), "Historic conference focuses on creating a new discipline", describes a conference sponsored by APA and the Canadian Psychological Association that was held in Londonderry, Northern Ireland. Conference participants were challenged to establish "a bedrock of scholarship on which could be built a brand new discipline of psychology" that was to "focus on how to prevent, resolve and intervene in conflicts" such as "the deadly wars of places like Bosnia, Cambodia and Rwanda that have claimed 30 million lives across the world and made refugees of another 45 million since 1990" (p. 1).

Discontinuity defined and illustrated

Interindividual–intergroup discontinuity is the tendency in the context of some social situations for relations between groups to be more competitive, or less cooperative, than are relations between individuals. Most, but not all, of the discontinuity investigations have used a Prisoner's Dilemma Game

(PDG) matrix (see the two matrices in Figure 9.1) with monetary outcomes to provide a context for the intergroup and interindividual interaction. Many of these experiments were conducted in a suite with a central area, or hall, between three smaller rooms on either side. Interactions between individuals were structured so that each participant in a room on one side of the suite interacted with another participant on the opposite side of the suite. Prior to the first trial, and between all subsequent trials, the individuals communicated regarding what choices they might make. Typically, the communication occurred through a face-to-face meeting in the central room, but in some instances there was an exchange of notes, or the use of an intercom. In most of these experiments there were ten trials; in some there was only one trial.

In the typical group session, six participants were randomly assigned to one of two groups, each composed of three individuals. The procedure for groups differed from that for individuals in several respects. First, the three participants on either side of the suite were seated in a common room. Second, the group members were required to reach agreement on a single choice for each trial. Third, the amount of money in the matrix was increased by a factor of three. Fourth, communication with the opposite groups typically occurred between representatives but, as with individuals, sometimes occurred through the exchange of notes or by communicating through an intercom. In still other instances all six participants (three from each side) met in the central room for the communication period between each trial. The repeatedly found discontinuity effect is the tendency for there to be more competitive, or fewer cooperative, choices between groups than between individuals.

Initial studies and meta-analysis

Since an initial pair of investigations by McCallum et al. (1985), a sizeable number of studies have been conducted. In a quantitative review of this literature, Wildschut, Pinter, Vevea, Insko, and Schopler (2003) identified 134 independent effect sizes extracted from 48 studies conducted at 11 different

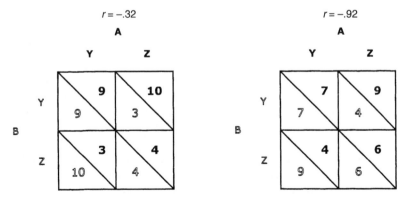

Figure 9.1 Two PDG matrices with differing degrees of correspondence.

laboratories in the US and Europe. The analysis tested and confirmed a number of theory-based predictions regarding the magnitude of the discontinuity effect.

The predictions regarding variation in the magnitude of the discontinuity effect flowed partially from three hypotheses: (1) fear, or schema-based distrust; (2) greed, or social support for shared self-interest; and (3) an ingroup-favouring norm.

The fear hypothesis accounts for discontinuity in terms of the greater distrust towards other groups than towards other individuals (Hoyle, Pinkley, & Insko, 1989; Insko & Schopler, 1998; Pemberton, Insko, & Schopler, 1996; Wildschut, Insko, & Pinter, 2004). This hypothesis assumes the existence of an outgroup schema implying wariness towards groups other than one's own.

The greed hypothesis accounts for discontinuity in terms of the social support for shared self-interested behaviour that may be explicitly available to group members but not to individuals (Insko, Schopler, Hoyle, Dardis, & Graetz, 1990; Schopler, Insko, Graetz, Drigotas, Smith, & Dahl, 1993; Wildschut, Insko, & Gaertner, 2002).

The ingroup-favouring norm hypothesis assumes that membership in a group implies normative pressure to act so as to benefit the ingroup. The distinction between the ingroup-favouring norm hypothesis and the greed hypothesis relates to the fact that the greed hypothesis assumes that social support, or influence, is explicit and flows only from self-interest, whereas the ingroup-favouring norm hypothesis assumes that social influence may be implicit or explicit and flows from group interest (Wildschut et al., 2002). Rabbie and associates are well known for emphasising the importance of a norm of group interest (Horwitz & Rabbie, 1982; Rabbie & Lodewijkx, 1994). Early reference to an ingroup-favouring norm can be found in Plato's *Republic*, where Polemarchus defends a traditional maxim of Greek morality that "justice is the art which gives good to friends and evil to enemies" (trans. 1891, p. 7). An assumption of the hypothesis is that, under some circumstances, the ingroup-favouring norm can overcome the norms of fairness (or outcomes associated with equal opportunity, Lind & Tyler, 1988; Thibaut & Walker, 1975) and reciprocity (Gouldner, 1960) that typically govern interindividual relations.

Four concerns

In the past different colleagues have expressed four different concerns regarding the discontinuity effect, each of which can be expressed as a question. First, would we obtain the discontinuity effect if the cells of the matrix contained larger sums of money? Second, would we obtain the discontinuity effect if the interaction were structured without a matrix? Third, would we obtain the discontinuity effect with "real" groups? Fourth, would we obtain the discontinuity effect in cultures outside the US? We have, in fact, obtained reassuring answers to all four questions.

First, we have found that the discontinuity effect does not change significantly when the values in the matrix vary from those we have typically used to values that are increased by a factor of 10, for example, $0.66 versus $6.60 for the highest possible outcome on one of the ten trials (Schopler, Insko, Graetz, Drigotas, & Smith, 1991, Experiment 3).

Second, we have found that the discontinuity effect obtained with a matrix does not differ significantly from the effect found in a condition in which participants were not shown a matrix but folded origami products and then made a binary decision to exchange or not exchange the products in a way that exactly duplicated the payoffs in the four cells of the matrix (Schopler et al., 2001).

Third, using a diary procedure developed by Reis and Wheeler (1991), we have obtained results in two studies indicating that recorded interactions between groups were judged as more competitive, or less cooperative, than recorded interactions between individuals (Pemberton et al., 1996).

Fourth, the above-described meta-analysis included several studies indicating that the discontinuity effect has been obtained in Europe. Additionally, we have published a study (Wildschut, Lodewijkx, & Insko, 2001) explicitly comparing American and Dutch participants in which we found no significant difference. But what about non-western participants?

During the summer of 2003 we received an email from Masaki Yuki, a social psychology colleague at Hokkaido University, requesting the materials necessary to replicate one of our discontinuity studies. On 30 September 2004 we received a draft of a manuscript in which the abstract contained the following statement: "The results of intergroup/interindividual prisoner's dilemma experiment ($n = 160$) indicated that there was in fact a discontinuity effect in Japan, showing that groups made more competitive choices than individuals" (Takemura & Yuki, 2004, p. 1).

Three questions

Because research on the discontinuity effect began in collaboration with John Thibaut, it is hardly remarkable that the research was guided by interdependence theory (Kelley & Thibaut, 1978; Thibaut & Kelley, 1959) and by game theory (Colman, 1995)—both of which share an initial outcome-maximisation assumption. On the other hand, it should be noted that neither interdependence theory nor game theory makes explicit reference to a difference between interindividual relations and intergroup relations.

Despite the lack of explicit references to the difference between interindividual and intergroup relations in interdependence theory or game theory, we have found that the concepts from these theoretical perspectives have proven useful in helping us to understand the discontinuity effect. In fact, as is explained below, in at least some contexts the concepts from interdependence theory and game theory account more obviously for intergroup relations than for interindividual relations. Recently, Bornstein, Kugler, and Ziegelmeyer

(2004) pointed out that research has amply demonstrated that game theory does a poor job of predicting individual behaviour, but it "may provide a better description of group behavior" (p. 599).

We have used interdependence theory and game theory concepts to aid in answering three research questions. First, what are the mechanisms responsible for the discontinuity effect? Second, what are some possible ways of reducing the effect, particularly by making groups less competitive? Third, what is the generality of the effect to various social contexts? The present chapter will focus on the third question, or on a subset of the issues relevant to the third question. These are issues relating to salient ways in which situations can differ.

Two ways in which matrices can differ

While there may be a tendency for intergroup relations to be more conflict prone than are interindividual relations, clearly such discontinuity does not always exist. One approach to examining the generality of the discontinuity effect is to examine different situations. Interdependence theory and game theory, of course, conceptualise different situations in terms of different matrices (see Kelley, Holmes, Kerr, Reis, Rusbult, & Van Lange, 2002, *Atlas of interpersonal situations*, pp. 4–11). Obviously matrices may differ in many ways, but we will focus on just two of these ways. These are, first, the extent to which the outcomes in the matrix are correspondent and, second, the extent to which maximising the outcomes in the matrix requires coordination. With symmetric outcomes for the two players (i.e., payoffs and strategies would not change if the column and row players switched roles), the first of these is indexed by the correlation between both players' outcomes across the four cells of the matrix, and the second is indexed by the magnitude of the difference in diagonal means in the matrix (the statistical interaction in the two-factor array).

Matrices differing in correspondence of outcomes

Our initial attempt to understand the generality of the discontinuity effect relied on a central theoretical concept in interdependence theory: Kelley and Thibaut's (1978) index of correspondence. With symmetric arrays this index is the correlation between the two players' outcomes across the four cells of the matrix; with nonsymmetric arrays Kelley and Thibaut provide a formula for correcting the correlation for the differing standard deviations of the outcomes for the two players.

Kelley and Thibaut placed major theoretical emphasis on the importance of this index—an index that they believed to be associated with conflict of interest. Why does the index relate to conflict of interest? Note quite simply that if the index is positive, an increase in one player's outcomes is associated with an increase in the other player's outcomes and that if the index is negative, an increase in one player's outcomes is associated with a decrease in the other player's outcomes.[1]

Our theoretical assumption was that the more negative the index, the greater the tendency of groups to be more competitive than individuals. Why is this? Note that with increasingly negative correspondence there is more reason for the norm of ingroup favouritism to require competitiveness and there is more reason for the group members to provide social support for being competitive. On the other hand, social support and the norm of ingroup favouritism are objectively absent for individuals. A possible reason why negative correspondence might increase competitiveness for both individuals and groups is that an increasing degree of negative correspondence might generally produce increasing distrust or fear. Past research, however, has found a strong tendency for individuals to trust other individuals when opportunities for communication are present (Insko et al., 1993; Insko & Schopler, 1998).

With the PDG the index is negative but can vary over a considerable range. In a 2 × 2 array the index can be manipulated by altering the ratio of the main effects. Consider the two PDG matrices in Figure 9.1. In the left-hand matrix the column main effect for the column player is 1 (10 vs 9 and 4 vs 3). This main effect is what Kelley and Thibaut (1978) refer to as "Reflexive Control" (RC), but Kelley et al. (2002) more recently label this as "Actor Control" (AC). On the other hand, the row main effect for the column players is 6 (9 vs 3 and 10 vs 4). This main effect was referred to by Kelley and Thibaut as "Fate Control" (FC), but is labelled "Partner Control (PC) by Kelley et al. Using the more recent terminology, the AC to PC ratio is 1/6. This ratio (for both players) produces a correlation of −.32.

Next consider the right-hand matrix in Figure 9.1. For this matrix the AC to PC ratio is 2/3 and the resultant correlation is −.92. Outcomes are more negatively correspondent for the right-hand matrix than for the left-hand matrix. Note that for the right-hand matrix the loss of 3 resulting from the partner's Z choice is contrasted with a gain of 2 resulting from an own Z choice. On the other hand, for the left-hand matrix the larger loss of 6 from the partner's Z choice is contrasted with a smaller gain of only 1 for an own Z choice.

Schopler et al. (2001) used the ratio of matrix main effects to vary the index of correspondence in four steps: −.92, −.60, −.32, and 0.[2] The results indicated that for groups, but not individuals, there was a linear decline in competitiveness as the index became less negative and approached 0. In fact, the discontinuity effect was nonsignificant and descriptively small when the index was 0.

A subsequent experiment by Wildschut et al. (2002, Experiment 2) also manipulated correspondence, but differed from the Schopler et al. (2001) experiment in several respects. For example, the experiment varied correspondence in only two levels (−.05 vs −.60) rather than four; the experiment involved only one trial rather than ten; the experiment only tested groups rather than group and individuals; the experimental groups consisted of five participants rather than three; the group members were seated in separate rooms rather than one room, and, as a consequence of the separate seating, reached a decision on the basis of a majority vote rather than agreed consensus. This experiment again found an effect of correspondence on intergroup competitiveness. Intergroup competition was greater with the more negative index. This experiment, however, went further and demonstrated that the reduced competitiveness of the less negative index could be partially overcome if the separated group members received social support for being competitive. In the no-social-support condition each of the five group members voted for the competitive or cooperative choice without knowledge of the votes of their fellow group members. In the social-support condition each group member voted third and believed that one of the other group members had voted to compete and one had voted to cooperate. In the social-support condition relative to the no-social-support condition competitiveness increased when correspondence was $-.05$, but not when correspondence was $-.60$ (i.e., there was a significant social support by correspondence interaction). Note that because one of the supposed votes by fellow group members was to compete and one was to cooperate, it is implausible that the increase in competitiveness was a simple conformity effect. Consistent with this argument, social support did not significantly increase the number of other group members who were expected to compete.

Further results came from mediational analyses. These analyses revealed that the tendency for social support to increase competitiveness in the $-.05$ correspondence matrix (the social support by correspondence interaction) was associated with a reported tendency to reduce the concern with the joint outcomes of both groups and to maximise the difference between ingroup and outgroup outcomes. An interpretation of this result is that the tendency of less negative correspondence to be associated with less competitiveness can be overcome when group members adopt a relativistic, social-comparative orientation, and that one cause of such an orientation is social support for competitiveness.

The obtained results for social support are possibly consistent with the theoretical argument that the effect of correspondence on intergroup competitiveness is due to the increasing social support for competitiveness produced by increasing negative correspondence. As Wildschut, Insko, and Gaertner point out, however, such consistency may require the additional assumption that social support for competitiveness in the context of near zero correspondence is particularly surprising and thus particularly likely to evoke questioning as to the reason for such a decision. The data suggest that the answer to such presumed questioning was relativistic social comparison; that is, the desire to be associated with the winning, or superior, group.

Wildschut et al. (2002) reported an additional experiment that did not manipulate correspondence but varied social support in the context of a matrix in which the correlation, or index of correspondence, was zero. This experiment again found an effect for social support, and mediational analyses again pointed to possible mediation by the desire to maximise relative differences between sides in one's own favour.

The Schopler et al. (2001) study and the Wildschut et al. (2002) study provide the only current experimental evidence relating to the correspondence effect. However, the Wildschut et al. (2003) meta-analysis did provide an opportunity to compare the results of reported experiments that had used different matrices with varying indices of correspondence. This analysis found that the more negative the index, the greater the discontinuity effect, and that this relationship was only significant for groups. When the conditions were optimal for producing a discontinuity effect (unconstrained communication between groups or individuals, unconstrained strategy by groups or individuals, and a group decision, rather than separate decisions by the individual group members, on each trial) the predicted effect size was 1.30 for an index of −.80 and 1.15 for an index of −.60. The obtained results provide an illustration of the fact that interdependence theory concepts do a better job of predicting intergroup relations than interindividual relations. Because game theory contains an index that makes predictions similar to those of the index of correspondence, Anatol Rapoport's (1967) index of cooperation, the same point also applies to game theory. As indicated above, Bornstein et al. (2004) have referred to the interesting possibility that game-theory predictions provide a better fit for intergroup than for interindividual relations.

Matrices differing in the magnitude of statistical interactions

While the above results might seem to settle the generality issue, it is important to note that the investigated matrices were either the PDG, or matrices similar to the PDG, in which the outcomes did not follow the above-mentioned statistical interaction pattern. Just as they placed major theoretical emphasis on the index of correspondence, so Kelley and Thibaut also placed major theoretical emphasis on matrices that differed in the presence or absence of statistical interactions. Kelley and Thibaut referred to matrices without interactions, or Behavioural Control (BC) in their language, as "exchange situations", and matrices with interactions as "coordination situations". More recently, Kelley et al. (2001) refer to matrix interactions as Joint Control (JC). (See the Kelley et al., 2001, discussion of coordination and exchange situations in their *Atlas of interpersonal situations*, pp. 18–23.)

So what should happen with matrices containing interactions? We have attempted to answer this question by looking at various possible matrices.

Anatol Rapoport and Guyer (1966) developed a well-known classification of 2 × 2 games by restricting attention to those games for which the ordinal relations among the payoffs are different. Using this ordinal assumption, Rapoport and Guyer demonstrated that there are exactly 78 possible games. Of these, 12 involve symmetric outcomes, and of the 12 symmetric matrices, 8 have similar patterns of payoffs for both players and thus are considered strategically uninteresting. This leaves four matrices—matrices that Rapoport and Guyer labelled Martyrs, Exploiter, Hero, and Leader. More conventional labels of the first three of the matrices are Prisoner's Dilemma Game, Chicken, and Battle of the Sexes (Colman, 1995). Examples of these matrices are presented in Figure 9.2.

Three of the matrices in Figure 9.2, Battle of the Sexes (BOS), Leader, and Chicken contain statistical interactions (JC), a difference in diagonal means. The classic example of the BOS matrix relates to the decisions a husband and wife make regarding how they spend their evening (Colman, 1995; Luce & Raiffa, 1957). In Luce and Raiffa's stereotyped example, the husband prefers going to a prizefight while the wife prefers going to the opera, but primarily both would prefer to be accompanied by the other rather than to attend either event alone. In Figure 9.2 the Y choice is the preferred choice of both spouses, but the highest outcome, 4, is only obtained when the partner selects his or her non-preferred choice. The cells in the upper-left to lower-right diagonal

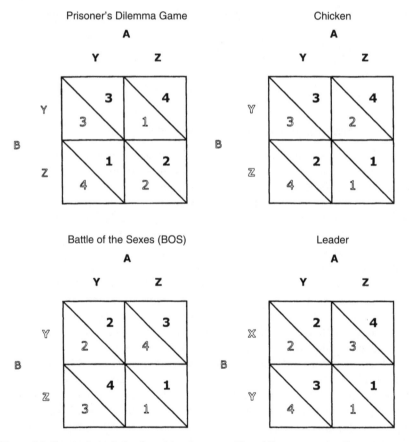

Figure 9.2 Examples of the four matrices considered important by Rapoport and Guyer (1966).

represent situations in which the spouses part company and attend different events, either the preferred events or non-preferred events. Maximisation of outcomes in the BOS matrix requires alternation between the cells in the lower-left to upper-right diagonal. Such alternation guarantees that the spouses are always together but take turns attending the preferred event.

Colman's (1995) example of the Leader matrix relates to the decisions that have to be made by two motorists that are both waiting to pull out into an intersection. If they pull out simultaneously a collision will occur; if they both wait they face an indefinite delay. The solution is for the "leader" to allow the other motorist to pull out first. In the context of repeated social interactions, this is again a matrix in which outcomes can be maximised through alternation.

Both the BOS and Leader matrices contain sizeable, identical interactions (2), and sizeable, identical correlations (+.80). For matrices such as these there is no obvious reason for groups and individuals to differ in the perceived advantage of alternation.

Poundstone (1992) credits Bertrand Russell (1959) with first using the example of the game of chicken as an illustration of what is labelled the "Chicken" matrix. The original game of "chicken run" from the movie *Rebel without a Cause* involved two teenagers driving their cars towards a cliff in order to see who would jump out first and thus be the "chicken". This movie was followed by many imitations, some of which adopted the variation of having the two teenagers drive their cars at each other in order to see who would swerve first. Russell adopted the latter example in what Poundstone characterises as the "canonical" game of chicken in game theory. Russell used the matrix to discuss the nuclear brinkmanship of the cold war.

Of the three Figure 9.2 matrices with statistical interactions, Chicken is, for present purposes, the most interesting. This is because Chicken has the smaller correlation (+.20 as opposed to +.80) and the smaller interaction (1 as opposed to 2), and these differences provide some reason for supposing that groups and individuals are more likely to differ with Chicken than with BOS and Leader.

The reason why groups and individuals might differ in the context of the Chicken matrix partially flows from interdependence theory's distinction between given and effective matrices. This distinction arose from the fact that matrices that were experimentally "given" did not always predict behaviour very well (McClintock, 1972). Kelley and Thibaut (1978, p. 16) do not pre-cisely define the term "given matrix," but began by giving an illustration. Here is the quote:

> For introductory purposes we propose to suggest the meaning of the *given* matrix by offering an illustration—the experimenter's game matrix. The experimenter specifies response choices and, in terms of kinds and quantities of incentive, the consequences of various combinations of choice.

Kelley and Thibaut then go on to indicate that the player's personal needs and other characteristics also play a role, and then state that: "The matrix is 'given' in the sense that the behavioral choices and the outcomes are strongly under the control of factors *external to the interdependence relationship itself*" (p. 16). This statement could be interpreted as implying that the given matrix relates solely to immediate self-interest. Kelley and Thibaut, however, do not quite go that far, possibly because, for example, in a parent–child relationship there may be an immediate self-interest in the outcomes of the child, along with, or even at the expense of, the parent's own individual cell preferences. Kelley et al. (2003), however, do offer the more clear-cut interpretation that the given matrix relates to the "'basic' person operating at the 'gut level' and solely concerned about immediate self-interest" (p. 75).[3]

Following McClintock's (1972) discussion, Kelley and Thibaut (1978) argue that the given matrix may be transformed to the effective matrix that actually controls behaviour. The transformation may occur through a concern with maximising the difference between own and other outcomes (max rel), a concern with minimising the difference between own and other outcomes (min diff), a concern with maximising joint own and other outcomes (max joint), or a concern with maximising the other's outcomes (max other). Despite the lack of conceptual clarity in the meaning of the given matrix, we as social observers are familiar with a transformation-like process. Kelley et al. (2003, p. 75) make this point rather well:

> As shown in everyday conversation, the phenomenon of "transformation" is widely recognized and understood. For example, we hear it said that "She's making a mountain out of a molehill," "He makes every game into a competitive contest," or "He treats her with more consideration than she deserves".

For present purposes the relevant question concerns the possibility of transformation of the given Chicken matrix to some kind of effective matrix. Interdependence theory primarily focuses on the matrix itself and, as a consequence, makes no predictions regarding the occurrence and type of transformation that should occur with particular people in particular situations. However, in the Kelley et al. (2003) chapter on Chicken (for which Norbert Kerr had primary responsibility) there is considerable discussion of the circumstances that might produce a "Death before Dishonour" transformation. Given our particular concern with the differences between groups and individuals, we find it particularly interesting that these circumstances include Bornstein, Budescu, and Zamir's (1997) finding that with an *n*-person version of Chicken, groups were more competitive than individuals.

If the "death before dishonour" transformation occurs with the ordinal Chicken matrix of Figure 9.2 (i.e., the payoff of "2" is transformed into a lower outcome than the payoff of "1", effectively "1" and "2" switch places), the given matrix is transformed to an effective PDG matrix. Assuming this happens, the effective matrix has a negative correspondence equal to that of the ordinal PDG ($r = -.80$). Due to the lack of explicit social support, however, such a transformation is less likely with individuals than with groups.

Why might groups be more competitive than individuals in the context of a Chicken matrix? Certainly no one of the three above hypotheses explicitly relates to the possibility that honour is of greater concern than death. However, the greed or social support for shared self-interest hypothesis could be interpreted as relevant to the concern with honour. How is this possible? Note that, as found in the above-described Wildschut et al. (2002) study, social support in the context of non-polarised correspondence in the PDG matrix can produce a concern with max rel, that is, a concern with obtaining relatively higher outcomes. Further note that relatively higher outcomes may suggest winning, superiority, higher status, and even honour. Quite possibly the same might be true of the Chicken matrix.

In a recently completed study we compared the choices of groups and individuals for each of the four matrices (PDG, Chicken, BOS, Leader) across a number of trials. The matrices were the Figure 9.2 matrices in which the outcomes were multiplied by 10 US cents. A procedural complexity here involves how to score the choices for cooperation, or competition, when cooperation may occur through alternation of the Y and Z choices. Note from Figure 9.2 that if the two players alternate Y and Z choices rather than make mutual Y choices, outcomes are reduced with the PDG (4 plus 1 is less than 3 plus 3), remain the same with Chicken (4 plus 2 equals 3 plus 3), but are increased with BOS and with Leader (3 plus 4 is greater than 2 plus 2). In the past we have noted occasional instances of such alternation with the PDG, and have scored the sequence as cooperation if this alternation was explicitly agreed upon and conformed to. In the present experiment alternation was only slightly greater with Chicken than with the PDG, but was very common with BOS and with Leader. In all instances such alternation was scored as cooperation—consistent with obvious intent.

After correcting for alternation the results revealed, in addition to a main effect for groups versus individuals, an interaction with type of matrix such that the tendency of groups to be more competitive (or less cooperative) than individuals was larger, and only significant, for the PDG and Chicken. There was no reason to expect a difference between BOS and Leader and, in fact, the difference was not significant. On the other hand, the tendency of groups to be more competitive than individuals was greater for the PDG than for Chicken. Still, the smaller difference for Chicken was significant. The interesting result here is that with Chicken there was a discontinuity effect. Although perhaps surprising, a similar result was previously obtained by Bornstein et al. (1997) with an *n*-person version of Chicken.

Mediational analyses revealed that the tendency for the PDG and Chicken matrices to show a larger discontinuity effect than BOS and Leader matrices might have been due to more max rel with the former matrices. These results are consistent with a possible max rel transformation and thus a possible involvement of status and honour for Chicken and also the PDG.

The significant discontinuity effect for Chicken clearly indicates that it is incorrect to only expect groups to be more competitive than individuals when the index of correspondence is negative. How then shall we generalise about the occurrence of the discontinuity effect when the index is positive? One possibility is to use the magnitude of the interaction. Note that the discontinuity effect did not occur with BOS and Leader and these matrices have larger interactions than Chicken (see Figure 9.2). The problem here, of course, is that BOS and Leader also have more positive correlations. Still, we find it plausible that a larger interaction would make the advantage of alternating cooperation more obvious. In order to follow this suggestion, we conducted an experiment that varied the magnitude of the interaction across two different versions of the Chicken matrix but held the index of correspondence constant. The investigated matrices are presented in Figure 9.3. Note that both matrices had correlations of +.20, but one matrix had an interaction of 60 and one an interaction of 15. As expected, the discontinuity effect was absent for the Chicken matrix with the larger interaction, but not for the Chicken matrix with the smaller interaction (that is, a significant groups vs individuals by matrix interaction was obtained). It would appear that column groups become reluctant to risk the potential benefit of the Z choice in the top row as the interaction becomes greater and the Z choice in the bottom row yields a lower and lower outcome. In addition, mediational analyses of the groups versus individuals by matrix interaction were consistent with max rel as a mediator of competition. Groups were more relativistic than individuals with the low-interaction matrix. Overall the results provide support for the cold war doctrine of "mutually assured destruction" (Kissinger, 1956; Wohlstetter, 1959)—a result that we consider important and even fascinating.

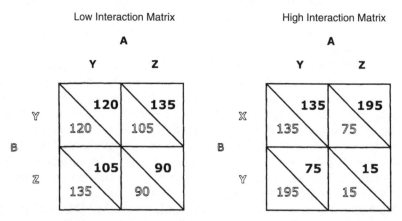

Figure 9.3 Two Chicken matrices with equal correspondence ($r = +.20$) but interactions of varying magnitude.

Three tentative conclusions

The above research provides some tentative basis for assuming a role for three situational variables affecting the presence and magnitude of the discontinuity effect. These are: first, the degree of correspondence (the correlation between the players' outcomes across the cells of the matrix), second, joint control of outcomes (the magnitude of the statistical interaction in the 2 × 2 array), third, social support for the competitive choice. The first two of these variables relate to the nature of the matrix and rely directly on interdependence theory concepts. The third does not relate to the nature of the matrix and is less directly related to interdependence theory.

The evidence for correspondence comes from the above-described two experiments and the meta-analysis. As the degree of correspondence becomes more negative, or the correlation becomes increasingly negative, the magnitude of the discontinuity effect increases. This effect could be interpreted as a function of the objective situation, or as a function of the "given" matrix.

To the extent that degree of correspondence relates to the objective situation, the postulated role for this index has an interesting parallel with Campbell's (1965) realistic-group-conflict theory. According to Campbell, intergroup conflict and ethnocentrism arise from conflict over objectively scarce resources such as territorial possessions, jobs, or political power. According to Campbell, "The observation that outgroup threat to the ingroup increases individual hostility toward the outgroup and individual loyalty is certainly one of the most agreed-upon observations of descriptive, non-experimental social science" (1965, p. 292). To the extent that this evidence complements the above experimental and meta-analytic evidence, support for the postulated role for degree of correspondence is greater than initially might have been assumed.

When the index of correspondence is zero and there is no conflict of interest, one might assume that there would be no discontinuity effect. While this assumption may have some validity in an exchange situation when there is no social support for competitiveness, it does not appear to hold in a coordination situation. In a coordination situation there is joint control of outcomes due to the presence of a statistical interaction. The evidence suggests that if the interaction is relatively small, even if the correlation is positive, a discontinuity effect can occur. This is, perhaps, the most tentative of the three conclusions, but the evidence from a single experiment suggests that with a larger interaction the discontinuity effect will no longer be significant. Presumably it is the increasingly low value of the bottom-right-hand cell that decreases the tendency to compete—consistent with the cold war doctrine of "mutually assured destruction" (Kissinger, 1956; Wohlstetter, 1959).

The third tentative conclusion regarding social support for competitiveness is potentially a qualification of both of the prior conclusions. The evidence from two experiments suggested that even with 0 or −.05 correlations, social support for competitiveness created a discontinuity effect. Stated less technic- ally, even when there was no objective basis for conflict, social support for competitiveness created conflict. Recognise, further, that the social support was not a simple conformity effect, because even though one of the prior group members had voted to compete, one had voted to cooperate. Why should such seemingly minimal support for competitiveness have an effect in a situation in which there was no objective basis for competing? A suggested answer comes from the fact that in both experiments there was evidence for the mediation of the social-support effect by max rel, or a concern with winning. This evidence in turn suggests that the influence of even minimal social support flows from consistency with self-esteem. Being a member of a superior group is consistent with positive self-evaluation. Such an interpret- ation is in agreement with the evidence of Gramzow and Gaertner (2005) that individual differences in self-esteem were correlated with the evaluation of novel ingroups and that this relationship held even when the behaviour of ingroup members was more negative than the behaviour of outgroup members.

If a consistency-with-self-esteem interpretation of the social-support effect is correct, then one might predict that social support would also qualify the effect of joint control; that is, that social support would produce a disconti- nuity effect even with a larger statistical interaction. Currently, there is no evidence for such a prediction and we get no comfort from considering the possibility that social support could lead to the risking of mutually assured destruction. On the other hand, one would hope that the grim prospect of mutually assured destruction would reduce the power of what could only be considered insane social support.

Conclusions

Interindividual–intergroup discontinuity is the tendency in the context of some social situations for relations between groups to be more competitive, or less cooperative, than relations between individuals. A meta-analysis has found that the effect is descriptively large, and it was argued that an under- standing of the circumstances in which this effect occurs is of obvious social significance. After considering various issues, such as whether this effect has been found outside the US and possible mechanisms responsible for the effect, the chapter focused on three situational variables that impact the generality of the effect. The first of these is the correspondence of outcomes (the correlation between the players' outcomes across the cells of the matrix). The second is the joint control of outcomes (the magnitude of the statistical interaction in the 2 × 2 array). The third is social support for the competitive choice.

Two experimental studies and a meta-analysis provide consistent evidence that for exchange matrices (matrices without statistical interactions) the dis- continuity effect decreases as the degree of correspondence becomes less and less negative. In fact, as the negative correspondence approaches zero the discontinuity effect becomes nonsignificant.

To explore the effect of statistical interaction, an experiment was completed in which the PDG, a matrix with no statistical interaction, was compared with three matrices, Chicken, Battle of the Sexes, and Leader, which do have statistical interaction, as well as positive correlations. These four matrices have received particular attention in the game-theory literature because, of all the possible matrices, they are the ones considered most theoretically interesting. With matrices containing statistical interactions the basic situation changes from one of exchange to one of coordination, because with such matrices outcomes are maximised through alternation or turn taking. The experiment revealed that the discontinuity effect was larger, and only significant, with the PDG and Chicken. The results were interpreted as indicating that the discontinuity effect with Chicken was due to the fact that the matrix has a smaller statistical interaction. This interpretation was supported with a further experiment demonstrating that the discontinuity effect decreased and became nonsignificant as the statistical interaction increased in magnitude. The results were interpreted as due to the fact that with a larger statistical interaction the bottom-right-hand cell becomes lower in magnitude and this made the group members reluctant to risk a competitive choice. On the other hand, when the statistical interaction was of lesser magnitude group members were willing to risk being competitive in order to achieve relative superiority—consistent with a max rel transformation to an "effective" matrix in which there is, indeed, negative correspondence. A mediation analysis yielded results consistent with this speculation.

A possible reason why group members are willing to take risks is the social support that they may provide each other for a competitive choice. This interpretation was based on a finding that when the degree of negative correspondence with the PDG approached zero, the tendency towards a smaller discontinuity effect was overcome with an experimental manipulation of social support for the competitive choice. If this can happen with matrices like the PDG with no statistical interactions, it was finally speculated that it might also happen with matrices, like Chicken, in which there is a statistical interaction.

Notes

1 A technical complexity here is that the argument concerning conflict of interest does not apply to the simple difference between cooperative and competitive choices when the index is polarised at either +1 or −1. Why is that? With a +1 correlation the "Y" choice does not benefit one player over the other and hence cannot involve competitive intent. With a −1 correlation mutual "X" choices do not benefit both players more than mutual the "Y" choice and hence cannot involve cooperative intent.
2 With a zero index of correspondence the matrix is not a PDG, but what Kelley and Thibaut (1978) refer to as a Mutual-Fate Control (MFC) matrix.

3 From the perspective of socio-biology (Wilson, 1957) the given matrix might be considered a matrix in which there is an immediate reaction either to the self or to genetically related kin. Such a perspective, however, would not obviously account for the fact that in military situations soldiers sometimes act in a self-sacrificial manner, for example by falling on a hand grenade. Another possibility would be to define the given matrix in terms of the preference of the average person outside the interdependent relationship. Such an approach would abandon the assumption that the given matrix always involves more immediate reactions than the effective matrix, but the distinction between immediate and delayed reactions would still be an interesting cross-cutting variable (cf. Yovetich & Rusbult, 1994).

References

Allport, F. H. (1920). The influence of the group upon association and thought. *Journal of Experimental Psychology*, *3*, 159–182.

Allport, F. H. (1924). *Social psychology*. Boston: Houghton-Mifflin.

Allport, F. H. (1962). A structuronomic concept of behavior: Individual and collective; 1. Structural theory and the master problem of social psychology. *Journal of Abnormal and Social Psychology*, *64*, 1–30.

Allport, G. W. (1985). The historical background of social psychology. In G. Lindzey & E. Aronson (Eds.), *The handbook of social psychology* (Vol. 1, pp. 1–46). New York: Random House.

Bornstein, G., Budescu, D., & Zamir, S. (1997). Cooperation in intergroup, n-person, and two-person games of chicken. *Journal of Conflict Resolution*, *41*, 384–406.

Bornstein, G., Kugler, T., & Ziegelmeyer, A. (2004). Individual and group decisions in the centipede game: Are groups more "rational" players? *Journal of Experimental Social Psychology*, *5*, 599–606.

Campbell, D. T. (1965). Ethnocentrism and other altruistic motives. In D. Levine (Ed.), *Nebraska symposium on motivation* (Vol. 13, pp. 283–311). Lincoln, NE: University of Nebraska Press.

Colman, A. M. (1995). *Game theory and its application in the social and biological sciences*. London: Butterworth-Heinemann.

Diehl, M., & Stroebe, W. (1991). Productivity loss in idea-generating groups. *Journal of Personality and Social Psychology*, *61*, 392–403.

Durkheim, E. (1898). Représentations individuelles et représentations collectives. *Revue de Metaphysique*, *6*, 274–302.

Freud, S. (1922). *Group psychology and the analysis of the ego* (Trans. J. S., 1960). New York: Bantam Books.

Gouldner, A. W. (1960). The norm of reciprocity: A preliminary statement. *American Sociological Review*, *25*, 161–178.

Gramzow, R., & Gaertner, L. G. (2005). Self-esteem and favoritism toward novel ingroups: The self as an evaluative base. *Journal of Personality and Social Psychology*, *88*, 801–815.

Horwitz, M., & Rabbie, J. M. (1982). Individuality and membership in the intergroup system. In H. Tajfel (Ed.), *Social identity and intergroup relations* (pp. 241–274). New York: Cambridge University Press.

Hoyle, R. H., Pinkley, R. L., & Insko, C. A. (1989). Perceptions of behavior: Evidence of differing expectations for interpersonal and intergroup interactions. *Personality and Social Psychology Bulletin*, *15*, 365–376.

Insko, C. A., & Schopler, J. (1998). Differential distrust of groups and individuals. In C. Sedikides, J. Schopler, & C. A. Insko (Eds.), *Intergroup cognition and intergroup behavior* (pp. 75–108). Mahwah, NJ: Lawrence Erlbaum Associates Inc.

Insko, C. A., Schopler, J., Drigotas, S. M., Graetz, K., Kennedy, J., Cox, C. et al. (1993). The role of communication in interindividual–intergroup discontinuity. *Journal of Conflict Resolution, 37*, 108–138.

Insko, C. A., Schopler, J., Hoyle, R. H., Dardis, G. J., & Graetz, K. A. (1990). Individual–group discontinuity as a function of fear and greed. *Journal of Personality and Social Psychology, 58*, 68–79.

Kelley, H. H., Holmes, J. G., Kerr, N. L., Reis, H. T., Rusbult, C. E., & Van Lange, P. A. M. (2003). *An atlas of interpersonal situations*. Cambridge, UK: Cambridge University Press.

Kelley, H. H., & Thibaut, J. W. (1978). *Interpersonal relations*. New York: Wiley.

Kissinger, H. A. (1956). Force and diplomacy in the nuclear age. *Foreign Affairs, 34*, 349–366.

Latané, B., & Darley, J. M. (1970). *The unresponsive bystander: Why doesn't he help?* New York: Appleton-Century Crofts.

Latané, B., Williams, K., & Harkins, S. (1979). Many hands make light the work: The causes and consequences of social loafing. *Journal of Personality and Social Psychology, 37*, 822–832.

LeBon, G. (1895). *The crowd*. London: Unwin. [Original work published 1895.]

Lind, E. A., & Tyler, T. R. (1988). *The social psychology of procedural justice*. New York: Plenum Press.

Luce, R. D., & Raiffa, H. (1957). *Games and decisions: Introduction and critical survey*. New York: Wiley.

McCallum, D. M., Harring, K., Gilmore, R., Drenan, S., Chase, J., Insko, C. A. et al. (1985). Competition between groups and between individuals. *Journal of Experimental Social Psychology, 21*, 301–320.

McClintock, C. G. (1972). Social motivation—a set of propositions. *Behavioral Science, 17*, 438–454.

McDougall, W. (1920). *The group mind*. Cambridge, UK: Cambridge University Press.

McGuire, P. A. (1998, August). Historic conference focuses on creating a new discipline. *APA Monitor, 29*, 1 & 15.

Pemberton, M. J., Insko, C. A., & Schopler, J. (1996). Memory for and experience of differential competitive behavior of individuals and groups. *Journal of Personality and Social Psychology, 71*, 953–966.

Plato. (1891). Republic (F. Cornford, Trans.). In B. Jowett (Ed.), *The dialogues of Plato* (Vol. 3, pp. 1–338). Oxford, UK: Oxford University Press.

Poundstone, W. (1992). *Prisoner's dilemma*. New York: Anchor Books.

Rabbie, J. M., & Lodewijkx, H. G. M. (1994). Conflict and aggression: An individual–group continuum. In B. Markovsky, K. Heimer, & J. O'Brien (Eds.), *Advances in group processes* (Vol. 11, pp. 139–174). Greenwich, CT: JAI Press.

Rapoport, An. (1967). A note on the "index of cooperation" for prisoner's dilemma. *Journal of Conflict Resolution, 11*, 101–103.

Rapoport, An., & Guyer, M. (1966). A taxonomy of 2 × 2 games. *General Systems, 11*, 203–214.

Reis, H. R., & Wheeler, L. (1991). Studying social interaction with the Rochester interaction record. In M. P. Zanna (Ed.), *Advances in experimental social psychology* (Vol. 24, pp. 269–318). New York: Academic Press.

Schopler, J., Insko, C. A., Graetz, K. A., Drigotas, S. M., & Smith, V. A. (1991). The generality of the individual–group discontinuity effect: Variations in positivity–negativity of outcomes, players' relative power, and magnitude of outcomes. *Personality and Social Psychology Bulletin, 17*, 612–624.

Schopler, J., Insko, C. A., Graetz, K. A., Drigotas, S., Smith, V. A., & Dahl, K. (1993). Individual–group discontinuity: Further evidence for mediation by fear and greed. *Personality and Social Psychology Bulletin, 19*, 419–431.

Schopler, J., Insko, C. A., Wieselquist, J., Pemberton, M., Witcher, B., Kozar, R. et al. (2001). When groups are more competitive than individuals: The domain of the discontinuity effect. *Journal of Personality and Social Psychology, 80*, 632–644.

Shaw, C. (1932). A comparison of individuals and small groups in the rational solution of complex problems. *American Journal of Psychology, 54*, 491–504.

Takemura, K., & Yuki, M. (2004). *Are intergroup relations competitive in Japan? A test of interindividual–intergroup discontinuity effect in a "collectivist" society.* Unpublished manuscript.

Thibaut, J., & Walker, L. (1975). *Procedural justice.* New York: John Wiley & Sons.

Thibaut, J. W., & Kelley, H. H. (1959). *The social psychology of groups.* New York: John Wiley & Sons, Inc.

Wildschut, T., Insko, C. A., & Gaertner, L. (2002). Intragroup social influence and intergroup competition. *Journal of Personality and Social Psychology, 82*, 975–992.

Wildschut, T., Insko, C. A., & Pinter, B. (2004). The perception of outgroup threat: Content and activation of the outgroup schema. In V. Yzerbyt, V. Judd, & O. Corneille (Eds.), *The psychology of group perception: Contributions to the study of homogeneity, entitativity, and essentialism.* Philadelphia, PA: Psychology Press.

Wildschut, T., Lodewijkx, H. F. M., & Insko, C. A. (2001). Toward a reconciliation of diverging perspectives on interindividual–intergroup discontinuity: The role of procedural interdependence. *Journal of Experimental Social Psychology, 37*, 273–285.

Wildschut, T., Pinter, B., Vevea, J. L., Insko, C. A., & Schopler, J. (2003). Beyond the group mind: A quantitative review of the interindividual–intergroup discontinuity effect. *Psychological Bulletin, 129*, 698–722.

Wilson, E. (1975). *Sociobiology.* Cambridge, MA: Harvard University Press.

Wohlstetter, A. (1959). The delicate balance of terror. *Foreign Affairs, 37*, 211–234.

Yovetich, N. A., & Rusbult, C. E. (1994). Accommodative behavior in close relationships: Exploring transformation of motivation. *Journal of Experimental Social Psychology, 30*, 138–164.

10 Group creativity and the stages of creative problem solving

Bernard A. Nijstad
University of Amsterdam, The Netherlands

John M. Levine
University of Pittsburgh, USA

Everybody probably agrees that people like Einstein, Edison, or Van Gogh were extremely creative. Many people are fascinated with these creative geniuses, and a large psychological literature exists that aims to explain why some people are more creative than others (see, e.g., Simonton, 1999). As a consequence of this fascination with highly creative people, creativity is often conceived to be an individual-level phenomenon (e.g., the "lone genius"). Mumford and Gustafson (1988, p. 28), for example, define creativity as:

> . . . a syndrome involving a number of elements: (a) the processes under-lying the *individual's* capacity to generate new ideas or understandings, (b) the characteristics of the *individual* facilitating process operation, (c) the characteristics of the *individual* facilitating the translation of these ideas into action, (d) the attributes of the situation conditioning the *individual's* willingness to engage in creative behavior, and (e) the attrib-utes of the situation influencing evaluation of the *individual's* productive efforts [italics added].

This fascination with highly creative people is often coupled with the assumption that groups cannot be creative. As Alfred Whitney Griswold (1906–1963), a US historian, said:

> Could Hamlet have been written by a committee, the Mona Lisa painted by a club? Could the New Testament have been composed as a confer-ence report? Creative ideas don't spring from groups. They spring from individuals.[1]

Similarly, in psychology a long-standing idea is that crowds reduce rational thought, lead to slavish conformity, and leave no room for independent, creative thought (e.g., LeBon, 1895). Indeed, some authors see individual reflection and social isolation as the key elements in creative achievement (e.g., Ochse, 1990; Simonton, 1988).

These assumptions can be challenged, however. Oftentimes creativity involves the cooperation of several minds (Levine & Moreland, 2004; Stroebe, Diehl, & Abakoumkin, 1992; see also Farrell, 2001; John-Steiner, 2000). One recently studied example is the making of feature films (Simonton, 2004). As can easily be seen in film credits, directors cannot make movies without the creative input of actors, screenwriters, art directors, costume designers, composers, and many others. Using data from 1327 movies made between 1968 and 1999, Simonton (2004) found that collaboration within the "dramatic cluster", consisting of director, actors, screenwriters, and film editors, was especially important for a film's artistic success. Indeed, one can argue that a "lone genius" could never make a great movie without the inputs of a number of other creative people.

In this chapter we consider creativity in groups (see Levine & Moreland, 2004; Nijstad, Rietzschel, & Stroebe, 2006; Paulus & Nijstad, 2003; Stroebe & Diehl, 1994; Thompson & Choi, 2006). In particular we address the question of how group interaction might relate to the creativity of a final product (or set of products). Can group interaction be helpful during the creative process? If so, when will this be the case? Like many authors (e.g., Amabile, 1996; Osborn, 1963; Parnes, 1992; West, 2002), we assume that creativity does not consist of one single act. Rather, we distinguish three stages in the creative process: problem finding, idea finding, and solution finding (Osborn, 1963). In each of these stages, some form of collaboration may occur, and we examine the (possible) effects of group collaboration for each stage. In doing so, we pay special attention to a specific kind of group member: newcomers. We will argue that newcomers can play a unique role in the creative process (see Levine, Choi, & Moreland, 2003). Before we discuss the first stage, problem finding, we must clarify what we mean by "group creativity".

What is group creativity?

Creativity can be defined as the introduction of ideas that are both novel and useful (e.g., Amabile, 1996; Diehl & Stroebe, 1987; Mayer, 1999). Although originality or novelty is often seen as the hallmark of creativity, it is essential that an idea is also useful or appropriate—otherwise it would just be unusual or even bizarre. Some authors make the distinction between "big C creativity" and "little c creativity" (e.g., Simonton, 2004). In big C creativity, creative products have a genuine impact on culture or society—this is the type of creativity we associate with Einstein or Van Gogh (or movies such as *The Wizard of Oz* or *Star Wars*). Little c creativity occurs when people solve rather mundane problems at home or at work (or in the psychological laboratory). Ideas in this latter category do not need to be novel in an absolute sense, as long as they are novel to the person who introduces them. Most of the studies we review are studies of little c creativity. However, we assume that by and large the same processes underlie big C creativity (as in the making of a classic movie).

We talk about *group* creativity when group interaction took place during the creative process and when the final product or products could not have been completed without the input of different group members. Sometimes a group of people collaboratively work towards one (creative) end product, as in the case of movie makers producing feature films or R&D project teams developing new products (e.g., Cohen & Bailey, 1997). In other cases groups or teams do not work towards one specific end product, but do occasionally collaborate in (at least one of the stages of) the creative act. An example would be a team of scientists who work on some projects together but not on others (e.g., Dunbar, 1995, 1997). It is important to realise that in all these cases collaboration does not mean that people *always* work as a group— rather, some activities (e.g., writing the screenplay) are performed individually, whereas others are performed as a group (e.g., shooting the movie).

Group problem finding

Problem finding is the process of defining the goals and objectives of the problem-solving effort and designing a plan to structure and direct problem solving (Reiter-Palmon, Mumford, O'Connor Boes, & Runco, 1997). The importance of problem finding can be illustrated with the following example (taken from Getzels, 1982, p. 38):

> An automobile is traveling on a deserted country road and blows a tire. The occupants of the automobile go to the trunk and discover that there is no jack. They define their dilemma by posing the problem: "Where can we get a jack?" They look about, see some empty barns but no habitation, and recall that, several miles back they had passed a service station. They decide to walk back to the station to get a jack. While they are gone, an automobile coming from the other direction also blows a tire. The occupants of this automobile go to the trunk and discover that there is no jack. They define their dilemma by posing the problem: "How can we raise the automobile?" They look around and see, adjacent to the road, a barn with a pulley for lifting bales of hay to the loft. They move the automobile to the barn, raise it on the pulley, change the tire, and drive off.

The example nicely illustrates that how the problem is defined will determine what solutions will be found. It has consequently been argued that the stage of problem finding (or problem identification) is the most important stage of the creative process (e.g., Reiter-Palmon et al., 1997).

Despite its importance, not many studies have addressed the issue of problem finding. There are, however, some studies at the individual level, the most famous of which is Getzels and Csikszentmihalyi's (1976) study of young artists. They invited art students to a studio and asked them to make a drawing. In the studio was a table on which there were 27 objects, such as a small manikin, a bunch of grapes, and a brass horn. There was also one empty table. The students were asked to arrange the objects on the empty table and then make a drawing they liked. While they were working on this, a researcher observed their behaviour. Getzels and Csikszentmihalyi found that those students who took more time looking at the different objects, feeling them, and arranging them in different ways eventually made drawings of higher creativity (as judged by different sets of expert and lay judges). The investigators argued that people who take more time defining and constructing a problem are subsequently more creative.

Problem finding at the group level has also been neglected (see Moreland & Levine, 1992). However, there is some relevant evidence. For example, Dunbar (1995) studied teams of researchers (microbiologists). He attended their weekly lab meetings and found that many of their discussions focused on unexpected and inconsistent findings. Of course, these anomalies present scientific problems and (sometimes) force one to reconsider one's theories. Interestingly, Dunbar observed that this often led to a revision of a hypothesis. Further, he noted that major revisions and conceptual changes rarely occurred outside these lab meetings. Whereas individuals tended to discard anomalous evidence or hope that inconsistencies would go away, groups tended to focus on inconsistent findings during meetings, which sometimes led to conceptual change and real discoveries. Dunbar's observations therefore point at the interesting possibility that groups might be especially suited for problem finding or for identifying those problems that are really important.

Although systematic work on group problem finding has been sparse, several authors have commented on the importance of this process to group productivity. Perhaps the most comprehensive analysis of problem identification at the group level was offered by Moreland and Levine (1992). They argued, for example, that a group's success in identifying a problem will be influenced by characteristics of (a) the problem (e.g., its severity, familiarity, and complexity), (b) the group (e.g., its problem-solving norms, propensity to scan the environment, and level of performance), and (c) the environment (e.g., its uncertainty, the presence of outgroups, and the involvement of outsiders). In addition, they suggested that the likelihood of particular members identifying group problems will vary as a function of several individual characteristics, including status, expertise, commitment, and personality. Finally, they suggested several response options available to people who identify a problem, including denying and distorting the problem, hiding the problem, waiting and watching the problem, trying to solve the problem alone, seeking assistance from other group members, and soliciting outside involvement.

In addition to arguing that groups may be especially suited for finding problems, we suggest that newcomers may play a special role when it comes to problem identification. Why might this be? For one thing, because newcomers have not spent time using the group's task strategy, their commitment to it may be low, which in turn may allow them to be relatively "objective" in identifying problems with it. This may be particularly true if newcomers had prior experience in other groups that used different (and perhaps more successful) strategies. In addition, the fact that newcomers have relatively distant personal relationships with older members may make it easier for them to be objective in identifying problems with these members' task performance. It is important to note, however, that these factors do not guarantee that newcomers will reveal the problems they discover to older members. As noted above, people who identify problems in groups have various options for responding to them, some of which involve saying nothing. Given that newcomers are often anxious about how they will be treated by older members (Moreland & Levine, 1989), it would not be surprising if they often kept their concerns about problems to themselves.

Group idea finding

Group idea finding is concerned with finding alternative solutions to a problem. Contrary to problem finding, a fairly large research literature exists on group idea finding (for reviews, see Lamm & Trommsdorff, 1973; Paulus, Dugosh, Dzindolet, Coskun, & Putman, 2002; Stroebe & Diehl, 1994). Let us briefly summarise the major findings.

Research on group idea generation began in the 1950s. In 1953 Alex Osborn, an advertising executive, suggested a technique called "brainstorming" to improve the creativity of groups. He argued that creativity is enhanced considerably when group members adhere to some simple rules. One rule, based on the notion that "quantity breeds quality", is that people should try to generate as many ideas as possible, because generating more ideas increases the chance that good ideas are among them. A second rule is that idea generation and idea evaluation should be strictly separated ("deferment of judgement"). Osborn argued that when people are concerned with negative evaluation of their ideas, they become less creative and are hesitant to mention their more unusual ideas. Research has generally confirmed that Osborn was right: Quantity does lead to quality, and a concern with negative evaluation does have a detrimental effect on creativity (see, e.g., Bartis, Szymanski, & Harkins, 1988; Camacho & Paulus, 1995; Diehl & Stroebe, 1987).

One question that has received a lot of research attention is whether groups are better idea generators than individuals. To answer this question, researchers have compared the performance of real groups with the performance of "nominal" groups, in which people work separately and their nonredundant ideas are pooled after the session. If group interaction facilitates performance, real groups (in which people can hear each other's ideas) should outperform nominal groups. However, it has consistently been found that nominal groups generate more total ideas and more good ideas than do real groups of the same size (e.g., Diehl & Stroebe, 1987; Mullen, Johnson, & Salas, 1991; Taylor, Berry, & Block, 1958). This so-called *productivity loss* of real groups is quite large, and the difference between real and nominal groups increases with group size. Thus, contrary to what many people think, group interaction not only fails to stimulate, but actually inhibits, idea generation.

There are several reasons why this is the case, but the most important cause of the productivity loss found in brainstorming groups is "production blocking" (Diehl & Stroebe, 1987, 1991). Production blocking arises because people in interacting groups have to take turns when expressing their ideas, since usually only one person speaks at any given time. Thus, group members must often wait for their turns, and this directly interferes with their ability to generate and express ideas (Nijstad, Stroebe, & Lodewijkx, 2003). Obviously, this is not a problem when working alone in a nominal group.

If production blocking is so important, it can be expected that eliminating blocking, by using procedures that do not require turn taking, will reduce the productivity loss. This is indeed the case: If ideas are not shared orally but rather on pieces of paper ("brainwriting") or through computers ("electronic brainstorming"), and turn taking is not necessary, productivity loss disappears (e.g., Gallupe, Bastianutti, & Cooper, 1991). Even more interesting is recent evidence that sometimes *productivity gains* can be found: Writing or electronic groups with idea sharing outperformed individuals who could not read each other's ideas (e.g., Dennis & Valacich, 1993; Paulus & Yang, 2000). Thus, in the absence of production blocking, the ideas of others can be stimulating (see also Dugosh, Paulus, Roland, & Yang, 2000; Nijstad, Stroebe, & Lodewijkx, 2002).

Recently, Choi and Thompson (2006) obtained evidence that newcomers can stimulate idea generation in brainstorming groups. In their first study, they initially had three-person teams perform an idea-generation task. Then they either did or did not change the team's composition by randomly replacing one member with a person from another team. On a second idea-generation task, teams with new members generated more unique ideas and more conceptually different kinds of ideas than did teams without new members. In their second study, which used similar procedures, Choi and Thompson again found more creativity when newcomers were present rather than absent. In addition, they found that the entry of newcomers increased the creativity of older members in the team.

Now what do these findings imply for group creativity? Some time ago researchers advised people not to use groups for idea generation: "the emphatic conclusion to be drawn from the findings of the research reported here [. . .] is that group sessions should not be used to generate ideas" (Diehl & Stroebe, 1991, p. 402). It has become clear, however, that this advice was premature: Groups can be effective when it comes to idea generation, as long as production blocking is eliminated. Further, being exposed to the ideas of others, including newcomers, can stimulate idea generation. Therefore, it seems that some forms of group interaction can be useful during idea generation.

Rather than continue to focus on the question of *whether* groups should be used for idea generation, researchers should focus on *when* to use groups

(Nijstad et al., 2006). Thus, although it may not be productive to generate all of one's ideas in a group, interaction with other group members at some point in the process might be helpful. For example, after some time generating ideas alone there almost inevitably comes a moment in which one gets stuck. Input from other group members might be very valuable in that case. Indeed, it has been found that group members can keep each other going during brainstorming, producing longer periods of idea generation than occur when individuals work alone (Nijstad, Stroebe, & Lodewijkx, 1999). In other words, whereas idea generation is something that can be done by an individual, we would suggest that at times it is helpful to turn to other group members (such as newcomers) for some input.

Group solution finding

Finding ideas is not the end of the creative process. Some ideas are better than others, and the good ideas have to be selected for further development, while the bad ideas have to be rejected. But that is not the end of the story either. Others might have to be convinced of the usefulness of certain ideas, and the chosen ideas have to be implemented. How does group interaction affect this process of solution finding and implementation?

Like problem finding, solution finding has long been ignored. However, recently this has begun to change. Thus, some researchers have asked themselves: What happens after a brainstorming session? Three studies have compared groups and individuals in terms of their idea selection performance (Faure, 2004; Putman & Paulus, 2003; Rietzschel, Nijstad, & Stroebe, 2006). In these studies, people first generated ideas either as individuals or in groups, after which they were asked to select their best ideas for further development. The quality of the selected ideas was then determined by having independent judges rate these ideas on different quality dimensions, including originality (the extent to which the idea is novel or unusual) and feasibility (the extent to which an idea can be implemented and contribute to solving a certain problem; cf. our earlier definition of creativity).

Theoretically, idea selection performance (i.e., the quality of the selected idea) depends on two factors: the extent to which ideas of high quality were generated in the idea generation stage, and the extent to which the best ideas are selected in the selection stage (see Rietzschel, Nijstad, & Stroebe, 2005). Thus, when no good ideas have been generated, it is not possible to select good ideas. Alternatively, if good ideas have been generated but are not selected, the quality of the selected ideas is below what would have been possible.

As we discussed in the previous section, members of interacting groups generally generate fewer ideas (and fewer high-quality ideas) than do members of nominal groups. For example, after a brainstorming session, a group of three will have fewer high-quality ideas available to it than will three individuals who worked separately during idea generation (i.e., a nominal group). Does this difference also imply that groups choose ideas of lower quality than do individuals? Both Faure (2004) and Putman and Paulus (2003) investigated this question. In both studies, three-person groups generated ideas together and then selected their best ideas as a group. The results were compared with groups of three who generated their ideas separately, but selected the best ideas as a group from their combined pool of ideas. Results were mixed. In the Putman and Paulus study, the three individuals generated more ideas and more high-quality ideas and eventually also selected ideas of higher quality. However, Faure found that, although the three individuals on average produced more ideas, this did not lead them to select ideas of higher quality. So, although groups are less productive than individuals, this does not always mean that they end up with worse ideas.

To interpret these findings, one has to know how good groups and individuals actually were at selecting their best ideas. Rietzschel et al. (2006) addressed this question. Similar to the two prior studies, they had three-person groups generate ideas and then select their best ideas as a group. However, unlike the other studies, this performance was compared with that of three individuals who both generated ideas and selected their best ideas individually. Rietzschel et al. found that groups generated fewer ideas and fewer good ideas than three individuals combined. However, there was no difference in the quality of the selected ideas, similar to what Faure (2004) had found. Further, Rietzschel et al. observed that selection was not very effective: There was no difference between the average quality (defined as originality and feasibility) of the generated ideas and the average quality of the selected ideas for either groups or individuals. Take a moment to consider this. It actually implies that people might just as well have made a *completely random selection*: The quality of the chosen ideas would not have been worse! Apparently, there is no difference between individuals and groups in the quality of selected ideas because both make a poor selection.

Why is this the case? Are people not capable of recognising their best ideas? In later research, Rietzschel et al. (2005) considered this question. They had participants rate ideas on the two dimensions—originality and feasibility—and then compared the ratings of the participants with those of trained judges. These ratings were very similar, indicating that participants were capable of recognising originality and feasibility. However, Rietzschel et al. found that participants did not spontaneously use both criteria when making their selection. While participants did think that feasibility was important, they did not see originality as important. They were therefore likely to select useful and feasible (and boring) ideas at the expense of original ones. However, they were capable of selecting original ideas when explicitly instructed to use originality as a criterion, but in that case were not very happy with their selection. Thus, people seem biased against originality when choosing among their ideas.

What are we to make of this? On the one hand, a good idea that solves a problem need not be original. Thus, why bother with originality per se? On the other hand, why go through the trouble of having a brainstorming session in the first place and trying to come up with many ideas if eventually the same old boring ideas are selected? Further, one could argue that it is probably easier to take an original idea and try to make it feasible than to take a feasible idea and try to make it original. These are interesting questions for future research.

Of course, even when high-quality ideas have been identified, the creative problem-solving process is not over. Instead, other people have to be convinced that the ideas are sound, and these ideas need to be worked out and implemented. Under what conditions will group members accept and implement a creative idea, particularly when it is offered by a newcomer? In seeking to provide an initial answer to this question, Levine et al. (2003) recently proposed a model of newcomer innovation in work teams. They suggested that characteristics of both newcomers and the team they are entering will affect older members' receptivity to newcomers' creative ideas. These characteristics include, among others, the newcomers' external social status, faction size, and persuasive ability (e.g., behavioural style), as well as the team's openness to membership change, staffing level, leadership, and performance.

Recent research has demonstrated that, at least under certain conditions, newcomers can indeed influence the groups they enter. For example, Choi and Levine (2004) found that newcomers entering a work team were more influential when the team had been assigned rather than chosen its initial task strategy and had failed rather than succeeded when using this strategy. In addition, Kane, Argote, and Levine (2005) found that when newcomers in work teams shared a superordinate identity with other team members, they were more influential when they suggested a superior rather than an inferior task strategy. In contrast, when newcomers did not share a superordinate identity with other team members, they had little influence regardless of the quality of their suggested task strategy. Finally, Levine and Choi (2004) found that teams performed better when newcomers had high rather than low ability, and this was particularly true when newcomers had high status.

Conclusion

We have argued that in order to understand group creativity, one needs to consider the different stages of the creative process. We have discussed three: problem finding (i.e., identifying and defining the problem), idea finding (generating solutions to the problem), and solution finding (choosing the best idea and then developing and implementing it). Group creativity, we have argued, occurs if people collaborate in at least one of these stages and if the final product(s) would not have been possible without that collaboration.

So, what do we know about group creativity in these different stages? About group problem finding, we have a number of plausible hypotheses but very little empirical data (Moreland & Levine, 1992). Nevertheless there is some evidence that groups might be useful in this stage: Whereas individuals often ignored problems hoping they would go away, groups tended to confront problems and recognise their importance (Dunbar, 1995). Clearly, more research on group problem finding in the context of creativity is needed.

Unlike group problem finding, we know quite a bit about group idea finding. Studies of group brainstorming have shown that, when left to their own devices, groups are not very good at generating ideas (e.g., Stroebe & Diehl, 1994). However, recent research has shown that groups can be effective, and hearing (or reading) ideas of others can be stimulating (see e.g., Dugosh et al., 2000; Nijstad et al., 2002). We argued that group interaction might be helpful in the stage of idea finding, especially when individuals get "stuck in a rut".

Finally, research about group solution finding is beginning to gain momentum. Several recent studies have addressed group idea selection. Results have been somewhat inconsistent, but at this point it appears that there is no systematic advantage of selecting ideas in a group (e.g., Faure, 2004). The reason appears to be that people are not very good at selecting their best ideas, whether alone or in a group (Rietzschel et al., 2006). People seem to have a bias against selecting original ideas and in favour of selecting feasible and useful ideas, which severely limits the creativity of their final choice (Rietzschel et al., 2005). Clearly, more research is needed about how to improve idea selection performance. Further, more research is needed to identify factors that influence the actual implementation of ideas.

Throughout the chapter, we have discussed the role that newcomers can play in the creative process. We made this point, in part, to dispel the common belief that newcomers are invariably targets, rather than sources, of influence in the groups they enter. Although it is true that newcomers are often hesitant to suggest new ideas, we would argue that, under certain conditions, they have both the motivation and ability to produce change (Levine et al., 2003). In such cases, they can make useful contributions in all three stages of the creative process.

One major conclusion to be drawn from our overview of the stages of creative group problem solving is that much work remains to be done. While we know a lot about group idea generation, we know next to nothing about group problem finding and only a little more about group solution finding. The second major conclusion is that we should focus more research effort on the question of *when* it is useful to have input from other group members, rather than on the question of *whether* such input is useful. It may not be necessary to work as a group throughout the creative process, but it often helps to get input from others at some points in time. The question of when that is the case needs to be addressed.

Note

1   Retrieved 6 February 2006 from http://quoteworld.org/quotes/5769

References

Amabile, T. M. (1996). *Creativity in context*. Boulder, CO: Westview Press.

Bartis, S., Szymanski, K., & Harkins, S. (1988). Evaluation and performance: A two-edged knife. *Personality and Social Psychology Bulletin, 14*, 242–251.

Camacho, L. M., & Paulus, P. B. (1995). The role of social anxiousness in group brainstorming. *Journal of Personality and Social Psychology, 68*, 1071–1080.

Choi, H. S., & Levine, J. M. (2004). Minority influence in work teams: The impact of newcomers. *Journal of Experimental Social Psychology, 40*, 273–280.

Choi, H. S., & Thompson, L. L. (2006). Membership change in groups: Implications for group creativity. In L. L. Thompson & H. S. Choi (Eds.), *Creativity and innovation in organizational teams* (pp. 87–107). Hillsdale, NJ: Lawrence Erlbaum Associates Inc.

Cohen, S. G., & Bailey, D. E. (1997). What makes teams work: Group effectiveness research from the shop floor to the executive suite. *Journal of Management, 23*, 239–290.

Dennis, A. R., & Valacich, J. S. (1993). Computer brainstorms: More heads are better than one. *Journal of Applied Psychology, 78*, 531–537.

Diehl, M., & Stroebe, W. (1987). Productivity loss in brainstorming groups: Toward the solution of a riddle. *Journal of Personality and Social Psychology, 53*, 497–509.

Diehl, M., & Stroebe, W. (1991). Productivity loss in idea-generating groups: Tracking down the blocking effect. *Journal of Personality and Social Psychology, 61*, 392–403.

Dugosh, K. L., Paulus, P. B., Roland, E. J., & Yang, H.-C. (2000). Cognitive stimulation in brainstorming. *Journal of Personality and Social Psychology, 79*, 722–735.

Dunbar, K. (1995). How scientists really reason: Scientific reasoning in real-world laboratories. In R. J. Sternberg & J. E. Davidson (Eds.), *The nature of insight* (pp. 365–395). Cambridge, MA: MIT Press.

Dunbar, K. (1997). How scientists think: On-line creativity and conceptual change in science. In T. B. Ward, S. M. Smith, & J. Vaid (Eds.), *Creative thought: An investigation of conceptual structures and processes* (pp. 461–493). Washington, DC: American Psychological Association.

Farrell, M. P. (2001). *Collaborative circles: Friendship dynamics and creative work*. Chicago: University of Chicago Press.

Faure, C. (2004). Beyond brainstorming: Effects of different group procedures on selection of ideas and satisfaction with the process. *Journal of Creative Behavior, 38*, 13–34.

Gallupe, R. B., Bastianutti, L. M., & Cooper, W. H. (1991). Unblocking brainstorms. *Journal of Applied Psychology, 76*, 137–142.

Getzels, J. W. (1982). The problem of the problem. In R. M. Hogarth (Ed.), *Question framing and response consistency* (pp. 37–49). San Francisco: Jossey-Bass.

Getzels, J. W., & Csikszentmihalyi, M. (1976). *The creative vision: A longitudinal study of problem finding in art*. New York: Wiley.

John-Steiner, V. (2000). *Creative collaboration*. New York: Oxford University Press.

Kane, A. A., Argote, L., & Levine, J. M. (2005). Knowledge transfer between groups via personnel rotation: Effects of social identity and knowledge quality. *Organizational Behavior and Human Decision Processes, 96*, 56–71.

Lamm, H., & Trommsdorff, G. (1973). Group versus individual performance on a task requiring ideational proficiency (brainstorming): A review. *European Journal of Social Psychology, 3*, 362–388.

LeBon, G. (1895). *The crowd*. London: Unwin.

Levine, J. M., & Choi, H. S., (2004). Impact of personnel turnover on team perform-ance and cognition. In E. Salas & S. M. Fiore (Eds.), *Team cognition: Understanding the factors that drive process and performance* (pp. 153–176). Washington, DC: American Psychological Association.

Levine, J. M., Choi, H. S., & Moreland, R. L. (2003). Newcomer innovation in work teams. In P. B. Paulus & B. A. Nijstad (Eds.), *Group creativity: Innovation through collaboration*. New York: Oxford University Press.

Levine, J. M., & Moreland, R. L. (2004). Collaboration: The social context of theory development. *Personality and Social Psychology Review*, *8*, 164–172.

Mayer, R. E. (1999). Fifty years of creativity research. In R. J. Sternberg (Ed.), *Handbook of creativity* (pp. 449–460). New York: Cambridge University Press.

Moreland, R. L., & Levine, J. M. (1989). Newcomers and oldtimers in groups. In P. B. Paulus (Ed.), *Psychology of group influence* (2nd ed., pp. 143–186). Hillsdale, NJ: Lawrence Erlbaum Associates Inc.

Moreland, R. L., & Levine, J. M. (1992). Problem identification by groups. In S. Worchel, W. Wood, & J. A. Simpson (Eds.), *Group process and productivity* (pp. 17–47). Newbury Park, CA: Sage.

Mullen, B., Johnson, C., & Salas, E. (1991). Productivity loss in brainstorming groups: A meta-analytic integration. *Basic and Applied Social Psychology*, *12*, 3–24.

Mumford, M. D., & Gustafson, S. G. (1988). Creativity syndrome: Integration, application, and innovation. *Psychological Bulletin*, *103*, 27–43.

Nijstad, B. A., Rietzschel, E. F., & Stroebe, W. (2006). Four principles of group creativity. In L. L. Thompson & H. S. Choi (Eds.), *Creativity and innovation in organizational teams* (pp. 161–179). Hillsdale, NJ: Lawrence Erlbaum Associates Inc.

Nijstad, B. A., Stroebe, W., & Lodewijkx, H. F. M. (1999). Persistence of brainstorm-ing groups: How do people know when to stop? *Journal of Experimental Social Psychology*, *35*, 165–185.

Nijstad, B. A., Stroebe, W., & Lodewijkx, H. F. M. (2002). Cognitive stimulation and interference in groups: Exposure effects in an idea generation task. *Journal of Experimental Social Psychology*, *38*, 535–544.

Nijstad, B. A., Stroebe, W., & Lodewijkx, H. F. M. (2003). Production blocking and idea generation: Does blocking interfere with cognitive processes? *Journal of Experimental Social Psychology*, *39*, 531–548.

Ochse, R. (1990). *Before the gates of excellence: The determinants of creative genius*. New York: Cambridge University Press.

Osborn, A. F. (1953). *Applied imagination* (first edition). New York: Scribner.

Osborn, A. F. (1963). *Applied imagination* (third edition). New York: Scribner.

Parnes, S. J. (Ed.). (1992). *Sourcebook for creative problem solving: A fifty-year digest of proven innovation processes*. Buffalo, NY: Creative Education Foundation Press.

Paulus, P. B., Dugosh, K. L., Dzindolet, M. T., Coskun, H., & Putman, V. L. (2002). Social and cognitive influences in group brainstorming: Predicting production gains and losses. In W. Stroebe & M. Hewstone (Eds.), *European review of social psychology* (Vol. 12, pp. 299–325). Chichester, UK: Wiley.

Paulus, P. B., & Nijstad, B. A. (Eds.). (2003). *Group creativity: Innovation through collaboration*. New York: Oxford University Press.

Paulus, P. B., & Yang, H. C. (2000). Idea generation in groups: A basis for creativity in organizations. *Organizational Behavior and Human Decision Processes*, *82*, 76–87.

Putman, V. L., & Paulus, P. B. (2003). *Brainstorming, brainstorming rules, and decision making*. Unpublished manuscript, University of Texas at Arlington, USA.

Reiter-Palmon, R., Mumford, M. D., O'Connor Boes, J., & Runco, M. A. (1997). Problem construction and creativity: The role of ability, cue consistency, and active processing. *Creativity Research Journal, 10*, 9–23.

Rietzschel, E. F., Nijstad, B. A., & Stroebe, W. (2005). *The selection of creative ideas after brainstorming: Overcoming the bias against originality*. Unpublished manuscript, University of Amsterdam, The Netherlands.

Rietzschel, E. F., Nijstad, B. A., & Stroebe, W. (2006). Productivity is not enough: A comparison of interactive and nominal groups on idea generation and selection. *Journal of Experimental Social Psychology, 42*, 244–251.

Simonton, D. K. (1988). *Scientific genius: A psychology of science*. New York: Cambridge University Press.

Simonton, D. K. (1999). *Origins of genius: Darwinian perspectives on creativity*. Oxford, UK: Oxford University Press.

Simonton, D. K. (2004). Group artistic creativity: Creative clusters and cinematic success in feature films. *Journal of Applied Social Psychology, 34*, 1494–1520.

Stroebe, W., & Diehl, M. (1994). Why groups are less effective than their members: On productivity losses in idea-generating groups. In W. Stroebe & M. Hewstone (Eds.), *European review of social psychology* (Vol. 5, pp. 271–303). London: Wiley.

Stroebe, W., Diehl, M., & Abakoumkin, G. (1992). The illusion of group effectivity. *Personality and Social Psychology Bulletin, 18*, 643–650.

Taylor, D. W., Berry, P. C., & Block, C. H. (1958). Does group participation when brainstorming facilitate or inhibit creative thinking? *Administrative Science Quarterly, 3*, 23–47.

Thompson, L. L., & Choi, H. S. (Eds.). (2006). *Creativity and innovation in organizational teams*. Mahwah, NJ: Lawrence Erlbaum Associates Inc.

West, M. A. (2002). Sparkling fountains or stagnant ponds: An integrative model of creativity and innovation implementation in work groups. *Applied Psychology: An International Review, 51*, 355–387.

11 Contrasting and integrating social identity and interdependence approaches to intergroup discrimination in the minimal group paradigm

Katherine Stroebe
Leiden University, The Netherlands

Russell Spears
Cardiff University, UK

Hein Lodewijkx
Open University, The Netherlands

The history of social psychology would have been less interesting in many ways without the heated debate between social identity and interdependence researchers concerning the primacy of each approach in explaining intergroup differentiation in the minimal group paradigm. Why do people who have been assigned to initially meaningless categories allocate more rewards to members of their own than to members of the other category? This question, so many years later, still provides food for debate (e.g., Gaertner & Insko, 2000; Scheepers, Spears, Doosje, & Manstead, 2002; K. Stroebe, Lodewijkx, & Spears, 2005). The interdependence approach argues that discrimination is the result of realistic conflicts, and perceptions of outcome dependence on ingroup and outgroup members, which trigger a tendency, among others, to reciprocate allocations that are expected from other ingroup (or outgroup) members (Rabbie, Schot, & Visser, 1989; Yamagishi, Jin, & Kiyonari, 1999). Social identity theory, on the other hand, proposes that discrimination is the result of attempting to achieve a positive social identity, or positive distinctiveness for the own group (Leonardelli & Brewer, 2001; Spears, Jetten, & Scheepers, 2002; Tajfel, Flament, Billig, & Bundy, 1971). But to what extent are these approaches distinct from each other and what do they share in their explanation of intergroup discrimination in the minimal group paradigm (MGP)?

In this chapter we will argue that both approaches can, in part, explain intergroup discrimination in the MGP and that it can be fruitful to consider them jointly. After an introduction to the history of the social identity and interdependence approaches, we will discuss studies that have considered these approaches, as well as, in two cases (Scheepers et al., 2002; K. Stroebe et al., 2005), proposing an integration of these approaches. Building on both integrations, we provide a theoretical framework within which both inter-dependence and social identity processes can operate, while determining factors that can indicate the relative strength of each process in a given context. We do not claim to be able to resolve the debate, but would like to argue that a joint approach, both in theory and in practice (the second and third authors being, respectively, a social identity and an interdependence researcher), may provide interesting theoretical avenues in future research on intergroup discrimination in the MGP.

Social identity

The minimal group paradigm, developed by Tajfel and colleagues (Tajfel et al., 1971) was, ironically, inspired by research by Rabbie, a formidable critic of the social identity account of the minimal group effect. Tajfel had noticed something interesting in the control condition of the classic study by Rabbie and Horwitz (1969). In this condition there was no interdependence between group members, and Tajfel used this condition as the model for the minimal group paradigm itself. Although there was no reliable evidence for ingroup bias in this "control" condition, Tajfel noted that there was actually a small difference in the evaluations favouring the ingroup and that this could become reliable with a larger sample.

The features of minimal groups, and the forms of ingroup bias, are well known and so will be described very briefly. Minimal groups are groups without any history or future, based on some minimal, even trivial, categor-isation criterion, where group members do not even know who else is a member of their own or the other group. Importantly they also always allo-cate rewards to other individual group members, not to the groups as a whole, and (thus) never to themselves. To assess evidence of this ingroup favourit-ism, Tajfel and colleagues developed the so-called Tajfel matrices (actually designed by Claude Flament) as a way to measure this favouritism and to distinguish between different allocation strategies that group members could adopt. In particular these matrices made it possible to distinguish strategies of fairness, maximum joint profit, maximum ingroup profit, and maximum differentiation. By means of "pull scores" different strategies could be con-trasted with competing strategies (Tajfel et al., 1971; Turner, Brown, & Tajfel, 1979; see Bourhis, Sachdev, & Gagnon, 1994).

What do we mean when we speak of the ingroup bias in the MGP? Ingroup bias actually covers two potentially distinct strategies, namely maximising ingroup profit, and maximising the positive difference between groups at the expense of ingroup profit. This latter strategy can be seen as a more aggressive or outgroup-derogating form of ingroup bias than maximum ingroup profit (which technically just favours the ingroup). However, a second property is that this maximising difference strategy also serves to *differentiate* between the groups. This tension (or, more strongly, confound) between differentiation and derogation has never been satisfactorily addressed with these measures.

It is important to note at the outset the contingent and probabilistic nature of ingroup bias in the MGP. To say that minimal categorisation can produce reliable ingroup bias (either maximum ingroup profit or maximum differentiation) is not to say that all people so categorised reveal evidence of such strategies. A good proportion of group members use fairness or maximum joint profit strategies (or indeed a mixture of strategies). However, it is also clear that there is sufficient evidence of ingroup bias in minimal group literature taken as a whole (see also Mullen, Brown, & Smith's, 1992, meta-analysis). Before focusing on explanations of the minimal ingroup bias effect, a point of definition needs to be addressed. In the present chapter we refer to *ingroup bias* and *ingroup favouritism* as forms of intergroup discrimination which may be motivated by different needs and encompass differing allocation strategies. Thus ingroup bias can be seen to correspond with the maximum differentiation or maximum ingroup profit strategy, and ingroup favouritism with the maximum ingroup profit strategy.

Social identity theory developed partly out of a quest to find an explanation for the ingroup bias shown in the MGP, although it is important to recognise that the theory is much more than this. It is also a normative theory in the prescriptive sense, designed to explain social change and in particular how status disadvantage motivates the quest for such change. The social identity explanation focuses on a *social* motive to seek positive distinctiveness for groups to which one belongs. In the minimal group paradigm the only way to achieve this is through favouring the ingroup over the outgroup, through positive enhancement and positive distinctiveness (maximum ingroup profit and maximum differentiation).

The central concepts of social identity theory (SIT) are (1) social categorisation, (2) social identity (a self-definition in terms of one's own group), (3) social comparison with other groups, motivated by a preference for having a positive social identity, and (4) the quest for psychological distinctiveness for the ingroup. An important assumption here is that people internalise their social identity to some degree (indeed, this is what makes a social category a social identity). Social identity theory should therefore not be read as saying that mere categorisation will automatically produce discrimination—it will only do this to the degree that group members accept and internalise the basis for categorisation (Turner, 1988). This is consistent with the fact that not all people exhibit ingroup bias in the MGP.

The assumption that some identification is necessary for ingroup bias in the MGP is also key to our attempt to test the predictions of social identity theory compared to interdependence accounts described below (see Stroebe et al., 2005). However, it is worth noting here that although identification may be a precondition for ingroup bias, the hypothesis that increased or high identification should predict (more) ingroup bias remains contested, and is not stated directly in social identity theory (but see Hinkle & Brown, 1990;

cf. Spears, Doosje, & Ellemers, 1999; Turner, 1999). Given that the MGP is an intergroup context where we expect group membership to be salient and other group norms are not evident, we might expect the relation between identification and ingroup bias to be plausible. However, to say that identification is a precondition for ingroup bias does not necessarily mean that they will be related in a linear sense, and this may depend on the more detailed process account. Matters are complicated by the fact that the social identity explanation arguably consists of (at least) two related elements: enhancement and distinctiveness. We now consider these in turn.

The focus on the motive for positive distinctiveness has been translated by some theorists into the so-called "self-esteem hypothesis" (Abrams & Hogg, 1988; Hogg & Sunderland, 1991; see also Oakes & Turner, 1980). While it is true that the original statements of the theory predict that enhancing social identity could be manifested in more positive self-esteem, it is probably wrong to locate this empirical prediction too centrally within the theory, as it can detract from the more central theme of positive group distinctiveness. If the motive for positive group distinctiveness is reduced to a quest for positive self-esteem alone, then this would return us to individualistic drive theories that social identity theory was expressly designed to contest. In this respect, focusing on self-esteem detracts from the arguably more group-level notion of distinctiveness addressed in the original statements of the theory (Spears et al., 2002). Having said this, there does seem to be general support for the notion that intergroup differentiation can enhance self-esteem, especially when this is defined at the level of the group (Long & Spears, 1997; Rubin & Hewstone, 1998).

As we have indicated, the self-esteem hypothesis tends to neglect the importance of the distinctiveness motive in focusing primarily on enhancement. This distinctiveness element may be particularly important in minimal groups that have no knowledge or content associated with them, raising the need for a distinct group identity perhaps in its starkest form. This is the argument that is developed by Spears et al. (2002), who elaborate a process called "creative distinctiveness", the drive to create group distinctiveness where none previously existed. This is particularly relevant for new or unestablished group identities and therefore applies to the MGP. In line with the original theorising of Tajfel, the idea here is that participants differentiate in order to create a meaningful and distinct identity, not only to gain a positive identity but one that makes sense of one's location within this minimal social context. We discuss some research by Scheepers et al. (2002) that provides evidence for this line of reasoning in the section on theoretical integration below. Further studies that provide a test of this idea were conducted by Spears, Jetten, and colleagues (see Spears et al., 2002; Spears, Scheepers, Jetten, Doosje, Ellemers, & Postmes, 2004). Spears and colleagues showed that participants who were assigned to a meaningful group, and thus were provided with a distinctive identity, showed less differentiation than participants in less meaningful groups. Additional studies showed that this effect was not explained by uncertainty principles.

In the meantime a number of other explanations of the minimal group effect, outside the social identity explanations relating to self-esteem and distinctiveness, have been proposed and examined down the years. An early study ruled out the possibility of demand characteristics (St. Claire & Turner, 1982). Diehl (1990) considered the possibility that equity principles may play a role, but concluded that this could not account for the effect. However, the idea that we reward others by taking into account the expectation of how others might reward us is a powerful idea that has not gone away and anticipates the reciprocity theme.

Before reviewing the reciprocity approach to the minimal group effects, it is important to note that the contemporary reciprocity explanations were only applied to the MGP some time after the social identity explanation was proposed, so SIT did not originally address these alternative possibilities. However, the social identity explanation of intergroup discrimination arose in contrast to another interdependence explanation of intergroup phenomena, namely realistic group conflict theory (e.g., LeVine & Campbell, 1972; Sherif, 1967). Realistic group conflict theory explains discrimination as resulting from real conflicts of interest concerning the distribution of scarce and valued resources. Clearly, assuming that material conflicts of interest are necessary for ingroup bias does little to explain (at least at first sight) the results of the minimal group paradigm. One of the important legacies of this paradigm and the theory that it inspired is the acknowledgement of more identity-based and symbolic forms of competition ("social competition"; Turner, 1975). It needs to be emphasised that Tajfel and Turner were well aware of the value of materialist explanations of intergroup conflict and saw the social identity approach as complementary to these, designed to explain as yet unexplained phenomena, rather than seeing these as competing theories in an all or nothing sense.

We now move on to consider the other leading contemporary contender for explaining intergroup discrimination in the MGP, the interdependence and reciprocity approach. We then address the question of under which conditions these different processes or "routes" to intergroup discrimination are most likely to prevail.

Interdependence and reciprocity

In this section we argue that various processes related to reciprocity may determine—at least partially—intergroup discrimination in the minimal group paradigm. As such, the present approach may enrich the main theories and hypotheses advocated to explain this phenomenon, such as social identification and self-categorisation processes. As will be outlined below, the reciprocity approach strongly rests in the interdependence perspective (e.g., Rabbie & Lodewijkx, 1994). More specifically, it focuses on processes of perceived within-group and between-group outcome dependencies that may influence MGP ingroup favouritism.

The sociologist Gouldner (1960) was the first to propose the existence of a generalised norm of reciprocity, arguing that most societies endorse some form of the reciprocity norm. The norm regulates the exchanges of goods and services between people in ongoing group or individual relationships. It dictates that people should help those who have helped them, and that penalties may be imposed on those who fail to reciprocate. Reciprocity thus calls for positive reactions to favourable treatment, and for negative reactions to unfavourable treatment. The norm has been found to influence diverse behaviours varying from helping behaviour, cooperation, ethnocentrism, compliance with requests in economic exchanges, to health impairment in organisational settings.

According to Gouldner, the norm has important social functions. It increases social stability in social groups or systems, and it structures and maintains social relationships. Additionally, the norm may function as a facilitating "*starting mechanism*" for the development of stable and enduring social relations in newly formed groups or pair bondings. This last proposition is of relevance here, since the MGP group members are all new and anonymous to each other. Thus, reciprocal exchanges among the members may foster initial group formation (see below). This idea formed the basis for the reciprocity approach to intergroup discrimination in the MGP.

The basis for the reciprocity approach to explaining MGP ingroup favouritism was provided by Rabbie, Schot, and Visser (1989). They argued that the effects of social categorisation in the MGP were confounded by outcome dependence. In the MGP, participants are specifically instructed to allot monetary rewards to, and receive allocated rewards from, anonymous members of both groups. Therefore allocation behaviour may not only be determined by categorisation but also by the existing outcome dependence between group members. Rabbie et al. (1989) further argued that these dependencies would overrule the effects of the category division. Moreover, they put forward that these dependencies constituted the basis for reciprocity, which, in turn, would determine ingroup members' ingroup-favouring reward allocations. Thus, in the view of these authors, ingroup reciprocity served as the mediating behavioural mechanism to account for intergroup discrimination. The importance of reciprocity processes within the MGP was also acknowledged by Tajfel et al. (1971) in their original MGP paper. Reciprocal expectations were said to constitute a possible rival explanation of MGP intergroup discrimination. They noted that ingroup members might "assume others to behave as they themselves do, and that this assumption in turn affects their own behavior" (1971, p. 175).

Since the seminal work of Rabbie et al. (1989), two versions of the reciprocity approach have been put forward. They are referred to as the *unbounded* and the (*generalised*) *bounded reciprocity hypothesis* (see Gaertner & Insko, 2000; Lodewijkx, Rabbie, & Syroit, 1999; Yamagishi et al., 1999). Basically, if the relationship between people in a given relationship is characterised only by outcome dependence, the *unbounded reciprocity hypothesis* would propose

an equitable link (Locksley, Ortiz, & Hepburn, 1980) between people's allocation of valued resources. Thus, in its unbounded form, people will have
higher reciprocal expectations of, and allocate more valued resources to,
those others upon whom they perceive themselves to be dependent. In this
approach, participants' designated category membership is irrelevant in the
allocation of the rewards. This means that participants may make allocations
to both ingroup and *outgroup* members. On the other hand, the *bounded
reciprocity hypothesis*, also referred to as *generalised bounded reciprocity*
(Yamagishi et al., 1999; Yamagishi & Kiyonari, 2000), maintains that the
effects of reciprocity are bounded or restricted by participants' designated
category membership. In other words, participants' reciprocal expectations
are determined not only by their perceived outcome dependence but also
by their category membership: Participants have higher expectations of
reciprocity from fellow ingroup as opposed to outgroup members. The predictions of the bounded version of the reciprocity hypothesis for allocation
behaviour are that participants who are ingroup outcome dependent have
stronger ingroup reciprocal expectations and make more ingroup-favouring
allocations than participants who are not. Participants who are outgroup
outcome dependent, on the other hand, in contrast to predictions by the
unbounded version, do not have outgroup reciprocal expectations or make
outgroup-favouring allocations. In several MGP experiments differential
ingroup and outgroup outcome dependencies were manipulated to show
their influence on bounded and/or unbounded reciprocal exchanges—and,
through these exchanges—on MGP intergroup discrimination. Importantly,
in all these studies, before introducing the outcome dependence conditions,
participants were categorised into two distinct units. This procedure allows for
the examination of the effects of the category division on intergroup discrimination, as well as for the proposed overruling effects of differential outcome
dependencies. The findings of the most relevant studies are summarised below.

Rabbie et al. (1989; see also Rabbie & Schot, 1990), after categorising
participants, created three outcome dependence conditions in their MGP
study: A one-sided ingroup outcome dependence condition (ID), a one-sided
outgroup outcome dependence condition (OD), and a two-sided ingroup–
outgroup outcome dependence condition (IOD), which parallels the standard
MGP situation. The findings showed that participants allotted the most
money to those ingroup or outgroup members on whom they perceived
themselves to be the most dependent. They observed ingroup favouritism in
the ID condition, outgroup favouritism in the OD condition, and inter-
mediate values of ingroup favouritism in the IOD condition. The *outgroup
favouritism* obtained in the OD condition reveals a favourable pro-outgroup
treatment, at the *expense* of the ingroup. Additional effects of the experimental conditions on measures of perceived dependence and reciprocal
expectations corresponded with the effects obtained on reward allocations.
The outgroup favouritism observed in this study cannot, as yet, be sufficiently
explained by SIT and related approaches. However, it can be explained by the

reciprocity approach, because it reflects the operation of unbounded reciprocity such that perceived outcome dependence overrules the effects of social categorisation. However, the findings of this study did not allow the drawing of clear conclusions about whether bounded or unbounded reciprocity processes (or both) were responsible for the occurrence of ingroup favouritism. The experimental manipulations did not disentangle the effects of the two distinct processes. Follow-up studies therefore tried to disentangle these processes.

In general, these studies found more support for the bounded reciprocity approach. For instance, Lodewijkx et al. (1999) varied outcome dependencies between the categorised groups in the MGP, namely the IOD and OD conditions of Rabbie et al. (1989). The usual ingroup favouritism was found in the two-sided ingroup–outgroup outcome dependence (IOD) condition (i.e., the condition that is comparable to the standard MGP). In the one-sided outgroup outcome dependence condition (OD), ingroup favouritism was significantly reduced. In support of the bounded version, the effect of the IOD versus OD condition on ingroup favouritism was more strongly mediated by reciprocal ingroup than by reciprocal outgroup expectations. These findings suggest a stronger effect of bounded compared to unbounded reciprocity processes on ingroup favouritism.

In a conceptual replication of these experiments, Gaertner and Insko (2000, Study 2) told participants that they, and one other person, would allocate bonus money; the other person allocating the money was either an ingroup or an outgroup member. Participants were thus either dependent (or not) on an ingroup member or on an outgroup member for receiving rewards. According to the bounded reciprocity hypothesis, participants should show ingroup favouritism, but only in the case where they could reciprocate favourable allocations received from other ingroup members. The findings of this study supported this hypothesis showing that "category members preferred the ingroup favoring strategies only when an ingroup member could reciprocate their allocations" (Gaertner & Insko, 2000, p. 89). The authors further observed that the reciprocity hypothesis held more for males, whereas the identity hypothesis was more applicable to females. This issue will be addressed in later sections.

Lacunae in the social identity and interdependence approaches

Part of the integrative aim of this chapter is to view intergroup discrimination in the minimal group paradigm as not necessarily the product of one single process, but as being potentially multiply determined ("over-determined"), or being subject to different processes in different contexts. With this in mind it is useful to highlight the features of the SIT and reciprocity approach that cannot easily account for some aspects of minimal group effects. Rather than undermining competing theories, this highlights the utility of complementary approaches.

A first issue concerns the reciprocity explanation of ingroup bias, which is seen as the result of greater expectation of reciprocity within the ingroup. The question that remains open is, what is special about the *ingroup* as the source of interdependence? In other words, why is *ingroup* bounded reciprocity stronger than outgroup bounded reciprocity? Some seek the answer in evolutionary psychology (see, e.g., Gaertner & Insko, 2000), or in the cultural transmission of the reciprocity norm (see Sober & Wilson, 1998, for a review), while others, such as Horwitz and Rabbie (1982), propose learning experiences. The latter researchers advocate a normative ingroup schema, defined as learned beliefs and expectations that a more favourable treatment can be expected from members of one's own group than from members of the other group, and that greater weight should be given to desires of own group members than to desires of other group members. At this moment, research findings do not give a definite answer to the question raised above, nor do they specify boundary conditions or conditions that may activate, strengthen, or weaken the operation of the reciprocity norm, or substantiate the content of the norm.

Concerning allocation strategies within the MGP, the reciprocity hypothesis has difficulty explaining the maximum differentiation strategy. Explanations based on reciprocity within the group are good at explaining why group members maximise the resources within the ingroup (especially when explicitly interdependent with this group), but they are perhaps less well placed to explain why people might disadvantage the ingroup, simply to disadvantage the outgroup even more.

While social identity theory addresses these issues more explicitly, its focus on positive differentiation and distinctiveness mechanisms leaves little room for the role of interdependence and reciprocal expectations as underlying intergroup discrimination within the MGP.

These considerations are not designed to create problems for individual theories so much as to reinforce the case for a multi-pronged theoretical approach. It has become clear that neither approach can provide a single process or all-encompassing analysis of intergroup behaviour in general nor in the minimal group paradigm in particular. This suggests that the theoretical net needs to be cast wider to include a range of processes.

Contrasting the two approaches

Surprisingly few studies have attempted to actually compare the categorisation/identification and interdependence/reciprocity approaches. In the following sections we briefly discuss studies that have done so (Gaertner & Insko, 2000; Gagnon & Bourhis, 1996). Above all, we capitalise on the studies integrating the two approaches, namely Scheepers et al. (2002) and K. Stroebe et al. (2005).

In previous attempts to delineate the effects of interdependence and identification on the occurrence of intergroup discrimination, Gagnon and Bourhis

(1996) manipulated the presence/absence of interdependence and measured identification. These authors predicted that "perceived interdependence may only contribute to discriminatory behavior to the degree that group members first identify with their category membership within the MGP" (p. 1292). Results were said to be in support of SIT, as participants who identified highly with their group discriminated on relevant allocation strategies such as the maximising differentiation strategy, whereas low identifiers showed little discrimination and were fairness oriented. There was little evidence for the effects of interdependence in this study, as reciprocal expectations did not influence intergroup discrimination.

Although their findings may seem to provide conclusive support for SIT, a number of methodological shortcomings have been raised concerning this study (see also Gaertner & Insko, 2000; K. Stroebe et al., 2005). Most importantly—and acknowledged by the authors—identification was measured after participants allocated the rewards, rather than manipulated before allocations were made. While identification was predicted to be a precursor of discrimination, clearly a measure of identification after discrimination cannot be said to test the same process, all the more because SIT claims that positive differentiation affects the social identity of group members. Therefore the identification effects of the Gagnon and Bourhis study (1996) may be a consequence of discrimination rather than an antecedent.

A follow-up study to investigate the relative influence of a SIT versus a reciprocity approach was conducted by Gaertner and Insko (2000, Study 1). These authors manipulated both the presence/absence of dependence structure, as well as, in line with SIT, categorisation (none/random/meaningful). This enabled the test of whether indeed mere categorisation is a necessary and sufficient basis for intergroup discrimination.

Due to gender differences, results of this study provided support for both SIT and the reciprocity approach. In support of SIT, categorised females favoured the ingroup regardless of the dependence structure. This intergroup discrimination was strongest for meaningfully categorised females. In contrast, and in support of a reciprocity approach, categorised males favoured the ingroup only in the presence of dependence.

Gaertner and Insko cannot provide a conclusive theoretical explanation of these gender differences and rely on possible evolutionary explanations. However, to resolve the debate concerning the relative importance of interdependence and SIT, a gender-based explanation is not sufficient. Furthermore, other studies within the MGP did not reveal these gender differences (Scheepers et al., 2002; K. Stroebe et al., 2005).

While Gaertner and Insko had already provided indications that a reciprocity and SIT approach might be able to jointly explain intergroup discrimination in the MGP, the aim of integrating the two approaches provided the basis of Scheepers et al.'s (2002) research. Scheepers et al. (Study 2) examined the effects of goal interdependence versus a social identity approach by manipulating the presence/absence of a group goal and the opportunity to differentiate the own from the other group via the opportunity to rate or not rate the other group at an early point in the study (i.e., differentiation at Time 1). According to Scheepers et al., two motives, an identity and an instrumental motive, operate to explain intergroup discrimination. When satisfying an identity motive, participants will discriminate in order to "place the own group within a social structure" (p. 1455). An instrumental motive is "linked to achieving certain goals" (p. 1455). The identity motive was assessed with a measure of participants' self-esteem after the allocation task, the instrumental motive with a number of items measuring goal-related motivation to differentiate (e.g., differentiating to make the group stronger). In line with SIT, Scheepers et al. stated that "in a relatively meaningless context (e.g. minimal groups), SIT may frequently offer the most plausible explanation, whereas under more meaningful conditions, with resources, outcomes or goal interdependence at stake, the instrumental function may prevail" (2002, p. 1457).

Scheepers et al. expected strongest differentiation from the outgroup (i.e., differentiation at Time 2), albeit for different motives, when participants either were in the no goal/no differentiation condition (referred to as the minimal condition) or in the goal/differentiation condition (referred to as the instrumental condition). Results largely supported the authors' predictions. Participants in the minimal and instrumental conditions indeed discriminated more than in the other two conditions and discriminated on the basis of different motives. Further support for the operation of the identity and instrumental motives was provided by mediation analyses. Scheepers et al. predicted that, if the identity motive drove intergroup discrimination in the minimal condition, differentiation should serve as a mediator for the identity motive in the minimal but not in the instrumental condition. Mediational analyses revealed the predicted mediation in the identity but not the instrumental condition. If, on the other hand, instrumental motives play a role in the instrumental condition and not in the minimal condition, the effect of group goal on differentiation should be mediated by instrumental motives in the instrumental condition only. This was indeed the case. Thus intergroup discrimination in the minimal condition could be explained by identity motives, whereas in the instrumental condition instrumental motives underlay discrimination.

The above study was the first to propose an integration of social identity theory and an interdependence approach. The findings provided stronger support for the social identity side in showing that the identity function is more basic, needing to be fulfilled before an instrumental function can operate. Note that, strictly speaking, this study does not examine reciprocity effects but rather considers the presence/absence of a group goal in influencing intergroup discrimination. Thus, it is more in line with realistic conflict theory.

A direct test and integration of the interdependence versus SIT approach was provided by K. Stroebe et al. (2005). This study orthogonally manipulated identification and ingroup–outgroup outcome dependence, and allowed an examination of the independent effects of identification and of the bounded versus unbounded reciprocity approach in one experiment. We focus on the test of the relative importance of the SIT and reciprocity approaches. Importantly, the experiment included a no-dependence (ND) condition, in which participants were not outcome dependent on either the ingroup or the outgroup. This condition is relevant to examine the SIT approach. The basis for reciprocity is absent in this condition: participants could only allot to, but not receive rewards from, other ingroup or outgroup members.

Results provided support for both a SIT and a reciprocity approach. In line with the SIT approach, participants within the ND condition who identified strongly with their group made marginally more ingroup-favouring allocations than those who identified less strongly. In support of the reciprocity hypothesis, participants who were ingroup outcome dependent made significantly more ingroup-favouring allocations. This effect was mediated by reciprocal expectations of ingroup members, providing evidence for the operation of bounded reciprocity. In support of the unbounded reciprocity hypothesis, participants also made marginally more outgroup-favouring allocations when outgroup outcome dependent. This effect was mediated by outgroup reciprocal expectations, supporting the unbounded reciprocity hypothesis.

Based on these results K. Stroebe et al. provide a possible integration for the reciprocity hypothesis and SIT based on two main factors: (1) the salience of the context, and (2) congruence/incongruence of identification or outcome dependence with categorisation. As the first is more relevant to explaining the strength of allocation behaviour and integrating the unbounded and bounded reciprocity hypothesis we only focus on the first factor here. The salience of the context refers to whether interdependence or identification is more salient within the MGP and determines the relative strength of interdependence or identification mechanisms. Thus, in the absence of other information to give meaning to a situation, the strength of perceived outcome dependence or identification with a category determines whether allocation behaviour is guided by reciprocal expectations and instrumental concerns or by identification and identity concerns respectively. Based on this line of reasoning, K. Stroebe et al. state that in their study identification was most contextually salient in the ND condition, when outcome dependence was absent, while outcome dependence/reciprocity concerns were salient in all other conditions that provided some explicit ingroup and/or outgroup outcome dependence.

A framework for integration

What can be distilled from the above studies for explaining intergroup discrimination in the MGP? Below we propose a framework that allows for both social identity and interdependence processes to take place within the MGP.

The previous sections of this chapter have shown that evidence in favour of these processes has been conflicting. While many studies may have claimed the importance of one approach above the other, the previous sections have already indicated that there is considerable empirical evidence speaking for each approach and that therefore both approaches may be equally relevant in explaining intergroup discrimination in the MGP (see also Scheepers et al., 2002). The advantage of the integrative framework outlined below is that it does not contest the importance of either approach but provides a framework in which both reciprocity/interdependence and social identity processes can take place. We argue that the relative strength of each process is determined by the intergroup context within which the MGP takes place. As will become clear below, this "contextual salience" of either process can influence the strength of manipulations within the MGP and dominance of certain allocation strategies.

Before outlining our integration, it is important to note that similar processes seem to be found for both goal interdependence (Scheepers et al., 2002) and reward interdependence (K. Stroebe et al., 2005) and that the proposed integration thus should be seen as applicable to both types of interdependence. Furthermore, it should be clear that, given the few studies comparing SIT and interdependence processes, the proposed integration still requires further empirical examination.

Contextual salience

We believe an important aspect in determining the relative influence of identity or interdependence concerns within the MGP is the intergroup context within which intergroup discrimination takes place. Note that the MGP is a fairly meaningless context, to which a participant will contrive to attach his/ her own meaning. Consequently, any manipulation or adaptation of the intergroup context that may attach meaning to the MGP can have strong effects on participants' allocation behaviour. We argue that aspects of the intergroup context can make either identity or interdependence concerns salient within the MGP. These aspects can be the task instructions, type of allocations to be made, amount of information given about the groups, or simply the order in which information is presented to participants. Taking a closer look at the Scheepers et al. (2002) study, identity concerns may be found to be primary compared to instrumental concerns, due to the fact that the intergroup context strengthened categorisation/group membership more than perceived goal interdependence, thus making identity concerns salient. This requires a redefinition of the Scheepers et al. study. While Scheepers et al. refer to the salience of a context as the presence/absence of an identity versus an instrumental motive, we regard the context of the Scheepers et al. study from a more abstract position whereby the MGP itself takes place in an intergroup context in which identity concerns are more salient. The Scheepers et al. study consists of an enriched MGP, wherein all group members are engaged in a joint task, thus making group membership more meaningful than in the standard MGP, and possibly even creating a group identity. This makes for a strong induction of category membership, irrespective of the manipulation that creates the possibility of discriminating between the groups (predicted to activate the identity motive). In contrast, goal interdependence (i.e., the instrumental motive) is only salient in the group goal condition. Therefore one can argue that, compared to the K. Stroebe et al. (2005) study (see below), identity rather than interdependence concerns may be relatively more salient within the intergroup context of the Scheepers et al. (2002) study.

In contrast, the K. Stroebe et al. study (2005) takes place in an intergroup context in which interdependence concerns may have been more salient. Here the manipulations of outcome dependence on the ingroup and on the outgroup were possibly stronger than the manipulation of identification: Participants could allocate the rewards immediately after receiving the outcome dependence and allocation instructions, and these manipulations and allocations took place after the manipulation of identification.

Predominance of forces

Whether identity or interdependence concerns are relatively more salient has consequences for the predominance of these concerns within the MGP, such that one concern will be primary above or predominate over the other. The salience of the context can therefore be seen to fit either the manipulation of identity or interdependence concerns and consequently determine which manipulation has stronger effects on allocation behaviour. In a context in which identity concerns are salient, manipulations that fit this concern by matching the needs related to identity concerns (e.g., categorisation, identification, or differentiation opportunity) will have a stronger effect on allocation behaviour than will manipulations related to interdependence (e.g., outcome dependence, goals). The findings of Scheepers et al. (2002), in which identity concerns are contextually salient, are in agreement with these contentions, revealing that participants favoured their own group more when an identity motive was induced, and that the effects of the instrumental motive were strongest when the identity motive had been satisfied.

The same conclusion holds for the K. Stroebe et al. (2005) study. As interdependence was contextually salient and the manipulation of outcome dependence fitted the salient context, outcome dependence influenced allocation behaviour irrespective of the identification with the group (i.e., identity concern). Identification only had an effect on allocation behaviour in the condition in which outcome dependence was absent (i.e., the ND condition).

Building on our predominance of forces argument it is important to realise that contextual salience not only influences the predominance of identity or interdependence-related manipulations, but also the relative importance of allocation strategies. When identity concerns are salient, the dominant allocation strategy will be maximum differentiation. Thus, allocations are determined by group differentiation, at the cost of sacrificing maximum profit of the ingroup. When interdependence is salient, the strategies for maximising ingroup profit allocation are likely to be dominant.

In consequence, our integration solves a number of problems mentioned earlier. It can explain why, even when allocation behaviour within the MGP seems based on interdependence processes, participants make use of the maximising differentiation strategy, which is seen as strongly related to identity rather than instrumental concerns. Our framework allows for allocation strategies related to both social identity and interdependence processes, predicting when and why one strategy will be stronger than the other. Furthermore our framework provides a solution for what has been regarded as a shortcoming of social identity theory, namely the theory's inability to explain why group members have reciprocal expectations based on their group membership and why subsequent allocations are the result of reciprocity/outcome dependence rather than the predicted distinctiveness or differentiation processes. Our integration allows for both processes to play a role, their primacy being determined by the relative salience of the processes within the MGP intergroup context.

In conclusion, it is important to note that while providing an *integrative* framework we view interdependence and social identity *processes* (i.e., motivated by instrumental or identity concerns respectively) as functionally separate. This idea is supported by studies by Gaertner and Insko (2000, Study 1), Scheepers et al. (2002), and K. Stroebe et al. (2005), wherein interdependence and social identity processes do not seem to interact and intensify each other. In fact, the studies by both K. Stroebe et al. and Scheepers et al. provide indications that one concern can inhibit or block the other, depending on the relative contextual salience. In the Scheepers et al. study (2002) instrumental motives became strongest only when identity motives had been fulfilled, while K. Stroebe et al. (2005) showed that identity concerns only played a role when there was no outcome dependence. This may explain why SIT and interdependence approaches have remained separate and conflicting perspectives over the decades.

Conclusions

Clearly it is possible to design studies that provide evidence for the primacy of either a SIT or an outcome dependence/reciprocity approach without necessarily contesting the content of either approach. The framework we propose here shows that a functional integration of SIT and interdependence approaches can provide an explanation for seemingly contradictory research while acknowledging the importance of each approach.

In the present chapter we have given an overview of the interdependence and social identity approaches to intergroup discrimination within the MGP. The approaches have instigated much heated debate over the past decades. Despite this long history of "inter-approach" conflict, our overview of studies that were conducted to compare both approaches revealed a surprisingly small amount of research in this area. In the present chapter we have tried to show that an integration of these approaches can provide the key to explaining intergroup discrimination in the MGP that neither approach alone can offer.

We have argued that, rather than an interdependence or a social identity approach being primary, the intergroup context may serve to determine which approach is salient and thus contextually primary within the MGP. Depending on the contextual salience of either instrumental or identity concerns, either concern may predominate and provide a match with one of the manipulations to determine allocation behaviour within the MGP. We have shown that our integration can be applicable to the studies by both Scheepers et al. (2002) and K. Stroebe et al. (2005), but we are aware that our integration needs further empirical support.

While it has become clear that interdependence concerns can play an important role in determining MGP allocation behaviour, it is not yet clear why categorisation plays such a strong role in this process. Taking this one step further, while the SIT and interdependence approaches agree that when persons are categorised, they discriminate between groups, each approach provides a different reason for this discrimination. SIT sees discrimination as a need to achieve a positive social identity, while the interdependence approach explains it by a need to reciprocate towards other ingroup and outgroup members. What protagonists from both camps are unwilling to acknowledge is that assigning persons to a category has the potential to raise both needs. Therefore it would seem that an integration in which categorisation is regarded as a central concept, which is unrelated to either approach, could be more fruitful (see also K. Stroebe et al., 2005). Yet, this would require reconceptualising both theories and developing a joint model. Perhaps, when we learn not to categorise ourselves as interdependence *or* social identity researchers, the time will be ripe to design an integrative model to explain intergroup discrimination in the MGP.

References

Abrams, D., & Hogg, M. (1988). Comments on the motivational status of self-esteem in social identity and intergroup discrimination. *European Journal of Social Psychology, 18*, 317–334.

Bourhis, R. Y., Sachdev, I., & Gagnon, A. (1994). Intergroup research with the Tajfel matrices: Methodological notes. In M. P. Zanna & J. M. Olson (Eds.), *The social psychology of prejudice: The Ontario symposium* (Vol. 7, pp. 209–232). Hillsdale, NJ: Lawrence Erlbaum Associates Inc.

Diehl, M. (1990). The minimal group paradigm: Theoretical explanations and empirical findings. In W. Stroebe & M. Hewstone (Eds.), *European review of social psychology* (Vol. 1, pp. 263–292). Chichester, UK: Wiley.

Gaertner, L., & Insko C. A. (2000). Intergroup discrimination in the minimal group paradigm: Categorization, reciprocation or fear? *Journal of Personality and Social Psychology*, *79*, 77–94.

Gagnon, A., & Bourhis, R. Y. (1996). Discrimination in the minimal group paradigm: Social identity or self interest? *Personality and Social Psychology Bulletin*, *22*, 1289–1301.

Gouldner, A. W. (1960). The norm of reciprocity: A preliminary statement. *American Sociological Review*, *25*, 161–178.

Hinkle, S., & Brown, R. J. (1990). Intergroup comparisons and social identity: Some links and lacunae. In D. Abrams & M. A. Hogg (Eds.), *Social identity theory: Constructive and critical advances* (pp. 48–70). London: Harvester Wheatsheaf.

Hogg, M. A., & Sunderland, J. (1991). Self-esteem and intergroup discrimination in the minimal group paradigm. *British Journal of Social Psychology*, *30*, 51–62.

Horwitz, M., & Rabbie, J. M. (1982). Individuality and membership in the intergroup system. In H. Tajfel (Ed.), *Social identity and intergroup relations* (pp. 89–101). Cambridge, UK: Cambridge University Press.

Leonardelli, G. J., & Brewer, M. B. (2001). Minority and majority discrimination: When and why. *Journal of Experimental Social Psychology*, *37*, 468–485.

LeVine, R. A., & Campbell, D. T. (1972). *Ethnocentrism*. New York: Wiley.

Locksley, A., Ortiz, V., & Hepburn, C. (1980). Social categorization and discriminatory behavior: Extinguishing the minimal intergroup discrimination effect. *Journal of Personality and Social Psychology*, *39*, 773–783.

Lodewijkx, H. F. M., Rabbie J. M., & Syroit, J. E. M. M. (1999). Don't bite the hand that feeds you: Mediation of minimal group discrimination by reciprocal expectations. *Representative Research in Social Psychology*, *23*, 28–41.

Long, K., & Spears, R. (1997). The self-esteem hypothesis revisited: Differentiation and the disaffected. In R. Spears, P. J. Oakes, N. Ellemers, & S. A. Haslam (Eds.), *The social psychology of stereotyping and group life* (pp. 296–317). Oxford, UK: Blackwell.

Mullen, B., Brown, R., & Smith, C. (1992). Ingroup bias as a function of salience, relevance, and status: An integration. *European Journal of Social Psychology*, *22*, 103–122.

Oakes, P. J., & Turner, J. C. (1980). Social categorization and intergroup behaviour: Does minimal intergroup discrimination make social identity more positive? *European Journal of Social Psychology*, *10*, 295–301.

Rabbie, J. M., & Horwitz, M. (1969). The arousal of ingroup–outgroup bias by a chance win or loss. *Journal of Personality and Social Psychology*, *13*, 269–277.

Rabbie, J. M., & Lodewijkx, H. F. M. (1994). Conflict and aggression: An individual–group continuum. *Advances in Group Processes*, *11*, 139–174.

Rabbie, J. M., & Schot, J. (1990). Group behavior in the minimal group paradigm: Fact or fiction? In P. J. D. Drenth, J. A. Sergeant, & R. J. Takens (Eds.), *European perspectives in psychology* (Vol. 3, pp. 251–263). Chichester, UK: Wiley.

Rabbie, J. M., Schot, J., & Visser, L. (1989). Social identity theory: A conceptual and empirical critique from the perspective of a behavioral interaction model. *European Journal of Social Psychology*, *19*, 171–202.

Rubin, M., & Hewstone, M. (1998). Social identity theory's self-esteem hypothesis: A review and some suggestions for clarification. *Personality and Social Psychology Review*, *2*, 40–62.

Scheepers, D., Spears, R., Doosje, B., & Manstead, A. S. R. (2002). Integrating identity and instrumental approaches to intergroup differentiation: Different contexts, different motives. *Personality and Social Psychology Bulletin*, *28*, 1455–1467.

Sherif, M. (1967). *Group conflict and co-operation: Their social psychology*. London: Routledge & Kegan Paul.

Sober, E., & Wilson, D. S. (1998). *Unto others: The evolution and psychology of unselfish behavior*. Cambridge, MA: Harvard University Press.

Spears, R., Doosje, B., & Ellemers, N. (1999). Commitment and the context of social perception. In N. Ellemers, R. Spears, & B. Doosje (Eds.), *Social identity: Context, commitment, content* (pp. 59–83). Oxford, UK: Blackwell.

Spears, R., Jetten, J., & Scheepers, D. (2002). Distinctiveness and the definition of collective self: A tripartite model. In A. Tesser, J. V. Wood, & D. A. Stapel (Eds.), *Self and motivation: Emerging psychological perspectives* (pp. 147–171). Lexington: APA.

Spears, R., Scheepers, D., Jetten, J., Doosje, B., Ellemers, N., & Postmes, T. (2004). Entitativity, group distinctiveness and social identity: Getting and using social structure. In V. Yzerbyt, C. M. Judd, & O. Corneille (Eds.), *The psychology of group perception: Contributions to the study of homogeneity, entitativity and essentialism* (pp. 293–316). Philadelphia: Psychology Press.

St. Claire, L., & Turner, J. C. (1982). The role of demand characteristics in the social categorization paradigm. *European Journal of Social Psychology*, *12*, 307–314.

Stroebe, K. E., Spears, R., & Lodewijkx, H. F. M. (2005). Do unto other as they do unto you: Reciprocity and social identification as determinants of ingroup favoritism. *Personality and Social Psychology Bulletin*, *31*, 831–845.

Tajfel, H., Flament, C. I., Billig, M. G., & Bundy, H. P. (1971). Social categorization and intergroup behavior. *European Journal of Social Psychology*, *1*, 149–178.

Turner, J. C. (1975). Social comparison and social identity: Some prospects for intergroup behaviour. *European Journal of Social Psychology*, *5*, 5–34.

Turner, J. C. (1988). Comments on Doise's individual and social identities in intergroup relations. *European Journal of Social Psychology*, *18*, 113–116.

Turner, J. C. (1999). Some current issues in research on social identity and self-categorization theories. In N. Ellemers, R. Spears, & B. Doosje (Eds.), *Social identity: Context, commitment, content* (pp. 6–34). Oxford, UK: Blackwell.

Turner, J. C., Brown, R. J., & Tajfel, H. (1979). Social comparison and group interest in ingroup favouritism. *European Journal of Social Psychology*, *9*, 187–204.

Yamagishi, T., Jin, N., & Kiyonari, T. (1999). Bounded generalized reciprocity: Ingroup boasting and ingroup favoritism. *Advances in Group Processes*, *16*, 161–197.

Yamagishi, T., & Kiyonari, T. (2000). The group as container of generalized reciprocity. *Social Psychology Quarterly*, *62*, 116–132.

Part 4

Health behaviour and health behaviour change

12 Positive affect and meaning-focused coping during significant psychological stress

Susan Folkman and Judith Tedlie Moskowitz
Osher Center for Integrative Medicine,
University of California—
San Francisco, USA

Stress and coping theory is organised around two important processes: appraisal and coping (Lazarus & Folkman, 1984). Appraisal refers to the individual's evaluation of the significance of an event for his or her well-being and the adequacy of resources for coping. Situations that threaten or harm well-being and that also tax or exceed the individual's coping resources are appraised as stressful. Coping refers to thoughts and behaviours that people use to regulate their emotions and address underlying problems. The concepts of appraisal and coping help to explain why people respond differently to the same or comparable events. Both appraisal and coping are tightly linked to emotions. Emotions go hand-in-hand with appraisal, and coping efforts are directed at managing these emotions, especially emotions that are stress related.

All three qualities—appraisal, coping, and emotion—are dynamic and change as a specific encounter unfolds over a relatively short time or as a chronic condition unfolds over long periods of time. Lazarus's (1966) early statement of stress theory dealt primarily with the appraisal of threat, and highlighted coping that was directed primarily at the regulation of distress emotions, reflecting both his earlier training in psychodynamic models and his later interest in cognitive approaches to stress that evolved during his laboratory research in the 1950s and 1960s.

In 1980 Lazarus, Kanner, and Folkman published a chapter about the possible roles of positive emotions in the stress process. Despite that chapter, and some mention of positive emotions by a handful of investigators, until recently there has been little interest in this question. Basically, this essay begins where the 1980 chapter left off. We review evidence that positive emotion occurs with negative emotion during the stress process and consider whether its presence merits attention. Then we get to the central issues: How positive affect is generated and sustained during periods when people experience harm, loss, and threat, and how positive affect in turn helps to sustain coping, especially over time in enduring stressful situations or conditions.

Positive emotions and the stress process

Most studies of coping have been concerned primarily with the regulation of distress. This emphasis harks back to the concern with the regulation of anxiety that characterises the ego-psychology approach to coping as a higher-order defensive process (e.g., Vaillant, 1977). The concern with the regulation of distress also reflects the mounting evidence linking distress to disease, especially cardiovascular disease (see May/June 2005 supplement to *Psychosomatic Medicine*, Sheps & Rozanski, 2005).

Our programme of research followed in the tradition of examining distress and the processes that contributed to and protected against it. We studied these processes in the context of AIDS-related caregiving and bereavement, which enabled us to consider profound stress, both acute and chronic. However, we also included measures of positive mood (for a summary of this research, see Folkman, 1997; Folkman & Moskowitz, 2000). The first of the studies, in which we followed 253 caregivers for up to 5 years, yielded both expected and unexpected findings, which were first reported in a keynote address at Rolduc in 1995 at the first conference of the Dutch Research Institute of Psychology and Health. In that presentation, Folkman described two sets of expected findings and two sets of unexpected findings. The expected findings pertained to high levels of depressed mood reported by caregivers throughout caregiving, and the even higher levels reported by the 156 caregivers whose partners died, for whom levels of depressed mood reached two standard deviations above the general population norms. These findings were consistent with other research on conjugal bereavement.

What were unexpected were the findings regarding the frequency of positive affect. With the exception of the period surrounding the partner's death, throughout caregiving and bereavement participants reported experiencing positive affect at a frequency comparable to negative affect. Affect was assessed with two measures: the Bradburn Positive and Negative Affect Scales and the Positive States of Mind measure (Horowitz, Adler, & Kegeles, 1988). The data from the two measures told the same story. We looked in the literature to see whether our findings were aberrational and learned they were not. Co-occurrence was reported in at least three studies that involved intensely stressful circumstances (Bonanno & Keltner, 1997; Viney, 1986; Wortman & Silver, 1987). Subsequently, we replicated the finding in two additional caregiver studies. We were intrigued and wanted to learn more about positive affect and the stress process.

Historical perspective: Positive emotion in the stress process

Positive emotions have not been entirely neglected in stress research. They have been discussed in relation to the primary appraisal of stressful situations as a challenge. Challenge signals the possibility of mastery or gain, is characterised by positively toned emotions such as eagerness, excitement, and confidence (Folkman & Lazarus, 1985; Skinner & Brewer, 2002), and has been perceived as beneficial for performance.

Discussions of positive emotions in the stress process, however, have been relatively patchy until recently, when developments in contemporary psychology fuelled an interest in this topic. "Positive Psychology", which was highlighted by Martin Seligman during his presidency of the American Psychological Association in 1998, seeks to advance knowledge about human virtues and states of well-being. A literature on these topics is growing rapidly. This new emphasis has renewed interest in processes such as resilience and thriving, which are complementary to our interest in positive emotion and stress.

A second development that helped to foster interest in positive affect in the stress process is the controversy about the extent to which positive and negative affect are two sides of the same coin or independent constructs. Although the controversy has not been definitively resolved, there is evidence that positive and negative affect have distinct biological substrates and that they are relatively independent constructs except under conditions where the implications for well-being are unambiguously positive or negative (see Zautra, 2003, for full review of these issues).

Why care about positive affect?

Just because positive affect is present does not necessarily mean that it adds anything to our understanding of the stress process over and above what we learn from distress. Does positive affect matter? A good place to start answering this question is by looking at recent studies linking positive affect and health, including morbidity, mortality, and survival.

There is substantial evidence of an association of positive affect and morbidity (for recent review, see Pressman & Cohen, 2005). Ostir, Markides, Peek, and Goodwin (2001), for example, found that lower positive affect at baseline was associated with a greater risk of stroke incidence after adjusting for potential confounders in a 6-year follow-up of healthy seniors. Negative affect was not associated with stroke occurrence, and controlling for negative affect did not reduce the association of positive affect with stroke. Positive affect was also found to be associated with lower risk of recurrence of stroke (Middleton & Bird, 1996) and the occurrence of infectious illness in initially health adults after controlling for potential confounders, including negative affect (Cohen, Doyle, Turner, Alper, & Skoner, 2003). Pressman and Cohen conclude their review of positive affect and morbidity by saying "Both cross-sectional and prospective studies of PA [positive affect] and illness virtually unanimously support an association between high PA and health . . . the near unanimity of results supporting a beneficial association of PA on health is impressive" (p. 933). Positive affect has also been linked with other health-related outcomes including improved immune function, lower basal cortisol levels, and reduced inflammatory responses to stress, among other outcomes (for review, see Fredrickson & Losada, 2005).

Studies of positive affect and mortality that have been conducted with older community-residing samples also show an association between positive affect and mortality. One of the more rigorous studies, conducted by Ostir, Markides, Black, and Goodwin (2000), found that people with higher positive affect at baseline were half as likely to die during the 2-year follow-up compared to those with low levels of positive affect, after controlling for baseline medical conditions, body mass index, smoking and drinking, age, and levels of negative affect. In another interesting study, Levy, Slade, Kunkel, and Kasl (2002) followed a sample of 660 adults for 23 years in a study that included attitudes towards ageing. Those with more positive self-perceptions of ageing at baseline lived 7.5 years longer than those with less positive perceptions, after controlling for a number of possible confounders. Moskowitz (2003) found that positive affect, and not negative affect or other potential confounders, predicted survival in AIDS patients over 7.5 years. Studies of cancer patients provide mixed findings, with only one finding a beneficial effect of state positive affect while other studies did not find evidence of a beneficial effect (reviewed in Pressman & Cohen, 2005). Thus, the evidence linking positive emotion and survival is mixed, but the evidence that does exist is sufficient to merit further investigation of this link.

Functions of positive emotions

That positive emotions are frequently, although not always, associated with important health outcomes provides a basis for pursuing the question to the next step—what do positive emotions "do" for us? What are the possible functions of positive emotions, particularly functions relevant to the stress process?

Work by Isen and her colleagues suggests that positive affect has a facilitative effect on motivation and performance in laboratory tasks (Erez & Isen, 2002). Further, their studies show that positive affect interacts with task conditions in influencing motivation, and that the influence of positive affect is through its beneficial effects on cognitive processes related to motivation, especially instrumentality and the attractiveness of the task.

Fredrickson (1998) has developed the "Broaden and Build Model of Positive Emotions", which is premised on evidence that positive emotions broaden the scope of attention, cognition, and action, and help to build physical, intellectual, and social resources. Positive emotions, such as joy, interest, contentment, pride, and love, broaden people's momentary thought–action repertoires and widen the array of thoughts and actions that come to mind. For example, joy creates the urge to play, push limits, and be creative. Interest creates the urge to explore, take in new information, and expand the self. Pride creates the urge to share news of the achievement and envision even greater future achievements.

Another important feature of positive emotions is that they "undo" lingering negative emotions (Fredrickson & Levenson, 1998). The undoing occurs by lessening the hold that a negative emotion has gained on that person's mind and body by dismantling or undoing preparation for specific action (Fredrickson, 2001). Tugade and Fredrickson (2004) found that for resilient individuals—individuals who have the capacity to modify responses to changing situational demands, especially frustrating or stressful encounters—positive emotions accelerated cardiovascular recovery from negative emotional arousal in response to the threat of a public speech. These findings are consistent with the "undoing effect" posited by Fredrickson.

In a study of positive thoughts and experiences, Reed and Aspinwall (1998) found that recalling past acts of kindness led to less avoidance of negative information in another, unrelated domain. Other studies have found that success on an initial task makes participants more willing to examine weaknesses or failures on subsequent, unrelated tasks (Trope & Pomerantz, 1998). So positive emotion may serve to facilitate more effective self-regulation by making the examination of weaknesses or shortcomings less aversive.

However, the typical context in which positive emotion has been studied is often a contrived laboratory stressor. As we have shown, positive emotions do in fact occur during intensely stressful situations, and based on findings with laboratory models, they should provide resources that can facilitate important coping similar to those found in laboratory settings.

Finally, we view all emotions that are expressed during a stressful situation as indicators of something that matters to the person, whether it be internal or in a transaction with the environment, whether in the past, the present, or the anticipated future, whether with positive, negative, or combined implications for well-being (Lazarus, 1991). Positive emotions are indicators of benign or beneficial appraisals of what is happening. Such indicators, when they occur during chronic stress, draw the investigator's attention to lines of inquiry that differ from those we follow when looking only at distress.

Positive emotions and coping

Stress and coping theory (Lazarus & Folkman, 1984) posits two major functions or purposes of coping: to regulate distress (emotion-focused coping) and to manage the problems causing the distress (problem-focused coping). Based on our programme of research and analyses of narratives which described stressful events that included positive emotions as well as narratives describing positive daily events, we realised we needed a way to describe coping processes that focus on the reappraisal of meaning, especially positive reappraisals of meaning. The processes we observed appeared to be distinct from processes used to regulate distress, such as distancing and escape avoidance, and seemed to be about the reappraisal of meaning. We called this meaning-focused coping (Folkman, 1997; Park & Folkman, 1997a).

Meaning-focused coping is not orthogonal to problem- and emotion-focused coping. Rather, it provides another way to group coping responses based on reappraisals of meaning. Our coping inventory, the Ways of Coping

(Folkman & Lazarus, 1988), and other widely used inventories such as the COPE (Carver, Scheier, & Weintraub, 1989) include coping strategies that are meaning focused and that are likely to generate positive affect. For example, the Ways of Coping includes a positive reappraisal scale that is usually grouped with emotion-focused coping. It includes items such as "I changed or grew as a person" and "I came out of the situation better than when I went in", but items such as these seemed to tap only one aspect of what we were seeing in the narratives.

Park and Folkman (1997a) discussed meaning-focused coping in terms of global meaning and situational meaning. Global meaning refers to the person's enduring values, beliefs about the self in the world and how the world works, and highest-order goals. Global meaning, for example, influences major choices the person makes, the overarching goals that he or she pursues, and his or her expectations regarding cause and effect. Situational meaning refers to the person's appraisal of a proximal stressful encounter in relation to proximal goals and implications for the person's well-being.

Profound stress can occur when a proximal stressful situation violates global meaning. For instance, a person who believes he is healthy with a long life ahead is very likely to experience profound stress if he is told he has a life-threatening disease. His global belief about his health and longevity becomes discrepant with the new understanding of the threat to his health. A discrepancy between global and situational beliefs can be reduced by changing situational meaning, global meaning, or both, although in general global meaning is not as easily changed (Park & Folkman, 1997a). Discrepancies can also be tolerated. For example, caregiving partners of men dying of AIDS continued to score high on a measure of optimism even when their partners were very sick and nearing death (Park & Folkman, 1997b).

The process of the reappraisal of meaning that we observe in narratives is rarely linear and usually emotionally complex, in that it often involves loss of meaning as well as the gain of new or renewed meaning. Here we are interested in exploring meaning-focused coping in terms of the actual coping processes through which meaning—both global and situational—changes to help the person deal with stressful situations that are chronic and for which there are no readily available fully satisfactory outcomes.

A tricky issue has to do with the often "automatic" nature of reappraisal. Effort or reflective deliberation is not always involved. By definition, however, coping involves awareness and effort (Lazarus & Folkman, 1984). Not all reappraisal processes, therefore, can necessarily be considered coping. While recognising this issue, we feel it is important to understand reappraisal of meaning, regardless of whether it is technically coping, because ultimately we believe that people can be taught to engage in this type of reappraisal. For now, we refer to these processes as coping.

The small but growing literature on meaning-focused coping, which deals almost exclusively with the perception of positive change following trauma and adversity, indicates a consistent association with positive affect and an inconsistent and usually weaker association to the management of negative affect (Linley & Joseph, 2004). As we will point out, we believe that positive affect facilitates subsequent meaning-focused coping and helps sustain problem-focused coping efforts over the long term. In these respects, positive affect has adaptational significance, especially in coping with enduring, chronic stress.

Here we discuss five kinds of meaning-focused coping, drawing on observations from our programme of research on caregiving and end-of-life, as well as the work of others who have observed meaning-focused coping in their studies of people with chronic illness.

Realigning priorities

The realisation that a stressful situation is not going to be resolved in the foreseeable future often leads to a reordering of priorities in order to deal with the altered reality. This reordering can be experienced as a shift in perspective, and it can "just happen", or it can happen as the result of reflection. It generally involves a reappraisal of what is important, what matters in terms of the individual's values and beliefs. The reordering of priorities itself involves an acceptance that things have changed, which is essentially an acceptance of loss, but it should also provide the basis for a renewed sense of purpose as the individual moves forward (Stroebe & Schut, 2001).

Theoretically, the reordering of priorities reflects underlying values that comprise general meaning. Values add the "mattering" quality to priorities. People find strength in focusing on what is really important to them in terms of what really matters. Sometimes this clarification "just happens", at other times it is the result of reflection, and sometimes it is both. In a study of maternal caregivers of children with chronic conditions, for example, 47% quit working outside the home in order to care for their child (Wilson et al., 2005). Presumably, this change reflected a shift in priorities regarding working outside the home and caring for a child in the home. A shift in priorities and the reallocation of resources, however, can exact a toll. In the case of the mothers of chronically ill children, for example, the decision to quit work may have created financial strain, which then becomes an additional stressor over time. The toleration of the additional stressor will depend in large part on the strength of commitment to the priority of caregiving (how much it matters) as well as having options for living within a reduced budget. Thus, in real life the reordering of priorities is likely to be complex, with the process generating secondary stressors, and thus negative affect as well as positive affect.

Adaptive goal processes

The pursuit of realistic goals in efforts to resolve a stressful situation, what we call "planful problem solving", is consistently associated with positive affect, as noted also by Carver and Scheier (1998) in their discussion of the self-regulation of behaviour. However, head-on problem-solving effort is often unsuccessful in chronically stressful conditions. There may be no realistic way to improve the overall situation. An adaptive response is to reappraise the tenability of the pursued goal, relinquish untenable goals, and substitute new goals that are both realistic and meaningful. We have referred to the process of goal evaluation, relinquishment, and substitution as "Adaptive Goal Processes" (Stein, Folkman, Trabasso, & Richards, 1997).

We emphasise that the new goal has to be valued; it needs to matter to the person. As demonstrated in the literature on goals, valuing a goal affects motivation and the ability to pursue the goal over time. For example, Sheldon and Elliot (1999) have shown that people whose goals are consistent with their core values (self-concordant goals) put more sustained effort into achieving those goals and are more likely to attain them. Further, people who attain goals that are self-concordant experience greater well-being than those whose goals are not self-concordant.

Others have formulated similar approaches to dealing with unattainable goals. Wrosch, Scheier, Miller, Schulz, and Carver (2003), for example, studied associations between goal disengagement, goal re-engagement, and subjective well-being in three samples: undergraduates, young adults, and parents of children with cancer or healthy children. Their findings indicated that disengagement from specific unattainable goals has beneficial effects on well-being and, importantly, that the "capacity to find, commit to, and pursue new goals is a protective factor that may help a person manage unattainable goals" (p. 1505).

The following narrative from a study of mothers of autistic children illustrates this process in real life, where the process is not always linear and often takes time to unfold (Epel et al., 2005).

> *Mom of 9 year old son with autism, diagnosed at age 2½*
> I remember going through my daily routine and feeling like, oh there's something I forgot about that's really bad and then I remember, oh yeah, he's got autism. And it was just like . . . I wish I hadn't remembered it [chuckling]. I'd think, oh yeah there's something that's not right. And then you remember, and you're like awwhh, right, and I went through that, and there's a little bit of grieving, but I pretty much lived through that and just kind of got it aside and I didn't have time to deal with that. I had to get help and I just dove right into what I could do for him and how I could help him to be the best person he could be.
>
> So when the first therapist came, she said, oh, you know, he's going to be speaking in sentences by the time he's five, and I just felt like she gave me the whole world.

Benefit finding

Tennen and Affleck's (2002, for review) seminal research on benefit finding, and the growing interest of others in the general theme of the ways in which people find benefit in their stressful experiences, have led to a literature on the beneficial effects of stress (see Linley & Joseph, 2004, for review). Of particular interest to us is that benefit finding is consistently related to positive affect (Linley & Joseph 2004; Pakenham, 2005).

Benefits are often framed in terms of personal growth, especially in relation to traumatic events (Tedeschi, Park, & Calhoun, 1998). "Personal growth" is a general term that can refer to a number of qualities such as growth in wisdom, patience, and competence; greater appreciation for life, greater clarity about what matters; strengthened faith or spirituality; and improved quality of social relationships.

The qualities that people find beneficial should reflect their underlying values, goals, and beliefs. Individuals from Asian cultures, for example, in which the collective (family, the company one works for) may be valued above the well-being of the individual, may identify benefits in relation to the well-being of the collective, whereas for westerners, the most salient benefits might be those that affect their individual personal growth.

Benefit finding, by definition, occurs when a stressful transaction has unfolded to the point that the individual can reflect on the possible beneficial effects of what he or she has experienced. Several studies found that the longer the time since the critical event, the greater the benefit finding (Linley & Joseph, 2004).

> *Bereaved male, about 3 years after partner's death*
> I have learned that I am a stronger person than I probably ever imagined and that I have more resources within me than I could have ever imagined. . . . I would have never chosen to go through the loss of him. But it has been a very positive thing for my life because I am a much stronger, much better person going through this side of it all.

Benefit reminding

Closely related to benefit finding is the concept of benefit reminding (Tennen & Affleck, 2002). Benefit reminding depends on benefits already having been found. Tennen and Affleck define benefit reminding as effortful cognitions in which the individual reminds himself/herself of the possible benefits stemming from the stressful experience. They studied patients suffering from fibromyalgia and asked these patients to keep a daily diary and to indicate how much that day they had reminded themselves of the benefits of their chronic pain. On days when these patients made greater efforts to remind themselves of the benefits that had come from their illness, they were more likely to experience pleasurable mood, regardless of the pain they had experienced that day. This finding is highly relevant to the notion of co-occurrence of negative and positive state that we discussed earlier.

Infusing ordinary events with meaning

Early in the data collection for a longitudinal study of AIDS-related caregiving that was conducted in the years before effective antiretroviral treatments were available, participants told us that we were asking only about the stresses associated with caregiving. These men said they had positive moments too, and wanted to tell us about them. We constructed a question that asked about something meaningful that had happened which had helped them get through the day, with follow-up questions concerning what it was about and what about the event made them feel good. The question was asked in nearly 1800 interviews, and positive events were described in 99% of them.

An analysis of these events indicated that most were ordinary events of daily life, such as a kind word offered by a friend, an expression of appreciation by a sick partner, seeing a good movie with a friend, meeting a deadline at work, or seeing something beautiful in nature, such as a sunset (Folkman, Moskowitz, Ozer, & Park, 1997). Although these events were ordinary, the narratives of these events indicated that they were in fact personally meaningful in terms of values, goals, and beliefs. We have asked about meaningful events in subsequent studies and have found that they are common in the lives of people living with chronic stress (Moskowitz, Wrubel, Barton, & Grant, 2005). Thus, positive meaningful events are of interest as a component of the process through which situational meaning is positively appraised, creating positive affect, during stressful times.

> *Meaningful event reported by mother of a child with HIV*
> . . . all the stuff my son wanted, the wrestling stuff, I found everything on sale. Things that were $40 I got for $10, and these are things he asked me for. I felt really good. And like I did something really good then. I went downtown and took care of what I had to take care of . . . Like I really accomplished something.

Amplifying positive affect

Our analyses of meaningful events led us to consider the idea that people "create" these positive events, whether deliberately or not, as a way of gaining momentary relief from distress. An interesting question is whether people direct their attention in a way that intensifies or prolongs these momentary breaks from distress. Langston (1994), for example, introduced the notion of "capitalising", which refers to the process of beneficially interpreting positive events. Ways of capitalising include enhancing self-regard through the interpretation of personal accountability or control of a positive event, marking an event in some expressive fashion such as jumping for joy, describing the event and one's role in it to others, or celebrating with friends. Langston found that capitalising was associated with higher levels of positive affect while it was not associated with negative affect.

More recent findings reported from a series of studies by (Gable, Impett, Reis, & Asher, 2004) supported the association of positive events with positive but not negative affect, and illustrated the beneficial effects of capitalising by sharing the events with others. Langston points out that by capitalising positive events, people can parlay a single positive experience into a series of them. We have seen capitalising in our research on maternal care-givers, as shown in this excerpt from an interview about positive events (Moskowitz et al., 2005, unpublished):

INTERVIEWER (I): Now I'm interested in hearing about something that was positive, that made you feel good—something that happened to you or that you did that sort of just helped you get through the day, in the last week. Or something that someone did for you.

PARTICIPANT (P): Something that we did. We took the kids to the snow last Saturday. And they really, really enjoyed it. It was probably one of the nicer trips that they—just the two—well, the three. The baby and C and L. And the other two girls had gone to their Grandma's. And it just made me feel good that we took the time to do that for them, because neither one of them had ever seen the snow. And they had such a good time. They just enjoyed it so much.

I: So they really enjoyed themselves a lot.

P: Yeah, oh, they did.

I: So how did it make you feel?

P: I was tickled. I was glad that I was able to do that for them. And it was a nice day. It was just really—we took them to Denny's for dinner—or lunch—and then we went and played in the snow and then it wore them out. [laughs]

I: They slept well? [laughs]

P: They slept on the way home. Yeah, it was just a day trip, and I'd really wanted to go for overnight, but it just didn't work out. And so we just went for the day.

I: So did you do anything in response to the event, like tell other people about it?

P: Oh yeah. Oh yeah, we took pictures and we shared the pictures with the kids. And they just gleam when they talk about it, how much fun they had. And we're trying to make arrangements to do it again. They want to do it again.

The adaptive functions of positive emotions in the coping process

Stress and coping theory is based on the assumption that the stress process is dynamic. Appraisals and coping change as an encounter unfolds (Folkman &

Lazarus, 1985). Further, the process is suffused with emotion. Emotions are generated by initial appraisals of stress, regulated by coping, and associated with outcome appraisals. The dynamic nature of the model means that appraisals of encounter outcomes and their emotions can set the stage for the next stressful encounter. The effects of the first round of coping on psychological resources, for example, can affect for better or worse the person's resources for coping on subsequent rounds.

We address just one facet of this process by identifying pathways through which the positive affect and the meaning-focused coping that generates it can have beneficial effects on coping resources and subsequent appraisals and coping effort.

Restores resources

We discussed Fredrickson's Broaden and Build Model of Positive Emotion earlier. Fredrickson (2001) makes the important point that the growth of personal resources during states of positive emotions is durable. "They outlast the transient emotional states that led to their acquisition" (p. 220).

With respect to physiological resources, earlier we noted studies by Fredrickson and her colleagues indicating that positive affect is associated with the recovery of stress-related physiological reactions in laboratory studies. Extrapolating to acute stressful events in naturalistic settings, we would hypothesise that positive affect can contribute to adaptive physiological stress responses to those events. These beneficial effects may be especially relevant to physical health over the long term, particularly in the case of chronic stress that is characterised by recurring acute events.

With respect to psychological resources, we would anticipate that events in which benefit is perceived, especially benefits that favour a positive evaluation of the self, contribute to the restoration of psychological resources relevant to those benefits. The perceived benefit of growth, for example, can reinforce psychological resources related to wisdom, knowledge, and improved interpersonal relationships.

Psychological resources should also be restored when individuals who pursue meaningful realistic goals achieve the desired positive outcomes. Even if these outcomes are modest and don't change the overall stressful dynamic, they can still produce a sense of accomplishment that should feed back to personal resources such as the perception of self-efficacy, mastery, and control. With respect to social resources, processes such as capitalising, which can promote closeness, or adaptive goal processes that are applied to stressful interpersonal situations, can reinforce social bonds and strengthen perceived social support.

Motivates and sustains coping

Meaning-focused coping that draws on deeply held values, and leads to a reordering of priorities and goals, creates or renews a sense of purpose that is essential to sustaining coping over the long term. We hypothesise that the awareness and valuing of purpose is heightened by positive emotion and that both the revised appraisal of purpose and the positive emotion that is generated by it help to sustain instrumental coping on a day-to-day basis. This hypothesis is consistent with laboratory studies described earlier.

Interestingly, the positive emotion that is generated by meaning-focused coping may in turn foster subsequent meaning-focused coping (Tugade & Fredrickson, 2004) and may increase sensitivity to the meaning relevance of a situation (King, Hicks, Krull, & Del Gaiso, 2006). These findings suggest a feedback process in which positive emotion and meaning-focused coping reinforce each other.

Conclusion

A strong case can now be made that positive affect occurs during stressful situations that are chronic, and there is good reason to believe that the presence of positive affect over time can affect health, independent of negative affect. We have continued to develop an understanding of the meaning-focused coping processes that play a major role in the regulation of positive affect, especially in chronically stressful situations where favourable outcomes are not readily available. We have proposed feedback loops through which both positive affect and meaning-focused coping can restore coping resources and motivate coping effort over the long term. However, the study of positive emotions in the stress process is still in its early stages of development. We look forward to further work by ourselves and others that will help elaborate our understanding of positive emotions in enabling individuals to maintain well-being under highly stressful, even dire, circumstances.

Acknowledgement

We thank Judith Wrubel for her thoughtful comments on drafts of this chapter.

References

Bonanno, G. A., & Keltner, D. (1997). Facial expression of emotion and the course of conjugal bereavement. *Journal of Abnormal Psychology, 106*, 126–137.

Carver, C. S., & Scheier, M. F. (1998). *On the self-regulation of behavior*. New York: Cambridge University Press.

Carver, C. S., Scheier, M. F., & Weintraub, J. K. (1989). Assessing coping strategies: A theoretically based approach. *Journal of Personality and Social Psychology, 56*, 267–283.

Cohen, S., Doyle, W. J., Turner, R. B., Alper, C. M., & Skoner, D. P. (2003). Emotional style and susceptibility to the common cold. *Psychosomatic Medicine, 65*, 652–657.

Epel, E., Moscowitz, J., Wrubel, J., Follkman, S. (2005). *Stress processes in mothers of autistic children.* University of California, San Francisco. Unpublished manuscript.

Erez, A., & Isen, A. (2002). The influence of positive affect on the components of expectancy motivation. *Journal of Personality and Social Psychology, 87*, 1055–1067.

Folkman, S. (1997). Positive psychological states and coping with severe stress. *Social Science and Medicine, 45*, 1207–1221.

Folkman, S., & Lazarus, R. S. (1985). If it changes it must be a process: Study of emotion and coping during three stages of a college examination. *Journal of Personality and Social Psychology, 48*, 150–170.

Folkman, S., & Lazarus, R. S. (1988). *Ways of Coping Questionnaire.* Palo Alto, CA: Consulting Psychologists Press.

Folkman, S., & Moskowitz, J. T. (2000). Positive affect and the other side of coping. *American Psychologist, 55*, 647–654.

Folkman, S., Moskowitz, J. T., Ozer, E. M., & Park, C. L. (1997). Positive meaningful events and coping in the context of HIV/AIDS. In B. H. Gottlieb (Ed.), *Coping with chronic stress* (pp. 293–314). New York: Plenum.

Fredrickson, B. L. (1998). What good are positive emotions? *Review of General Psychology, 2*, 300–319.

Fredrickson, B. L. (2001). The role of positive emotions in positive psychology: The broaden-and-build theory of positive emotions. *American Psychologist, Special Issue, 56*, 218–226.

Fredrickson, B. L., & Levenson, R. (1998). Positive emotions speed recovery from the cardiovascular sequelae of negative emotions *Cognition & Emotion, 12*, 191–220.

Fredrickson, B. L., & Losada, M. (2005). Positive affect and the complex dynamics of human flourishing. *American Psychologist, 60*, 678–686.

Gable, S. L., Impett, E. A., Reis, H. T., & Asher, E. R. (2004). What do you do when things go right? The intrapersonal and interpersonal benefits of sharing positive events. *Journal of Personality and Social Psychology, 87*, 238–245.

Horowitz, M., Adler, N., & Kegeles, S. (1988). A scale for measuring the occurrence of positive states of mind: A preliminary report. *Psychosomatic Medicine, 50*, 477–483.

King, L. A., Hicks, J. A., Krull, J. L., & Del Gaiso, A. K. (2006). Positive affect and the experience of meaning in life. *Journal of Personality and Social Psychology, 90*, 179–196.

Langston, C. A. (1994). Capitalizing on and coping with daily-life events: Expressive responses to positive events. *Journal of Personality and Social Psychology, 67*, 1112–1125.

Lazarus, R. S. (1966). *Psychological stress and the coping process.* New York: McGraw Hill.

Lazarus, R. S. (1991). *Emotion and adaptation.* New York: Oxford University Press.

Lazarus, R. S., & Folkman, S. (1984). *Stress, appraisal, and coping.* New York: Springer.

Lazarus, R. S., Kanner, A. D., & Folkman, S. (1980). Emotions: A cognitive-phenomenological analysis. In R. Plutchik & H. Kellerman (Eds.), *Theories of emotion. Vol 1. Emotion: Theory, research, and experience* (pp. 189–217). New York: Academic Press.

Levy, B. R., Slade, M., Kunkel, S. R., & Kasl, S. V. (2002). Longevity increased by positive self-perceptions of aging. *Journal of Personality and Social Psychology, 83,* 261–270.

Linley, P. A., & Joseph, S. (2004). Positive change following trauma and adversity: A review. *Journal of Traumatic Stress, 17,* 11–21.

Middleton, R. A., & Bird, E. K. (1996). Psychosocial factors and hospital readmission status of older persons wth cardiovascular disease. *Journal of Applied Rehabilitation Counseling, 27,* 3–10.

Moskowitz, J. T. (2003). Positive affect predicts lower risk of AIDS mortality. *Psychosomatic Medicine, 65,* 620–626.

Moskowitz, J. T., Wrubel, J., Barton, L., & Grant, J. (2005). [*Unpublished data.*]

Ostir, G. V., Markides, K. S., Black, S. A., & Goodwin, J. S. (2000). Emotional well-being predicts subsequent functional independence and survival. *Journal of the American Gerontological Society, 48,* 473–478.

Ostir, G. V., Markides, K. S., Peek, M. K., & Goodwin, J. S. (2001). The association between emotional well-being and the incidence of stroke in older adults. *Psychosomatic Medicine, 63,* 210–125.

Pakenham, K. I. (2005). Benefit finding in multiple sclerosis and associations with positive and negative outcomes. *Health Psychology, 24,* 123–132.

Park, C. L., & Folkman, S. (1997a). The role of meaning in the context of stress and coping. *General Review of Psychology, 2,* 115–144.

Park, C. L., & Folkman, S. (1997b). Stability and change in psychosocial resources during caregiving and bereavement in partners of men with AIDS. *Journal of Personality, 65,* 421–447.

Pressman, S., & Cohen, S. (2005). The influence of positive affect on health: A review. *Psychological Bulletin, 131,* 925–971.

Reed, M. B., & Aspinwall, L. G. (1998). Self-affirmation reduces biased processing of health-risk information. *Motivation and Emotion, 22,* 99–132.

Sheldon, K. M., & Elliot, A. J. (1999). Goal striving, need satisfaction, and longitudinal well-being; The self-concordance model. *Journal of Personality and Social Psychology, 76,* 482–497.

Sheps, D. S., & Rozanski, A. (Eds.). (2005). *Depression and heart disease: Epidemiology, pathophysiology and treatment* (Vol. 67). New York: Lippincott Williams & Wilkins.

Skinner, N., & Brewer, N. (2002). The dynamics of threat and challenge appraisals prior to stressful achievement events. *Journal of Personality and Social Psychology, 83,* 678–692.

Stein, N., Folkman, S., Trabasso, T., & Richards, T. A. (1997). Appraisal and goal processes as predictors of psychological well-being in bereaved caregivers. *Journal of Personality and Social Psychology, 72,* 872–884.

Stroebe, M. S., & Schut, H. (2001). Meaning making in the dual process model of coping with bereavement. In R. A. Neimeyer (Ed.), *Meaning reconstruction and the experience of loss* (pp. 55–73). Washington, DC: American Psychological Association.

Tedeschi, R. G., Park, C. L., & Calhoun, L. G. (Eds.). (1998). *Posttraumatic growth.* Mahwah, NJ: Lawrence Erlbaum Associates Inc.

Tennen, H., & Affleck, G. (2002). Benefit-finding and benefit-reminding. In C. R. Snyder & S. J. Lopez (Eds.), *Handbook of positive psychology* (pp. 584–597). London: Oxford University Press.

Trope, Y., & Pomerantz, E. M. (1998). Resolving conflicts among self-evaluative motives: Positive experiences as a resource for overcoming defensiveness. *Motivation and Emotion, 22*, 53–72.

Tugade, M. M., & Fredrickson, B. L. (2004). Resilient individuals use positive emotions to bounce back from negative emotional arousal. *Journal of Personality and Social Psychology, 86*, 320–333.

Vaillant, G. E. (1977). *Adaption to life*. Boston, MA: Little, Brown.

Viney, L. L. (1986). Expression of positive emotion by people who are physically ill: Is it evidence of defending or coping? *Journal of Psychosomatic Research, 30*, 27–34.

Wilson, L., Moskowitz, J., Acree, M., Heyman, M. B., Harmatz, P., Ferrando, S. J. et al. (2005). The economic burden of home care for children with HIV and other chronic illnesses. *American Journal of Public Health, 95*, 1445–1452.

Wortman, C., & Silver, R. (1987). Coping with irrevocable loss. In G. R. VandenBos & B. K. Bryant (Eds.), *Cataclysms, crises, and catastrophies: Psychology in action* (Vol. 6, pp. 189–235). Washington, DC: American Psychological Association.

Wrosch, C., Scheier, M. F., Miller, G. E., Schultz, R., & Carver, C. S. (2003). Adaptive self-regulation of unattainable goals: Goal disengagement, goal reengagement, and subjective well-being. *Personality and Social Psychology Bulletin, 29*, 1494–1508.

Zautra, A. (2003). *Emotions, stress, and health*. London: Oxford University Press.

13 Self-regulation of health communications

A motivated processing approach to risk perception and persuasion

John B.F. de Wit
Utrecht University, The Netherlands

Enny Das
Free University—Amsterdam,
The Netherlands

Natascha de Hoog
Friedrich Schiller University, Jena, Germany

Around the globe, millions of individuals die annually from causes that could have been prevented (World Health Organization, 2004). In our time and place, individuals are affected most often by health conditions resulting from their own behaviours, such as smoking, unhealthy diets, insufficient physical exercise, and unprotected sex (for an overview, see Stroebe, 2000). Thus, effective disease prevention and health promotion ultimately depend on the thoughtful promotion of effective self-regulation of health-related behaviours. Social and health psychologists contribute in important ways to health promotion, for instance by developing and testing theories to explain motivational processes and volitional strategies involved in the successful initiation and maintenance of health-related actions (for overviews see Cameron & Leventhal, 2003; De Ridder & De Wit, 2006).

Over the past decades, social psychological theorising has become a major foundation for successful approaches to the study and change of health behaviour (see De Wit & Stroebe, 2004; Stroebe, 2000; Stroebe & De Wit, 1996), and theory-based interventions have been developed and tested for a wide range of issues (see e.g., Rutter & Quine, 2002). In this chapter we focus on the important role of beliefs regarding personal risk or vulnerability in understanding health-related behaviours and promoting change. In particular, we address the biased nature of these perceptions and subsequent information processing. Classic social psychological theories of health and social behaviour have been mostly based on the assumption that health behaviour is guided by rational deliberation and cognitive processing of information (e.g., Rogers, 1983). By contrast, more recent perspectives emphasise the interplay of affect and cognition in predicting persuasion. The complex dynamics between emotions and thoughts constitute the main focus of this chapter.

An important part of the chapter is devoted to theory and research regarding the efficacy of communication strategies to promote awareness and acceptance of a personal health threat. This overview features recent work conducted by Stroebe and colleagues (Das, De Wit, & Stroebe, 2003; De Hoog, Stroebe, & De Wit, 2005a; Stroebe, 2000), who propose a novel theoretical conceptualisation of health-threat communication that sees persuasion as resulting from the biased processing of information, and helps to synthesise extant theory and research. We start, however, by discussing the motivated processing of health-risk information. Next, we present theory and findings regarding strategies to eliminate defensive biases in the health persuasion process, and possible positive effects of defensiveness.

Health beliefs and persuasion

Initial theorising of the effects of health communication, advanced in the 1950s, emphasised the affective properties of health-risk communication. The drive reduction model specifically saw persuasion as a product of the reinforcing decline in fear that may result from accepting a recommended protective action (Hovland, Janis, & Kelley, 1953). However, even in this period where instrumental-learning theorising was still dominant, cognitive accounts were proposed that saw individuals' health behaviours as resulting from their expectancies, and served to derive persuasive interventions to promote health-related actions by changing individuals' beliefs. The health belief model (e.g., Rosenstock, 1974) emerged from this work, and became an important early member of a family of social-cognitive models of health behaviour that came to dominate the field (cf. Conner & Norman, 2005).

The health belief model distinguished two major types of beliefs that affect the likelihood of individuals engaging a specific health behaviour (De Wit & Stroebe, 2004): the perception of a threat to one's health, and the evaluation of the costs and benefits of any action to avert the danger. Personal health threat reflects a sense of susceptibility to the condition and the individual's appraisal of its seriousness. The experience of some threat is considered a prerequisite to change. Protection-motivation theory similarly assumes that individuals' perceptions of the severity of, and their vulnerability to, a health threat affect their appraisal of the threat and reduce the likelihood of maladaptive responses (Rogers, 1983). More recent models distinguish multiple stages of change and posit that deliberative behaviour change will only be initiated after individuals become aware of a personal danger (e.g., Weinstein, Lyon, Sandman, & Cuite, 1998), providing the motivational impetus for action.

Promoting individuals' perception of a serious health risk generally is thought to contribute to behaviour change, albeit that this may only be a first step (e.g., Schwarzer, 2001). Nevertheless, a (tacit) assumption underlying many health promotion programmes is that individuals want to avoid harm and will be motivated to adopt precautions when they become aware of their vulnerability to a potentially serious condition. However, as Weinstein (2003, p. 22) notes, "the links between risk perceptions and health behavior are far from obvious" (see also Gerrard, Gibbons, & Bushman, 1996; Weinstein & Nicolich, 1993). Moreover, "effectively communicating health information has been found deceptively difficult" (Rothman, Kelly, Hertel, & Salovey, 2003, p. 278). In part this is because the message needs to be accepted, and messages that convey a personally relevant health threat are likely to be actively counterargued (e.g., Liberman & Chaiken, 1992). People have many ways of discounting unwelcome messages, and their perceptions of vulnerability are substantially and persistently biased.

The motivated tendency to construct comforting assessments of personal vulnerability has been extensively studied by Croyle, Ditto, Jemmott, and colleagues (for an overview, see Ditto & Croyle, 1995). These authors assessed the impact of risk factor testing using a fictitious condition to ensure optimal experimental control. Their programme of research demonstrated two basic phenomena (e.g., Jemmott, Ditto, & Croyle, 1986). First, individuals respond defensively to information suggesting that they are at risk for a health problem. Evidence has been obtained for two forms of defensiveness or denial: a minimisation of the health threat, and a heightened scepticism regarding the validity of the diagnosis. Second, health problems that are highly prevalent in participants' immediate social comparison group are considered to be less serious. Thus, relatively rare health conditions are perceived as more serious. Furthermore, both lay persons and physicians tend to overestimate the prevalence of conditions they have personally experienced, which also contributes to reducing perceptions of seriousness (e.g., Jemmott, Croyle, & Ditto, 1988). Subsequent research has provided evidence to support the motivational nature of biased reactions. Notably, defensive reactions disappear when respondents are informed that the health condition is treatable (e.g., Ditto, Jemmott, & Darley, 1988).

Ditto and Lopez (1992) propose that biases in judgements of undesirable information result from "motivated skepticism", a tendency to process information that is inconsistent with desired conclusions relatively extensively. This active scrutiny of information results in a more critical appraisal of its validity. Eventually individuals may be persuaded, although this may require more time and information. In support of this amount of processing explanation, Ditto, Munro, Apanovitch, Scepansky, and Lockhart (2003) recently found that participants who received unfavourable (bogus) medical feedback took more time to accept the validity of the test result and were more likely to spontaneously recheck its validity.

Promoting open-minded responses to threatening health information

It appears, then, that individuals are often reluctant to face the truth about their health status. Accordingly, receivers of health messages are likely to minimise the seriousness of a health risk, deny its relevance, or engage in wishful thinking about potential solutions (e.g., Das et al., 2003; De Hoog et al., 2005a; Ditto & Croyle, 1995). From a self-regulation perspective, this defensive processing of threatening health information may serve several functions. For instance, defensive processing may protect an individual against negative emotions such as fear, irritation, anger, and disgust. Defensive processing of self-threatening information may also protect the integrity of the self, and help to maintain a positive self-image. Notwithstanding these potentially adaptive functions of defensive responses, they may have serious drawbacks when they prevent people from protecting their health.

Recent research efforts have hence focused on strategies that decrease defensive responses, and make individuals more accepting of personal health risks. These efforts have yielded two self-regulatory mechanisms that may positively affect the processing and acceptance of health information: self-affirmation, and mood. Self-affirmation can broadly be defined as the affirmation of values that are important to the self (Steele, 1988), and there is evidence that self-affirmation can increase the acceptance of threatening health information (e.g., Harris & Napper, 2005; Reed & Aspinwall, 1998; Sherman, Nelson, & Steele, 2000). Recent findings suggest that the induction of a positive mood can also enhance message acceptance (e.g., Das & Fennis, 2005; Raghunathan & Trope, 2002). There may, however, be limits to the positive effects of these self-regulatory mechanisms.

Self-affirmation and health persuasion

One motive underlying individuals' reluctance to accept self-relevant threatening health messages may be found in self-affirmation theory (Steele, 1988), which posits that a fundamental need of the human self-regulatory system is to maintain self-integrity. Self-relevant threatening health information can pose a serious threat to self-integrity, and thus motivate an individual to restore global self-integrity. Individuals may restore self-integrity directly, for instance by defensively processing threatening information. However, people may also restore self-integrity indirectly, by drawing upon alternative sources of self-integrity, such as reflecting on one's positive standing on an unrelated but important value. For instance, individuals may affirm their love of beautiful things to restore self-integrity.

Research has confirmed that such self-affirmation can increase people's attendance to, and acceptance of, threatening health information. For instance, self-affirmation has been shown to increase perceptions of personal risk (Harris & Napper, 2005; Reed & Aspinwall, 1998; Sherman et al., 2000).

Self-affirmation also promoted healthy behaviours, such as the purchase of condoms (Sherman et al., 2000, Study 2), and intentions to reduce alcohol consumption (Harris & Napper, 2005). Thus, the affirmation of an important value that is unrelated to health can function as a buffer against the self-regulatory costs of a threatening health message, and enhance positive responses to threatening health information. This may be similar to the way in which psychological resources of optimism, personal control, and meaning have been found to buffer people against psychological as well as physical adversity (see Taylor & Brown, 1988; Taylor, Kemeny, Reed, Bower, & Guenewald, 2000). However, some threats to self-integrity may be so severe that they exceed the buffering function of self-affirmation. In these cases, self-affirmation cannot completely restore self-integrity, and may cease to be effective in opening up a receiver's mind to threatening health information.

Recent evidence suggests that there may indeed be limits to the positive effects of self-affirmation (Das, Koole, & Van Koningsbruggen, 2005). Across three experiments, self-affirmation increased participants' sensitivity to the quality of the arguments in health messages for moderate threats to the self. When participants did not feel very vulnerable to serious health consequences (e.g., stomach ulcers, heart problems), self-affirmation induced more open-minded, intensive processing of a health message. By contrast, when participants felt vulnerable to serious health problems, self-affirmation negatively affected message processing, message acceptance, and motivations to act upon a health message. Similar findings have been reported for the effects of self-esteem (e.g., Heatherton & Vohs, 2000; Vohs & Heatherton, 2004), which can be considered a chronic self-affirmation resource (Steele, Spencer, & Lynch, 1993).

Mood and health persuasion

Health messages contain important self-regulatory information, but also threaten the integrity of the self. In addition, open-minded processing of health messages is likely to generate negative emotions such as fear, anxiety, or guilt. Clearly, these are emotions that individuals prefer to avoid (e.g., Aspinwall, 1998; Trope & Fishbach, 2000; Trope & Neter, 1994). According to the mood-as-a-resource perspective (for an overview, see Trope, Ferguson, & Raghunathan, 2001), positive mood can function as a buffer against threatening health information, and thus increases an individual's openness to this information. According to this perspective, situations that offer individuals self-relevant information can create a motivational conflict. New information may provide guidance for self-improvement, but it can also uncover threatening weaknesses. The resolution of this self-control dilemma is thought to depend on individuals' mood. In a negative mood, people will be mainly motivated to improve their mood, and hence avoid information that contains threatening self-relevant elements. A positive mood is posited to act as a buffer against the short-term affective costs of self-threatening information, and thus increase processing of self-relevant information.

Recent studies support the proposition that a positive mood can motivate individuals to face self-threatening health information. For instance, a positive mood has been shown to enhance recall of the negative effects of caffeine intake for coffee drinkers, induce less favourable attitudes towards caffeine intake, and increase intentions to cut down caffeine intake (Raghunathan & Trope, 2002). In addition, a positive mood increased differentiation between strong and weak arguments in a study of participants' thoughts and attitudes regarding a health message (Das & Fennis, 2005), which is thought to reliably indicate intensive, open-minded message processing (e.g., Petty & Wegener, 1999). Thus, like self-affirmation, a positive mood can buffer against the self-regulatory costs of a threatening health message.

However, there may similarly be limits to the buffering effect of a positive mood. Specifically, a positive mood may not be sufficient to compensate the affective costs of a severely threatening and relevant health message. In such cases, a positive mood may cease to be effective in opening up a receiver's mind to threatening health information. Recent evidence suggests that the beneficial effects of a positive mood may indeed be limited to moderate threats (Das, 2005). Specifically, a positive mood increased more open-minded, intensive processing of a moderately threatening health message about a known health risk (i.e., smoking). By contrast, when a health message constituted a severe and unknown threat to the self, a positive mood decreased participants' sensitivity to the content of a health message, and decreased persuasion. Thus, when participants were confronted with new information regarding a severe health risk, the induction of a positive mood backfired, and negatively affected message processing and acceptance.

Limits of mood and self-affirmation: A functional perspective

Self-affirmation and positive mood, two distinct self-regulation resources, appear to have analogous effects on the processing and acceptance of threatening health information. Specifically, they buffer against the costs of moderately threatening health messages, and increase open-minded processing and acceptance of such messages. In addition, both self-regulation mechanisms may backfire when it comes to the processing and acceptance of seriously threatening health information. These similarities are all the more intriguing when considering the marked differences between self-affirmation and a positive mood. For instance, self-affirmation involves the confirmation of some aspect of the self that is important to an individual, whereas a positive mood may be prompted by a cue unrelated to the self. In addition, positive mood is linked to measures of explicit affect, while self-affirmation typically is not (e.g., Steele, 1988).

However, on a more implicit level, there are some interesting parallels between the effects of self-affirmation and mood. Self-affirmation is thought to restore self-integrity on a general level, and consequently functions as a resource or buffer against threatening information (Steele, 1988). This proposition is in line with recent conceptions of the self as a parallel processing network (Kuhl, 2000; Kuhl & Koole, 2004). According to this perspective, the self is capable of neutralising moderate threats by integrating the information into a larger cognitive network of related experiences. Self-activation, for instance through the affirmation of values that are central to the self, stimulates this integrative processing of incoming threats, and thus serves a highly adaptive mechanism that buffers threats to self-integrity. There is evidence that a positive mood can do the same, and equally stimulates the integration of new information into the self-system (Bolte, Goschke, & Kuhl, 2003). Specifically, compared with negative mood, positive mood has been shown to stimulate a holistic processing mode that involves the activation of wider semantic fields in memory, including weak or remote associates. The activation of a large network of (strongly or weakly) related self-experiences, in turn, can function as a buffer against incoming threats to the self.

Parallel distributed processing models may also explain why the effects of self-affirmation and positive mood may backfire for higher levels of threat. When threat levels become increasingly severe and uncontrollable, the integrative functions of the self become inhibited (Baumann & Kuhl, 2003). This integration inhibition under severely threatening conditions prevents the self-system from becoming flooded with negative experiences, which may result in a breakdown in global self-integrity. When global self-integrity breaks down, the self's cognitive, affective, and executive functions can no longer be performed, leaving the person in a state of "functional helplessness" that is accompanied by impaired self-regulation, passivity, and alienation (Kuhl, 1981; Kuhl & Beckmann, 1994). To prevent a breakdown in self-integrity, the self is equipped with powerful mechanisms that shield the system from becoming flooded by negative information (Koole, 2004; Nowak, Vallacher, Tesser, & Borkowski, 2000; Sedikides & Green, 2004). This shielding mode is likely to be activated when the incoming information poses a serious threat to self-integrity. Thus, when incoming threats are very severe, self-affirmation and a positive mood will not stimulate integrative processing, but rather trigger a shielding mode.

Parallel distributed processing models of the self may equally explain the effects of self-affirmation and positive mood on information processing and persuasion. Self-affirmation and positive mood may support the processing mode that is most adaptive in a given context. When the self is relatively safe, self-affirmation and a positive mood promote open-minded processing of self-threatening information (e.g., Raghunathan & Trope, 2002; Sherman et al., 2000). When the self is seriously threatened, self-affirmation and a positive mood promote shielding against self-threatening information, and decrease intensive information processing (Das, 2005; Das et al., 2005). In these instances, self-affirmation and a positive mood are likely to backfire, and can have detrimental effects on persuasion.

Positive effects of defensive reactions

A tentative and possibly counterintuitive conclusion that seems to emerge from recent work on the effects of self-affirmation and mood on persuasion is that open-minded processing may not always be beneficial for optimal self-regulation. In fact, open-mindedly facing severely threatening health information seems to increase individuals' vulnerability to a breakdown in self-integrity that can only be countered by shielding responses. Fortunately, there is evidence that defensive responses need not always be eliminated in order to increase persuasion. Under some conditions, defensive responses actually may increase persuasion.

Defensive reactions have been observed in a range of studies examining judgements about fictitious as well as actual health conditions, using survey formats and experimental designs, and providing self-administered as well as professionally administered tests in a formal medical context or not (for an overview, see Ditto & Croyle, 1995; also see Wiebe & Korbel, 2003). Importantly, the work on defensive reactions to health-risk feedback suggests that their relations to measures of coping behaviours, notably intentions, interest in additional information, and choice of information service, are not as straightforward as is typically assumed (Ditto & Croyle, 1995). The assumption that defensiveness promotes maladaptive responses is not supported, and defensive respondents are often *more* likely to request information and to have more favourable intentions for behaviour change. This suggests that defensive reactions can be requisite for, rather than contrary to, adaptive behavioural responding.

Wiebe and Korbel (2003) elaborate this reasoning in addressing how individuals accomplish the dual self-regulation tasks of managing sometimes extreme distress, while simultaneously taking action to reduce the danger (cf. Trope & Pomerantz, 1998). Their proposition is that defensive processes often actually enhance the effectiveness of the dynamic system designed to manage health threats. According to Leventhal's (1970) Parallel Response model, affective and cognitive reactions to a health threat may operate relatively independently, and threat can consequently be represented at two related levels: an abstract, rational, long-term, and "cool" level, and a more concrete, emotional, impulsive, and "hot" level (Wiebe & Korbel, 2003; also see Metcalfe & Mischel, 1999). When negative emotional arousal becomes too high, affect regulation becomes primary and this can interfere with management of the health risk. Defensive denial processes may work to cool the health threat representation, which diminishes the need for affect to become the primary target of self-regulation and should facilitate the management of objective danger. Wiebe and Korbel (2003) note that defensive processes seem to be elicited automatically and have an ongoing influence on self-regulation efforts, but should not be viewed as active self-regulation mechanisms per se. Effective defensive biases do not include avoidance or outright denial of facts that allow fears and vulnerability beliefs to remain active (Wiebe & Korbel,

2003), but refer to more subtle and malleable cognitive distortions that are responsive to new information and the constraints of reality. This is suggestive of motivated reasoning (Kunda, 1990).

The theorising advanced by Wiebe and Korbel (2003) maintains that relatively benign (i.e., subtly biased) interpretations of risk-factor information may not hinder adaptive health behaviour but actually facilitate problem-focused responses by keeping potentially disruptive emotions in check (cf. Ditto & Croyle, 1995). At first glance this reasoning seems at odds with other recent work which suggests that anxiety and worry may actually be adaptive (for overviews, see Cameron, 2003; McCaul & Mullens, 2003). This apparent contradiction can, however, be resolved when considering that it is extreme distress that is particularly debilitating and most likely to arouse defensive bias, as a result of which negative emotions may become attenuated and thus do not disrupt effective self-regulation.

Some interesting findings have emerged from studies addressing the influence of worry (for an overview, see McCaul & Mullens, 2003) and anxiety (for an overview, see Cameron, 2003). Worry was noted to promote self-protective behaviours in a range of contexts (e.g., screening for several types of cancer, using sunscreen, obtaining vaccination), and to do so independently of perceptions of vulnerability, even though distress and risk perception are obviously correlated (McCaul & Mullens, 2003). Worrying may reflect a concern over control, and behaviour change may restore a sense of control over outcomes. Anxiety, an emotion often held responsible for inducing irrational and maladaptive responses (Cameron, 2003), may equally play a crucial role in successful self-regulation, through its proposed *beneficial* effects on perception and attention, and information processing, and its informational value. Rather than promoting avoidance, anxiety arousal is posited to enhance attention to health threat cues (Cameron, 2003), although direct evidence is currently lacking.

What is better known is that negative affect, including (trait) anxiety automatically promotes the substantive processing of information (Forgas, 2000), albeit that this may be motivated in the service of mood repair. Furthermore, anxiety has an energising nature that can promote adequate coping responses (Cameron, 2003), although anxiety may impair reasoned decision making because it provokes more impulsive, dominant, and well-learned responses. Nevertheless, anxiety can also foster sustained, vigilant coping over time by enhancing accessibility to representations and coping plans (Cameron, 2003). These different strategic behaviours may result from different affect-related information-processing modes (Forgas, 2000). What seems particularly influential in determining the nature of strategic responding is the extent to which self-regulation of distress (i.e., affect regulation) is effective, which may be promoted by a tendency to alternate between substantive (i.e., open-minded) and motivated processing (see Forgas, 2000). Forgas (2000, p. 276) maintains that (negative) affect and information processing are intricately linked, and "different cognitive information-processing strategies may not only mediate affect infusion, but could also function as an effective and self-correcting affect management system".

Presently data regarding the behavioural consequences of defensive biases and regulation of negative affect are limited. Despite this, the conceptual analyses proposed by Wiebe and Korbel (2003), as well as by Cameron (2003), underscore the adaptive function of positive illusions (cf. Taylor & Brown, 1988), and affect infusion processes (cf. Forgas, 2000). They also speak to the paradox of how biased perceptions can promote psychological well-being, while simultaneously not putting the individual at risk as a result of overly optimistic (health) decision making. Some pertinent data supporting the reasoning advanced by Ditto and Croyle (1995) and elaborated by Wiebe and Korbel (2003) were collected to test our model of the processing of sequential health message components.

Processing health information

From the early days of the field, theories of the effects of health messages proposed that cognitive processes mediate persuasion. However, specific predictions about the nature of information processing generally were not made and measures of information processing (e.g., cognitive responses) have been virtually absent in this research. Information-processing predictions and measures can be derived from dual-process theories of attitude change (Chaiken, 1980; Petty & Cacioppo, 1986) that have also been applied to account for the impact of health communications (e.g., Gleicher & Petty, 1992; Liberman & Chaiken, 1992).

According to dual-process theories, messages conveying a serious threat to a person's health can have two effects, namely to act as a motivator for individuals to engage in intensive and thoughtful message processing, and to simultaneously induce defence motivation, which will lead to biased message processing (Gleicher & Petty, 1992; Liberman & Chaiken, 1992). Whereas the unbiased or accuracy-motivated individual assesses the validity of attitude-relevant information in the interest of achieving a well-founded position, the processing goal of defence-motivated individuals is to confirm the validity of a preferred position and disconfirm the validity of non-preferred positions. Thus, defence-motivated individuals will process and perceive information in ways that best support their own beliefs.

The stage model of processing of fear-arousing communications advanced by Stroebe and colleagues (Das et al., 2003; De Hoog et al., 2005a, 2005b; Stroebe, 2000) integrates these ideas from dual-process theories (e.g., Chaiken, 1980) with those of earlier theories of fear-arousing communications (e.g., Leventhal, 1970; Rogers, 1983; Witte, 1992). The stage model assumes that individuals who are exposed to fear-arousing communications engage in two types of appraisal, namely an appraisal of the threat, and an appraisal of coping strategies available for reducing or eliminating the threat. Based on assumptions of dual-process theories of attitude change (e.g., Chaiken,

1980), the stage model makes specific predictions that are partly different for the distinct appraisal processes. The stage model predicts that when a risk is trivial and individuals do not feel vulnerable, they are unlikely to invest much effort in thinking about the contents of the communication, and they rely on heuristic processing modes. When individuals do feel vulnerable to a minor risk, this feeling of vulnerability should induce sufficient motivation to systematically process the communication. This is in line with the assumption of dual-process theories that personal relevance, a concept similar to vulnerability, is a key motivator of systematic processing.

When individuals do not feel vulnerable, but a risk is depicted as severe, they are also assumed to invest effort in processing the contents of a communication. This is because it is useful to be well informed about a serious risk, even if the danger is not imminent. In other words, the stage model proposes that severity of a risk can also operate as a motivational factor that increases the likelihood of systematic processing. At first glance this may seem to differ somewhat from dual-process theories which hold that personal relevance (i.e., vulnerability) is an important precondition for the motivation for systematic processing. However, dual-process theories also specify other motivational variables that may promote systematic processing (Petty & Cacioppo, 1986), and we suggest that severity of a risk may be such a factor. Indeed, one of the ways in which the resulting negative affect can influence persuasion is that it may promote information processing (Petty, DeSteno, & Rucker, 2001).

The situation the stage model is most concerned with is when individuals feel vulnerable to a severe risk. This will seriously threaten self-definitional beliefs of being healthy, and consequently arouse defence motivation. It is further assumed that message processing under defence motivation will be systematic and not heuristic, because any communication describing a serious personal threat is likely to require a thorough and critical evaluation (Chaiken, Liberman, & Eagly, 1989). The stage model hence proposes that defence motivation induced by high perceptions of threat is manifest not in avoidance reactions as previous models have proposed (e.g., Witte, 1992), but in biased systematic processing. The direction of this defensive-motivated bias depends on the type of appraisal.

In appraising a threat, defence-motivated individuals will attempt to minimise the threat by looking critically at the content of a fear appeal. They will scrutinise the message to find ways to criticise and downplay the information in order to reduce the threat. As a body of research shows, defence-motivated individuals engage, for instance, in a biased search for inconsistencies, and evaluate the evidence with a bias in the direction of their preferred conclusion (e.g., Ditto & Lopez, 1992; Liberman & Chaiken, 1992; Sherman et al., 2000). However, the stage model proposes that this threat-minimising strategy often will not be fully successful, because biased processing is constrained by evidence and rules of inference (Kunda, 1990). In such situations, individuals will have to accept that they are personally at risk, and the stage model proposes that the subsequent processing of the action recommendation will then be biased as well. This bias is assumed to be in a *positive* direction. When processing the action recommendation, the processing goal of defence-motivated individuals will be to find the protective action effective, because they can then feel safe. Biased processing of the action recommendation will involve attempts to make the recommendation appear highly effective, such as by means of a biased search for arguments that support the effectiveness of the protective action, or through a biased evaluation of these arguments. In other words, defence motivation will increase the likelihood of accepting a solution to a particular threat, regardless of the quality of the arguments supporting this recommendation. These predictions can explain earlier observations that defensive biases do not interfere with adaptive behavioural responses (Ditto & Croyle, 1995), and, more importantly, illustrate how defensive biases are functional (cf. Wiebe & Korbel, 2003).

Studies conducted by Das et al. (2003), and De Hoog et al. (2005a, 2005b) provide direct support for the predictions of the stage model. These studies assessed the effects of the severity of and vulnerability to a health risk on the processing of a fear appeal, and on the processing and acceptance of an action recommendation, which was supported by high or low quality arguments. The pattern of findings observed in these experiments is consistent with the main prediction derived from the stage model: Stressing vulnerability to a severe health risk induces defence motivation, which demonstrates itself in the negatively biased processing of a fear-arousing communication. Vulnerable, defence-motivated respondents report more minimising thoughts about the fear appeal than non-vulnerable respondents do. Importantly, these studies also reveal a positive bias in the processing of the action recommendation: Vulnerable, defence-motivated respondents report more positive thoughts about the recommended action than non-vulnerable respondents, regardless of argument quality.

Furthermore, in all experiments measures of persuasion that had behavioural implications (i.e., intentions and behaviour) were solely determined by individuals' sense of vulnerability. Vulnerable respondents had higher intentions, requested more information, and subscribed to a recommendation more often than non-vulnerable respondents did, regardless of argument quality. The experiments also showed that the effect of vulnerability on intention was mediated by negative affect and cognitive responses, whereas the effect of vulnerability on behaviour was mediated by intentions. In sum, it was found that fear-arousing communications are most effective when perceptions of vulnerability to a severe health risk are high. In this situation defence motivation is induced, which shows itself not only in a negative bias in processing a fear appeal, but also in a positive bias in processing an action recommendation, which results in intention and behaviour change. These findings support the theorising advanced by Ditto and Croyle (1995) and Wiebe and Korbel (2003).

Conclusions

The seeming irrationality of many health-risk behaviours continues to intrigue social and health psychologists and lay persons alike, and the complex relation between perceptions of vulnerability and behaviour remains a major concern for health education practitioners. Two issues are particularly important in understanding how health-risk messages "work": the nature of the influence exerted by defensive bias, and the processes instigated by affect, in particular by the distress resulting from the message. Specious as biases may seem, positive illusions serve as important adaptive resources that can promote psychological as well as physical health (Taylor et al., 2000), and subtle defensive responses are thought to be beneficial to successful persuasion by attenuating negative affect (Wiebe & Korbel, 2003).

Moreover, affective influences on memory, judgement, and persuasion are no longer seen as merely promoting maladaptive biases, but rather adequate decision making is thought to be informed by feelings unmediated by higher-order cognitive processes. The risk-as-feeling hypothesis proposes that adaptive responses to risky situations, notably decision making under uncertainty, result in part from direct emotional influences (Loewenstein, Weber, Hsee, & Welch, 2001), and these "hunches" may operate as somatic markers of the value of our actions (cf. Adolphs & Damasio, 2001). Feelings are assumed to respond to factors that do not enter the cognitive evaluation of risk, such as the immediacy of a risk, and may represent some of the more impulsive or implicit determinants of behaviour (cf. Strack & Deutsch, 2004). Furthermore, affect can infuse substantive processes through priming mechanisms (e.g., Forgas, 2000), modulate information-processing mode (e.g. Petty et al., 2001), and motivate biased processing (cf. Forgas, 2000). Different cognitive information-processing strategies, in turn, may function as affect management system (Forgas, 2000).

Current theorising underscores that affect and cognition are interactively linked in a myriad of ways (for an overview, see Clore & Schnall, 2005). This novel work is mostly concerned with affect unrelated to the persuasive message, and understanding the reciprocal influences between message-induced affect regulation and information processing would advance health-risk communication theory and practice. We propose that responses to health communications first and foremost depend on prepotent affective processes that serve important psychological needs, and our stage or sequential processing model provides a starting point for an integration of this self-regulation in information-processing perspectives of persuasion. The central importance of affect regulation in human functioning is underscored in recent work suggesting that individuals' flourishing (i.e., an optimal range of functioning) depends on their ratio of positive to negative affect (Fredrickson & Losada, 2005). How individuals respond to health information may well depend on their flourishing.

References

Adolphs, R., & Damasio, A. R. (2001). The interaction of affect and cognition: A neurobiological perspective. In J. P. Forgas (Ed.), *Handbook of affect and social cognition* (pp. 27–49). Mahwah, NJ: Lawrence Erlbaum Associates Inc.

Aspinwall, L. G. (1998). Rethinking the role of positive affect in self-regulation. *Motivation and Emotion, 22*, 1–32.

Baumann, N., & Kuhl, J. (2003). Self-infiltration: Confusing assigned tasks as self-selected in memory. *Personality and Social Psychology Bulletin, 29*, 487–498.

Bolte, A., Goschke, T., & Kuhl, J. (2003). Emotion and intuition: Effects of positive and negative mood on intuitive judgments of semantic coherence. *Psychological Science, 14*, 416–421.

Cameron, L. D. (2003). Anxiety, cognition, and responses to health threats. In L. D. Cameron & H. Leventhal (Eds.), *The self-regulation of health and illness behaviour* (pp. 157–183). London: Routledge.

Cameron, L. D., & Leventhal, H. (2003). *The self-regulation of health and illness behaviour*. London: Routledge.

Chaiken, S. (1980). Heuristic versus systematic information processing and the use of source versus message cues in persuasion. *Journal of Personality and Social Psychology, 39*, 752–766.

Chaiken, S., Liberman, A., & Eagly, A. H. (1989). Heuristic and systematic information processing within and beyond the persuasion context. In J. S. Uleman & J. A. Bargh (Eds.), *Unintended thought* (pp. 212–252). New York: Guilford Press.

Clore, G. L., & Schnall, S. (2005). The influence of affect on attitude. In D. Albarracín, B. T. Johnson, & M. P. Zanna (Eds.), *The handbook of attitudes* (pp. 437–489). Mahwah, NJ: Lawrence Erlbaum Associates Inc.

Conner, M., & Norman, P. (2005). *Predicting health behavior* (2nd ed.). Maidenhead, UK: Open University Press.

Das, E. (2005). *Mood as a limited resource: Threat level moderates the impact of a positive mood on the processing of threatening health messages*. Manuscript in preparation. Vrije Universiteit Amsterdam.

Das, E., & Fennis, B. M. (2005). *In the mood to face the facts: A positive mood increases systematic processing of self-threatening health messages*. Manuscript submitted for publication.

Das, E., Koole, S. L., & Van Koningsbruggen, G. M. (2005). *When self-affirmation promotes closed-mindedness: Vulnerability to health risks moderates the impact of self-affirmation on responses to threatening health information*. Manuscript submitted for publication.

Das, E. H. H. J., De Wit, J. B. F., & Stroebe, W. (2003). Fear appeals motivate acceptance of action recommendations: Evidence for a positive bias in the processing of persuasive messages. *Personality and Social Psychology Bulletin, 29*, 650–664.

De Hoog, N., Stroebe, W., & De Wit, J. B. F. (2005a). The impact of fear appeals on processing and acceptance of action recommendations. *Personality and Social Psychology Bulletin, 31*, 24–33.

De Hoog, N., Stroebe, W., & De Wit, J. B. F. (2005b). *The processing of fear-arousing communications: How biased processing leads to persuasion*. Manuscript submitted for publication.

De Ridder, D. D. R., & De Wit, J. B. F. (2006). *Self-regulation of health behaviour*. Chichester, UK: Wiley.

De Wit, J., & Stroebe, W. (2004). Social cognition models of health behaviour. In A. Kaptein & J. Weinman (Eds.), *Health psychology* (pp. 52–83). Malden, MA: Blackwell.

Ditto, P. H., & Croyle, R. T. (1995). Understanding the impact of risk factor test results: Insights from a basic research program. In R. T. Croyle (Ed.), *Psychosocial effects of screening for disease prevention and detection* (pp. 144–181). New York: Oxford University Press.

Ditto, P. H., Jemmott, J. B. III, & Darley, J. M. (1988). Appraising the threat of illness: A mental representational approach. *Health Psychology, 7*, 183–200.

Ditto, P. H., & Lopez, D. F. (1992). Motivated skepticism: The use of differential decision criteria for preferred and non-preferred conclusions. *Journal of Personality and Social Psychology, 63*, 568–584.

Ditto, P. H., Munro, G. D., Apanovitch, A. M., Scepansky, J. A., & Lockhart, L. K. (2003). Spontaneous skepticism: The interplay of motivation and expectation in responses to favorable and unfavorable medical diagnoses. *Personality and Social Psychology Bulletin, 29*, 1120–1132.

Forgas, J. P. (2000). Affect and information processing strategies: An interactive relationship. In J. P. Forgas (Ed.), *Feeling and thinking: The role of affect in social cognition* (pp. 253–280). New York: Cambridge University Press.

Fredrickson, B. L., & Losada, M. F. (2005). Positive affect and the complex dynamics of human flourishing. *American Psychologist, 60*, 678–686.

Gerrard, M., Gibbons, F. X., & Bushman, B. J. (1996). Relation between perceived vulnerability to HIV and precautionary sexual behavior. *Psychological Bulletin, 119*, 390–409.

Gleicher, F., & Petty, R. E. (1992). Expectations of reassurance influence the nature of fear-stimulated attitude change. *Journal of Experimental Social Psychology, 28*, 86–100.

Harris, P. R., & Napper, L. (2005). Self-affirmation and the biased processing of threatening health-risk information. *Personality and Social Psychology Bulletin, 31*, 1250–1263.

Heatherton, T. F., & Vohs, K. D. (2000). Interpersonal evaluations following threat to the self. *Journal of Personality and Social Psychology, 78*, 725–736.

Hovland, C. I., Janis, I. L., & Kelley, H. H. (1953). *Communication and persuasion: Psychological studies of opinion change*. New Haven, CT: Yale University Press.

Jemmott, J. B., Croyle, R. T., & Ditto, P. H. (1988). Commonsense epidemiology: Self-based judgments from lay persons and physicians. *Health Psychology, 7*, 55–73.

Jemmott, J. B. III, Ditto, P. H., & Croyle, R. T. (1986). Judging health status: Effects of perceived prevalence and personal relevance. *Journal of Personality and Social Psychology, 50*, 899–905.

Koole, S. L. (2004). Volitional shielding of the self: Effects of action orientation and external demands on implicit self-evaluation, *Social Cognition, 22*, 117–146.

Kuhl, J. (1981). Motivational and functional helplessness: The moderating effect of state versus action orientation. *Journal of Personality and Social Psychology, 40*, 155–170.

Kuhl, J. (2000). A functional-design approach to motivation and self-regulation: The dynamics of personality systems interactions. In M. Boekaerts, P. R. Pintrich, & M. Zeidner (Eds.), *Handbook of self-regulation* (pp. 111–169). San Diego, CA: Academic Press.

Kuhl, J., & Beckmann, J. (1994). Alienation: Ignoring one's preferences. In J. Kuhl

& J. Beckmann (Eds.), *Volition and personality: Action versus state orientation* (pp. 375–390). Göttingen: Hogrefe & Huber.

Kuhl, J., & Koole, S. L. (2004). Workings of the will: A functional approach. In J. Greenberg, S. L. Koole, & T. Pyszczynski (Eds.), *Handbook of experimental existential psychology* (pp. 411–430). New York: Guilford Press.

Kunda, Z. (1990). The case for motivated reasoning. *Psychological Bulletin, 108,* 480–498.

Leventhal, H. (1970). Findings and theory in the study of fear communications. In L. Berkowitz (Ed.), *Advances in experimental social psychology* (Vol. 5., pp. 119–186). New York: Academic Press.

Liberman, A., & Chaiken, S. (1992). Defensive processing of personally relevant health messages. *Personality and Social Psychology Bulletin, 18,* 669–679.

Loewenstein, G. F., Weber, E. U., Hsee, C. K., & Welch, N. (2001). Risk as feeling. *Psychological Bulletin, 127,* 267–286.

McCaul, K. D., & Mullens, A. B. (2003). Affect, thought and self-protective health behavior: The case of worry and cancer screening. In J. Suls & K. A. Wallston (Eds.), *Social psychological foundations of health and illness* (pp. 137–168). Malden, MA: Blackwell.

Metcalfe, J., & Mischel, W. (1999). A hot/cool-system analysis of delay of gratification: Dynamics of willpower. *Psychological Review, 106,* 2–19.

Nowak, A., Vallacher, R. R., Tesser, A., & Borkowski, W. (2000). Society of self: The emergence of collective properties in self-structure. *Psychological Review, 107,* 39–61.

Petty, R. E., & Cacioppo, J. T. (1986). The elaboration likelihood model of persuasion. In L. Berkowitz (Ed.), *Advances in experimental social psychology* (Vol. 19, pp. 123–205). New York: Academic Press.

Petty, R. E., DeSteno, D., & Rucker, D. D. (2001). The role of affect in attitude change. In J. P. Forgas (Ed.), *Handbook of affect and social cognition* (pp. 212–233). Mahwah, NJ: Lawrence Erlbaum Associates Inc.

Petty, R. E., & Wegener, D. T. (1999). The elaboration likelihood model: Current status and controversies. In S. Chaiken & Y. Trope (Eds.), *Dual-process theories in social psychology* (pp. 37–72). New York: Guilford Press.

Raghunathan, R., & Trope, Y. (2002). Walking the tightrope between feeling good and being accurate: Mood as a resource in processing persuasive messages. *Journal of Personality and Social Psychology, 83,* 510–525.

Reed, M. B., & Aspinwall, L. G. (1998). Self-affirmation reduces biased processing of health-risk information. *Motivation and Emotion, 22,* 99–132.

Rogers, R. W. (1983). Cognitive and physiological processes in fear appeals and attitude change: A revised theory of protection motivation. In J. T. Cacioppo & R. E. Petty (Eds.), *Social psychophysiology: A sourcebook* (pp. 153–176). New York: Guilford Press.

Rosenstock, I. M. (1974). Historical origins of the health belief model. *Health Education Monographs, 2,* 1–8.

Rothman, A. J., Kelly, K. M., Hertel, A. W., & Salovey, P. (2003). Message framing and illness representations: Implications for interventions to promote and sustain health behavior. In L. D. Cameron & H. Leventhal (Eds.), *The self-regulation of health and illness behaviour* (pp. 278–296). London: Routledge.

Rutter, D., & Quine, L. (2002). *Changing health behaviour.* Buckingham, UK: Open University Press.

Schwarzer, R. (2001). Social-cognitive factors in changing health-related behavior. *Current Directions in Psychological Science, 10*, 47–51.

Sedikides, C., & Green, J. D. (2004). What I don't recall can't hurt me: Information negativity versus information inconsistency as determinants of memorial self-defense. *Social Cognition, 22*, 4–29.

Sherman, D. A. K., Nelson, L. D., & Steele, C. M. (2000). Do messages about health risks threaten the self? Increasing the acceptance of threatening health messages via self-affirmation. *Personality and Social Psychology Bulletin, 26*, 1046–1058.

Steele, C. M. (1988). The psychology of self-affirmation: Sustaining the integrity of the self. In L. Berkowitz (Ed.), *Advances in experimental social psychology* (Vol. 21, pp. 261–302). New York: Academic Press.

Steele, C. M., Spencer, S. J., & Lynch, M. (1993). Self-image resilience and dissonance: The role of affirmational resources. *Journal of Personality and Social Psychology, 64*, 885–896.

Strack, F., & Deutsch, R. (2004). Reflective and impulsive determinants of social behavior. *Personality and Social Psychology Review, 8*, 220–247.

Stroebe, W. (2000). *Social psychology and health* (2nd ed.). Buckingham, UK: Open University Press.

Stroebe, W., & De Wit, J. (1996). Health-impairing behaviours. In G. Semin & K. Fiedler (Eds.), *Applied social psychology* (pp. 113–144). Thousand Oaks, CA: Sage.

Taylor, S. E., & Brown, J. D. (1988). Illusion and well-being: A social psychological perspective on mental health. *Psychological Bulletin, 110*, 193–210.

Taylor, S. E., Kemeny, M. E., Reed, G. M., Bower, J. E., & Gruenewald, T. L. (2000). Psychological resources, positive illusions, and health. *American Psychologist, 55*, 99–109.

Trop, Y., Ferguson, M., & Raghunathan, R. (2001). Mood as a resource in processing self-relevant information. In J. P. Forgas (Ed.), *Handbook of affect and social cognition* (pp. 256–274). Mahwah, NJ: Lawrence Erlbaum Associates Inc.

Trope, Y., & Fishbach, A. (2000). Counteractive self-control in overcoming temptation. *Journal of Personality and Social Psychology, 79*, 493–506.

Trope, Y., & Neter, E. (1994). Reconciling competing motives in self-evaluation: The role of self-control in feedback seeking. *Journal of Personality and Social Psychology, 66*, 646–657.

Trope, Y., & Pomerantz, E. M. (1998). Resolving conflicts among self-evaluative motives: Positive experiences as a resource for overcoming defensiveness. *Motivation and Emotion, 22*, 53–72.

Vohs, K. D., & Heatherton, T. F. (2004). Ego threat elicits different social comparison processes among high and low self-esteem people: Implications for interpersonal perceptions. *Social Cognition, 22*, 168–191.

Weinstein, N. D. (2003). Exploring the links between risk perceptions and preventive health behavior. In J. Suls & K. A. Wallston (Eds.), *Social psychological foundations of health and illness* (pp. 22–53). Malden, MA: Blackwell.

Weinstein, N. D., Lyon, J. E., Sandman, P. M., & Cuite, C. L. (1998). Experimental evidence for stages of health behavior change: The precaution adoption process model applied to home radon testing. *Health Psychology, 17*, 445–453.

Weinstein, N. D., & Nicolich, M. (1993). Correct and incorrect interpretations of correlations between risk perceptions and risk behavior. *Health Psychology, 12*, 235–245.

Wiebe, D. J., & Korbel, C. (2003). Defensive denial, affect, and the self-regulation of health threats. In L. D. Cameron & H. Leventhal (Eds.), *The self-regulation of health and illness behaviour* (pp. 184–203). London: Routledge.

Witte, K. (1992). Putting the fear back into fear appeals: The extended parallel process model. *Communication Monographs, 59,* 329–349.

World Health Organization. (2004). *World health report: 2004.* Geneva, CH: World Health Organization.

14 An organisational and social psychological perspective on burnout and work engagement

Arnold B. Bakker, Wilmar B. Schaufeli,
Evangelia Demerouti, and
Martin C. Euwema
Utrecht University, The Netherlands

Burnout is a metaphor that is commonly used to describe a state of mental weariness. In the pioneer phase of burnout research, researchers chose to study employees in healthcare professions, because of the chronically taxing emotional demands they experience in their jobs. However, gradually it became clear that burnout also exists outside the human services (Maslach, Schaufeli, & Leiter, 2001). Employees who are burned out by their work are characterised by feelings of exhaustion, negative attitudes (cynicism), and reduced professional efficacy.

Work engagement is assumed to be the positive antipode of burnout. Or, as Maslach and Leiter (1997, p. 34) put it: "Energy, involvement, and efficacy— these are the direct opposites of the three dimensions of burnout." According to Maslach and Leiter, work engagement is assessed by the opposite pattern of scores on the three burnout dimensions. However, this way of operational- ising burnout and engagement is questionable in view of the debate on the polarity of positive and negative affect (Diener, 1999). It could be argued that instead of being two opposite poles, burnout and engagement are independ- ent yet negatively correlated states of mind. For instance, feeling emotionally drained from one's work "once a week" by no means excludes that in the same week one may feel bursting with energy. Thus, instead of perfectly com- plementary and mutually exclusive states, burnout and engagement should be seen as conceptually different states that, because of their antithetical nature, are supposed to be negatively related.

We define engagement separate from burnout, as a positive, fulfilling, work-related state of mind in its own right that is characterised by vigour, dedication, and absorption (Schaufeli, Salanova, González-Romá, & Bakker, 2002; for an overview, see Schaufeli & Salanova, in press). *Vigour* is character- ised by high levels of energy and mental resilience while working, the willing- ness to invest effort in one's work, and persistence in the face of difficulties. *Dedication* is characterised by a sense of significance, enthusiasm, pride, inspiration, and challenge. The third dimension of engagement is called absorption, which was found to be a constituting element of engagement in 30 in-depth interviews (Schaufeli, Taris, Le Blanc, Peeters, Bakker, & De Jonge, 2001; see also Rothbarth, 2001). *Absorption* is characterised by being fully concentrated and happily engrossed in one's work, whereby time passes quickly and one has difficulties with detaching oneself from work.

Since, in contrast to Maslach and Leiter (1997), burnout and work engagement are defined independently from each other, their relationship can be studied empirically. A recent study showed that burnout and engagement are indeed each other's opposite poles (González-Romá, Schaufeli, Bakker, & Lloret, 2006). More specifically, vigour and exhaustion span a continuum that is dubbed "energy", whereas dedication and cynicism similarly constitute the endpoints of a continuum that is labelled "identification". Hence, engagement is characterised by high levels of energy and identification, whilst burnout is characterised by low levels of energy and identification. This finding agrees with Demerouti, Bakker, Nachreiner, and Schaufeli's (2001) conceptualisation and measurement of burnout and engagement. Reduced professional efficacy and absorption both play a somewhat different role, and seem to be the *outcomes* of burnout and engagement, respectively.

An organisational psychological perspective

Several scholars have pointed out the "laundry list" of burnout antecedents that have been found in empirical research (e.g., Halbesleben & Buckley, 2004; Lee & Ashforth, 1996). Moreover, it seems as if every occupation has its own specific risk factors regarding burnout. For example, whereas for employees in call centres burnout is mainly caused by the dissonance between their genuine feelings and those that can openly be shown towards clients (Zapf, Vogt, Seifert, Mertini & Isic, 1999), for production workers the combination of work overload and lack of autonomy seems the most important problem (De Jonge & Kompier, 1997). For teachers the interaction with their pupils appears the most important determinant of burnout (Van Horn, Schaufeli, & Enzmann, 1999).

At the heart of Demerouti et al.'s (2001) *job demands–resources (JD–R) model* lies the premise that, whereas each occupation may have its own specific risk factors associated with burnout, these factors can be classified in two general categories (i.e., job demands and job resources), thus constituting an overarching model that may be applied to various occupational settings, irrespective of the particular demands and resources involved. *Job demands* refer to those physical, psychological, social, or organisational aspects of the job that require sustained physical and/or psychological (cognitive and emotional) effort or skills, and are therefore associated with certain physiological and/or psychological costs. Examples are a high work pressure, an unfavourable physical environment, and emotionally demanding interactions with clients.

Job resources refer to those physical, psychological, social, or organisational aspects of the job that are either/or: (1) functional in achieving work goals; (2) reduce job demands and the associated physiological and psychological costs; (3) stimulate personal growth, learning, and development. Hence, not only are resources necessary to deal with job demands, they are also important in their own right. This agrees with Hackman and Oldham's (1980) *job characteristics theory* that emphasises the motivational potential of job resources at the task level, including autonomy, feedback, and task significance. In addition, this agrees on a more general level with *conservation of resources (COR) theory* (Hobfoll, 2001), which states that the prime human motivation is directed towards the maintenance and accumulation of resources. Accordingly, resources are valued in their own right or because they are means to the achievement or protection of other valued resources. Job resources may be located at the level of the organisation at large (e.g., pay, career opportunities, job security), interpersonal and social relations (e.g., supervisor and co-worker support, team climate), the organisation of work (e.g., role clarity, participation in decision making), and at the level of the task (e.g., skill variety, task identity, task significance, autonomy, performance feedback).

A second premise of the JD–R model is that two different underlying psychological processes play a role in the development of burnout and work engagement. In the first process, chronic job demands (e.g., work overload or conflicts) lead in the long term to exhaustion. According to Hockey (1993), individuals use performance-protection strategies under the influence of environmental demands. Performance protection is achieved through the mobilisation of sympathetic activation (autonomic and endocrine) and/or increased subjective effort (use of active control in information processing). Hence, the greater the activation and/or effort, the greater the physiological costs for the individual. Even though the use of this strategy makes it difficult to demonstrate overt decrements in primary task performance, according to Hockey's theory, several different patterns of *indirect* degradation may be identified. These are referred to as compensatory costs (increased activation and/or subjective effort), strategy adjustments (narrowing of attention, increased selectivity, redefinition of task requirements), and fatigue after-effects (risky choices, high levels of subjective fatigue). The long-term effect of such a compensatory strategy may be a draining of an individual's energy, eventually resulting in a breakdown.

The second process is motivational in nature, whereby it is assumed that job resources have motivational potential and lead to high work engagement, low cynicism, and excellent performance. As follows from our definition, job resources may either play an intrinsic motivational role because they foster employees' growth, learning, and development, or they may play an extrinsic motivational role because they are instrumental in achieving work goals. In the former case, job resources fulfil basic human needs, such as the needs for autonomy (DeCharms, 1968), competence (White, 1959), and relatedness (Baumeister & Leary, 1995). For instance, proper feedback fosters learning, thereby increasing job competence, whereas decision latitude and social support satisfy the need for autonomy and the need to belong, respectively. Job resources may also play an extrinsic motivational role, because, according to the *effort-recovery model* (Meijman & Mulder, 1998), work environments that offer many resources foster the willingness to dedicate one's efforts and abilities to the work task. In that case it is likely that the task will be completed successfully and that the work goal will be attained. For instance, supportive colleagues and proper feedback from one's superior increase the likelihood of being successful in achieving one's work goals. In either case, be it through the satisfaction of basic needs or through the achievement of work goals, the presence of job resources leads to engagement, whereas their absence evokes a cynical attitude towards work.

In addition to the main effects of job demands and resources, the JD–R model proposes that the *interaction* between job demands and job resources is important for the development of burnout and work engagement as well. More specifically, it is proposed that job resources may *buffer* the impact of job demands on burnout (Bakker, Demerouti, Taris, Schaufeli, & Schreurs, 2003d). This assumption is consistent with the *demand-control model* (DCM; Karasek, 1979, 1998), but expands this model by claiming that several *different* job resources can play the role of buffer for several *different* job demands. Which job demands and resources play a role in a certain organisation depends on the specific job characteristics that prevail. Thus, whereas the DCM states that control over the execution of tasks (autonomy) may buffer the impact of work overload on job stress, the JD–R model expands this view and states that *different* types of job demands and job resources may interact in predicting job strain.

Social support is probably the most well-known situational variable that has been proposed as a potential buffer against job stress (e.g., Johnson & Hall, 1988; Stroebe & Stroebe, 1995; but see Deelstra, Peeters, Schaufeli, Stroebe, Zijlstra, & Van Doornen, 2003). Other characteristics of the work situation that may act as moderators are: (a) the extent to which the onset of a stressor is predictable (e.g., role ambiguity and performance feedback), (b) the extent to which the reasons for the presence of a stressor are understandable (e.g., through information provided by supervisors), (c) the extent to which aspects of the stressor are controllable by the person who must experience it (e.g., job autonomy) (Kahn & Byosiere, 1992).

The final proposition of the JD–R model is that job resources particularly influence work engagement when job demands are high. This is consistent with Hobfoll (2002), who has argued that resource gain has only a modest effect in itself, but instead acquires its saliency in the context of resource loss. Indeed, Riolli and Savicki (2003) showed that information service workers' personal resources (optimism and control coping) were particularly beneficial when their work resources were low. The full JD–R model is depicted graphically in Figure 14.1.

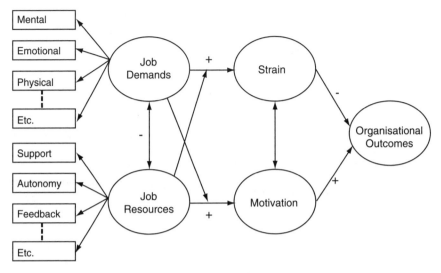

Figure 14.1 The job demands – resources model.

Empirical evidence for the JD–R model

EVIDENCE FOR THE DUAL PROCESS

Several studies have provided evidence for the hypotheses put forward by the JD–R model. Specifically, a number of studies supported the dual pathways to employee well-being proposed by the model, and showed that it can predict important organisational outcomes. Bakker, Demerouti, and Schaufeli (2003b) applied the model to call-centre employees of a Dutch telecom company, and investigated its predictive validity for self-reported absenteeism and turnover intentions. Results of a series of structural equation modelling analyses largely supported the dual processes. In the first energy-driven process, job demands (i.e., work pressure, computer problems, emotional demands, and changes in tasks) were the most important predictors of health problems, which, in turn, were related to illness absence (duration and long-term absence). In the second motivation-driven process, job resources (i.e., social support, supervisory coaching, performance feedback, and time control) were the only predictors of dedication and organisational commitment, which, in turn, was related to turnover intentions.

Hakanen, Bakker, and Schaufeli (2006) found comparable results in their study among Finnish teachers. More specifically, they found that burnout mediated the effect of job demands on ill-health, and that work engagement mediated the effect of job resources on organisational commitment. Furthermore, Bakker, Demerouti, De Boer, and Schaufeli (2003a) applied the JD–R model to nutrition production employees, and used the model to predict future company-registered absenteeism. Results of structural equation modelling analyses showed that job demands were unique predictors of burnout, and indirectly of absence duration, whereas job resources were unique predictors of organisational commitment, and indirectly of absence spells. Finally, Bakker, Demerouti, and Verbeke (2004) used the JD–R model to examine the relationship between job characteristics, burnout, and other-ratings of performance. They hypothesised and found that job demands (e.g., work pressure and emotional demands) were the most important antecedents of the exhaustion component of burnout, which, in turn, predicted in-role performance. In contrast, job resources (e.g., autonomy and social support) were the most important predictors of extra-role performance, through their relationship with (dis)engagement. Taken together, these findings support the JD–R model's claim that job demands and job resources initiate two different psychological processes, which eventually affect important organisational outcomes.

Most studies providing evidence for the dual processes suggested by the JD–R model have been based on subjective evaluations of job demands and resources increasing the risk of common method variance. Two additional studies utilised an alternative methodology for the assessment of job demands and resources. The study of Demerouti et al. (2001) among employees working with people, next to the self-reports, also included observer ratings of job demands and resources. Results of a series of structural equation analyses, both with self-report data and with observer ratings of job charac-teristics, provide strong and consistent evidence for the validity of this model. Job demands were primarily and positively related to exhaustion, whereas job resources were primarily and negatively related to disengagement from work.

Bakker (2005, Study 1) approached employees from seven different organ-isations, who were asked to fill in the Utrecht Work Engagement Scale (the UWES). In the next step, 20 employees high in engagement and 20 employees low in engagement were visited at their workplace, and exposed to short video clips of about 30 seconds. In these video clips, professional actors role-played two aspects of work engagement (vigour, dedication), three job demands, and four job resources. The participants were asked to indicate how often they experienced each of the situations shown in the video clips. Results showed that the engaged group more often reported experi-encing work engagement (vigour and dedication), as role-played by the actors. Importantly, the low- and high-engagement groups also differed sig-nificantly regarding the prevalence of several of the working conditions shown in the video clips. As predicted, job resources particularly (not job demands) were higher among the high (vs low) engagement group. The high-engagement group scored significantly higher on three of the four job resources (autonomy, feedback, and supervisory coaching; the effect was nonsignificant for social support). There were no differences between both groups regarding the job demands.

Two recent studies explicitly focused on the buffer function of job resources, and found clear evidence for the proposed interaction. Bakker, Demerouti, and Euwema (2005a), in their study among 1000 employees of a large institute for higher education, found that the combination of high demands and low job resources significantly added to the prediction of burnout (exhaustion and cynicism). Specifically, they found that work overload, emotional demands, physical demands, and work–home interference did not result in high levels of burnout if employees experienced autonomy, received feedback, had social support, or had a high-quality relationship with their supervisor. Psychologically speaking, different processes may have been responsible for these interaction effects. Thus, autonomy may have helped in coping with job demands because employees could decide for themselves when and how to respond to their demands, whereas social support and a high-quality relationship with the supervisor may have buffered the impact of job demands on levels of burnout because employees received instrumental help and emotional support. In contrast, feedback may have helped because it provided employees with the information necessary to maintain their performance and to stay healthy (see Kahn & Byosiere, 1992, for a further discussion).

Similar findings were reported by Xanthopoulou, Bakker, Demerouti, and Schaufeli (2005), who tested the JD–R interaction hypothesis among employees from Dutch home-care organisations. The findings revealed, for instance, that patient harassment interacted with autonomy and support in predicting exhaustion; and with autonomy, support, and professional development in predicting cynicism. In cases where the levels of job resources were high, the effect of job demands on the core dimensions of burnout was significantly reduced.

Two studies have shown that job resources particularly have an impact on work engagement when job demands are high. Hakanen, Bakker, and Demerouti (2005) tested this interaction hypothesis in a sample of Finnish dentists employed in the public sector. It was hypothesised that job resources (e.g., variability in the required professional skills, peer contacts) are most beneficial in maintaining work engagement under conditions of high job demands (e.g., workload, unfavourable physical environment). The dentists were split into two random groups in order to cross-validate the findings. A set of hierarchical regression analyses resulted in 17 out of 40 significant interactions (40%), showing, for instance, that variability in professional skills mitigated the negative effect of qualitative workload on work engagement, and boosted work engagement when qualitative workload was high.

Conceptually similar findings have been reported by Bakker, Hakanen, and Demerouti (2005c). In their study among Finnish teachers working in elementary, secondary, and vocational schools, they found that job resources particularly influence work engagement when teachers are confronted with high levels of pupil misconduct. A series of hierarchical regression analyses resulted in 13 out of 18 possible two-way interaction effects. Particularly supervisor support, innovativeness, appreciation, and organisational climate were important job resources for teachers that helped them cope with demanding interactions with students.

Conclusion

The JD–R model, which represents an organisational psychological perspective, proposes that burnout and work engagement may be caused by a wide variety of different aspects of the work environment that can be integrated into a relatively simple model (see Figure 14.1). Exposure to job demands is predictive of exhaustion, whereas job resources are the most important predictors of work engagement and reduced cynicism. Furthermore, job demands and resources interact such that the influence of job demands on burnout can be buffered by job resources. In addition, job resources particularly gain their salience in the context of high job demands.

A social psychological perspective

While the organisational psychological perspective explains how burnout and engagement originate in the work environment, the social psychological perspective emphasises the social nature of this environment and explains how both states may transfer[1] among individuals. The notion that *burnout* may transfer from one employee to another is not new. Several authors have used anecdotal evidence to argue that job-induced strain and burnout may cross over between colleagues (e.g., Cherniss, 1980; Edelwich & Brodsky, 1980; Schwartz & Will, 1953). We will describe recent more systematic studies that have provided empirical evidence for this phenomenon. Moreover, the central aim of the second part of this chapter is to give an overview of theories that can explain the transference of burnout *and* work engagement.

Research on the symptomatology of burnout has shown that the syndrome may manifest itself in various ways. Schaufeli and Enzmann (1998) counted more than 100 burnout symptoms in the literature, including such highly visible symptoms as hyperactivity, physical fatigue, and enhanced irritability. Moreover, researchers have identified several "social symptoms" of burnout, most notably negative or cynical attitudes towards clients and work (for an overview see Burisch, 1989). Such negative attitudes may take the form of reduced empathy, cynicism, black humour, and stereotyping. Burnout symptoms expressed by colleagues may therefore transfer to individual employees when they socialise with one another on the job or in informal meetings.

Emotional contagion

Emotional contagion has been defined as "the tendency to automatically mimic and synchronize facial expressions, vocalizations, postures, and movements with those of another person and, consequently, to converge emotionally" (Hatfield, Cacioppo, & Rapson, 1994, p. 5). The emphasis in this definition is on non-conscious emotional contagion. Research has indeed shown that, in conversations, people "automatically" mimic the facial expressions, voices, postures, and behaviours of others (Bavelas, Black, Lemery, & Mullett, 1987; Bernieri, Reznick, & Rosenthal, 1988), and that people's conscious experience may be shaped by such facial feedback (e.g., Laird, 1984).

There is, however, a second way in which people may "catch" another person's emotions. Contagion may also occur via a conscious cognitive process by "tuning in" to the emotions of others. This will be the case when a person tries to imagine how they would feel in the position of another, and, as a consequence, experiences the same feelings. Thus, the realisation that another person is happy or sad may trigger memories of the times we have felt that way, and these reveries may spark similar emotions (Hsee, Hatfield, Carlson, & Chemtob, 1990). Particularly the attitude of helping professionals of showing empathic concern is likely to foster such a process of consciously "tuning in" to others' emotions.

Regardless of why such contagion might occur, researchers from a wide range of disciplines have described phenomena suggesting that emotional contagion does exist (for overviews, see Hatfield et al., 1994; McIntosh, Druckman, & Zajonc, 1994). Hsee and his colleagues (Hsee et al., 1990; Uchino, Hsee, Hatfield, Carlson, & Chemtob, 1991) documented convincing evidence for emotional contagion using controlled laboratory studies. In these experiments, college students were asked to observe video tapes of another (fictitious) participant relating an emotional experience. They were then asked what emotions they felt as they watched the person describe the happiest and saddest event in his life. The results of these experiments showed that participants "caught" the emotions of the stimulus person. In each of the experiments, both participants' self-reports, and judges' ratings of participants' facial expressions of emotions showed that they were happier when they were watching a stimulus person expressing happy emotions than when they were watching him expressing sad feelings.

Contagious depression

One may assume that the mechanisms involved in burnout contagion processes are comparable to those involved in emotional contagion processes. Moreover, there is also evidence for contagious depression, and depression is a syndrome that is related to burnout, most notably the emotional exhaustion dimension (Glass, McKnight, & Valdimarsdottir, 1993). More specifically, depression accounts for approximately 20% of the variance in emotional exhaustion, the core symptom of burnout. In a classic study of contagious depression, Howes, Hokanson, and Lowenstein (1985) assessed first-year college students twice using the Beck Depression Inventory, at the start of the semester and 3 months later. The students were randomly assigned to a room with a mildly depressed roommate or with a non-depressed roommate. Those who were assigned to a room with a depressed roommate became increasingly depressed over time. Joiner (1994) reported similar evidence for contagious depression in an independent roommate study. Importantly, this latter study showed that the contagion effect persisted when baseline levels of roommate depression and roommate negative life events were controlled for (see also Westman & Vinokur, 1998).

Burnout contagion

The first empirical indication for a socially induced burnout effect came from Rountree (1984), who investigated 186 task groups in 23 local settings of organisations. He found that 87.5% of employees with the highest scores on burnout worked in task groups in which at least 50% of the staff was in a similar advanced burnout phase. Low-scoring, less burned-out employees showed a similar but less marked tendency to cluster. Rountree concluded that ". . . the affinity of work groups for extreme scores seems substantial" (p. 245). Thus, individuals with very high or very low burnout scores can often be found within one task group, suggesting the possibility that task group members "infect" each other with the burnout "virus". After reviewing similar additional studies, Golembiewski, Munzenrider, and Stevenson (1986, p. 184) concluded that "Very high and very low scores on burnout tend to concentrate to a substantial degree." They added that "these findings suggest 'contagion' or 'resonance' effects" (p. 185).

However, this concentration of burnout in particular work groups may also be explained by a negative change in the working conditions, because burnout has been related to a wide range of detrimental behaviours. For example, Freudenberger (1974) observed that burned-out individuals do not perform efficiently, independently of how hard they try. Indeed, it has been found that they make more on-the-job mistakes, misuse work breaks, and have higher absenteeism rates (e.g., Bakker et al., 2003a; Kahill, 1988). In a team, each of these behaviours may increase the workload of the other team members, as they will have to compensate for the inefficient or disruptive behaviours of their burned-out colleagues.

To rule out the third variable explanation, Bakker and his colleagues set up a series of studies including measures of working conditions, burnout, and/or work engagement. Evidence for direct *and* indirect routes of socially induced burnout was found in a study that included nurses from 80 European intensive care units (Bakker, Le Blanc, & Schaufeli, 1997; see also Bakker, Le Blanc, & Schaufeli, 2005d). In addition to a *direct* effect from unit burnout to individual nurses' burnout, unit burnout had an *indirect* effect through its influence on individual nurses' workload and job autonomy. More specifically, structural equation modelling analyses revealed that unit burnout had a positive influence on the workload reported by individual nurses, and a negative impact on their autonomy. These changed working conditions, in turn, had a significant impact on their experience of burnout. That is, workload had a positive, and job autonomy a negative influence on individual nurses' feelings of exhaustion, depersonalisation (a specific form of cynicism), and reduced personal accomplishment (i.e., professional efficacy). This indirect influence of unit burnout on individual burnout can be explained by assuming that individual nurses had more work to do because of the impaired job performance of their burned-out colleagues. Conceptually similar findings have been reported by Bakker, Demerouti, and Schaufeli (2003b) among a sample of employees of a large banking and insurance company, working in one of 47 teams. They showed that burnout at the team level is related to individual team members' burnout scores, both directly and indirectly, through its relationship with individual members' job demands, job control and perceived social support.

Bakker, Van Emmerik, and Euwema (in press) investigated the crossover of burnout and *work engagement* among Dutch constabulary officers, working in one of 85 teams. On the basis of theories on crossover and emotional contagion, it was hypothesised that both types of work-related feelings and attitudes may transfer from teams to individual team members. The results of multilevel analyses confirmed this crossover phenomenon by showing that team-level burnout and work engagement were related to individual team members' burnout (i.e., exhaustion, cynicism, and reduced professional efficacy) and work engagement (vigour, dedication, and absorption), after controlling for individual members' job demands and resources.

Transference of burnout and work engagement has also been observed in studies among working *couples*. For example, Westman and Etzion (1995) examined burnout contagion among couples of male military officers and their wives. They found that wives' burnout had a direct impact on husbands' burnout, after controlling for the husbands' own job stress and coping resources. In addition, husbands' burnout likewise affected their wives' burnout.

Furthermore, Bakker, Demerouti, and Schaufeli (2005b) tested the hypothesis that burnout and *work engagement* may cross over from husbands to wives and vice versa. Data were collected among couples working in a variety of occupations. The job demands–resources model was used to simultaneously examine possible correlates of burnout and engagement for each partner separately. The results of a series of hierarchical regression analyses provided evidence for the crossover of burnout (exhaustion and cynicism) and work engagement (vigour and dedication) among partners. The crossover relationships were significant and about equally strong for both partners, after controlling for important characteristics of the work and home environment.

Moderators of the contagion effect

Hatfield et al. (1994) have argued that there are several circumstances under which people should be especially likely to catch others' emotions. Emotional contagion is particularly likely, for example, if individuals pay close attention to others, and if they construe themselves as interrelated to others rather than as independent and unique. Given the increased models of teamwork in modern organisations, it is likely that employees indeed experience higher levels of interdependence, and therefore are more sensitive to the emotional states of their colleagues. Furthermore, a number of studies have shown that stable individual differences exist in people's susceptibility to emotional stimuli (Doherty, Orimoto, Singelis, Hatfield, & Hebb, 1995; Stiff, Dillard, Somera, Kim, & Sleight, 1988), and that these individual differences are good predictors of the extent to which people catch positive and negative emotions from others. What are the conditions under which contagion of burnout and work engagement is most likely?

EMPATHY

Westman and Vinokur (1998) have argued that empathy can be a moderator of the crossover process. Literally, the root meaning of the word empathy is "feeling into". Starcevic and Piontek (1997) define empathy as interpersonal communication that is predominantly emotional in nature. It involves the ability to be affected by the other's affective state, as well as to be able to read in oneself what that affect has been. Similarly, Lazarus (1991) defined empathy as "sharing another's feelings by placing oneself psychologically in that person's circumstances" (p. 287). The core relational theme for empathy would have to involve a sharing of another person's emotional state, distressed or otherwise. Accordingly, strain in one partner produces an empathic reaction in the other that increases his or her own strain, by way of what may be called *empathic identification*. Social learning theorists (e.g., Bandura, 1969; Stotland, 1969) support this view, and have explained the transmission of emotions as a conscious processing of information. They suggest that individuals imagine how they would feel in the position of another (i.e., empathic identification), and thus come to experience and share the other's feelings. Eckenrode and Gore (1981) suggested that the effect of one's strain on the spouse's distress might be the result of empathy as expressed in reports such as "We feel their pain is our own" (p. 771).

SUSCEPTIBILITY

Bakker, Schaufeli, Sixma, and Bosveld (2001) observed that general practitioners' individual susceptibility to emotional contagion was positively related to burnout. That is, they were most vulnerable to catching the negative emotions expressed by their patients, such as fear, anxiety, depressed mood, and worry. Interestingly, and in line with Hatfield et al.'s (1994) predictions, susceptibility to the emotions of others particularly showed a relationship with burnout when doctors reported many colleagues with burnout symptoms. That is, practitioners who perceived burnout complaints among their colleagues *and* who were susceptible to the emotions expressed by their colleagues reported the highest emotional exhaustion scores. A similar finding was reported by Bakker and Schaufeli (2000), who found that teachers who were most vulnerable to the emotions and negative attitudes expressed by their colleagues were most likely to become burned out.

FREQUENCY OF EXCHANGING VIEWS

In their study among teachers, Bakker and Schaufeli (2000) also found that teachers who frequently talked with their burned-out colleagues about problematic students had the highest probability of catching the negative attitudes expressed by their colleagues. In repeatedly trying to understand the problems their colleagues were facing, teachers presumably had to tune in to the negative attitudes expressed by their colleagues (about themselves as well as about students). This creates a condition under which central or systematic processing of information is likely to occur (Petty & Cacioppo, 1986; Stroebe, 1999). The result is negative attitude change, particularly when the burned-out colleague (the "source") has evidence or strong arguments to bolster their frustration and uncaring attitudes.

SIMILARITY TO THE SOURCE

Classic social comparison theory regards uncertainty as the main motive for social comparison activity (Festinger, 1954; Schachter, 1959). Festinger stated that people have a drive to evaluate their motives and opinions. He argued that when objective sources of information for self-evaluation are lacking, people would turn to others in their environment. Schachter (1959) stated that when individuals feel uncertain about the appropriateness of their emotions, they tend to reduce this uncertainty by socially comparing and by adjusting their emotional reactions to those of others. Indeed, Groenestijn, Buunk, and Schaufeli (1992) found that nurses who perceived burnout complaints among their colleagues and who felt a strong need for social comparison were more susceptible to burnout compared to those who had a low need for social comparison.

In addition, an important assumption in Festinger's (1954) theory is that others who are similar will be preferred for comparison, because information about similar others is most informative for self-evaluation (see also Tesser, 1988; Tesser, Millar, & Moore, 1988). Levy, Freitas, and Salovey (2002) maintain that perceiving similarity between oneself and others can lead one to take the others' perspectives, thus prompting experience of empathic emotions (empathic identification). Keinan, Sadeh, and Rosen (2003) investigated the attitudes and reactions to media coverage of terrorist acts. They suggest that the experience of stress responses in reaction to media coverage stems from identification with the victims of violence, and this identification is related to the degree of similarity between the media consumer and the victim: The greater the number of shared characteristics, the greater the probability of identifying with the victim.

Bakker, Westman, and Schaufeli (2005e) tested this hypothesis in the context of burnout and work engagement crossover among a sample of soldiers. The participants were randomly exposed to a videotape of a burned-out or an engaged colleague who was either similar in profession and status (soldier), or who had a considerably higher status (squadron leader). The results confirmed the crossover of burnout (cynicism and reduced professional efficacy). In addition, consistent with the hypothesis, a significant interaction effect for cynicism revealed that the crossover of burnout was moderated by similarity with the stimulus person. Figure 14.2 shows the pattern of the interaction, and shows that soldiers were particularly susceptible to the negative attitudes endorsed by those who were similar in rank.

Conclusion

The notion of emotional contagion, which represents a social psychological perspective, proposes that burnout and work engagement are, at least to some extent, socially induced. That means that employees are likely to "catch" burnout symptoms that are displayed by others in their work team, irrespective of the experienced workload. Also, it has been observed that in couples burnout crosses over from one spouse to the other. In a similar vein, employees and couples seem to be "infected" with work engagement. Several moderators have been identified that may increase the "risk of infection",

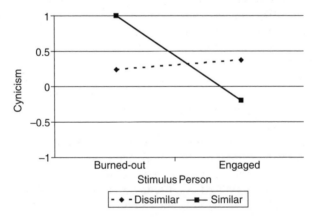

Figure 14.2 Interaction effect of stimulus person's well-being and similarity on cynicism.

such as empathy, susceptibility to emotional contagion, frequency of exposure, and similarity with the source.

Avenues for future research

Based on the overview presented above, three main avenues for future research may be distinguished. These pertain to the extension and refinement of the organisational JD–R model, the extension and refinement of the social psychological notion of "emotional contagion", and the integration of the JD–R model and the emotional contagion approach, respectively. It is important to note that work in all three areas is currently in progress, which is illustrated by the fact that in this section we often refer to papers that have recently been submitted for publication.

Extension and refinement of the JD–R model

Most studies on the JD–R model have relied exclusively on self-report measures. Some exceptions to this rule are reported by Demerouti et al. (2001), who employed expert ratings to assess job demands and job resources, Bakker et al. (2004) and Salanova, Agut, and Peiró (2005), who used other-ratings of performance, and Bakker (2005), who used video clips of job demands and resources. As argued by Schaufeli (2005), it is crucial for the development of the field of occupational health psychology to include in research models objective measures that play a role in business. For instance, Harter, Schmidt, and Hayes (2002) showed that levels of employee engagement were positively related to business-unit performance (i.e., customer satisfaction and loyalty, profitability, productivity, turnover, and safety) across almost 8000 business units of 36 companies. The authors conclude that engagement is ". . . related to meaningful business outcomes at a magnitude that is important to many organizations" (p. 276). In addition, using the JD–R model among employees of a temporary agency, Van Riet and Bakker (2004) showed that cynicism mediated the relationship between job resources and objective financial performance. Future research should further illuminate to what extent objective business indicators (e.g., work performance, customer satisfaction, sickness absenteeism, sales) are predicted by the JD–R model.

An important extension of the JD–R model is the inclusion of personal resources in the model. Recently, Xanthopoulou et al. (2005) examined the role of three personal resources (self-efficacy, organisational-based self-esteem, and optimism) in predicting exhaustion and work engagement. Results of structural equation modelling analyses showed that personal resources did *not* manage to offset the relationship between job demands and exhaustion. However, as predicted, personal resources partly mediated the relationship between job resources and work engagement, suggesting that job resources foster the development of personal resources. The inclusion of self-efficacy has opened the window for the "dynamisation" of the JD–R model, in the sense that it seems that self-efficacy may precede, as well as follow, employee well-being (Llorens, Salanova, Schaufeli, & Bakker, in press; Salanova, Bakker, & Llorens, in press). This suggests the existence of an upward spiral: self-efficacy that results from the availability of job resources and optimal job demands fuels engagement, which in turn increases efficacy beliefs, and so on. This is in line with *social cognitive theory* (Bandura, 2001) that predicts reciprocal relationships between self-efficacy and positive affective–cognitive outcomes, such as work engagement. In addition, these reciprocal relationships are compatible with the notion of so-called "gain spirals" as described by COR theory (Hobfoll & Shirom, 2000). Simultaneously, the existence of a downward "loss spiral" has been confirmed in which high job demands lead to exhaustion, which in turn leads to higher job demands over time (Demerouti, Bakker, & Bulters, 2004; Demerouti, Le Blanc, Bakker, & Schaufeli, 2005). Future research should investigate the dynamics of the JD–R model using the concepts of loss and gain spirals.

Extension and refinement of the notion of "emotional contagion"

So far, emotional contagion of employee well-being has been studied exclusively in field studies or in the laboratory, using between-subjects designs. An innovation would be to study emotional contagion using a within-subjects design in which respondents are followed closely during their working day, for instance by asking them to keep an electronic diary (Van Eerde, Holman, & Totterdell, 2005). In doing so, emotional contagion might be studied from a slightly broader perspective of emotional labour (Hochschild, 1983). Traditionally, emotional labour has been studied in relation to customers or clients (Heuven & Bakker, 2003), but linking it to our notion of emotional contagion would open the possibility of studying how employees manage the emotions of other employees they are working with.

Another interesting avenue for research would be to investigate the relative impact of negative and positive emotional contagion. So far, the contagious nature of burnout and work engagement has been studied separately. Only two exceptions exist in which both are studied simultaneously; one of these studies was on working couples (Bakker et al., 2005b; Bakker et al., in press). So it remains to be seen if the effect of negative emotions on burnout levels of team members is equally as strong as the effect of positive emotions on engagement. Based on arguments from evolutionary psychology, one could argue that negative contagion effects might be stronger than positive effects because the former have greater survival value compared to the latter (Fredrickson, 1998). That is, negative emotions signal danger, damage, or threat, and thus a potential assault on one's mental and physical integrity. Hence, they have greater immediate relevance for survival than positive emotions that broaden one's scope and initiate learning and development (Frederickson, 2001).

Integration of the JD–R model and the emotional contagion approach

The most challenging avenue for future research is the integration of the organisational and social psychological approaches to employee well-being. Although stemming from different backgrounds, both approaches may be integrated using the JD–R model as a general framework. This means that perceptions of positive or negative emotions of other colleagues at work could be considered as "job demands" and "job resources", respectively. More specifically, negative emotions of other colleagues are likely to foster interpersonal conflicts and a poor team spirit (De Dreu, 2005); in short, they are demanding. Contrarily, team members' positive emotions are associated with mutual support and a good team spirit (West, 2004); in short, they are motivating. In addition to including other colleagues' negative and positive emotions as job demands and job resources, respectively, a specific kind of self-efficacy, namely the belief that one can deal effectively with other colleagues' emotions (Heuven, Bakker, Schaufeli, & Huisman, in press), could be included as well. This would offer the possibility to study "loss" and "gain" spirals related to the management of emotions in the workplace.

Practical implications

We have argued that burnout and work engagement are not only characteristics of the individual employee, but can also be meaningfully interpreted at the group level. Moreover, burnout and engagement are socially induced, and should be seen as processes that are contagious. This approach both illustrates risks, as burnout can be transferred as an "infectious disease", and offers opportunities, as social relations can be used to foster engagement as an antidote for burnout in organisations. Human resource policies and practices should be aimed at reducing those risks, and creating opportunities, through the use of team structures in organisations (Baron & Krepps, 1999; Cummings & Worley, 2001).

The rise of team-based work structures is perhaps one the most salient characteristics of contemporary workplaces and the shift from individualised work structures to teamwork has spread all over the organisation (Committee on Techniques for the Enhancement of Human Performance: Occupational Analysis, 1999). Moreover, the use of teams in the workplace can only be expected to grow in the future (Stout, Salas, & Fowlkes, 1997). Teams bring together diverse groups of employees, who incorporate a variety of backgrounds, ideas, and personalities (Jehn, Northcraft, & Neale, 1999). This diversity also relates to the work attitude in terms of burnout or work engagement of team members. Recently, the effects and management of diversity in teams has received a great deal of attention (Van der Vegt & Bunderson, 2005; West, Tjosvold, & Smith, 2005). These insights should be combined with the knowledge on stress management in organisations, to minimise risks of burnout contagion and foster the development of engagement in work teams. We describe two types of interventions, in addition to the more traditional individual interventions.

Firstly, burnout assessment should be done not only at the individual level, but also at team or unit levels (Bakker et al., in press). When teams demonstrate relatively high levels of burnout, interventions should be aimed primarily at the team. Interventions may include introduction of communication norms (e.g., limitations to cynical communications, encouragement of positive communication, and working norms and attitudes). The literature on team development suggests that this can be done effectively (West et al., 2005). A more rigorous intervention at the team level is the replacement of team members. Introduction of new team members, with an enthusiastic attitude and positive energy, can change mood at the team level, particularly when at the same time some members with high burnout are distributed over other teams. This is old wisdom, applied by many schoolteachers, who place problematic kids at the back benches, over the classroom, and couple them with those who have a positive learning attitude. At the organisational level, the assessment of team-level burnout and related team processes (e.g., lowered innovation and cohesion, increased interpersonal conflicts, and reduced productivity) should be a key element in team management. Whereas leadership is still too often focused on the management of individuals, team leadership really should be focused on creating stimulating social work environments, by promoting positive social influence in teams. Training managers to do this is applied social psychology by definition.

Overall conclusion

The present chapter aimed to integrate an organisational with a social psychological perspective on the experience of burnout and work engagement. As was shown, aspects of work (the organisational psychological perspective) and of individuals within groups (the social psychological perspective) were both able to predict the development and sustenance of occupational well-being or unwell-being. While we saw that some studies have aimed to integrate both perspectives in the study of employee well-being, more systematic work should be conducted in this direction. Each of these perspectives can be enriched by the insights gained in the other perspective, and their simultaneous consideration may promote a more systemic view on occupational health and well-being. This will help research and practice to find more workable solutions, which are beneficial for well-being and for all involved parties.

Note

1 The terms transference, contagion, and crossover are used interchangeably in order to use the same terminology as the studies that we are referring to. While there

might be some differences between these terms, for instance in their underlying mechanisms, they all describe the situation that the well-being of two persons covaries.

References

Bakker, A. B. (2005). *Job resources as predictors of work engagement and employee retention.* Manuscript submitted for publication.

Bakker, A. B., Demerouti, E., De Boer, E., & Schaufeli, W. B. (2003a). Job demands and job resources as predictors of absence duration and frequency. *Journal of Vocational Behavior, 62*, 341–356.

Bakker, A. B., Demerouti, E., & Euwema, M. C. (2005a). Job resources buffer the impact of job demands on burnout. *Journal of Occupational Health Psychology, 10*, 170–180.

Bakker, A. B., Demerouti, E., & Schaufeli, W. B. (2003b). Dual processes at work in a call centre: An application of the Job Demands – Resources model. *European Journal of Work and Organizational Psychology, 12*, 393–417.

Bakker, A. B., Demerouti, E., & Schaufeli, W. B. (2003c). The socially induced burnout model. In S. P. Shohov (Ed.), *Advances in psychology research* (Vol. 25, pp. 13–30). New York: Nova Science Publishers.

Bakker, A. B., Demerouti, E., & Schaufeli, W. B. (2005b). Crossover of burnout and work engagement among working couples. *Human Relations, 58*, 661–689.

Bakker, A. B., Demerouti, E., Taris, T., Schaufeli, W. B., & Schreurs, P. (2003d). A multi-group analysis of the Job Demands – Resources model in four home care organizations. *International Journal of Stress Management, 10*, 16–38.

Bakker, A. B., Demerouti, E., & Verbeke, W. (2004). Using the Job Demands – Resources model to predict burnout and performance. *Human Resource Management, 43*, 83–104.

Bakker, A. B., Hakanen, J. J., & Demerouti, E. (2005c). *Job resources boost work engagement, particularly when job demands are high.* Manuscript submitted for publication.

Bakker, A. B., Le Blanc, P. M., & Schaufeli, W. B. (1997). *Burnout contagion among nurses who work at intensive care units.* Paper presented at the fifth European Conference on Organizational Psychology and Health Care, Utrecht, The Netherlands.

Bakker, A. B., Le Blanc, P. M., & Schaufeli, W. B. (2005d). Burnout contagion among nurses who work at intensive care units. *Journal of Advanced Nursing, 51*, 276–287.

Bakker, A. B., & Schaufeli, W. B. (2000). Burnout contagion processes among teachers. *Journal of Applied Social Psychology, 30*, 2289–2308.

Bakker, A. B., Schaufeli, W. B., Sixma, H., & Bosveld, W. (2001). Burnout contagion among general practitioners. *Journal of Social and Clinical Psychology, 20*, 82–98.

Bakker, A. B., Van Emmerik, IJ. H., & Euwema, M. C. (in press). Crossover of burnout and engagement in work teams. *Work & Occupations.*

Bakker, A. B., Westman, M., & Schaufeli, W. B. (2005e). *Crossover of burnout: An experimental design.* Internal report; Utrecht University, Department of Social and Organizational Psychology, The Netherlands.

Bandura, A. (1969). *Principles of behavior modification.* New York: Holt, Rinehart, & Winston.

Bandura, A. (2001). Social cognitive theory: An agentic perspective. *Annual Review of Psychology, 52,* 1–26.

Baron, J. N., & Kreps, D. M. (1999). *Strategic human resources: Frameworks for general managers* (Vol. 41). New York: Wiley.

Baumeister, R. F., & Leary, M. R. (1995). The need to belong: Desire for interpersonal attachments as a fundamental human motivation. *Psychological Bulletin, 117,* 497–529.

Bavelas, J. B., Black, A., Lemery, C. R., & Mullett, J. (1987). Motor mimicry as primitive empathy. In N. Eisenberg & J. Strayer (Eds.), *Empathy and its development* (pp. 317–338). New York: Cambridge University Press.

Bernieri, F. J., Reznick, J. S., & Rosenthal, R. (1988). Synchrony, pseudosynchrony, and dissynchrony: Measuring the entrainment process in mother–infant interactions. *Journal of Personality and Social Psychology, 54,* 1242–1253.

Burisch, M. (1989). *Das burnout-syndrom: Theorie der inneren Erschöpfung* [The burnout syndrome: A theory of inner exhaustion]. Berlin: Springer.

Cherniss, C. (1980). *Professional burnout in human service organizations.* New York: Praeger.

Committee on Techniques for the Enhancement of Human Performance: Occupational Analysis. (1999). *The changing nature of work: Implications for occupational analysis.* Washington, DC: National Academy Press.

Cummings, T. G., & Worley, C. G. (2001). *Organizational development and change.* Cincinnati, OH: South-Western College Publishing.

DeCharms, R. (1968). *Personal causation: The internal affective determinants of behavior.* New York: Academic Press.

De Dreu, C. K. W. (2005). *Bang voor conflict* [Afraid of conflict]? Assen: Van Gorcum.

Deelstra, J. T., Peeters, M. C. W., Schaufeli, W. B., Stroebe, W., Zijlstra, F. R. H., & Van Doornen, L. P. (2003). Receiving instrumental support at work: When help is not welcome. *Journal of Applied Psychology, 88,* 324–331.

De Jonge, J., & Kompier, M. A. J. (1997). A critical examination of the Demand-Control-Support Model from a work psychological perspective. *International Journal of Stress Management, 4,* 235–258.

Demerouti, E., Bakker, A. B., & Bulters, A. J. (2004). The loss spiral of work pressure, work–home interference and exhaustion: Reciprocal relations in a three-wave study. *Journal of Vocational Behavior, 64,* 131–149.

Demerouti, E., Bakker, A. B., Nachreiner, F., & Schaufeli, W. B. (2001). The job demands–resources model of burnout. *Journal of Applied Psychology, 86,* 499–512.

Demerouti, E., Le Blanc, P., Bakker, A. B., & Schaufeli, W. B. (2005). *The costs of "working through" sickness: A three-wave study on presenteeism.* Manuscript submitted for publication.

Diener, E. (1999). Introduction to special section: The structure of emotion. *Journal of Personality and Social Psychology, 76,* 803–804.

Doherty, R. W., Orimoto, L., Singelis, T. M., Hatfield, E., & Hebb, J. (1995). Emotional contagion: Gender and occupational differences. *Psychology of Women Quarterly, 19,* 355–371.

Eckenrode, J., & Gore, S. (1981). Stressful events and social support: The significance of context. In B. Gottlieb (Ed.), *Social networks and social support* (pp. 43–68). Beverly Hills, CA: Sage.

Edelwich, J., & Brodsky, A. (1980). *Burnout: Stages of disillusionment in the helping professions.* New York: Human Sciences Press.

Festinger, L. (1954). A theory of social comparison processes. *Human Relations, 7,* 117–140.

Fredrickson, B. L. (1998). What good are positive emotions? *Review of General Psychology, 2,* 300–319.

Fredrickson, B. L. (2001). The role of positive emotions in positive psychology: The broaden-and-build theory of positive emotions. *American Psychologist, 56,* 218–226.

Freudenberger, H. J. (1974). Staff burn-out. *Journal of Social Issues, 30,* 159–166.

Glass, D. C., McKnight, D., & Valdimarsdottir, H. (1993). Depression, burnout, and perceptions of control in hospital nurses. *Journal of Consulting and Clinical Psychology, 61,* 147–155.

Golembiewski, R. T., Munzenrider, R. F., & Stevenson, J. G. (1986). *Stress in organizations: Towards a phase model of burnout.* New York: Praeger.

González-Romá, V., Schaufeli, W. B., Bakker, A. B., & Lloret, S. (2006). Burnout and work engagement: Independent factors or opposite poles? *Journal of Vocational Behavior, 62,* 165–174.

Groenestijn, E., Buunk, B. P., & Schaufeli, W. B. (1992). Het besmettingsgevaar bij burnout: De rol van sociale vergelijkingsprocessen [The danger of burnout contagion: The role of social comparison processes]. In R. W. Meertens, A. P. Buunk, P. A. M. van Lange, & B. Verplanken (Eds.), *Sociale psychologie en beïnvloeding van intermenselijke en gezondheidsproblemen* (pp. 88–103). The Hague, The Netherlands: VUGA.

Hackman, J. R., & Oldham, G. R. (1980). *Work redesign.* Reading, MA: Addison-Wesley.

Hakanen, J. J., Bakker, A. B., & Demerouti, E. (2005). How dentists cope with their job demands and stay engaged: The moderating role of job resources. *European Journal of Oral Sciences, 113,* 479–487.

Hakanen, J. J., Bakker, A. B., & Schaufeli, W. B. (2006). Burnout and work engagement among teachers. *Journal of School Psychology, 43,* 495–513.

Halbesleben, J. R. B., & Buckley, M. R. (2004). Burnout in organizational life. *Journal of Management, 30,* 859–879.

Harter, J. K., Schmidt, F. L., & Hayes, T. L. (2002). Business-unit-level relationship between employee satisfaction, employee engagement, and business outcomes: A meta-analysis. *Journal of Applied Psychology, 87,* 268–279.

Hatfield, E., Cacioppo, J. T., & Rapson, R. L. (1994). *Emotional contagion.* New York: Cambridge University Press.

Heuven, E., & Bakker, A. B. (2003). Emotional dissonance and burnout among cabin attendants. *European Journal of Work and Organizational Psychology, 12,* 81–100.

Heuven, E., Bakker, A. B., Schaufeli, W. B., & Huisman, N. (in press). The role of self-efficacy in performing emotion work. *Journal of Vocational Behavior.*

Hobfoll, S. E. (2001). The influence of culture, community, and the nested-self in the stress process: Advancing conservation of resources theory. *Applied Psychology: An International Review, 50,* 337–370.

Hobfoll, S. E. (2002). Social and psychological resources and adaptation. *Review of General Psychology, 6,* 307–324.

Hobfoll, S. E., & Shirom, A. (2000). Conservation of resources theory: Applications to stress and management in the workplace. In R. T. Golembiewski (Ed.), *Handbook of organization behavior* (2nd ed., pp. 57–81). New York: Dekker.

Hochschild, A. R. (1983). *The managed heart: Commercialization of human feeling.* Berkeley, CA: University of California Press.

Hockey, G. R. J. (1993). Cognitive-energetical control mechanisms in the management of work demands and psychological health. In A. Baddeley & L. Weiskrantz (Eds.), *Attention: Selection, awareness, and control* (pp. 328–345). Oxford, UK: Clarendon Press.

Howes, M. J., Hokanson, J. E., & Lowenstein, D. A. (1985). Induction of depressive affect after prolonged exposure to a mildly depressed individual. *Journal of Personality and Social Psychology, 49*, 1110–1113.

Hsee, C. K., Hatfield, E., Carlson, J. G., & Chemtob, C. (1990). The effect of power on susceptibility to emotional contagion. *Cognition and Emotion, 4*, 327–340.

Jehn, K. A., Northcraft, G. B., & Neale, M. A. (1999). Why differences make a difference: A field study of diversity, conflict, and performance in workgroups. *Administrative Science Quarterly, 44*, 741–763.

Johnson, J. V., & Hall, E. M. (1988). Job strain, work place social support and cardio-vascular disease: A cross-sectional study of a random sample of the Swedish working population. *American Journal of Public Health, 78*, 1336–1342.

Joiner, T. F. Jr. (1994). Contagious depression: Existence, specificity to depressive symptoms, and the role of reassurance seeking. *Journal of Personality and Social Psychology, 67*, 287–296.

Kahill, S. (1988). Symptoms of professional burnout: A review of the empirical evidence. *Canadian Psychology, 29*, 284–297.

Kahn, R. L., & Byosiere, P. (1992). Stress in organizations. In M. D. Dunette & L. M. Hough (Eds.), *Handbook of industrial and organizational psychology* (Vol. 3, pp. 571–650). Palo Alto, CA: Consulting Psychologists Press.

Karasek, R. A. (1979). Job demands, job decision latitude, and mental strain: Implications for job design. *Administrative Science Quarterly, 24*, 285–308.

Karasek, R. A. (1998). Demand/Control Model: A social, emotional, and physio-logical approach to stress risk and active behaviour development. In J. M. Stellman (Ed.), *Encyclopaedia of occupational health and safety* (pp. 34.6–34.14). Geneva: ILO.

Keinan, G., Sadeh, A., & Rosen, S. (2003). Attitudes and reaction to media cover-age on terrorist acts. *Journal of Community Psychology, 31*, 149–168.

Laird, J. D. (1984). The real role of facial response in the experience of emotion: A reply to Tourangeau and Ellsworth, and others. *Journal of Personality and Social Psychology, 47*, 909–917.

Lazarus, R. S. (1991). *Emotion and adaptation.* New York: Oxford University Press.

Lee, R. T., & Ashforth, B. E. (1996). A meta-analytic examination of the correlates of the three dimensions of job burnout. *Journal of Applied Psychology, 81*, 123–133.

Levy, S., Freitas, A., & Salovey, P. (2002). Construing actions abstractly and blurring social distinctions: Implications for perceiving homogeneity among, but also empathizing with helping others. *Journal of Personality and Social Psychology, 83*, 1224–1238.

Llorens, S., Schaufeli, W. B., Bakker, A. B., & Salanova, M. (in press). Does a positive gain spiral of resources, efficacy beliefs and engagement exist? *Computers in Human Behavior.*

Maslach, C., & Leiter, M. P. (1997). *The truth about burnout: How organizations cause personal stress and what to do about it.* San Francisco: Jossey-Bass.

Maslach, C., Schaufeli, W. B., & Leiter, M. P. (2001). Job burnout. *Annual Review of Psychology, 52*, 397–422.

McIntosh, D. N., Druckman, D., & Zajonc, R. B. (1994). Socially induced affect. In

D. Druckman & R. A. Bjork (Eds.), *Learning, remembering, believing: Enhancing human performance* (pp. 251–276). Washington, DC: National Academy Press.

Meijman, T. F., & Mulder, G. (1998). Psychological aspects of workload. In P. J. Drenth, H. Thierry, & C. J. de Wolff (Eds.), *Handbook of work and organizational psychology* (2nd ed., pp. 5–33). Hove, UK: Lawrence Erlbaum Associates Inc.

Petty, R. E., & Cacioppo, J. T. (1986). The elaboration likelihood model of persuasion. In L. Berkowitz (Ed.), *Advances in experimental social psychology* (Vol. 19, pp. 124–205). Orlando, FL: Academic Press.

Riolli, L., & Savicki, V. (2003). Optimism and coping as moderators of the relation between work resources and burnout in information service workers. *International Journal of Stress Management, 10*, 235–252.

Rothbarth, N. P. (2001). Enriching or depleting? The dynamics of engagement in work and family roles. *Administrative Science Quarterly, 46*, 655–684.

Rountree, B. H. (1984). Psychological burnout in task groups. *Journal of Health and Human Resources Administration, 7*, 235–248.

Salanova, M., Agut, S., & Pieró, J. M. (2005). Linking organizational resources and work engagement to employee performance and customer loyalty: The mediation of service climate. *Journal of Applied Psychology, 90*, 1217–1227.

Salanova, M., Bakker, A. B., & Llorens, S. (in press). Flow at work: Evidence for a gain spiral of personal and job resources. *Journal of Happiness Studies.*

Schachter, S. (1959). *The psychology of affiliation.* Palo Alto, CA: Stanford University Press.

Schaufeli, W. B. (2005). The future of occupational health psychology. *Applied Psychology: An International Review, 53*, 502–517.

Schaufeli, W. B., & Enzmann, D. (1998). *The burnout companion to research and practice: A critical analysis.* London: Taylor & Francis.

Schaufeli, W. B., & Salanova, M. (in press). Work engagement: An emerging psychological concept and its implications for organizations. In S. W. Gilliland, D. D. Steiner, & D. P. Skarlicki (Eds.), *Research in social issues in management: Managing social and ethical issues in organizations* (Volume 5). Greenwich, CT: Information Age Publishers.

Schaufeli, W. B., Salanova, M., González-Romá, V., & Bakker, A. B. (2002). The measurement of engagement and burnout: A confirmative analytic approach. *Journal of Happiness Studies, 3*, 71–92.

Schaufeli, W. B., Taris, T., Le Blanc, P., Peeters, M., Bakker, A. B., & De Jonge, J. (2001). Maakt arbeid gezond? Op zoek naar de bevlogen werknemer. *De Psycholoog, 36*, 422–428.

Schwartz, M. S., & Will, G. T. (1953). Low morale and mutual withdrawal on a hospital ward. *Psychiatry, 16*, 337–353.

Starcevic, V., & Piontek, C. M. (1997). Empathic understanding revisited: Conceptualization, controversies, and limitations. *American Journal of Psychotherapy, 51*, 317–328.

Stiff, J. B., Dillard, J. P., Somera, L., Kim, H., & Sleight, C. (1988). Empathy, communication, and prosocial behavior. *Communication Monographs, 55*, 198–213.

Stotland, E. (1969). Exploratory investigations of empathy. In L. Berkowitz (Ed.), *Advances in experimental social psychology* (Vol. 4, pp. 271–314). New York: Academic Press.

Stout, R. J., Salas, E., & Fowlkes, J. E. (1997). Enhancing teamwork in complex environment through team training. *Journal of Group Psychotherapy, Psychodrama and Sociometry*, *49*, 163–187.

Stroebe, W. (1999). The return of the one-track mind. *Psychological Inquiry*, *10*, 173–176.

Stroebe, W., & Stroebe, M. S. (1995). *Social psychology and health*. Buckingham, UK: Open University Press.

Tesser, A. (1988). Towards a self-evaluation maintenance model of social behavior. In L. Berkowitz (Ed.), *Advances in experimental social psychology* (Vol. 21, pp. 181–227). San Diego, CA: Academic Press.

Tesser, A., Millar, M., & Moore, J. (1988). Some affective consequences of social comparison and reflection processes: The pain and pleasure of being close. *Journal of Personality and Social Psychology*, *54*, 49–61.

Uchino, B., Hsee, C. K., Hatfield, E., Carlson, J. G., & Chemtob, C. (1991). *The effect of expectations on susceptibility to emotional contagion*. Unpublished manuscript, University of Hawaii.

Van der Vegt, G., & Bunderson, J. S. (2005). Learning and performance in multidisciplinary teams: The importance of collective team identification. *Academy of Management Journal*, *48*, 532–547.

Van Eerde, W., Holman, D., & Totterdell, P. (2005). Editorial: Diary studies in work psychology. *Journal of Occupational and Organizational Psychology*, *78*, 151–154.

Van Horn, J. E., Schaufeli, W. B., & Enzmann, D. (1999). Teacher burnout and lack of reciprocity. *Journal of Applied Social Psychology*, *29*, 91–108.

Van Riet, P., & Bakker, A. B. (2004). Financiële omzet als een functie van werkstressoren en energiebronnen [Financial performance as a function of job demands and resources]. *Gedrag en Organisatie*, *6*, 487–504.

West, M. A. (2004). *Effective teamwork* (2nd ed.). Oxford, UK: Blackwell.

West, M. A., Tjosvold, D., & Smith, K. G. (Eds.). (2005). *The essentials of teamworking: International perspectives*. Chichester, UK: Wiley.

Westman, M., & Etzion, D. (1995). Crossover of stress, strain and resources from one spouse to another. *Journal of Organizational Behavior*, *16*, 169–181.

Westman, M., & Vinokur, A. (1998). Unraveling the relationship of distress levels within couples: Common stressors, emphatic reactions, or crossover via social interactions? *Human Relations*, *51*, 137–156.

White, R. (1959). Motivation reconsidered: The concept of competence. *Psychological Review*, *66*, 297–333.

Xanthopoulou, D., Bakker, A. B., Demerouti, E., & Schaufeli, W. B. (2005). *The role of personal resources in the Job Demands–Resources model*. Manuscript submitted for publication.

Zapf, D., Vogt, C., Seifert, C., Mertini, H., & Isic, A. (1999). Emotion work as a source of stress: The concept and development of an instrument. *European Journal of Work and Organizational Psychology*, *8*, 371–400.

Part 5

Bereavement and coping

15 Reflections on extended Bowlby theory

Robert S. Weiss
University of Massachusetts, Boston, USA

Wolfgang Stroebe and his colleagues, in a study of widows and widowers, found that while supportive friends effectively ameliorated the distress associated with social isolation, they did little to reduce the loneliness associated with marital loss (Stroebe, Stroebe, Abakoumkin, & Schut, 1996). The inference Stroebe and his colleagues drew was that the emotional partnership of a marriage, on the one hand, and the support of friends and kin, on the other, made independent contributions to well-being.

I would like here to offer a theoretical and empirical context for the Stroebe et al. findings. The theoretical context stems from the work of Bowlby and extends his work to include a concern for relationships he treated as of secondary importance. It also includes a theory of loneliness. I will refer to it as "extended Bowlby theory". In this theory both the relationships of attachment that were Bowlby's primary concern and the relationships of community to which he gave much less attention foster feelings of security, but in different ways and under different circumstances. Bowlby did not especially concern himself with loneliness, but loneliness tends now to be seen as either of two states: one made possible by the absence of attachment relationships, the other by the absence of relationships of community.

The empirical context for the Stroebe et al. findings includes efforts to establish that the emotional partnership of a marriage and the linkages to others that can be categorised under the heading of relationships of community make different provisions to individual well-being. It also includes efforts to establish that the loneliness that is associated with the absence of a marriage or similar relationship is different from the loneliness that is associated with the absence of relationships of community.

Theory

John Bowlby, on the basis of observations of small children undergoing separation from their parents, augmented by the literature on imprinting and other relational phenomena among animals, proposed that children establish a bond with their parents which he called attachment. The function of the attachment bond was to foster proximity to the parents when the children felt themselves threatened, and it operated by fostering anxiety in the children when they felt themselves distant from their parents under conditions of threat.

Bowlby suggested that attachments had three primary identifying characteristics. They provided children with a secure base from which to explore the world by strengthening their confidence in the ultimate safety of their situations; they provided a safe haven to which the children could retreat when they felt threatened; and their interruption gave rise to separation distress. Separation distress, as Bowlby described it, was a state in which the child did his or her utmost to regain the parent's presence and, should this prove unavailing, remained tensely and unhappily focused on the parent's return.

Bowlby further proposed that when children believed that their parents were reliably accessible they were able to give their attention to play and exploration. His view was that one could discern two distinct states in children, one of them dominated by attachment strivings, the other by exploratory impulses (Bowlby, 1969, 1973, 1980; see also Weiss, 1974).

Bowlby did not especially attend to the relational implications of a child's exploratory impulses, but it is easy to imagine what they must be. They would include friends, especially, who might share exploratory goals and serve as companions and allies. The presence of friends would assure the child that he or she wasn't alone, and so reduce the child's sense of vulnerability, and might actually provide useful support should there be threat. Friends, like attachment figures, would bolster the child's feelings of security, though in a different way and undoubtedly with less effectiveness.

Extended Bowlby theory has extrapolated from Bowlby's discussions to the setting of adult life. The parental security-providing attachment relationships of childhood are seen as having an analogue in committed adult partnerships, of which marriage might be seen as the model. Such relationships are seen as providing participants with a secure base and safe haven (often with, literally, a home). Furthermore, threat of loss in these relationships gives rise to a syndrome of protest together with effort at prevention of the loss, just as did the threat of parental loss earlier in life. Indeed, the response of adults to the threat of loss of what might be called "attachments of adult life" so strongly resembles the response of children to the inaccessibility of their parents that it too might be called a form of separation distress. The absence of an attachment of adult life makes for vulnerability to feelings of separation distress, except that efforts to regain a particular figure have been replaced by a yearning for an unidentified potential attachment figure. Thus the loneliness associated with absence of an attachment figure can be seen as separation distress without an object.

These observations raise the question of how the child's attachment feelings, directed towards a parent, can have been transmuted into the adult's attachment feelings directed towards an age peer. One approach to answering this question is to suppose that in the process of maturation, attachment feelings towards the parent become ever less present, and eventually arise primarily under conditions of threat. As this is happening, there is a corresponding development, perhaps impelled by sexual maturation, to form bonds of attachment with age peers. It seems likely that proximity can foster the development of such bonds, so long as the proximity is not so close and constant that it triggers an incest taboo, but it also seems likely that sudden infatuations are possible. Attachments in formation tend to absorb energy and attention, and the energy and attention may contribute to the relationships becoming established in the individual's emotional economy.

Just as adult attachment can be seen as a development of attachment in childhood, so the companionships and alliances of adulthood can be seen as developments of the companionships and alliances that strengthened children's self-confidence in play and exploration. In adulthood these companionships and alliances can take the form of occupational relationships, friendships, and relationships with kin. I will refer to the inclusive category as relationships of community.

Attachments tend towards exclusivity: one invests one's trust in specific others. Relationships of community tend towards inclusiveness: several allies are preferable to one, and many of the social activities of adulthood are better managed with sets of others rather than specific others. The provisions of attachment tend to be associated with a single figure; the provisions of relationships of community tend to be associated with a number of figures, often themselves interconnected (Weiss, 1998).

Extended Bowlby theory sees both attachments and relationships of community as necessary for effective functioning. An absence of either is then believed to foster vulnerability to loneliness. However, the loneliness syndrome associated with an absence of relationships of attachment is different from that associated with the absence of relationships of community. Although each syndrome may be called loneliness, their component elements are different.

Let us turn now to empirical materials that have some bearing on the validity of extended Bowlby theory. While I cannot review all relevant materials, I believe I can suggest typical findings and concerns.

Relational taxonomies

It is inescapable that a relationship with a friend is different in some fundamental way from a relationship with a child or parent, and different again, though in a different way, from a relationship with one's spouse. There have been several efforts to establish a taxonomy of relationships, identifying relationships that are fundamentally different, one from another.

Argyle and Henderson asked Oxford undergraduates to rate the importance of particular rules—rules such as trying to make an encounter pleasant, or refraining from touching the other person—for maintenance of a particular kind of relationship. They used the cluster analysis statistical technique to identify which of a set of relationships were like each other. They found an attachment cluster: "living together", "dating", "husband", and "wife". They also found a separate family and kin cluster that included "close friend", "sibling", "parent", "adolescent", "parent-in-law", and "son or daughter-in-law". All other relationships—among them work colleague, neighbour, and teacher—were in a distinctly different cluster (Argyle & Henderson, 1984).

An issue is whether respecting the same rules is an appropriate basis for developing a relational typology. For example, sexual accessibility can be available both in marriage and in a commercial relationship of much less importance to functioning. Nevertheless, the approach produces a distinction between, on the one hand, attachments of adult life and, on the other, relationships of community. That it seems also to distinguish between different relationships of community—between close friends and work colleagues— should be noted. I argue, below, that while one may behave differently with friends and work colleagues (and with kin as well,) each of these kinds of relationships can supply allies with whom to explore some sector of reality.

Fiske and his colleagues (Fiske, Haslam, & Fiske, 1991) have proposed a taxonomy of relationships based on participants' understanding of underlying principles that govern the relationships. One of Fiske's types of relationships, "communal sharing", appears largely to overlap with attachments. Another of his types, "equality matching", largely overlaps with relationships of community. (The remaining categories are, essentially, commercial relationships and relationships in which one person has formal authority over another.)

Fiske et al. investigated the way in which people made interpersonal errors: called a familiar person by the wrong name, failed to remember with whom they had interacted, or mistakenly directed an action at an inappropriate person. They found that such mistakes tended to be within relational categories: for example, one friend's name might mistakenly be used for another's, but not for an attachment figure's. This can be seen as a demonstration that people maintain cognitive or emotional distinctions between attachment relationships and relationships of community.

I have used functional substitutability as a criterion for proposing a classification of relationships. In particular, I have found that absence of attachments makes for vulnerability to distress despite the presence of relationships of community, and absence of relationships of community makes for vulnerability to distress despite the presence of attachments (Weiss, 1974).

I have also shown that friendships together with other non-work associations can provide a community that is functionally equivalent (in that it fends off feelings of social isolation) to the community of work (Weiss, 2005). This suggests that there is a functional distinction between attachments and relationships of community that corresponds to Bowlby's distinction between attachment and exploratory modes of functioning, and also that relationships of community, although they differ in many important ways, are functionally similar (Weiss, 1998).

Contributions to well-being

A good many studies have been done with the intention not of developing a classification of relationships but rather of deciding whether attachments and relationships of community make different contributions to well-being. The study of relational contributions to allaying loneliness conducted by Stroebe et al. (1996) is one such. Perhaps most dramatic of the findings of such studies are those reported by Sorkin, Rook, and Lu (2002). They found that the support provided by attachment figures and the support provided by companions independently lessened the likelihood of heart conditions. Whatever the pathways to cardiac disability, they seemed independently accessible to absence of attachments and absence of relationships of community. (One possible explanation is that each deficit independently contributes to physiological stress.)

Phenomenology of loneliness

Extended Bowlby theory sees vulnerability to loneliness as a consequence of relational deficit. It anticipates that there will be two forms of loneliness corresponding to the two potential relational deficits. At the very least, the lonely person will be aware of the kind of deficit that has made loneliness possible.

To judge the validity of this aspect of extended Bowlby theory we need instances of the loneliness syndromes associated with the two deficit conditions. Because loneliness is a subjective experience, this requires detailed introspective descriptions. Unfortunately, there have been few such phenomenological studies. What I believe to be the most valuable such study was conducted about 30 years ago, at the advent of loneliness as a topic of research interest. In this study Rubenstein and Shaver (1982a, 1982b) developed descriptions of the experience of loneliness using three different approaches: they interviewed 50 adult Americans living in different parts of the United States, collected survey data from students, and analysed responses to an advertisement for descriptions of loneliness placed in several newspapers.

The interview materials produced such evocative descriptions of loneliness as "I was eating too much—like I was filling up an empty spot somewhere". People said of themselves that they felt left out and unwanted, felt bored, felt drowsy and down, and that they got in their cars and drove restlessly and aimlessly. Factor analysis of newspaper responses produced four dimensions, of which two seemed descriptive of the loneliness syndrome and two descriptive of what might be causes or consequences of loneliness.

One of the dimensions described a loneliness syndrome whose items might be seen as aspects of emotional loneliness in that they suggested absence of an attachment figure. They included feeling desperate, panicked, helpless, afraid, hopeless, abandoned, and vulnerable. The other dimension seemed descriptive of the syndrome of social loneliness in that its items suggested absence of a place in a valued community. They included: feeling impatient, bored, desiring to be elsewhere, feeling uneasy, angry, and unable to concentrate. Of the two dimensions that described a syndrome that seemed associated with loneliness rather than being loneliness itself, one was labelled depression, and included as items feeling sad, depressed, empty, isolated, sorry for oneself, melancholy, alienated, and longing to be with a special person; the other was labelled self-deprecation, and included as items feeling unattractive, being down on oneself, feeling stupid, ashamed, or insecure.

The correspondence between what might be expected to be components of emotional and social isolation and the dimensions produced by factor analysis was not quite one-to-one. I would have expected "longing to be with a special person" to load on the emotional isolation dimension rather than on the depression dimension. I am surprised, too, that inability to concentrate loaded on the social loneliness dimension rather than the emotional loneliness dimension. In my own work on loneliness, which was qualitative and at times impressionistic, it seemed to me that inability to concentrate was strongly associated with absence of attachment figures. However, being unable to care about current activities did seem an aspect of social loneliness, and perhaps this is what was being tapped. Finally, I would have anticipated that self-deprecation would overlap social loneliness as the lonely person partially accepted the apparent rejection of by the social world. In general, however, the results of the Rubenstein–Shaver factor analysis seem remarkably supportive of what might be anticipated by extended Bowlby theory.

Rubenstein and Shaver asked their respondents to state causes for their loneliness. Appropriately enough, those whose descriptions of their loneliness corresponded to emotional loneliness spoke of being unattached, being without a spouse, being without a sexual partner, or having broken up with a spouse or lover. They were more likely than others actually to be separated or divorced. Those whose descriptions of their loneliness corresponded to social loneliness were more likely to give as reasons for their state feeling different, not being needed, and having no close friends. Again, this is remarkably supportive of extended Bowlby theory.

Loneliness scales

There have been several efforts to develop scales to measure loneliness. For the most part the motivation for such scales is to have a measurement device that can be correlated with dependent variables such as morbidity, or with situational variables such as age or region of residence. There have also been studies whose concern was simply to decide whether there were one, two, or more distinct forms of loneliness.

By far the best-established of the loneliness scales is the UCLA Loneliness Scale, a third version of which was published in 1996. Russell, the author of the UCLA Scale, conducted factor analyses of responses to scale items which led him to believe that loneliness is a single condition, whatever its causes. The factor analysis identified three factors, of which one was a global "loneliness" factor and the other two response set factors, one for negative items and one for positive items (Russell, 1996).

One possible explanation for the inconsistency between Russell's factor-analytic finding and extended Bowlby theory is that the items of the UCLA Loneliness Scale are mostly concerned with social loneliness. They include such items as "How often do you feel that you are 'in tune' with the people around you?" and "How often do you feel that you lack companionship?", but no item that asks anything like "How often do you yearn for someone who would share your life?". Furthermore, because most of the items seem to relate to relationships of community rather than attachments, items that might refer either to an absence of an attachment figure or to absence of relationships of community, such as "How often do you feel alone?", are apt to be interpreted as referring to an absence of relationships of community.

The many scales based on the UCLA Scale also seem to elicit information regarding social loneliness alone. One example is the three-item short scale intended for inclusion in survey schedules. Here the items are ". . . how often do you feel that you lack companionship?", "How often do you feel left out?", and "How often do you feel isolated from others?", all clearly asking about relationships of community (Hughes, Waite, Hawkley, & Cacioppo, 2004).

An 11-item scale that attempts to elicit material on emotional loneliness as well as social loneliness has been developed by De Jong-Gierveld (De Jong-Gierveld & Kamphuis, 1985). Her scale includes only one item that seems on theoretical grounds to be closer to emotional than to social loneliness: "I experience a general sense of emptiness". There are no items that ask about yearning for someone who would share one's life, nor about hoping a romantic partner may appear. Nevertheless, statistical analysis of responses to the 11-item set found support for a two-dimensional model in which the dimensions could be seen as emotional loneliness and social loneliness (Van Baarsen, Snijders, Smit, & Van Duijn, 2001). Most strongly linked to emotional loneliness was often feeling rejected (which I would have thought a component of both emotional and social loneliness), and next most strongly the sense of emptiness. Most strongly linked to social loneliness was having many people who can be counted on and having plenty of people who can be leaned on. Appropriately enough, living alone was correlated more highly with emotional loneliness than with social loneliness, and network size and support were correlated more strongly with social loneliness than emotional loneliness. But it is worth noting that the scale scores for emotional loneliness and social loneliness were themselves correlated.

If the UCLA Loneliness Scale suggests only a single loneliness syndrome and the De Jong-Gierveld loneliness scale supports the existence of two loneliness syndromes, a scale developed by DiTomasso, Brannen, and Best (2004), itself a shorter form of an earlier scale developed by DiTomasso and Spinner (1993), suggests that there are three loneliness syndromes. It does so by finding two sub-syndromes within the syndrome of emotional loneliness: a romantic loneliness in which it is a life partner or sexual partner that is pined for, and a family loneliness in which it is closeness to family that is pined for.

The DiTommaso and Spinner (1993) scale was developed and tested with students in introductory psychology classes functioning as respondents. There is theoretical reason for expecting that these students, many of them newly separated from home, would be experiencing an upsurge of feelings of attachment to parents. DiTomasso and Spinner (1993) go on to find that this form of loneliness is linked to a desire for a guiding figure, which supports the idea that the students miss their parents.

When we look at the scale items used by DiTomasso and Spinner (1993) we see that they ask about the actual or desired state of social ties much more than about feeling states. There are no items about restlessness or yearnings, about feeling rejected or marginal. Instead the items are about relationships, existent or wished for: "I do not have any friends who understand me, but I wish I did", "I feel part of my family", "I have a romantic or marital partner who gives me the support and encouragement I need". I suspect that had the scale included items eliciting attachment to motor vehicles, such as "I have a car I really like", and "I wish I had a BMW", the authors' factor analysis would have identified auto-loneliness as a fourth dimension. It is the items in the scale that decide what factors are produced.

This review of scales leads us to consider again what it is we mean by loneliness. I would propose that we mean a syndrome of distress that is generally recognised as loneliness by those who experience it, and that, in addition, is linked to an experienced relational deficit. What defines loneliness is the nature of the experience as well as its source.

The work of Rubenstein and Shaver seems to me enormously valuable in specifying the content of loneliness syndromes and in linking syndromes to deficits. I believe we need scales based on phenomenological study of the loneliness experience. We also need careful phenomenological examination of the conditions under which loneliness develops and the thoughts that accompany it. Rubenstein and Shaver (1982a, p. 221) end their paper with the observation that "Social psychology is, unfortunately, remarkable for its ability to reduce profound and fascinating human issues to rather superficial and uninteresting generalizations . . . One safeguard would be to return regularly to the complexities of phenomenology". I agree.

Where are we now?

The work of Stroebe et al. has established that the contribution of relationships to well-being requires that we understand how specific relationships function. Extended Bowlby theory seems to provide us as robust a basis for that understanding as any we have. However, like everything in science, it is a work in progress. In particular I would note the following about extended Bowlby theory:

The theory is as yet incomplete. We know little about how attachment develops and, assuming the attachment system in adulthood is lodged in the same cognitive-emotional neural network as the attachment system in child-hood, how the change in object occurs. We know little about the ways in which relationships of community change over the course of development, although it does seem as if they experience nothing as dramatic as the attachment system's change of object. We know too little about what makes any relation-ship, whether potential attachment or potential linkage to community, satis-factory to the individual. And while we know a good deal about the relational determinants of vulnerability to loneliness, we know too little about the personality, cultural, and situational (apart from relational) determinants.

It might be noted that there has been an extraordinary amount of research, much of it produced by Mary Ainsworth, her students, and her students' students, dealing with forms of insecure attachment. There is nothing at all like this in connection with relationships of community. And yet it is com-mon observation that some people have easier relationships with co-workers, friends, and family than do others. Some effort has been made to link peer relationships to attachment styles, but it would seem useful to treat peer relationships as having their own developmental course.

Even as extended Bowlby theory needs much more elaboration, it may already overreach. There seems to be good evidence that there is a syndrome of emotional loneliness and a syndrome of social loneliness, but they may not be entirely distinct. Sadness, restlessness, and questioning of self may occur in each—may indeed be central to each—even while some elements, such as a sense of emptiness, may characterise emotional loneliness but not social lone-liness, and other elements, such as boredom, may characterise social loneli-ness. It may be that while there are two distinct forms of loneliness, each linked to a relational deficit, the syndromes nevertheless have much in common.

I have noted the importance of understanding subjective experience in the study of loneliness. We may yet be able to link information regarding brain functioning with information about subjective experience. Recently brain-imaging techniques have examined attachments in formation—that state in which a new couple's focusing of energy and attention on their relationship helps to establish bonds of attachment between them (Bartels & Zeki, 2000). These techniques have led to the conclusion that attachments in formation engage different brain regions from those engaged by ongoing friendships. We can hope that further brain-imaging studies will provide information regarding the regions used by attachments in place, and whether they are different from the regions used by relationships of community.

Still, it may be attention, rather than attachment, that is at issue in the brain-imaging work done so far: the regions of the brain activated by pictures of romantic partners have a high concentration of receptors for dopamine, a neurotransmitter thought to focus attention. In any event, as the work of Wolfgang Stroebe exemplifies, whether or not we are helped by neuropsychology, we have much useful work to do.

References

Argyle, M., & Henderson, M. (1984). The rules of friendship. *Journal of Social and Personal Relationships, 1*, 209–235.

Bartels, A., & Zeki, S. (2000). The neural basis of romantic love. *Neuroreport, 11*, 3829–3834.

Bowlby, J. (1969). *Attachment* (Vol. 1 of *Attachment and loss*). London: Hogarth Press.

Bowlby, J. (1973). *Separation: Anxiety & anger* (Vol. 2 of *Attachment and loss*). London: Hogarth Press.

Bowlby, J. (1980). *Loss: Sadness & depression* (Vol. 3 of *Attachment and loss*). London: Hogarth Press.

De Jong-Gierveld, J., & Kamphuis, F. H. (1985). The development of a Rasch-type loneliness scale. *Applied Psychological Measurement, 9*, 289–299.

DiTommaso, E., Brannen, D., & Best, L. A. (2004). Measurement and validity characteristics of the short version of the social and emotional loneliness scale for adults. *Educational and Psychological Measurement, 64*, 99–119.

DiTommaso, E., & Spinner, B. (1993). The development and initial validation of the Social and Emotional Loneliness Scale for Adults (SELSA). *Personality and Individual Differences, 14*, 127–134.

Fiske, A. P., Haslam, N., & Fiske, S. T. (1991). Confusing one person with another: What errors reveal about the elementary forms of social relations. *Journal of Personality and Social Psychology, 60*, 656–674.

Hughes, M. E., Waite, L. J., Hawkley, L. C., & Cacioppo, J. T. (2004). A short scale for measuring loneliness in large surveys. *Research on Aging, 26*, 655–672.

Rubenstein, C., & Shaver, Ph. (1982a). The experience of loneliness. In L. A. Peplau & D. Perlman (Eds.), *Loneliness: A sourcebook of current theory, research and therapy* (pp. 206–223). New York: John Wiley & Sons.

Rubenstein, C., & Shaver, Ph. (1982b). *In search of intimacy*. New York: Delacorte Press.

Russell, D. W. (1996). UCLA Loneliness Scale (Version 3): Reliability, validity, and factor structure. *Journal of Personalitty Assessment, 66*, 20–40.

Sorkin, D., Rook, K. S., & Lu, J. L. (2002). Loneliness, lack of emotional support, lack of companionship, and the likelihood of having a heart condition in an elderly sample. *Annals of Behavioral Medicine, 24*, 290–298.

Stroebe, W., Stroebe, M., Abakoumkin, G., & Schut, H. A. W. (1996). The role of loneliness and social support in adjustment to loss: A test of attachment versus stress theory. *Journal of Personality and Social Psychology, 70*, 1241–1249.

Van Baarsen, B., Snijders, T. A. B., Smit, J. H., & Van Duijn, M. A. J. (2001). Lonely but not alone: Emotional isolation and social isolation as two distinct dimensions of loneliness in older people. *Educational and Psychological Measurement, 61*, 119–135.

Weiss, R. S. (1974). *Loneliness: The experience of emotional and social isolation*. Cambridge, MA: MIT Press.

Weiss, R. S. (1998). A taxonomy of relationships. *Journal of Personal and Social Relationships, 15*, 671–684.

Weiss, R. S. (2005). *The experience of retirement*. Ithaca, NY: Cornell University Press.

16 A scientist's role in bereavement research

The case of Wolfgang Stroebe

Georgios Abakoumkin
University of Thessaly, Volos, Greece

Kenneth Gergen
Swarthmore College, Swarthmore, PA, USA

Mary Gergen
Penn State University, Media, PA, USA

Robert Hansson
University of Tulsa, USA

Henk A. W. Schut and Margaret S. Stroebe
Utrecht University, The Netherlands

How did it all start?

Writings on the health consequences of bereavement can be traced back across many centuries, with fascinating contributions as long ago as the seventeenth century. One widely read and highly influential book, first published in 1621, was Robert Burton's *The anatomy of melancholy* (republished in 1977). Burton drew the conclusion that grief can have negative effects on those smitten with it. He cited cases such as the suicide of Aegeus, who drowned himself, "impatient of sorrow for his son's death" (p. 360). Another landmark was the publication of probably the first systematic examination of differential mortality rates across marital statuses by William Farr (1858), who reported excesses in deaths among widowed persons and went on to comment: if "unmarried people suffer from disease in undue proportion the have been married [by whom he meant the widowed] suffer still more" (p. 440).

Clinical investigations of bereavement began in earnest, though, only during the early part of the twentieth century (Freud, 1917). Attention initially focused on the implications of bereavement for mental health and pathological reactions. In the 1930s and 40s, however, investigators began to broaden that focus to examine more normal grieving reactions and how they might differ from pathological grief. Clinical work by Lindemann (1944), for example, led to a formulation of the nature of grief as a syndrome, its component symptom clusters, and its course. The most striking features of the grief response were established through his work not only with patients suffering from ulcerative colitis, but also bereaved victims of the so-called Coconut Grove fire disaster. Despite the unusual composition of his sample, Lindemann was able to identify most of the features of the grief response typically observed with recently bereaved individuals, including somatic distress, preoccupation with the image of the deceased, guilt feelings, hostile reactions to others, and loss of usual patterns of activity.

This focus on normal grief raised a host of related questions among researchers from many disciplines; Lindemann's conceptualisation of grief-related symptomatology was generally replicated, expanded, and refined using diverse samples of persons experiencing normal bereavements (e.g., Parkes, 1972/1996; Parkes & Weiss, 1983). Particular attention focused on short- and long-term consequences for physical and psychological health, potential social and economic consequences of widowhood (e.g., Lopata, 1993, 1996), and the identification of individuals (or classes of individuals) who might be at greater risk for poor outcome (e.g., Sanders, 1989). Ethnographic studies offered insights into cultural factors that shape the experience and symptomatology of grief (Rosenblatt, Walsh, & Jackson, 1976). Studies of informal and formal interventions began, targeting bereaved persons experiencing both complicated and uncomplicated bereavements (e.g., Marmar, Horowitz, Weiss, Wilner, & Kaltreider, 1988; Raphael, 1977). Theory development progressed within many disciplines to account for the increasing complexity apparent in bereavement (M. Stroebe, Stroebe, & Hansson, 1993). Research relating bereavement phenomena to more fundamental topics in emotion, human development, and social-psychological process, and assessing the applicability to bereavement of broader models of stress and coping, began to appear. Demographers, epidemiologists, and health planners examined implications for the future of medical practice and for public institutions.

Originally, the burgeoning body of bereavement research was greatly fragmented, with investigators throughout the world often pursuing research questions specific to their clinical or academic discipline, publishing in their own disciplinary journals, and seldom locating their work in the context of other perspectives. Integration was much needed. From the 1980s onwards, this goal was furthered through a series of interdisciplinary volumes co-edited by Wolfgang Stroebe. Other major reviews across the decades include Archer, 1999; Genevro, Marshall, and Miller, 2004; Osterweis, Solomon, and Green, 1984, Parkes, 1972; Raphael, 1983; Walter, 1999. It was, in fact, about this time that Stroebe entered the field of bereavement research—but more of that shortly.

In the first of these co-edited volumes, *Bereavement and widowhood* (Hansson, Stroebe, & Stroebe, 1988), topics ranged from the psychobiology of loss to the social/cultural context of grief, risk factors, support systems, and counselling and therapy. This volume's special contribution to the field was its emphasis on the interpersonal implications of loss and adaptation, in addition to the more usual intra-personal focus on individual experience and coping. The volume focused solely on widow(er)hood—other types of intense loss experiences (including loss of a child, parent, or sibling, etc.) were beyond consideration.

The bereavement field expanded rapidly in the years following this first publication. This was reflected in the range of topics in the second integrative review, *Handbook of bereavement: Theory, research, and intervention* (M. Stroebe et al., 1993). One section of this work focused on contrasting conceptualisations of normal and pathological grief. Another expanded theoretical coverage of the nature of grief, contrasting social, cognitive, anthropological, and clinical perspectives. Topics addressed also included animal loss, neuroendocrine changes, mortality, late-life bereavement, and the different types of loss (death of a child, parent, partner to AIDS, and the experience of Holocaust survivors), all of which were absent in the previous volume. The field was expanding fast, not only with respect to the scope of subject matter available but also in provision of its review.

A completely new range of topics again was featured in the third volume *Handbook of bereavement research: Consequences, coping, and care* (M. Stroebe, Hansson, Stroebe, & Schut, 2001). Similarly reflecting developments in the field, emphasis was placed on novel theoretical approaches, as well as on stringent methodology and ethical rigour in empirical investigation. More sophisticated research had been conducted, particularly in the areas of coping, lifespan development, risk factors, psychotherapeutic and pharmacological interventions, and efficacy in treatment for bereavement. The fact that there were 29 robust chapters on such a range of topics, from authors across many countries of the world, shows that bereavement research had come a long way and could by then be considered an established scientific discipline.

An abiding topic of concern across the decades sketched above dealt with the most extreme consequence of the loss of a loved one, namely the mortality of bereavement: Is it really the case that people can die of a broken heart following the death of a loved one? This merits closer inspection.

Death causing death?

It was within this line of inquiry that Wolfgang Stroebe entered the field of bereavement research. It started like this, as Kenneth and Mary Gergen remember:

> In the spring of 1977 Wolfgang and Margaret Stroebe invited Kenneth and Mary Gergen, to visit Schwabia, Germany. Late one afternoon, they arrived in the village of Murrhardt, where they decided to take a walk. They discovered an ancient cemetery and started perusing the gravestones. They noticed among the husbands and wives buried next to each other how remarkably similar their death dates were. This observation became the focus of animated dinner conversation. Is it possible that the

death of one's mate could hasten the death of the remaining spouse? How could such a pattern be explained? A plan was made to re-visit the graveyard the following morning and take down birth and death dates of all the couples in the cemetery in order to do some later analysis. So out they went, roving among the gravestones (despite a raging rainstorm that soaked their pages), to collect their data. Little did they know what lay ahead.

As the data analysis subsequently demonstrated, their suspicions were confirmed. By comparing the death date of the remaining spouse with the death date of the deceased as opposed to a randomly selected individual with the same birth date, they found that, on average, losing one's mate could have a significant impact on one's lifespan. This generated much speculation regarding possible causes. Were these the results of loss of desire to live, with attendant loss in self-care? Perhaps the single individual during these early times could not manage adequately alone. Or, perhaps couples suffered similar diseases. Whatever the reason, both the findings and the causes deserved further attention. While gathering data they coined the phrase loss effect, to refer to the reduction in lifespan resulting from the loss of a loved one.

They first published the results of their review of the mortality research area in German (W. Stroebe, Stroebe, Gergen, & Gergen, 1980). Scanning further sources they were also able to reach the tentative conclusion that men were more vulnerable than women to the death of their spouse, and that the death of a child could significantly decrease the lifespan of a parent (M. Stroebe, Stroebe, Gergen, & Gergen, 1981). They then went on to formulate tentative conclusions as to the dynamics underlying the loss effect (W. Stroebe, Stroebe, Gergen, & Gergen, 1982). Subsequently, these early explorations led to what became known as the Tübingen longitudinal study of bereavement, a large-scale research project mounted by the Stroebes and their colleagues at the University of Tübingen to generate a more thorough understanding of the effects of bereavement on health.

Where did it all go?

The main objectives of the Tübingen study were the examination of (a) consequences of bereavement on the health of the widowed across time, and (b) factors associated with health risks in bereavement outcome (cf. W. Stroebe, Stroebe & Domittner, 1987). This project was theoretically based on the Stroebes' deficit model of partner loss (W. Stroebe & Stroebe, 1986, 1987; W. Stroebe et al., 1980; W. Stroebe et al., 1982), which was derived from cognitive stress theory (see Lazarus & Folkman, 1984, and Folkman & Moskowitz, Chapter 12, this volume). The Tübingen study was further designed to examine a series of more specific questions that were either derived from the deficit model of partner loss or were controversial issues raised in the literature, which needed careful investigation. The use of sophisticated design and methodology in addressing these issues was characteristic of the study, a central feature being the use of a carefully matched non-bereaved control group. Furthermore, it involved two data-collection techniques: questionnaires and interviews. Among other things, this allowed collection of questionnaire data from some of the bereaved who did not want to participate in the study (but who agreed to fill out a questionnaire); this made the examination of a probable selection bias possible (M. Stroebe & Stroebe, 1989). We return to this in the next section.

A sample of 30 widows and 30 widowers mostly in their early fifties was included in the study. These persons were individually matched by sex, age, socioeconomic status, and number of children to 60 married persons. Data were collected by extended structured interviews and questionnaires at three time points: 4–7 months after bereavement, and approximately 14 months and 2 years after loss (see W. Stroebe et al., 1987, or W. Stroebe & Stroebe, 1993).

Many variables were investigated in the Tübingen study, but here we focus on major issues to do with differential patterns of selection in bereavement research, bereavement-specific health trajectories (i.e., identifying individual difference factors in adjustment that are not just reflections of risk factors in the general population), and the role of coping in adaptation to loss. These selections serve to illustrate how an individual research programme such as the Tübingen study fits within the more general developments in bereavement research across the decades of the twentieth century, as outlined above.

Who participates in bereavement research?

At first, this question may seem mundane, but in fact it is critical in bereavement research. Bereaved people are frequently distressed and vulnerable. No pressure should be put on them to participate in research on bereavement, and in fact, large proportions choose to turn down such a request (M. Stroebe & Stroebe, 1989). When investigating the health consequences of loss, then, every researcher needs to ask the question how representative are the bereaved persons in their samples of the bereaved in general. The decision not to participate may have much to do with grief status and health status (frequently these are the very variables under investigation), but this may be related to different underlying health-related factors: Do they refuse because they have come to terms with their grief, are feeling good, and want to move on? Or is the opposite the case: are they so overwhelmed by their loss and suffering from health problems that they cannot face taking part in a bereavement study? Both alternatives seem plausible.

Surprisingly, these potential biases had (and still have) received very little empirical investigation. Such selection bias was a major worry in setting up the Tübingen study, but it is potentially, of course, a very difficult matter to investigate (most particularly for ethical reasons: those who refuse should be left in peace). However, what could be done (taking care not to put pressure on them) was to ask persons who refused participation, first, if they would share their reasons for refusal, and second, and uniquely in this study, if they did not want to be interviewed, whether they felt able to fill in a postal questionnaire. A sufficient number of "refusers" agreed to fill in question-naires, enabling comparisons with those who had participated in interviews on health measures.

At first glance, the results seemed reassuring: for example, there was no significant difference between interview participants and refusers in depres-sion levels. It seemed that, so far as could be evaluated on the basis of these data, results from the participants could be taken as representative of the bereaved in general. Closer examination, however, identified an interaction: when gender differences were examined, it emerged that while widows who were (significantly) more depressed more frequently agreed to participate in interviews, quite the opposite was the case for widowers: the more depressed men were refusing interviews and agreeing simply to answer the postal questionnaires.

These patterns were understood in terms of traditional gender roles, which would mostly pertain among these participants in southern Germany at the time of the study. Men would have felt more uncomfortable showing distress in front of strangers, whereas for women crying and expressing emotions would be less of a problem.

The implications for interpretation of gender differences in health follow-ing bereavement in the Tübingen study were far reaching: conclusions about well-being among widows based on the interview respondents would likely overestimate distress, while for widowers, they would underestimate it (M. Stroebe & Stroebe, 1989). There is every reason to believe that such biases are present in other data sets, and similar caution is always needed in inter-preting results.

Does help help?

Another important interaction effect that could be examined in the frame-work of the study was the well-known social support perspective's "buffering hypothesis". In fact, the results of the study could be evaluated from the perspectives of two very different—but both highly impactful—theories, namely the social support and attachment perspectives, as we shall see.

The buffering hypothesis (Cohen & Wills, 1985) proposed that social sup-port (support from family and friends) is a protective factor against stress. Applied to bereavement (W. Stroebe & Stroebe, 1987), one would assume that the widowed who have the supportive company of family and friends might be better able to deal with the loss experience and show fewer psychological symptoms than the widowed who lack social support. The idea here is that loss of a partner also means loss of social support; this deficit might be compensated to the extent that close others fulfil the supportive function of the lost partner. In other words, the crucial prediction here is that of an interaction between marital status and social support: Whereas the bereaved with high social support would be somehow protected against detrimental consequences of partner loss, the widowed with low social support should show an excess in psychological symptoms as compared to their married counterparts.

This turned out not to be the case (W. Stroebe & Stroebe, 1987; W. Stroebe, Stroebe, Abakoumkin, & Schut, 1996). Social support exhibited only a main effect on symptoms (depression and somatic complaints), which contradicts the buffering hypothesis. However, this result is compatible with attachment theory (Bowlby, 1969; Weiss, 1975). A marital partner is an attachment figure providing feelings of security. Losing such a person cannot be simply compensated by support from family and friends; an attachment figure is probably only to be replaced by another attachment figure. Nevertheless, it is important to keep in mind that a supportive social network plays a role in its own right.

Weiss (1975, Chapter 15, this volume) proposed that deficits either with respect to attachment figures or social network might result in two distinct types of loneliness: If an attachment figure is lacking, emotional loneliness occurs, while a deficit in social network is associated with social loneliness. Loneliness is seen as the mediating mechanism between a deficit and psychological symptoms. Yet, depending on the type of deficit, a different type of loneliness mediates the relation between deficit and symptomatology. According to this reasoning, both marital status and social support should have an impact on symptomatology, however via two distinct pathways, namely emotional and social loneliness respectively. That is in fact what emerged from the Tübingen study (W. Stroebe et al., 1996).

All in all, the pattern of results provided more support for the attachment than the social support perspective. Losing a partner means losing a major attachment figure, for which social support from family and friends (though generally useful to bereaved and non-bereaved alike) cannot compensate. This finding is consistent with sentiments expressed by bereaved persons in the Tübingen study, who explained to the investigators that, while they found their friends and other family members around them to be a great help, these persons could in no way replace the lost loved one.

Does grief work work?

Following Freud's early formulation, the notion that people have to do their grief work in order to come to terms with their loss became widely accepted. However, in the latter part of the twentieth century, a number of researchers called this notion into question (Rosenblatt, 1983; Wortman & Silver, 1989). The Tübingen study provided a testing ground for this hypothesis (M. Stroebe & Stroebe, 1991). The coping strategies of confrontation versus avoidance of grief could be examined in this data set, and their impact on depression across the 2-year period of bereavement evaluated. In this way, an indication of the impact of doing grief work during the early months of bereavement could be obtained. Contrary to expectations, depression among the widows was not related to grief work. On the other hand, widowers seemed to profit somewhat more from confronting their grief.

This finding was interpreted as being in line with traditional social roles, which do not encourage disclosure of emotions among men. As regards the grief work hypothesis, the Stroebes suggested that "working through grief may not be as essential for adjustment to loss as has been frequently assumed" (W. Stroebe & Stroebe, 1993, p. 225).

These and other early findings (e.g., Rosenblatt, 1983; Wortman & Silver, 1989) were to fuel subsequent research, to which other researchers have also contributed in more recent years (e.g., Bonanno, 2001), but the early findings on grief work and gender differences were more intriguing than conclusive. Next we examine how they led beyond the Tübingen study data to further reviewing of bodies of research and conceptual analyses. We give two examples.

Who suffers more?

Classic studies such as those of Parkes (1972/1996) had shown that both men and women suffered from poor health, distress, and depression following widowhood. But do widows or widowers suffer more, or are there similar responses between the genders? Impressions of caregiving professionals that, for example, widows show more depression and enter care programmes in greater numbers than widowers seemed to be confirmed by early research (M. Stroebe, Stroebe, & Schut, 2001), but we know that women in general get more depressed (Nolen-Hoeksema, 1987), that there are more widows than widowers, and that such factors as these—rather than a "true" excess in suffering—could account for the excessive number of widows, compared with widowers, in these statistics.

There was need for careful review of empirical studies on gender differences in the health consequences (including mental and physical health and mortality) of bereavement. Most of all, rates for non-bereaved counterparts need to be taken into account. This is because there are general (non-bereavement-specific) gender differences not only with respect to depression but also on other health consequences (e.g., mortality: males have higher rates). Thus, in such a review, *relative* rates of symptomatology need to be calculated in the following way: the rates of widower to married men's rates need to be compared with widow to married women's rates. When this was done, results were different from the impressions described above. If one compares carefully, controlling for the differences in total numbers in the different bereaved and control groups, it can be seen that what researchers have found is that widowers are *relatively* worse off than widows (M. Stroebe & Stroebe, 1983; M. Stroebe et al., 2001; M. Stroebe, Schut, & Stroebe, 2006).

In short, widowers suffer relatively higher rates of depression, and greater health consequences, most notably in their death rates, than widows.

Researchers need to conduct further empirical research to provide adequate explanation for this phenomenon. In all likelihood, leads will be found through further investigation of differences in sex roles and relationships, in coping styles of widows and widowers, and with respect to factors to do with the whole context within which bereavement takes place for males and females.

To continue or break bonds?

A second line of research that emerged from the earlier investigation of the grief work hypothesis had to do with the *functions* of grief work: should grief work be aimed at relinquishing dependency and re-establishing a full and productive life, or should it be directed towards continuing a healthy relationship with the deceased? In historical perspective, the former orientation was identified as modernist. Cultural modernism places a strong emphasis on rational decision making, autonomy, and continuous participation in the work force. From this perspective, continuous rumination on loss is maladaptive, and ultimately inimical to one's well-being. Yet, viewed in terms of cultural history, one could also locate the latter orientation. In this case life's meaning is located in one's intimate relationships. The loss of a loved one thus metaphorically threatens one with the breaking of the heart. The modernist pressure to "get one with life" is an intensification of the break, and counterproductive. Successful grieving means sustaining a relationship with the deceased. It seemed clear from this analysis that the relationship between health and grieving was culturally specific. Much depends on how loss is understood, and no one therapeutic formula for successful grief work was sufficient. These thoughts and their implications for multiple forms of successful grieving were then published in *American Psychologist* (M. Stroebe, Gergen, Gergen, & Stroebe, 1992).

The Stroebes and their colleagues then set out to explore these issues more extensively. At the present writing the question of healthy grieving still remains open. As M. Stroebe and Schut (2005) conclude in their comprehensive review of both clinical and empirical studies, "There is simply no choosing between the two apparent alternatives. Put simply, it has become evident . . . that certain types of continuing bonds may sometimes be helpful/ harmful, whereas certain types of relinquishing bonds may sometimes be helpful/harmful" (p. 13). One may suppose that the door remains open to more fine-grained analyses of the various modes of healthy grieving, and in fact empirically examining the links between types of bonds and health outcomes is a major interest in contemporary research (e.g., Field, Gal-Oz, & Bonanno, 2003). Yet, if the effects of loss are vitally dependent on the interpretive processes of the survivors, and this process is embedded within continuing conversations—with loved ones, within the sub-culture, and within the culture more generally—there may be no means of ultimately pinning down healthy forms of grieving. The challenge for the professional may be to contribute frames of meaning that can help these conversations to yield healthy benefits for all.

Where does it go from here?

Not only the continuing bonds issue just discussed, but also the other questions raised above, are still major concerns in bereavement research in general and for Wolfgang Stroebe in particular. An emerging topic that encompasses nearly all of these strands is emotional disclosure (see Zech, Rimé, & Pennebaker, Chapter 17, this volume). For example, in the most recent review, many of these lines of argument were brought together, as indicated in the title, *Grief work, disclosure and counselling: Do they help the bereaved?*. The answers that the authors (W. Stroebe, Schut, & Stroebe, 2005) provided to this question have already attracted considerable attention, not only in the bereavement research field, but also in the popular media and among counsellors.

The article reviewed four research domains: social support, emotional disclosure, experimentally induced disclosure, and grief intervention. Within each area, the empirical evidence was put to stringent methodological test: were the claims made by the authors in terms of the benefits of, say, social support or professional intervention, really justified on the basis of the data collected? In none of these areas did the authors find sound empirical evidence that emotional disclosure facilitates adjustment to loss in *normal* bereavement—it simply takes time to heal from the loss of a loved one and precious little can be done to speed up the process.

In conclusion

We have documented the development of scientific research on bereavement across several decades. We have illustrated the participation in this process of one scientist, Wolfgang Stroebe, posing here the sorts of questions that are typical of those that he himself asks. We have described the patterns of results that urged him on to further questions, mirroring the process of sequential exploration and discovery that is fundamental to scientific investigation. Fortunately for us, he did not do any of this work in isolation, but—quite typically—in interaction with others, including all of us. Thus, we have been able to reflect here with pleasure, from the inside of this particular scientific process.

References

Archer, J. (1999). *The nature of grief: The evolution and psychology of reactions to loss.* London: Routledge.

Bonanno, G. (2001). Grief and emotion: A social-functional perspective. In M. Stroebe, R. O. Hansson, W. Stroebe, & H. Schut (Eds.), *Handbook of bereavement research: Consequences, coping, and care* (pp. 493–515). Washington, DC: American Psychological Association Press.

Bowlby, J. (1969). *Attachment and loss. Vol. 1: Attachment.* London: Hogarth.

Burton, R. (1621/1977). *The anatomy of melancholy.* New York: Random House.

Cohen, S., & Wills, A. T. (1985). Stress, social support, and the buffering hypothesis. *Psychological Bulletin, 98,* 310–357.

Farr, W. (1858/1975). Influence of marriage on the mortality of the French people. In N. Humphreys, *Vital statistics: A memorial volume of selections from reports and writings of William Farr.* New York: Methuen; The Scarecrow Press.

Field, N. P., Gal-Oz, E., & Bonanno, G. (2003). Continuing bonds and adjustment at 5 years after the death of a spouse. *Journal of Consulting and Clinical Psychology, 71,* 110–117.

Freud, S. (1917). Trauer und Melancholie. *Internationale Zeitschrift für ärztliche Psychoanalyse, 4,* 288–301.

Genevro, J. L., Marshall, T., & Miller, T. (2004). Report on bereavement and grief research. *Death Studies, 28,* 491–575.

Hansson, R. O., Stroebe, M. S., & Stroebe, W. (1988). Bereavement and widowhood. *Journal of Social Issues, 44,* (whole issue).

Lazarus, R. S., & Folkman, S. (1984). *Stress, appraisal, and coping.* New York: Springer.

Lindemann, E. (1944). Symptomatology and management of acute grief. *American Journal of Psychiatry, 101,* 141–148.

Lopata, H. Z. (1993). The support systems of American urban widows. In M. S. Stroebe, W. Stroebe, & R. O. Hansson (Eds.), *Handbook of bereavement: Theory, research, and intervention* (pp. 381–396). Cambridge, UK: Cambridge University Press.

Lopata, H. Z. (1996). *Current widowhood: Myths and realities.* Thousand Oaks, CA: Sage.

Marmar, C. R., Horowitz, M. J., Weiss, D. S., Wilner, N. R., & Kaltreider, N. B. (1988). A controlled trial of brief psychotherapy and mutual-help group treatment of conjugal bereavement. *American Journal of Psychiatry, 145,* 203–209.

Nolen-Hoeksema, S. (1987). Sex differences in uni-polar depression: Evidence and theory. *Psychological Bulletin, 101,* 259–282.

Osterweis, M., Solomon, F., & Green M. (Eds.). (1984). *Bereavement: Reactions, consequences and care.* Washington, DC: National Academy Press.

Parkes, C. M. (1972). *Bereavement: Studies of grief in adult life* (1st ed.). New York: International Universities Press.

Parkes, C. M. (1996). *Bereavement: Studies of grief in adult life* (3rd ed.). London: Routledge.

Parkes, C. M., & Weiss, R. S. (1983). *Recovery from bereavement.* New York: Basic Books.

Raphael, B. (1977). Preventive interventions with the recently bereaved. *Archives of General Psychiatry, 34,* 1450–1454.

Raphael, B. (1983). *The anatomy of bereavement.* New York: Basic Books.

Rosenblatt, P. (1983). *Bitter, bitter tears: Nineteenth century diarists and twentieth century grief theorists.* Minneapolis: University of Minnesota Press.

Rosenblatt, P., Walsh, R., & Jackson, D. (1976). *Grief and mourning in cross-cultural perspective.* New Haven, CT: Human Relations Area Files Press.

Sanders, C. (1989). *Grief: The mourning after*. New York: Wiley.

Stroebe, M. S., Gergen, M., Gergen, K. J., & Stroebe, W. (1992). Broken hearts or broken bonds: Love and death in historical perspective. *American Psychologist, 47*, 1205–1212.

Stroebe, M. S., Hansson, R. O., Stroebe, W., & Schut, H. (Eds.). (2001). *Handbook of bereavement research: Consequences, coping, and care*. Washington, DC: American Psychological Association.

Stroebe, M. S., & Schut, H. (2005) To continue or relinquish bonds: A review of consequences for the bereaved. *Death Studies, 29*, 1–18.

Stroebe, M. S., Schut, H., & Stroebe, W. (2006). *The health consequences of bereavement: A review*. Manuscript submitted for publication.

Stroebe, M. S., & Stroebe, W. (1983). Who suffers more? Sex differences in health risks of the widowed. *Psychological Bulletin, 93*, 279–301.

Stroebe, M. S., & Stroebe, W. (1989). Who participates in bereavement research? A review and empirical study. *Omega, 20*, 1–29.

Stroebe, M., & Stroebe, W. (1991). Does "grief work" work? *Journal of Consulting and Clinical Psychology, 59*, 479–482.

Stroebe, M. S., Stroebe, W., Gergen, K. J., & Gergen, M. (1981) The broken heart: Reality or myth? *Omega, 12*, 87–106.

Stroebe, M. S., Stroebe, W., & Hansson, R. O. (Eds.). (1993). *Handbook of bereavement: Theory, research and intervention*. Cambridge, UK: Cambridge University Press.

Stroebe, M. S., Stroebe, W., & Schut, H. (2001). Gender differences in adjustment to bereavement: An empirical and theoretical review. *Review of General Psychology, 5*, 62–83.

Stroebe, W., Schut, H., & Stroebe, M. S. (2005). Grief work, disclosure and counseling: Do they help the bereaved? *Clinical Psychology Review, 25*, 395–414.

Stroebe, W., & Stroebe, M. S. (1986). Beyond marriage: The impact of partner loss on health. In R. Gilmour & S. Duck (Eds.), *The emerging field of personal relationships*. Hillsdale, NJ: Lawrence Erlbaum Associates Inc.

Stroebe, W., & Stroebe, M. S. (1987). *Bereavement and health: The psychological and physical consequences of partner loss*. Cambridge, UK: Cambridge University Press.

Stroebe, W., & Stroebe, M. S. (1993). Determinants of adjustment to bereavement in younger widows and widowers. In M. S. Stroebe, W. Stroebe, & R. O. Hansson (Eds.), *Handbook of bereavement: Theory, research, and intervention* (pp. 208–226). New York: Cambridge University Press.

Stroebe, W., Stroebe, M. S., Abakoumkin, G., & Schut, H. (1996). The role of loneliness and social support in adjustment to loss: A test of attachment versus stress theory. *Journal of Personality and Social Psychology, 70*, 1241–1249.

Stroebe, W., Stroebe, M. S., & Domittner, G. (1987). Kummerbewältigung und Kummereffekt: Psychische und physische Reaktionen von Verwitweten. *Abschlußbericht über das Projekt Str. 186/4–3*. University of Tübingen, Germany.

Stroebe, W., Stroebe, M. S., Gergen, K. J., & Gergen, M. (1980). Der Kummer Effekt: Psychologische Aspekte der Sterblichkeit von Verwitweten. *Psychologische Beiträge, 22*, 1–26.

Stroebe, W., Stroebe, M. S., Gergen, K. J., & Gergen, M. (1982). The effects of bereavement on mortality: A social psychological analysis. In J. R. Eiser (Ed.), *Social psychology and behavioural medicine* (pp. 527–560). Chichester, UK: Wiley.

Walter, T. (1999). *On bereavement: The culture of grief.* Buckingham, UK: Open University Press.

Weiss, R. S. (1975). *Loneliness: The experience of emotional and social isolation.* Cambridge, MA: MIT Press.

Wortman, C. B., & Silver, R. C. (1989). The myths of coping with loss. *Journal of Consulting and Clinical Psychology, 57*, 349–357.

17 The effects of emotional disclosure during bereavement

Emmanuelle Zech and Bernard Rimé
University of Louvain, Louvain-la-Neuve, Belgium

James W. Pennebaker
The University of Texas at Austin, USA

Any emotionally upsetting experience has the potential to aggravate mental and physical health problems. This is clearly the case after the death of a close friend or family member. Bereavement is associated with extended periods of anguish and pain, increased risk of depression, physical illness, and mortality (W. Stroebe, Schut, & Stroebe, 2005a). It is widely assumed in Western societies that people have to confront their feelings and reactions to the death of a loved one in order to adjust to the loss. Despite some dissenting voices (e.g., M. Stroebe & Stroebe, 1991; Wortman & Silver, 1989, 2001), it is widely accepted, not only by lay persons but also bereavement professionals, that the bereaved must do their "grief work".

The concept of grief work implies a process of confronting the reality of loss, of going over events that occurred before and at the time of the death, and of focusing on memories and working towards detachment from the deceased (M. Stroebe, 1992). The concept has been central in the major theoretical formulations on grief and bereavement since Freud's (1917) classic monograph. Freud's view that grief work was necessary for the resolution of grief was shared by other major theoreticians who dominated bereavement research, such as Lindemann (1944), Bowlby (1980), and Parkes (1996). Principles of counselling and therapy also assign a central role to grief work in adjustment to loss. Failure to confront and experience the intense emotions that accompany the loss is considered maladaptive.

Pathological grief is generally regarded as the failure to undergo or complete grief work. For example, many researchers and clinicians in the field of loss agree that the absence of grief following bereavement ("absent grief") indicates that the grieving process may be abnormal or "pathological" (e.g., Middleton, Raphael, Martinek, & Misso, 1993). It is assumed that if grief is not expressed due to an intrapsychic cause (such as denial or inhibition), it will surface at some later point or health problems will subsequently emerge (Worden, 2001). Thus, counselling and therapy programmes for the bereaved share the common goal of helping the bereaved to adapt to life without the loved one, by facilitating grief work (e.g., Worden, 2001).

Research conducted on the one hand by Pennebaker and colleagues on the effects of written self-disclosure on health and on the other hand by Rimé and colleagues on the effects of oral social sharing of emotion (i.e., talking to others about the emotions one experienced) on recovery, is highly relevant to this principle. Written disclosure and social sharing of emotions are not necessary conditions of grief work, because individuals can also confront their grief and work through it in isolation, nonverbally, or in thoughts. Nevertheless, verbal emotional expression and grief work are closely linked, because people will probably confront their loss when they write or talk about it. Confronting one's emotions in the course of a written or verbal disclosure task should thus be particularly helpful for the bereaved. Moreover, similarly to the grief work hypothesis, much of the early research conducted by Pennebaker and colleagues was based on an inhibitory model, which suggested that the act of inhibiting or holding back one's thoughts, feelings, or behaviours involved biological work that, in and of itself, was stressful. If individuals were forced to actively inhibit over long periods of time, it was argued, the greater the probability that they would suffer from a variety of psychosomatic diseases (for a discussion of this model, see Pennebaker, 1989). Not talking about a significant emotional experience or trauma with others could certainly invoke inhibitory processes: the active restraining of the urge to share one's story.

Writing about or sharing one's story may also produce a number of interesting cognitive side-effects. Talking with others about an important event may help the person to organise the experience, find meaning, and come to terms with it. This is why, in the "writing paradigm", respondents are typically asked to write for 15 to 30 minutes on several consecutive days, either about their deepest thoughts and feelings related to past traumatic experiences or about trivial control topics (e.g., Pennebaker & Beall, 1986).

By the same token, talking with others may also clarify one's psychological state for others. The person's social network, then, can make accommodations based on what the person is feeling and saying. For example, if a bereaved person expressed utter loneliness, friends or family members could phone, visit, or invite the bereaved person more regularly. Without talking, the traumatised individual would be less likely to come to terms with the event and would be more socially isolated. The work conducted by Rimé and colleagues on the effects of social sharing of emotion is thus also relevant for the grief work hypothesis. Rimé and colleagues mainly focused on the oral verbalisation of *emotional events* in the context of a social interaction (i.e., to someone listening—and in most cases responding—empathetically) and the effects it may have on the *emotional recovery from such events* (for reviews, see Rimé, Finkenauer, Luminet, Zech, & Philippot, 1998; Rimé, Philippot, Boca, & Mesquita, 1992). Emotional recovery was defined as the evolution over time of the arousal still elicited when a given emotional memory is reaccessed. It is now known that people who experience an emotion usually feel compelled to talk about it and to share it, preferably with their intimates. They do so quite willingly, despite the fact that the sharing process will reactivate the negative aspects of the emotional experience. There is widespread belief that sharing an emotion should bring emotional relief (Zech & Rimé, 2005). Yet both correlative and experimental studies which were conducted to test the validity of this belief consistently failed to support it. It does not seem that talking about an emotional memory has a significant impact on the emotional load associated with this memory. Nevertheless, people who share their emotions generally express the feeling that the process is beneficial (Zech & Rimé, 2005). Thus, while it is debatable whether sharing bereavement-related feelings would bring emotional relief, bereaved individuals may well feel that sharing their emotions with intimates is meaningful and beneficial for various reasons. In particular, the development and maintenance of close relationships that may be involved when one shares one's emotions, may be a fundamental function of social sharing of emotion.

The question still remains as to whether specifically writing or talking about the loss of a loved one would be associated with improved physical and mental health, including recovery from the loss. Literature reviews of the data on disclosure and coping among bereaved individuals are clearly mixed, if not negative (Pennebaker, Zech, & Rimé, 2001; M. Stroebe, Stroebe, Schut, Zech, & van den Bout, 2002; W. Stroebe et al., 2005a). There was no evidence from the three published experimental studies on non-suicide deaths that emotional disclosure facilitates adjustment (Range, Kovac, & Marion, 2000; Segal, Bogaards, Becker, & Chatman, 1999; M. Stroebe et al., 2002). It is noteworthy, however, that significant improvements of symptoms of distress, avoidance, intrusion, and doctor visits were found over time, suggesting that, in case of non-suicide deaths, time was a great healer. Only one study on bereavement after suicide deaths found evidence of a beneficial effect, but this effect was limited to one of several health measures included in that study (Kovac & Range, 2000).

These findings are in line with the pattern that emerged in a recent review of the efficacy of different types of general preventive interventions for bereaved individuals (Schut, Stroebe, van den Bout, & Terheggen, 2001). There is no evidence that counselling or therapy helps the normally bereaved (i.e., those who did not themselves seek professional help) to adjust to their loss. Preventive interventions seem to be only effective for bereaved people at high risk of complications in their grieving process.

These findings are also consistent with the pattern that emerged in several studies of the impact of social support in bereavement (e.g., W. Stroebe, Stroebe, Abakoumkin, & Schut, 1996; W. Stroebe, Zech, Stroebe, & Abakoumkin, 2005b). In these longitudinal studies of the influence of social support on psychological well-being of bereaved and non-bereaved men and women, no evidence of a *differential* effect of social support for the bereaved was found. Although individuals who perceived their level of social support as high were less likely to show depressive symptomatology than individuals who thought they had little support, this beneficial effect was of the same magnitude for bereaved and non-bereaved alike. Taken together, these findings suggest that in cases of uncomplicated bereavement, the help from others is a moderator rather than a mediator of the grieving process: there is a main effect, suggesting that support helps, but not more when the person is suffering from bereavement.

How can we reconcile the widely held assumption that in order to cope with loss, bereaved individuals have to confront and express their emotions, with the mainly negative findings that have been reviewed so far? Elsewhere, we have argued that the disclosure paradigm was usually—but not always —powerful enough to swamp individual differences between respondents (Pennebaker & Keough, 1999). We also acknowledged that the manipulation could not be viewed as helping everyone. Thus, it is important to identify individuals for whom disclosure would be more versus less likely to be associated with health and well-being. This suggests that not everyone will benefit, but that specific individuals might. The questions then arise: "who benefits?" and "under what conditions?". Next, we turn to the specific conditions that may enhance the likelihood of finding beneficial disclosure effects on health, well-being, and emotional recovery for bereaved individuals.

Moderators of the effects of emotional disclosure

Highly distressed bereaved individuals?

Previously, we suggested that the beneficial effects of writing-induced emotional disclosure might only emerge for bereavements that are relatively traumatic, such as sudden and unexpected losses (Pennebaker et al., 2001). This hypothesis was partially tested by M. Stroebe and colleagues (2002, Study 2). They divided the widowed participants into those whose loss was expected and those whose loss was not. They then examined the moderating effect of expectedness on the health benefits of the writing instructions. Results failed to indicate that writing-induced disclosure had more beneficial effects for bereaved people who suffered an unexpected loss than for those whose partner died expectedly after a long illness. Nevertheless, the bereaved individuals in the Kovac and Range (2000) study had lost a person to whom they had been close; in this case to suicide. It is possible that suicide deaths, as voluntary deaths, are characterised by a feature that sets them apart from normal losses. It is noteworthy that writing about their deepest feelings about this loss rather than a trivial topic decreased only suicide-specific grief symptoms but did not reduce general grief, intrusion or avoidance of the event, or health centre visits.

The question concerning who signs up to participate in an intervention study is also relevant. One of the most difficult aspects of studying bereavement is in collecting truly random samples. The Stroebe group has been doing this by directly contacting individuals 4 to 8 months after the death of their spouse. Other researchers, such as Segal et al. (1999), advertised for participants in the local newspaper. We suspect that those who seek out researchers (as in the Segal et al. project) could represent very different groups from those who are directly contacted. Because most people cope quite well with the death of a spouse—especially if it is not a traumatic death (cf. Wortman & Silver, 1989)—disclosure interventions may only be effective with those coping poorly. A randomly selected sample, then, will be less likely to show the benefits of disclosure, since most of the participants will be in relatively good shape. A sample that self-selects to participate in a study on spousal bereavement may, in fact, comprise the very people who have not had the opportunity to work through their emotions. In line with the research on the efficacy of bereavement counselling, those who might benefit the most are actually those who suffer the most.

Gender

Gender may also be a significant moderating factor in the effects. Indeed, in his review of the literature, Smyth (1998) reported that males are more likely to demonstrate health improvements after writing than females. Similarly, Schut, Stroebe, van den Bout, and de Keijser (1997) reported that the ways in which men versus women are *counselled* differentially predicts positive bereavement responses. Specifically, in this study, highly distressed bereaved persons entered a counselling programme. The interventions were done by trained and experienced social workers (seven times over a period of 10 weeks). When men were asked to focus on the acceptance of emotions and emotional discharge (client-centred type of counselling), they became less distressed than when asked to focus on problems (behaviour therapy type). Women showed the opposite pattern. It is thus possible that writing instructions focusing on specific aspects of the grieving process would be more beneficial to men than women (and vice versa). In other words, specific writing or talking instructions could benefit men more, while other instructions could benefit women more. Evidence that gender might be a good candidate for moderating the impact of emotional disclosure on health is also provided by the Stroebes, who demonstrated over 15 years ago that widowers who participate in research were less depressed than those who refused, while the reverse was true for widows (M. Stroebe & Stroebe, 1989). It is thus possible that men who agree to participate are actually better off and may not need help in the form of expressive writing or disclosure. On the contrary, women who participate in bereavement research tend to be more depressed than those who refuse and are thus likely to use more ruminative coping strategies. They might therefore need specific instructions that help them to reframe or reappraise, or see the loss and its consequences in a more positive light.

Insecurely attached individuals?

The attachment style of the bereaved person to the deceased may also be a major individual difference factor accounting for the effects of emotional disclosure on well-being and health. Indeed, attachment researchers have demonstrated that attachment styles were associated with patterns of both emotional disclosure and well-being (e.g., Mikulincer & Nachshon, 1991). Attachment theory claims that people's attachment styles evolve as a result of experiences related to communication and the expression of emotions within interpersonal relationship exchanges, especially with caregivers (Feeney, Noller, & Roberts, 1998; Kennedy-Moore & Watson, 1999). According to attachment theory, learning experiences involving emotional expression between caregiver and infant lead to the development of mental models (representations) of the self and of relationships (Bartholomew & Horowitz, 1991). These emerge as attachment styles and are, in turn, linked to patterns of (non)expressive emotional behaviour (Mikulincer & Shaver, 2003).

Persons with a *secure* style, which is characterised by relative ease in closeness to others and feeling comfortable both depending on and having others depend on oneself (Cassidy & Shaver, 1999), will be more likely to experience and express emotions to a moderate degree (M. Stroebe, Schut, & Stroebe, 2005b). There are three insecure attachment styles: avoidant or dismissive, ambivalent or preoccupied, and disorganised or fearful. People with a *dismissive-avoidant* attachment style are uncomfortable with closeness to others, find it difficult to trust others completely, or to allow themselves to depend on others, and present an apparent lack of anxiety about abandonment. They restrict expressions of distress and avoid seeking support from others. As a result they are found to report less emotional disclosure than other persons (e.g., Mikulincer & Nachshon, 1991). Adults with a *preoccupied* attachment style see others as reluctant to get as close to them as they would like. They worry about their attachment to others, about their own desire to stay very close to them, and about the fact that this sometimes scares others away. They tend to disclose highly and indiscriminately to persons. Finally, individuals classified as having a *disorganised* attachment style are uncomfortable with closeness to others, find it difficult to trust others or to depend on them, and tend to avoid seeking support from others. They would be likely to have difficulties talking coherently about their emotions and their loss (M. Stroebe et al., 2005b).

These attachment patterns and their disclosure correlates may be relevant for predicting well-being in general, but they are even more likely to be important in the case of bereavement, where the main problem is the loss of an attachment bond. According to Shaver and Tancredy (2001), people with different attachment styles cope with grief differently. M. Stroebe, Schut, and Stroebe (2005a) proposed that secure persons who are more at ease in disclosing emotional information, and who have less difficulty interacting with others, would be less distressed in such a situation. They should not benefit more from a written or oral disclosure session, since they already cope well with their loss and disclose coherently to others. On the contrary, the insecure attachment styles would require specific disclosure instructions. In line with Pennebaker's inhibition theory, dismissive individuals, who are the most reluctant to disclose personal information, would be predicted to benefit from any disclosure induction. Preoccupied individuals would be predicted not to benefit from an emotional disclosure intervention since they might just ruminate about their intense grief. They could benefit from instructions that would force reappraisal of the meaning of loss. Finally, disorganised individuals would also be predicted to benefit from an emotional disclosure, but provided that this could help the "development of a coherent account in terms of logic, fluency, and understanding" (M. Stroebe et al., 2005a, p. 25).

In a recent survey we investigated depressive affect among persons visiting their general practitioner (GP)—both patients and their accompanying persons—and a number of factors likely to be associated with depressive affect, including emotional disclosure and attachment style (Zech, de Ree, Berenschot, & Stroebe, 2006). Contrary to popular culture and clinical lore, but consistent with some previous research and our own predictions, we did not find evidence that disclosure was associated with well-being in general. However, when attachment dimensions were taken into account, this was indeed the case. This suggested that one needs to take people's attachment tendencies into account when examining the efficacy of emotional disclosure on affective states. As expected, avoidant attachment was associated with less depressive affect and less emotional disclosure. This could be indicative of the fact that patients who felt more discomfort depending on others—that is, who were more independent of others—were less depressed, or at least less willing to admit to negative feelings. The avoidant attachment style has indeed been related to the use of defensive strategies to suppress affective reactions (Mikulincer & Orbach, 1995). That avoidant attachment was associated with higher levels of self-perceived well-being was consistent with the image of this group as strong, silent types who can—or try to—get by without revealing their emotions.

These findings are particularly interesting when considering the relationship between avoidant attachment and the reason patients had for consulting their GP. Participants who visited their GP for severe *physical* reasons were those who were more avoidantly attached (suggesting that they may have delayed seeking help until problems became intense). Consistent with these findings, the attachment literature indicates that persons with an avoidant attachment style are less inclined to trust others, share their problems with others, or seek support from others (Bartholomew & Horowitz, 1991; Mikulincer & Nachshon, 1991). Thus, these findings were consistent with inhibition theory (Pennebaker, 1989) and with M. Stroebe et al.'s predictions.

Avoidantly attached people, who were also found to report discomfort with emotional disclosure of distressing information and to perceive that such disclosure is actually not useful, tend to seek less help from counsellors and have more negative attitudes towards help seeking (Vogel & Wester, 2003). Since they have a more negative view of others, a first step towards helping such persons could be to instruct them to write down their emotions. As a second step, early discussions could be useful in identifying and addressing likely problematic expectancies regarding their potential sharing partners' trustworthiness and dependability. A change in attitudes and sharing behaviours among this group would probably require repetitive as well as positive sharing interactions.

With respect to the other attachment dimension, the Zech et al. study (2006) found that those having high anxious attachment reported more depressed affect. Results also indicated that the anxiously attached individuals were more inclined to visit their GP for severe *psychological* problems. They were also found to disclose their emotions more frequently. This would suggest that, although anxiously attached persons disclose their emotions and problems to a great extent, this strategy was not efficient in reducing their depressive affect or severe psychological problems. On the other hand, patients high on anxiety may be more prone to seek help for their problems and report more psychological problems. Since they have a more negative view of themselves, we speculated that such individuals could be helped by reinforcing their own, independent treatment capacities (e.g., trying to involve them more in their treatment to improve their self-efficacy, giving them a more positive view of themselves). Using similar reasoning, anxiously attached persons could be helped by guidance to reinforce their self-efficacy and positive viewpoint.

Socially constrained individuals?

Another plausible moderator of the impact of disclosure could be the frequency with which the bereaved individuals have already engaged in social sharing before and have already disclosed their deepest emotions about the loss to others. It would seem plausible that the beneficial effects of induced disclosure are weakened to the extent that individuals have already engaged in disclosure outside the laboratory. This hypothesis was tested by M. Stroebe and colleagues (2002, Study 2). Results showed that there was no indication that the frequency with which the bereaved participants had previously talked about their loss to others and, in social sharing, had disclosed their emotions, moderated the impact of writing-induced disclosure. In fact, *low* disclosers were found to suffer less from intrusive thoughts and also had fewer visits to the doctor than high disclosers. This suggested that, rather than facilitating adjustment, the extent to which bereaved people disclose their emotions at a given point in time may be a symptom of poor recovery.

During bereavement, people usually work through grief naturally and do not need intervention strategies to help them to cope with their grief. There may be several reasons why some bereaved individuals continue to show extreme grief reactions several months or years after the death, including a hostile or non-existent social network that does not allow for the open discussion of the death. In this case, intervention may be needed and a written disclosure task might help to provide a situation for expressing emotions, without the direct evaluation of another person. Because the writing intervention does not need a real recipient to be present, such a tool may be particularly useful in cases where persons feel social constraints. This could then be further used in therapeutic sessions, if necessary (e.g., in the form of a diary or letters that would be discussed with a therapist).

Unsupported bereaved individuals

The assumption that support from family and friends is one of the most important moderators of bereavement outcome is still widely accepted among bereavement researchers and practitioners (e.g., W. Stroebe & Stroebe, 1987; Stylianos & Vachon, 1993). Indeed, the loss of a partner leads to deficits in areas that can be broadly characterised as loss of instrumental support, loss of validational support, loss of emotional support, and loss of social contact support (W. Stroebe & Stroebe, 1987). In the case of widowhood, the loss of a spouse also represents the loss of one's main sharing target (Rimé et al., 1998). These deficits could be partially compensated through social support from family and friends. This compensation assumption provides the theoretical basis for the buffering hypothesis (Cohen & Wills, 1985). Supportive reactions from a listener could thus be important in explaining beneficial effects of disclosure. Yet, as indicated above, there is little research supporting this view (W. Stroebe et al., 2005b).

In fact, attachment theory rejects the assumption that supportive friends can compensate for the loss of an attachment figure (Bowlby, 1969; Weiss, 1975). Bowlby (1969) proposed that the attachment figure was uniquely able to foster general feelings of security and that other people could not simply take over this function. Attachment theory also predicts that social support and partner loss affect health and well-being by separate pathways (Weiss, 1975). The loss of a partner, and thus of an important attachment figure, results in emotional loneliness—the feeling of utter aloneness, even when one is with others. Emotional loneliness can only be remedied by the integration of another emotional attachment or the reintegration (after separation) of the one who has been lost. However, social support should reduce social loneliness, which results from the absence of an engaging social network. Thus, even though attachment theory denies the possibility of buffering processes in bereavement, it would predict that social support has a general beneficial effect on health and well-being, which is independent of the stress situation (i.e., a main effect). These predictions were confirmed in several studies (e.g., W. Stroebe et al., 2005b).

Even if supportive family and friends do not *accelerate* the grieving process, it is possible that unsupportive family and friends are actually detrimental for one's adjustment to bereavement. In addition, it remains possible that specific types of supportive reactions may be beneficial for a particular index of health and well-being, while this would not be the case for a different dependent variable. Indeed, research conducted by Nils (2003) suggests that, although providing empathy and understanding when listening to someone who has just been exposed to an emotion-inducing film is perceived by the sharer as beneficial and helpful (especially for the quality of one's affiliation with the listener), this type of supportive response did not help the sharer to recover more quickly. However, when a listener answered to the disclosure with reappraising comments this was perceived as less beneficial for one's relationship, but actually helped the participant to gain cognitively and emotionally (for a review of types of supportive partners, their reactions and their effects, see Zech, Rimé, & Nils, 2004).

This research suggests that natural social sharing may not always address cognitive demands implied in recovering from an emotion (e.g., reappraisal). However, natural social sharing may actually fulfill socio-affective needs such as attention, interest, empathy, support, nonverbal comforting, and help (Rimé, 2005). Indeed, when shared emotions are intense, listeners' use of verbal mediators were found to be reduced, and listeners switched to the nonverbal mode (Christophe & Rimé, 1997). This leaves less opportunity for cognitive work and more place for manifestations of the socio-affective kind. Nils's research also suggests that there is a need to specify the dependent variable for which the beneficial effect would be most likely to occur (i.e., one could expect a beneficial effect on one dimension of well-being, but the reverse effect on another).

In fact, it is also possible that timing is very important during the grieving process. Bereaved individuals could be perceiving other persons' supportive attempts at one time as beneficial and at the next moment as detrimental. In other words, we suggest that one may need to see helpful or unhelpful disclosures as ongoing processes rather than as a present-or-absent phenomenon. Next, we will delineate such a viewpoint in more detail.

Mediators of the effects of emotional disclosure

In this section, we will propose not only that certain individuals might benefit more from disclosure than others, but that specific processes should be at hand when disclosing about the loss of a dear person. We will also propose that one specific individual may actually benefit more at certain moments from specific types of disclosure than at other times.

Coping with bereavement implies "working through grief"

As indicated above, grief work implies a process of confronting a loss, an active, ongoing, effortful attempt to come to terms with the loss (M. Stroebe, 1992). In contrast, ruminations reflect a passive repetition of events without any active attempts at reaching a detachment from the lost person. It is a truism that the best predictor of future depression is a prior episode of depression. Similarly, if we have a group of bereaved spouses 6 months post-loss, the best predictor of their grief responses 2 years later will be their current grief responses. It is thus important to distinguish between disclosure as an intervention versus a reflection of grief. Asking participants about their thoughts and feelings during a brief interview may be a reflection of their grief rather than an intervention. We found such effects with gay men who are dealing with the death of their lovers due to AIDS (Pennebaker, Mayne, & Francis, 1997). For a disclosure session to be an intervention, the person should be actively working through an upsetting experience.

In the writing paradigm, people write about emotional topics multiple times over several days. When the language of their writing samples is ana-lysed, the people who benefit most are the ones who show clear cognitive change from the first writing session to the last. Those who are highly emo-tional across all four days of writing but who do not show cognitive change do not experience any health benefits (cf. Pennebaker, 1997). Similarly, those who are able to change their perspectives in writing from one session to another are the ones who evidence greatest improvements (Campbell & Pennebaker, 2003). These perspective shifts are apparent in people's use of pronouns. That is, they switch from using first person singular pronouns (e.g., I, me, my) to other more social pronouns (he, they, we). Taken together, the language results indicate that the more that people change or "grow" in their writing, the more their health and adjustment improve.

Coping with bereavement implies more than "working through grief": *Loss- and restoration-oriented coping strategies*

In the last decade, some theoreticians and researchers have not supported the view that expressing the negative emotions associated with grief is essential for its successful resolution (e.g., Bonanno & Keltner, 1997; M. Stroebe & Stroebe, 1991). Depending on the theoretical view of bereavement, other tasks may be regarded as equally essential for the resolution of grief. The dual-process model of bereavement (DPM) developed by M. Stroebe and H. Schut (1999, 2001) postulates that adaptive coping with bereavement requires a fluctuation or oscillation between strategies aimed at addressing the loss of the deceased person (referred to as loss-oriented strategies) and strategies aimed at addressing the secondary stressors that come about as an indirect consequence of the bereavement, such as changing identity and role or mastering new skills (referred to as restoration-oriented strategies). Grief work corresponds essentially to loss-oriented strategies, such as expressing emotions related to the loss of one's loved one. The DPM also postulates that the bereaved person will have to deal with the situational changes and will have to rebuild "assumptions about the world and one's own place in it" (M. Stroebe et al., 2005b, p. 9). It thus proposes that both confronta-tion and distraction/avoidance strategies will be used to deal effectively with both loss- and restoration-stressors and tasks. Focusing on only one orientation would not be adaptive: exclusively focusing on loss would lead to chronic grief, while exclusively focusing on restoration would lead to absent or inhibited grief. A disturbance of the oscillation process, with extreme involuntary confrontation and avoidance of the stressors, would be indicative of traumatic grief.

The extension of this model (M. Stroebe et al., 2005a, 2005b) postulates that the disclosure paradigm will work for those who are unable, alone or in their daily interactions with others, to create a coherent discourse about their thoughts and feelings. Thus, flexible and smooth oscillation will be characteristic of securely attached individuals who should not benefit very much from a disclosure intervention. Again, the disclosure intervention should benefit according to one's attachment style, which should be related to loss-oriented (preoccupied), restoration-oriented (dismissive) coping strategies, or saccadic oscillation (disorganised). Thus, one of the important features of the DPM is the oscillation process. This could explain why a specific disclosure intervention would not work. There is a need to investigate the process as it develops over time and people need to (learn to) oscillate in a coherent manner. Instructions that would address these different coping strategies and restore a smooth oscillation when needed would most likely be beneficial.

Conclusions

The work of Wolfgang Stroebe and his colleagues (most notably Margaret Stroebe and Henk Schut) has been instrumental in debunking any simple models that have been put forward to explain grief reactions. More importantly, their research has clearly demonstrated that no interventions seem to work for most people in reducing the pain of bereavement. These conclusions are disturbing, but they also raise new challenges for the next generation of bereavement researchers.

Given the spectacular failings of grief counselling, written disclosure (except in cases of traumatic experiences), or other known interventions, should psychologists pack their bags and move on to other lines of research? Before closing, two questions must be addressed. Do people naturally seek out a grieving style that works best for them? If this is the case, we would expect that no intervention would ever work, since it would deviate from people's natural styles. Ironically, of course, it would mean that certain grieving styles *are* working effectively—we just cannot see them because life is not a function of random assignment. Let us consider a rather outrageous suggestion: Perhaps the best strategy to test this idea would be to actively block people from grieving in a natural way. Perhaps banning them from the funerals of loved ones, forcing them to be happy and not to think of their dead relatives could help to disentangle (un)helpful coping strategies. If the "people choose what's best for themselves" hypothesis is true, these dire interventions would prove to prolong long-term grief (of course, such a proposal for intervention would raise ethical concerns).

An equally provocative hypothesis hinted at by the Stroebe work is that the entire process of grief is a social construction that people actually would not need. If working through is not a viable hypothesis, perhaps we should assume that cultural working through is actually maladaptive. A logical intervention, then, would be some form of "snap-out-of-it" therapy: no funeral, get back to work, and no talking about the deceased.

The strength of the Stroebes' research has been in pointing to the short-comings of many of the basic assumptions most of us hold about death and loss. Through carefully controlled real-world studies, they have repeatedly demonstrated the difficulty of modifying grief reactions. Before throwing out the baby with the bath water as just proposed, one should remember that the potential moderators and mediators of the effects of emotional disclosure in coping with bereavement that were outlined in this chapter need further investigation. In short, in line with Stroebe's group, we have highlighted that understanding human reactions to bereavement is more complex than previously proposed: specific sharing interactions should work for specific individuals at a precise point in time of their grieving process.

Acknowledgement

Preparation of this chapter was made possible by a grant from the National Institutes of Health (MH-52391) and by grants 8.4506.98 and 2.4546.97 of the Belgian National Fund for Scientific Research.

References

Bartholomew, K., & Horowitz, L. M. (1991). Attachment styles among young adults: A test of a four-category model. *Journal of Personality and Social Psychology, 61*, 226–244.

Bonanno, G. A., & Keltner, D. (1997). Facial expressions of emotion and the course of conjugal bereavement. *Journal of Abnormal Psychology, 106*, 126–137.

Bowlby, J. (1969). *Attachment and loss. Vol. 1. Attachment.* London: Hogarth Press.

Bowlby, J. (1980). *Attachment and loss. Vol. 3. Loss: Sadness and depression.* London: Hogarth.

Campbell, R. S., & Pennebaker, J. W. (2003). The secret life of pronouns: Flexibility in writing style and physical health. *Psychological Science, 14*, 60–65.

Cassidy, J., & Shaver, P. (1999). *Handbook of attachment: Theory, research and clinical applications.* New York: Guilford Press.

Christophe, V., & Rimé, B. (1997). Exposure to the social sharing of emotion: Emotional impact, listener responses and the secondary social sharing. *European Journal of Social Psychology, 27*, 37–54.

Cohen, S., & Wills, T. A. (1985). Stress, social support and buffering. *Psychological Bulletin, 98*, 310–357.

Feeney, J. A., Noller, P., & Roberts, N. (1998). Emotion, attachment, and satisfaction in close relationships. In P. A. Andersen & L. K. Guerrero (Eds.), *Handbook of communication and emotion: Research, theory, applications, and contexts* (pp. 473–505). San Diego, CA: Academic Press.

Freud, S. (1917). Mourning and melancholia. In J. Strachey (Ed. & Trans.) *Standard edition of the complete psychological works of Sigmund Freud*. London: Hogarth Press, 1957.

Kennedy-Moore, E., & Watson, J. C. (1999). *Expressing emotion*. New York: Guilford Press.

Kovac, S. H., & Range, L. M. (2000). Writing projects: Lessening undergraduates' unique suicidal bereavement. *Suicide and Life-Threatening Behavior, 30*, 50–60.

Lindemann, E. (1944). Symptomatology and management of acute grief. *American Journal of Psychiatry, 101*, 141–148.

Middleton, W., Raphael, B., Martinek, N., & Misso, V. (1993). Pathological grief reactions. In M. S. Stroebe, W. Stroebe, & R. O. Hansson (Eds.), *Handbook of bereavement: Theory, research, and interventions* (pp. 44–61). Cambridge, UK: Cambridge University Press.

Mikulincer, M., & Nachshon, O. (1991). Attachment styles and patterns of self-disclosure. *Journal of Personality and Social Psychology, 61*, 321–331.

Mikulincer, M., & Orbach, I. (1995). Attachment styles and repressive defensiveness: The accessibility and architecture of affective memories. *Journal of Personality and Social Psychology, 68*, 917–925.

Mikulincer, M., & Shaver, P. R. (2003). The attachment behavioral system in adulthood: Activation, psychodynamics, and interpersonal processes. In M. P. Zanna (Ed.), *Advances in experimental social psychology* (Vol. 35, pp. 56–152). San Diego, CA: Academic Press.

Nils, F. (2003). *Le partage social des émotions: déterminants interpersonnels de l'efficacité de la communication des épisodes émotionnels* [Social sharing of emotion: interpersonal determinants of the efficacy of the communication of emotional episodes]. Unpublished doctoral dissertation, University of Louvain, Louvain-la-Neuve, Belgium.

Parkes, C. M. (1996). *Bereavement: Studies of grief in adult life*. London: Routledge.

Pennebaker, J. W. (1989). Confession, inhibition, and disease. In L. Berkowitz (Ed.), *Advances in experimental social psychology* (Vol. 22, pp. 211–244). New York: Academic Press.

Pennebaker, J. W. (1997). *Opening up: The healing power of expressing emotions* (Revised edition). New York: Guilford Press.

Pennebaker, J. W., & Beall, S. K. (1986). Confronting a traumatic event: Towards an understanding of inhibition and disease. *Journal of Abnormal Psychology, 95*, 274–281.

Pennebaker, J. W., & Keough, K. (1999). Revealing, organizing, and reorganizing the self in response to stress and emotion. In R. Contrada & R. Ashmore (Eds.), *Self, social identity, and physical health: Interdisciplinary explanations* (pp. 101–121). Oxford, UK: Oxford University Press.

Pennebaker, J. W., Mayne, T. J., & Francis, M. E. (1997). Linguistic predictors of adaptive bereavement. *Journal of Personality and Social Psychology, 72*, 863–871.

Pennebaker, J. W., Zech, E., & Rimé, B. (2001). Disclosing and sharing emotion: Psychological, social, and health consequences. In M. S. Stroebe, R. O. Hansson, W. Stroebe, & H. Schut (Eds.), *Handbook of bereavement research: Consequences, coping, and care* (pp. 517–543). Washington, DC: American Psychological Association.

Range, L. M., Kovac, S. H., & Marion, M. S. (2000). Does writing about bereavement lessen grief following sudden, unintentional death? *Death Studies, 24*, 115–134.

Rimé, B. (2005). *Le partage social des émotions* [The social sharing of emotions]. Paris: Presses Universitaires de France.

Rimé, B., Finkenauer, C., Luminet, O., Zech, E., & Philippot, P. (1998). Social sharing of emotions: New evidence and new questions. In W. Stroebe & M. Hewstone (Eds.), *European review of social psychology* (Vol. 8, pp. 145–190). Chichester, UK: Wiley.

Rimé, B., Philippot, P., Boca, S., & Mesquita, B. (1992). Long-lasting cognitive and social consequences of emotion: Social sharing and rumination. In W. Stroebe & M. Hewstone (Eds.), *European review of social psychology* (Vol. 3, pp. 225–258). Chichester, UK: Wiley.

Schut, H., Stroebe, M. S., van den Bout, J., & de Keijser, J. (1997). Gender differences in the efficacy of grief counselling. *British Journal of Clinical Psychology, 36*, 63–72.

Schut, H., Stroebe, M. S., van den Bout, J., & Terheggen, M. (2001). The efficacy of bereavement intervention: Who benefits? In M. S. Stroebe, R. O. Hansson, W. Stroebe, & H. Schut (Eds.), *Handbook of bereavement research: Consequences, coping, and care*. Washington, DC: American Psychological Association Press.

Segal, D. L., Bogaards, J. A., Becker, L. A., & Chatman, C. (1999). Effects of emotional expression on adjustment to spousal loss among older adults. *Journal of Mental Health and Aging, 5*, 297–310.

Shaver, P. R., & Tancredy, C. M. (2001). Emotion, attachment and bereavement: A conceptual commentary. In M. S. Stroebe, R. O. Hansson, W. Stroebe, & H. Schut (Eds.), *Handbook of bereavement research—Consequences, coping, and care* (pp. 63–88). Washington, DC: American Psychological Association Press.

Smyth, J. M. (1998). Written emotional expression: Effect sizes, outcome types, and moderating variables. *Journal of Consulting and Clinical Psychology, 66*, 174–184.

Stroebe, M. S. (1992). Coping with bereavement: A review of the grief work hypothesis. *Omega, 26*, 19–42.

Stroebe, M. S., & Schut, H. (1999). The dual process model of coping with bereavement: Rationale and description. *Death Studies, 23*, 197–224.

Stroebe, M. S., & Schut, H. (2001). Meaning making in the dual process model of coping with bereavement. In R. A. Neimeyer (Ed.), *Meaning reconstruction and the experience of loss* (pp. 55–73). Washington, DC: American Psychological Association Press.

Stroebe, M. S., Schut, H., & Stroebe, W. (2005a). Attachment in coping with bereavement: A theoretical integration. *Review of General Psychology, 9*, 48–60.

Stroebe, M. S., Schut, H., & Stroebe, W. (2005b). Who benefits from disclosure? Exploration of attachment style differences in the effects of expressing emotions. *Clinical Psychology Review, 26*, 66–85.

Stroebe, M. S., & Stroebe, W. (1991). Does grief work, work? *Journal of Consulting and Clinical Psychology, 59*, 479–482.

Stroebe, M. S., & Stroebe, W. (1989). Who participates in bereavement research? An empirical study of the impact of health on attrition. *Omega, 20*, 1–29.

Stroebe, M. S., Stroebe, W., Schut, H., Zech, E., & van den Bout, J. (2002). Does disclosure of emotions facilitate recovery from bereavement? Evidence from two prospective studies. *Journal of Consulting and Clinical Psychology, 70*, 169–178.

Stroebe, W., Schut, H., & Stroebe, M. S. (2005a). Grief work, disclosure and counseling: Do they help the bereaved? *Clinical Psychology Review, 25*, 395–414.

Stroebe, W., & Stroebe, M. S. (1987). *Bereavement and health: The psychological and physical consequences of partner loss.* New York: Cambridge University Press.

Stroebe, W., Stroebe, M., Abakoumkin, G., & Schut, H. (1996). The role of loneliness and social support in adjustment to loss: A test of attachment versus stress theory. *Journal of Personality and Social Psychology, 70,* 1241–1249.

Stroebe, W., Zech, E., Stroebe, M. S., Abakoumkin, G. (2005b). Does social support help in bereavement? The impact on vulnerability and recovery. *Journal of Social and Clinical Psychology, 24,* 1030–1050.

Stylianos, S. K., & Vachon, M. L. S. (1993). The role of social support in bereavement. In M. S. Stroebe, W. Stroebe, & R. O. Hansson (Eds.), *Handbook of bereavement: Theory, research and intervention* (pp. 397–410). New York: Cambridge University Press.

Vogel, D. L., & Wester, S. R. (2003). To seek help or not to seek help: The risks of self-disclosure. *Journal of Counseling Psychology, 50,* 351–361.

Weiss, R. S. (1975). *Loneliness: The experience of emotional and social isolation.* Cambridge, MA: MIT Press.

Worden, J. W. (2001). *Grief counseling and grief therapy: A handbook for the mental health practitioner* (3rd ed.). New York: Springer Publishing Company.

Wortman, C. B., & Silver, R. C. (1989). The myths of coping with loss. *Journal of Consulting and Clinical Psychology, 57,* 349–357.

Wortman, C. B., & Silver, R. C. (2001). The myths of coping with loss revised. In M. S. Stroebe, R. O. Hansson, W. Stroebe, & H. Schut (Eds.), *Handbook of bereavement research: Consequences, coping, and care* (pp. 405–429). Washington, DC: American Psychological Association.

Zech, E., de Ree, F. F., Berenschot, A. F., & Stroebe, M. S. (2006). Depressive affect among health care seekers: How it is related to attachment style, emotional disclosure, and health complaints. *Psychology, Health & Medicine, 11,* 7–19.

Zech, E., & Rimé, B. (2005). Is talking about an upsetting experience helpful? Effects on emotional recovery and perceived benefits. *Clinical Psychology & Psychotherapy, 12,* 270–287.

Zech, E., Rimé, B., & Nils, F. (2004). Social sharing of emotion, emotional recovery, and interpersonal aspects. In P. Philippot & R. Feldman (Eds.), *The regulation of emotion* (pp. 157–185). New York: Lawrence Erlbaum Associates Inc.

Part 6

Psychology in context

18 Social psychology is not enough

The Interdisciplinary Social Science Working Group

Karl-Dieter Opp
University of Leipzig, Germany

In a volume that honours Wolfgang Stroebe it is absolutely necessary to acknowledge his active membership for almost 30 (30!) years in a group that was founded to practise interdisciplinary work. How did this group come into being? How does the group engage in interdisciplinary work? These are the major questions that are addressed in this chapter.

It is highly unusual that a small group of eight members devoted to the exchange of scientific ideas from several social science disciplines should exist for such a long time. The history and activities of the group may therefore also be of interest to readers who are not mainly interested in Wolfgang's scientific career. Interdisciplinary work is rare, and this group has been committed to it for three decades. The group may therefore serve as an example indicating how a longstanding effort at interdisciplinary work may be set up.

Although there is general agreement that interdisciplinary work is a good thing, very few social scientists practise it. One reason is that it is not clear exactly what interdisciplinary work looks like. The second reason is that interdisciplinary endeavours—of whatever kind they may be—require great investments of time. It is much easier to specialise in a narrow field, and this probably increases the chances to publish in leading journals and to promote one's career. On the other hand, interdisciplinary work has a high reputation, and funding is more likely if a research project has some interdisciplinary quality. Although a focus on a narrow field may have short-term advantages, scientific progress in the social sciences seems more likely if a given problem such as explaining human behaviour is approached by a joint effort of scientists from different disciplines.

For such a joint effort to materialise four conditions must be met: (1) There must be explanatory problems shared by several social science disciplines, otherwise interdisciplinary work, in the sense that scholars of different disciplines work on joint explanatory problems, is not possible. (2) Engaging in interdisciplinary work will only have a chance to succeed if the members' fundamental methodological convictions are not too different. (3) The members must have a strong interest in interdisciplinary collaboration. (4) The likelihood that the group will persist increases if positive personal relationships between the members (and their spouses) develop. To what extent did these conditions obtain when the Interdisciplinary Social Science Working Group came into being, and to what extent do these conditions continue to exist?

The research programme of the group

It seems at first sight that the social sciences focus on different explanatory problems. For example, only economics deals with the formation of prices. However, there are numerous substantive explanatory problems that are addressed by several social science disciplines. Examples are crime (biology, criminology, economics, psychology, and sociology deal with crime), political participation (which is the subject of social psychology, political science, and sociology) and the family (which is addressed by economics, social psychology, and sociology). One approach to interdisciplinary work is to look at the existing explanations of the specific phenomena and examine which independent variables of the theories work best; i.e., to combine the independent variables. For example, in explaining crime one could measure biological variables such as gene aberrations, psychological variables such as personality characteristics, and sociological variables such as individual income or inequality of the country of the individuals in a sample. This is an eclectic approach that is favoured by many social scientists. One problem is that a collection of independent variables does not give any information about what specific phenomena are to be explained. For example, does income explain theft, murder, or white-collar crime? Such relationships between independent and dependent variables are usually specified ad hoc.

An alternative to this approach is to apply a general theory of human behaviour to explain a wide range of phenomena on the micro as well as on the macro level. Such an approach has already been developed by the Scottish moral philosophers Adam Ferguson (1723–1815), Adam Smith (1723–1790), and David Hume (1711–1776). The general theoretical principles they applied have then been narrowed down to explain only economic phenomena such as demand and supply of economic commodities. Beginning with the 1950s, the range of application of the general theory was again expanded to embrace all kinds of social phenomena. The theory we are referring to is the "economic model of man", also called "*homo oeconomicus*", or the theory of rational action, or rational choice theory. The pioneers of this renewed "economic imperialism" were Gary Becker in economics and George C. Homans in sociology. In political science, Anthony Downs, James Buchanan, and Gordon Tullock—all economists—were among those who founded the economic theory of politics or public choice theory.

This research programme, which is often called the "individualistic" research programme, consists of two parts. One is the idea of methodological individualism. It is held that macro-phenomena can and should be explained by applying a general theory of human behaviour. Thus, in order to explain revolutions one must explain the behaviour of individuals involved in a revolution. The other ingredient of the research programme is the theory of individual behaviour that is applied to carry out the explanation. Most adherents of this research programme apply the theory of rational action.

As everything in the social sciences, this research programme is controversial. It is first contested that macro-phenomena can be explained by a micro-theory (and, in addition, by certain "bridge assumptions"). For example, is it possible to explain phenomena like economic growth, revolutions, or institutions by applying theories about individuals? A further issue is the individual theory that is applied by most social scientists who work in this research programme. It is argued that the theory of rational action is wrong and should thus not be applied to solve explanatory problems. Another claim is that the theory is tautological. However, a huge amount of theoretical and empirical research has accumulated, which suggests that this theory and the individualistic research programme are fruitful, compared to other theories and research programmes.

The above research programme provided the intellectual foundation and general framework for the interdisciplinary group. However, although the members agree that rational choice theory is a fruitful theoretical frame, they are convinced that it has to be further developed. Therefore, examples that demonstrate certain limits of the general applicability of rational choice theory (e.g., the evolutionary basis of decisional processes, the Tversky–Kahneman ideas about decision heuristics, Gigerenzer's results concerning the effects of recognition heuristics, the hidden costs of reward, etc.) are vividly and sometimes controversially discussed. This also holds for the application of psychological ideas in economics by Bruno S. Frey, a member of our group (Frey, 1997).

But none of these controversies has had any negative influence on the group's motivation to get a step nearer to a satisfactory solution of problems. It is this common interest in general theory, its application to concrete explanatory problems, and its rigorous testing, that is probably the strongest unifying bond of the members of the group—a common interest that is by no means widely held in the social sciences in general.

The methodological orientation

This basic theoretical orientation is not compatible with any existing methodological convictions. On the one hand, one can hardly imagine that an adherent of the individualistic research programme is a constructivist. On the other hand, many methodological positions are compatible with pursuing the individualistic research programme. The members of the group share the methodology of critical rationalism, which is mainly based on the work of Karl R. Popper and further developed by Hans Albert (who has been a member of the group from the very beginning). The basic ideas can be summarised as follows.

(1) Everything is open to criticism, i.e., there are no dogmas or "final truths".
(2) Human knowledge is fallible; even if there is subjective certainty that specific theories are true, we cannot rule out that there will be evidence that provides a falsification.
(3) Theories cannot be verified, i.e., proven to be true, but only confirmed for the time being.
(4) Theories are deductively tested, i.e., research examines predictions that follow from theories; this implies that there is no induction that derives theories from singular statements.
(5) Testing theories means trying to falsify and not to confirm theories; one effective means is to empirically confront theories with alternative inconsistent theories. Thus, comparative theory testing is important.
(6) The aim is to provide "deep" explanations, i.e., to search for theories with high explanatory power.

It seems that the methodology of critical rationalism is surprisingly consistent with the individualistic research programme. Critical rationalism implies a focus on theories with explanatory power. This is exactly the goal of proponents of the individualistic programme: to apply a theory to a wide range of empirical phenomena. Furthermore, comparative theory testing—i.e., to confront alternative and inconsistent theories—is of central concern.

Critical rationalism is the second unifying bond of the group. This does not mean that everybody agrees with everything that Karl Popper or Hans Albert have written. But the basic claims mentioned above are accepted by all members of the group.

How everything began—and almost came to an end

There are many scholars who are interested in interdisciplinary work. But how did it happen that a few of them joined to found the group? Many groups originate because there is at least one "political entrepreneur". This happened here as well. In 1976, Kurt Stapf, Professor of Psychology at the University of Tübingen, received funding for a conference to be held in 1977 on the occasion of the 500-year anniversary of the University of Tübingen. Kurt Stapf talked about the preparation of the conference with Hans Albert. Both agreed about basic shortcomings of the social sciences, which will be outlined in more detail below. In short, they believed that economics had to some extent a good general theory that can be applied to explain phenomena from different social science disciplines. But psychology could improve that theory and provide the methods to test it. They decided to organise a conference that focused on these convictions. Those invited to give a talk at the conference—which took place in November 1977—largely shared those ideas. The conference volume (Albert & Stapf, 1979) includes all presentations. The introduction of the editors outlines the basic ideas of the research programme (see in particular the summary on p. 16). Apart from Hans Albert and Kurt Stapf, two other permanent members of the group participated in the conference: Wilhelm Meyer and Karl-Dieter Opp. In preparing the conference, the idea emerged that it would be fruitful to set up a group devoted to these issues, which should convene regularly.

The group was founded at the European Forum Alpbach in August 1976 (i.e., before the conference mentioned in the previous paragraph took place). Alpbach is a wonderful Austrian village near Wörgl (which is about 100 km south east of Munich). The Forum was founded by Simon Moser and Otto Molden in 1945 as the "International University Weeks" (*Internationale Hochschulwochen*) with the aim to promote an intellectual exchange "to develop the ideas of a peacefully united Europe and of free and independent universities and science" (see the website www.alpbach.org). Part of the Forum was a 2-week conference with seminars held by a wide range of individuals, mostly university professors, but also other intellectuals including managers, lawyers, artists, journalists, writers, and politicians. The topics were of general interest. The seminar groups convened in the morning; the afternoon consisted of lectures about timely topics or of art events. The audience was also very heterogeneous: participants were housewives as well as university professors. There was ample opportunity to meet participants informally outside the lectures and talks.

During the Forum in August 1977, such informal meetings took place between some economists and psychologists from several German and Swiss universities "who discovered joint research interests".[1] This group decided to meet again at the next Forum in Alpbach in 1978 "to hold a private seminar". "To prepare this seminar we will meet at a nice location in the spring of 1978 at a date to be arranged." The nice village was Weinheim an der Bergstraße (about 20 km from Mannheim), and the meeting took place on 14 January 1978.

At that time the group consisted of eight members: two psychologists (Kurt Stapf and Wolfgang Stroebe), four economists (Peter Bernholz, Bruno S. Frey, Gerd Fleischmann, and Michael Küttner), one philosopher (Hans Albert), and one sociologist (Karl-Dieter Opp). The original focus was on economics and psychology. The philosopher and the sociologist were recruited because they had a strong interest in economics and psychology. The name of the group was "Arbeitsgemeinschaft Ökonomie – Psychologie – Soziologie" (ÖPSAG: "Working group Economics – Psychology – Sociology"). There were further meetings in January 1978, November 1979, and May 1980.

What began as a promising start turned out to become increasingly problematic. The problems were more of a personal nature. One effect of these problems was that attendance was irregular. At the meeting in May 1980, only Hans Albert, Bruno Frey, Karl-Dieter Opp, Kurt Stapf, and Wolfgang Stroebe were present. It was decided that the group should be dissolved. But there was no doubt that the members who attended the meeting were interested in further collaboration. Therefore, the group was re-founded.

The new name that the group still has today was "Interdisciplinary Social Science Working Group" (ISAG, for *Interdisziplinäre Sozialwissenschaftliche Arbeitsgruppe*). The next meeting took place in November 1980. A new member was recruited: the economist Wilhelm Meyer. In 1985 the psychologist Klaus Foppa became a member of the group. Finally, Viktor Vanberg joined the group in June 2004. So at present the group has eight members again.

Recruiting new members was a difficult matter. One criterion a potential member had to fulfil was that he[2] would "fit" into the group in terms of his personality. This "fit" was certainly difficult to operationalise, but everybody had an opinion about what this meant. Another criterion was unanimity: if there was dissent, a potential member was not to be accepted. Furthermore, it was important that a new member should add some additional expertise, i.e., that he was specialised with regard to new substantive topics that could be discussed in the meetings. It goes without saying that the two basic orientations—positive valuation of the individualistic research programme and of critical rationalism—had to be present. This does not mean that the members' theoretical and methodological orientations matched perfectly. Opinions often differed with respect to details. But the basic orientations were the same and—in the opinion of the members—should be the same. Why? We have all experienced long and tiring discussions between completely incompatible orientations, such as between Marxists on the one hand and critical rationalists or adherents of the individualistic programme on the other. We wanted to avoid such debates. It was preferable to have peers from whom you can learn.

It has also turned out that the importance of good personal relationships between the members cannot be overemphasised. Over the years, the members of the group became friends. An indicator is that we celebrate birthdays and anniversaries or attend inaugural lectures of the members. Another indicator of the good personal "climate" is that our spouses attend the meetings as well. The division of labour is that the men work and the wives engage in various cultural or sightseeing activities. The fact that the wives somehow fit together as well may have contributed to the thriving of the group.

Our group meets—with few exceptions—twice a year. It is worth noting that it has been extremely rare that somebody misses a meeting. This has happened only in cases of illness, long-term-absence, or mix-up of a date (which happened once!). The next meeting is always planned in the last session of a previous meeting. Now we even plan a year ahead.

The schedule of the meetings that emerged is as follows. We meet on Friday for dinner at 7 pm (with spouses). There is normally a presentation on Saturday morning, Saturday afternoon, and Sunday morning. It sometimes happens that a session consists of two talks, but this is rare. In each session, there is extensive discussion. There is another joint dinner (again with spouses) on Saturday night. Departure is Sunday noon—mostly after a joint lunch.

The members of the group

There are currently eight members. In this section their affiliation and major areas of research and interest will be presented. Because of limitations of space only some information about status, affiliation, and area of research and interest is provided.

Hans Albert is Professor Emeritus of Sociology and Philosophy of Science at the University of Mannheim. He has worked on a range of problems of economics, sociology, jurisprudence, philosophy of science, and epistemology. He is author of *Ökonomische Ideologie und politische Theorie* (1954, 1972); *Marktsoziologie und Entscheidungslogik* (1967, 1998); *Traktat über kritische Vernunft* (1968, 1991)—English translation 1985: *Treatise on Critical Reason*; *Traktat über rationale Praxis* (1978); *Das Elend der Theologie* (1979, 2005); *Kritik der reinen Erkenntnislehre* (1987); *Kritik der reinen Hermeneutik* (1994); *Between Social Science, Religion and Politics* (1999); *Kritik des transzendentalen Denkens* (2004), and other books and articles.

Klaus Foppa is Professor Emeritus of Psychology at the University of Berne (Switzerland). He has worked in different problem fields. Starting with research on memory and learning, his book on "Learning, Retention, and Behaviour" (*Lernen, Gedächtnis, Verhalten*) was published in 1965 and has been reprinted several times. He has co-edited several books, e.g., with M. v. Cranach, W. Lepenies, and D. Ploog, *Human Ethology: Claims and limits of a new discipline* (1979); with Ivana Markovà, *The Dynamics of Dialogue* (1990); *Asymmetries in Dialogue* (1991); and with Ivana Markovà and Carl Graumann, *Mutualities in Dialogue* (1995). In addition, he has published many papers on retention and learning and on general methodological problems.

Bruno S. Frey was born in Basle, Switzerland, in 1941. He studied economics at the Universities of Basle and Cambridge (England). He was Professor of Economics at the University of Constance from 1970–77, and since 1977 has been Professor of Economics at the University of Zurich. He received an honorary doctorate in economics from the Universities of St. Gallen (Switzerland, 1998) and Goeteborg (Sweden, 1998). He is the author of numerous articles in professional journals and books, including *Not Just for the Money* (1997), *Economics as a Science of Human Behaviour* (1999), *Arts & Economics* (2000), *Inspiring Economics* (2001), *Successful Management by Motivation* (with Margit Osterloh, 2001), *Happiness and Economics* (with Alois Stutzer, 2002), and *Dealing with Terrorism—Stick or Carrot?* (2004).

Wilhelm Meyer is Professor Emeritus of Economic Thought and Methodology at the University of Marburg, Germany. His areas of interest include philosophy of science, economic methodology, utility theory and behaviour, institutions and economic theory, history of economic research programmes, the gender revolution. His main papers on epistemology, economic methodology, and economic research programmes are published in his *Grundlagen des ökonomischen Denkens* (2002).

Karl-Dieter Opp is Professor Emeritus of Sociology at the University of Leipzig, Germany. His areas of interest include collective action and political participation, rational choice theory, and the emergence and effects of norms and institutions. He is currently working on a book about the origins and effects of regional, national, and European identification. He is author of *The Rationality of Political Protest* (1989), co-author of *The Origins of a Spontaneous Revolution: East Germany 1989* (1995), and editor (with M. Hechter) of *Social Norms* (2001). His articles have been published in scholarly journals such as the *American Sociological Review*, *Social Forces*, *Rationality and Society*, *American Political Science Review*, and the *American Journal of Political Science*. He has also published numerous books and articles in German.

Kurt H. Stapf is Professor of Psychology at the University of Tübingen and Director of the Psychological Institute. He worked in the area of cognitive psychology on spatial orientation and the cognitive map, and published several articles and a monograph (1972, with Th. Herrmann) on parental educational style (*elterlicher Erziehungsstil*). From 1979 to 1986 he participated in a research group that constructed the first German university admission test for medical students (*Hochschulzulassungstest für das Medizinstudium*). Recently, he has been working in the field of applied psychology, especially on traffic and industrial psychology, pursuing several lines of research interests: psychological issues of safety in traffic, the working efficiency of older employees, issues of life-long learning, and work motivation. In 2005 he published a book (with R. Brinkmann) about the process of disengagement from work.

Wolfgang Stroebe is Professor of Social and Organisational Psychology at Utrecht University, The Netherlands. He received an honorary doctorate from the University of Louvain-la-Neuve in 2002. His research interests span social and health psychology. He has written and edited extensively in both these fields. Authored books include *Social Judgment and Categorization* (with J. R. Eiser), *Social Psychology and Health*, and *Bereavement and Health* (with M. Stroebe). Edited volumes include two handbooks on bereavement (with M. Stroebe, R. Hansson, and H. Schut), the long-standing series *European Review of Social Psychology*, and three editions of the *Introduction to Social Psychology* (both with Miles Hewstone). His articles, on topics ranging from group productivity, eating behaviour, attitudes, and attitude change, to bereavement, have been published in many leading journals (e.g., *Psychological Bulletin*, *Journal of Personality and Social Psychology*, *American Psychologist*, and *Journal of Consulting and Clinical Psychology*). He is currently working on a monograph on eating behaviour.

Viktor Vanberg is Professor of Economics at the University of Freiburg (Breisgau) and Director of the Walter Eucken Institut, Freiburg. In addition to economic policy, his "official" area of teaching and research, his areas of interest are, in particular, institutional and evolutionary economics, and the behavioural foundations of the social sciences, reflecting his background in sociology. He is author of *Die zwei Soziologien* (1975), *Markt und Organisation* (1982), *Rules and Choice in Economics* (1994), and *The Constitution of Markets* (2001). His articles have appeared in the *American Political Science Review*, *Constitutional Political Economy*, *Economics and Philosophy*, *Rationality and Society*, *Journal of Economic Methodology*, *Journal of Institutional Economics*, *Kyklos*, *Journal of Law Economics and Organization*, *Public Choice*, *Journal of Theoretical Politics*, *Review of Political Economy*, and other journals.

How the group works

The name of our group includes the term "interdisciplinary". However, it has never been an important or recurrent topic in the meetings to examine how "interdisciplinary" work could be defined or what alternative possibilities of "interdisciplinarity" exist. We simply practised interdisciplinary work in the following way. The initial interest of the group members was to explore the extent to which the economic model of man was appropriate to explain economic phenomena and social phenomena in general. We believed that this model could be improved by applying psychological theories or findings. The question then was which findings of psychology could improve the economic model. Due to these interests, the non-psychologists of the group were eager to learn what psychology (including social psychology) had to offer. The non-economists wanted to learn how economics worked and what economics—especially the model of economic man—had to offer. "Our" philosopher Hans Albert taught the rest of the group how critical rationalist philosophy of science is relevant for good social science.

However, the interest of the group members became broader. It turned out that each of us was also simply interested in the work of the other members. This meant that many presentations were reports on work in progress.

The first phase after the group was founded consisted of discussion of articles and books that seemed relevant as a common reference with regard to the economic model and relevant psychology. To get an impression of the wide variety of topics that were addressed in the sessions, some of the themes of the presentations of each member are listed below (the themes are translated into English). We further note the year in which the talk was given.

Hans Albert: Critique of jurisprudence (1983); the state of the controversy on critical rationalism (1986); hermeneutics and economics (1988); jurisprudence as a social science (1993); history as a hypothetico-deductive discipline (1996); problems of interdisciplinarity (1999); the development of critical rationalism (2001).

Klaus Foppa: From single cases to rules (1986); an economic-psychological model of man (with Frey) (1986); the ipsative process model (with Frey) (1989); problems of the ipsative behavioural model (1991); outline of a research project on determinants of environmental behaviour (1992); a new theory of learning (1993); the problem of freedom of choice and the ipsative theory of action (1995); restrictions of experience and their consequences for individual knowledge (1997); new findings about the psychology of verbal communication (1998); markets and ipsative opportunities (1999); model learning (2000); internalisation of informal norms (2001); effects of non-verbal communication (2002); explaining cultural evolution (2003); sociobiology (2004); social dimensions of knowledge (2005).

Bruno S. Frey: Recent economic models of bureaucracy (1980); crime (1982); economics of art (1986); an economic-psychological model of man (with Foppa) (1986); an economic theory of power (1987); the ipsative process model (with Foppa) (1989); monitoring and morals in shirking (1991); economics of art in international perspective (1992); empirical research on intrinsic motivation (1992); the NIMBY (Not In My Back Yard) problem (1993); moral standards in economics (1997); economic aspects of voluntary work (1998); economics and research on happiness (1999); a new idea of citizenship (2002); economic theory of terrorism (2003).

Wilhelm Meyer: The research programme of economics and the relevance of psychology (1982); critique of economics based on Boland (1983); economic modelling and the structuralist view of science (1986); G. Schmoller's research programme: his psychology and the autonomy of the social sciences (1988); history and economics (1989); falsificationism and economic theory (1991); knowledge and thinking in everyday life: cognition, intuition, and tradition (1992); problems of the research on anomalies in economics (1993); the explanation of unemployment in Europe (1995); an international comparison of determinants of unemployment (1997); the wealth of nations and the moral behaviour of economic subjects (1998); general theory of the market (1999); Nietzsche, Mill, and gender equality (2001); action against the best of one's knowledge (2002); tobacco advertisements and health politics (2004); women: equal rights and unequal chances in the labour market (2005).

Karl-Dieter Opp: Emergence of norms (with Stroebe) (1979); white-collar crime as a collective cost (1982); shadow economy (1982); rationality and political participation (1986); conditions for political protest (1987); a simulation of the dynamics of political action (1989); social change in the new German states (1991); causes of the collapse of the GDR (1992); is behaviour in high-risk situations "rational"? (1993); personality characteristics and the theory of rational action (1996); a new theory of the emergence of norms (1997); why do ordinary people think they are politically influential? (1998); the dynamics of political participation (1999); when may and when should one get a divorce? An application of the factorial survey (2002); the impact of institutions—the example of the European Union (2004); what are the effects of national and sub-national identities? (2005).

Kurt H. Stapf: Attitudes and behaviour (1979); the hidden costs of rewards (1980); models of test fairness (1986); patterns of behaviour and social situations (1986); a complementary experiment on goal setting (1987);

memory in old age: results of an experiment (1990); risk assessment and risk behaviour in a simulated behavioural environment (1994); psychological aspects of long-term unemployment (1995); the problem of "internal notice" (1997); deterioration of internal motivation (1998); firms on "internal notice" (2000); achievements of older employees (2001); new research on the psychological effects of long-term unemployment (2002); refutation of the deficit hypothesis of older employees (2003); stress in the workplace (2004).

Wolfgang Stroebe: Emergence of norms (with Opp) (1979); the free rider principle, the charity market, and the economics of blood spending (1982); the behavioural model of social psychology (1986); research on goal setting (1987); the influence of state measures on alcohol consumption (1989); test of the model of planned behaviour with outcomes of examinations (1990); determinants of the productivity of groups (1991); behaviour and health (1992); the Köhler effect (1994); reactions to the experience of loss (1995); cognitive control of eating behaviour (1997); determinants and consequences of health behaviour (1997); psychological aspects of eating behaviour (1999); new research on brainstorming (2000); fear-arousing communication and attitude change (2002); outcomes of the process of grieving (2004); new research on the psychology of eating (2005).

Viktor Vanberg: Rationality and evolutionary psychology (2004). (Viktor has been a member of the group since 2004.)

This overview shows the great variety of themes that have been addressed in the sessions. With regard to the two major unifying bonds—the individualistic research programme and critical rationalism—we see that not all themes were related to these topics. As was said before, some of the talks were reports on current research projects.

There was another topic addressed in many sessions. Scholars who are interested in the developments in several social science disciplines have a problem in keeping track of the recent literature. There is a general expectation that each member provides information to the other members about new literature if that seems to be of interest to the others. A recurrent theme is thus reports on new literature.

What the group did not do

It is instructive to think about what the group did not achieve, but which could have been accomplished. The group did not produce a book. However, there was a plan for a joint book project in 1983 with the preliminary title "The poverty of the social sciences", and there was even a table of contents, dated 12 December 1982, which was written by Hans Albert, based on a draft by Bruno Frey. Here is the table of contents:

I.   The Wealth of Nations and the poverty of the social sciences
II. The Poverty of Economics

The table of contents is a good summary of what we thought were the major deficits of the social sciences. These deficits were mainly of a theoretical nature. We thought that a systematic application of the individualistic research programme, including the relevant theories and findings of social psychology, could help to improve the social sciences. This includes tackling questions that have been neglected, such as the explanation of preferences or beliefs.

There was a deadline date for those chapters assigned to members: 31 December 1984. Why did the book not come out? Perhaps because there were several chapters that members were not willing to write because they had to invest time to delve into new fields. Each of us was very busy in pursuing his own research, so that there were heavy time constraints.

There is one edited book in which four members were involved: Wolfgang Stroebe and Wilhelm Meyer edited a special issue of the *British Journal of Social Psychology* in 1982 on "Social Psychology and Economics". This issue includes articles by Wilhelm Meyer, Wolfgang Stroebe and Bruno S. Frey, and Karl-Dieter Opp. Another joint book involving two members is Stapf, Stroebe, and Jonas (1986).

Writing a joint book is indeed a major investment. But might one not have expected at least a bulk of joint papers to have been written? Indeed, there were some collaborative efforts in regard to joint papers (see Frey & Foppa, 1986; Frey & Opp, 1979; Stroebe & Frey, 1980, 1982). In hindsight, however, it is surprising that there has been so little joint writing. Why is this? A plausible explanation is that the heterogeneity of the members is still too large. To be sure, there is theoretical and methodological homogeneity, but each of us is also a specialist in different substantive fields of inquiry. In this situation it is difficult to develop joint publications or research. It seems that the main benefits of the group activities were first a broadening of each member's knowledge about other disciplines. This certainly stimulated the contents of papers and research projects of the members. There was a more specific effect when presentations were first versions of papers that were published later (which was very often the case). The detailed discussions often led to major revisions. An indicator of the influence of the group discussions is that in many of the group members' papers and books there are acknowledgements of the contributions of the group.

Concluding remarks

This concludes a brief outline of the history of the Interdisciplinary Social Science Working Group of which Wolfgang Stroebe—who is to be honoured by this Festschrift—has been a member from the very beginning in 1977. We owe Wolfgang many thanks for excellent and stimulating talks and contributions to the discussions. His enormous knowledge about social psychological theories and research has provided us with many valuable suggestions for our own research. We learned other things from Wolfgang as well: the location of good hotels and restaurants, and what wine to order. How to explain the causal relationship between Wolfgang's scientific productivity and competence on the one hand, and his deep knowledge of the non-scientific (gastronomic) part of life on the other, may be a topic for the next Festschrift.

Acknowledgements

When the plan originated that a contribution on the "Inderdisciplinary Social Science Working group" should be included in the Festschrift for Wolfgang Stroebe, I became the author because I had collected all the programmes of the sessions and other documents about the development of the group as well. Nonetheless, my files were not complete. I would like to gratefully acknowledge the support of the other members of the group in writing this chapter: Hans Albert, Klaus Foppa, Bruno S. Frey, Wilhelm Meyer, Kurt H. Stapf, and Viktor Vanberg.

Notes

1 This and the following quotation is from a letter by Kurt Stapf, Professor of Psychology at the University of Tübingen. The letter was written to the sociologist Karl-Dieter Opp who participated in the Alpbach Forum in 1977 but did not join the informal meetings. In this letter Opp was invited to join the group.
2 As a matter of fact, there was never any discussion about gender. We just looked for persons who could meet the criteria mentioned. It turned out—as an unintended outcome of the decision process—that members were all men.

References

Albert, H., & Stapf, K. H. (1979). *Theorie und Erfahrung: Beiträge zur Grundlagenproblematik der Sozialwissenschaften.* Stuttgart: Klett-Cotta.
Frey, B. S. (1997). *Not just for the money: An economic theory of personal motivation.* Cheltenham and Brookfield, UK: Edward Elgar.

Frey, B. S., & Foppa, K. (1986). Human behavior: Possibilities explain action. *Journal of Economic Psychology, 7*, 137–160.

Frey, B. S., & Opp, K.-D. (1979). Anomie, Nutzen und Kosten. *Soziale Welt, 30*, 330–343.

Stapf, K. H., Stroebe, W., & Jonas, K. (1986). *Amerikaner über Deutschland und die Deutschen: Urteile und Vorurteile.* Opladen: Westdeutscher Verlag.

Stroebe, W., & Frey, B. S. (1980). In defense of economic man: Towards an integration of economics and psychology. *Schweizerische Zeitschrift für Volkswirtschaft und Statistik, 116*, 119–148.

Stroebe, W., & Frey, B. S. (1982). Self-interest and collective action: The economics and psychology of public goods. *British Journal of Psychology, 21*, 43–60.

Stroebe, W., & Meyer, W. (Eds.) (1982). *Social psychology and economics. A special issue of the British Journal of Social Psychology.* Letchworth, UK: The British Psychological Society.

19 Epilogue

Impressions of Wolfgang Stroebe

Lloyd H. Strickland, Jaap Rabbie,
Rein van der Vegt, and Lizet Hoekert

As a conclusion to this volume in honour of Wolfgang Stroebe, the editors invited a few of his most esteemed colleagues/friends to write down their personal impressions of him. As you will see, what has emerged is a set of very different contributions from very different persons. To start out with, Lloyd Strickland reflects back on decades of impressions, having known Wolfgang since his 20s when they were both at Bristol University, UK. Next, Jaap Rabbie, Wolfgang's predecessor at Utrecht University, gives his personal account of Wolfgang's role at the Department of Social and Organisational Psychology at this university. Following this, Rein van der Vegt describes how Wolfgang designed a new research institute at Utrecht. Finally Lizet Hoekert shares her impressions of Wolfgang as Director of the Research Institute for Psychology & Health.

Professor Lloyd H. Strickland
Psychology Department, Carleton University,
Ottawa, Canada

It was immediately easy to agree to offer some personal observations about Wolfgang Stroebe for this special volume, focusing on our joint work contexts. I can detail a few events, wondering as I write whether my observations, based as they must be on his "early days" in social psychology, will resemble those of his younger colleagues and co-authors.

One of Wolfgang's strengths, which I have observed in both formal and informal contexts, was apparent early on. It was an ability, perhaps manifest on the spur of the moment, to generate hypotheses linking apparently conflicting sets of empirical observations. Were a colleague to assert "He says that he found thus and so in his experiment, but my observations seem to show just the opposite", Wolfgang was likely to connect these incompatibilities with a testable hypothesis. A public example of this facility, one subsequently seen by many North American undergraduate students, took place at a NATO social psychology conference in Canada. He was interviewed by a prominent Canadian TV News figure, Warner Troyer, for a series of educational films on social psychology entitled "Parts of the Sum". During live filming, Troyer challenged Wolfgang with what in the early 1970s was a nagging contradiction in the research on interpersonal attraction, i.e., why should some research support the "opposites attract" hypothesis, while other research bore out the "birds of a feather . . ." or a similarity-based attraction assumption. Stroebe proposed and elaborated upon an explanation based on "ease of interaction"; while similarity of interests might make interaction easier than disparate ones with a newly acquainted couple, this interaction would be easiest when the couple had complementary social needs, say, one dominant and the other submissive. This interpretive skill seemed, then and since, representative of Wolfgang's psychological thinking.

At this same international conference, "Paradigms and Priorities for Social Psychology", Stroebe (1976) offered a sensitive analysis of the then highly provocative paper by Zajonc and Markus (1976) on the effects of birth order on intellectual development. In several brief paragraphs, Wolfgang pointed out (a) problems of employing the class "intelligence" scores on the Dutch Army personnel; (b) that it was not clear that physical or social factors could mediate a relationship between family intelligence, as one environmental factor, and the intelligence of a child in that family (the data were essentially correlational); and (c) that there were no data concerning the variables on which Zajonc and Markus's major assumptions rested. Nevertheless, Stroebe endorsed the type of analysis offered by Zajonc and Markus, proposing that it could be useful in other contexts and recalling the study of a decade and a half earlier, by Jacobs and Campbell (1961) on the establishment of "traditions" in small groups developing over several membership generations. He was able to link two vastly different studies, conducted 15 years apart, in terms of the novel methodological approach employed by Zajonc and Markus, and this immediately broadened the appeal of the study's methodology.

One of Wolfgang's most incisive papers, dealing with the "crisis in social psychology" of the 1960s and early 1970s, appeared—sadly for social psychology (and perhaps for Stroebe as well)—in one of the least frequently cited publishing efforts of that period (Strickland, 1979). In "The Level of Social Psychological Analysis: A Plea for a More Social Social Psychology" (1979), Stroebe reviewed the most important causes of social psychology's self-doubt. He noted that almost all of the recently proposed solutions for the field's problems had been cast hitherto in the language of different methodologies, while what was really needed was a new theoretical orientation, one in which social psychologists would study the individual in his or her social context rather than in relation to another individual. He then argued that social psychology should recall its starting place, as a field "between" individual psychology and sociology, offering Henri Tajfel's emerging theory (Tajfel, 1974) as the prime example of what we should have been doing. This pioneering essay anticipated by a decade more recent, better-known lines of argument concerning how experimental social psychologists should orient their research towards questions about the person in his or her "situation", in particular, about the person as a member of his or her social group.

I was invited to comment on Stroebe's career. What does one see? First, in the late 1960s two PhD degrees, one in German, one in English, granted just 2 years apart; second, a meteoric rise in academic rank to Professor within 5 years of the second doctorate; third, quickly using the crass, publication-counting strategy we are so often accused of employing, I noted that he had become author or co-author of 6 books, editor or co-editor of 29 books, and author or co-author of more than 130 articles and chapters by the time of my reading of his (no longer current) CV, in 2004. Many of these publications have been rendered through corresponding editors into one or more of half a dozen languages. I cannot calculate even a rough statistic for this next observation because, to my eternal shame, I cannot even pronounce, let alone translate, the titles of many of them. Nevertheless, I would wager that, since 1987 and the appearance of the book with Maggie (Stroebe & Stroebe, 1987), the ratio of theoretical/experimental articles to the clearly applied has been roughly 50–50, and many of his collaborators in these efforts have been, as they were in the "early" years discussed above, among the central figures in their fields.

The status of Stroebe's more familiar (to me) collaborators would suggest, even if I did not know them from personal experience, that their high output would be matched by high quality. These collaborators are not all members of the same geographical/cultural "club"—they are from all over the globe. He has been invited to give keynote addresses to major international conferences in nine different countries. I cannot think of another person who has contributed so much and so often in the "applied" fields, particularly in the realm of important interpersonal relationships and groups, while at the same time addressing the historically important theoretical issues with which social psychology has been concerned. This all comes together to make him one of the preeminent social psychologists of the Western world.

References

Jacobs, R. C., & Campbell, D. T. (1961). Perpetuation of an arbitrary tradition through several generations of laboratory microculture. *Journal of Abnormal and Social Psychology, 62*, 649–658.

Strickland, L. H. (1979) (Ed.). *Soviet and Western perspectives in social psychology.* Oxford, UK: Pergamon Press.

Stroebe, W. (1976). Critique: On Zajonc and Markus's "Birth order and intellectual development". In L. H. Strickland, F. E. Aboud, & K. J. Gergen (Eds.), *Social psychology in transition.* New York: Plenum Press.

Stroebe, W. (1979). The level of social psychological analysis: A plea for a more social social psychology. In L. H. Strickland (Ed.), *Soviet and Western perspectives in social psychology.* Oxford, UK: Pergamon Press.

Stroebe, W., & Stroebe, M. (1987). *Bereavement and health: The psychological and physical consequences of partner loss*. New York: Cambridge University Press.

Tajfel, H. (1974). *Intergroup behaviour, social comparison and social change*. Katz-Newcomb Lectures, University of Michigan.

Zajonc, R. B., & Markus, G. B. (1976). Birth order and intellectual development. In L. H. Strickland, F. E. Aboud, & K. J. Gergen (Eds.), *Social psychology in transition*. New York: Plenum Press.

Professor Jaap Rabbie
Emeritus Professor Department of Social and Organisational Psychology, Utrecht University, The Netherlands

In 1992 Wolfgang Stroebe was appointed Professor of Social and Organisational Psychology at Utrecht University, with especial attention to Health and Public Health. I was very pleased with his appointment as my successor. First of all, I admired him as an excellent social psychologist. In my farewell address in 1993, I called him "one of the top social psychologists in the world" and I still believe that to be true.

Second, I had the hope that Wolfgang, as an unbiased outsider, could help us to solve the ideological problems and conflicts at the psychology department. Utrecht was still suffering from the consequences of political activism and student protests that had taken place at universities in the early 1960s, in Paris, Berlin, and Berkeley for instance. The Dutch government had, as a reaction to this uproar, decided that students and staff needed more influence on university policy. Prior to this, professors had absolute power over research and teaching, and now they were forced to share that with their co-workers and students. Since I was appointed as dean of the psychology department, I can substantiate Van Hezewijk's (2005) claim that chaos and anarchy were stronger at the psychology department in Utrecht than anywhere else in the Netherlands. One of the most important issues leading to conflict was whether or not the curriculum of the study of psychology at Utrecht University should be guided by an empirical-analytic approach. I placed my hopes on Wolfgang for solving this issue.

As members of the European Association of Experimental Social Psychology (EASP), Wolfgang and I go back a long time. But I really got to know him better when we worked together on the executive committee of the association (from 1981 to 1983). He was elected as the president and I became the treasurer of the executive committee. In my view, he was a superb president, full of ideas and with a great sense of humour, which enabled him to unify the committee behind him. Thus, when I heard that Wolfgang was interested in coming to Utrecht, I was immediately very enthusiastic about it, because I felt that he was one of the few persons who would be capable of managing the ideological conflicts.

Chaos at the psychology department in Utrecht had reached such a level by 1986 that the Dutch Minister of Education had suggested the department should be abolished. This threat was not immediately implemented, but the situation remained unstable for years to come. These were the circumstances under which Wolfgang took over the department. Not a simple task!

In those days Wolfgang and his wife Maggie were working on a handbook of social psychology and health. This theme provided the department with the superordinate theme that was needed to induce cooperation between the different groups within the department. In view of my experiences with Wolfgang in the executive committee of the EASP, I felt that he was the best possible person to do this job too.

Over the years, the facts proved me right. Step by step, Wolfgang turned out not only to be capable of creating a cooperative élan in the psychology department, he was also effective in founding the Dutch National Research Institute for Psychology & Health. Therefore, it was no surprise that Wolfgang became the first director of the research institute. And I am convinced that Wolfgang played a key role in the development of experimental social psychology at Utrecht University and in the unity and quality of the psychology department.

I am very grateful to Wolfgang for all that.

References

van Hezewijk, R. (2005). De geschiedenis van de psychologie [The history of psychology]. In W. Koops, H. van Rinsum, & J. van Teunenbroek (Eds.), *De sociale wetenschappen in Utrecht; een geschiedenis [The social sciences in Utrecht: A history]* (pp. 67–127). Hilversum: Uitgeverij Verloren.

Professor Rein van der Vegt

Emeritus Professor Department of Social and Organisational Psychology, Utrecht University, The Netherlands

Building a new research institute

The task at hand

When Wolfgang took up his chair at Utrecht University, an exciting but formidable task lay ahead of him: directing the establishment of an innovative inter-university research and training institute for psychological research on issues of health and health care.

This task had three aspects. The first had to do with delineating the substance of the new programme, in essence defining its research focus and mission. It meant the development of a programme for research and training in a diverse and even fragmented domain of psychological research on health and health care. Second, the new programme had to be given an appropriate organisational structure; that is, a structure suitable for administering the core activities of the researchers who would eventually participate in the programme. Finally, the newly developed programme, once given its specific structural format, had to earn scientific credentials by accrediting agencies and acquire a viable niche in a competitive field of research institutes and funding agencies.

These three represent, respectively, the substantive programmatic, the organisational-administrative and the political-competitive aspect of an assignment to "build a new research institute". Thus, Wolfgang courageously accepted a formidable yet exciting task upon entering Utrecht University. And he brought this task to a successful conclusion.

The context

This major task had to be performed in the dynamics of the political arena of a (for him) "foreign" university. Actually, an important part of his job took place on the mundane "shop floor" of the psychology department. Here he was face to face with fellow researchers, most (though not all) well intentioned yet forcefully arguing about the mission, about the standards for research and, the overriding question, about their role in the new venture. These colleagues represented a broad range of work experiences, plans for research, and hopes for their faculty careers. Clearly, to get this project to fruition in a dynamic setting like this required a leader with an expert reputation. But it also demanded ambition with sufficient resilience to overcome numerous obstacles.

Upon entering this scene, Wolfgang showed firm commitment to his "construction job". His determination to make the institute "world class" was pursued with sincere forcefulness and with, occasionally, strongly held opinions. This unswerving approach at times led to clashes with colleagues when translating goals into achievement. After all, his very mandate to establish a solid institute inevitably lent his efforts a confrontational flavour. However, Wolfgang faced those confrontations. He also accepted his lost arguments and the setbacks in the building process. His sense of pragmatic exploration was nicely balanced by his conscientiousness and firmness of purpose. This and his solid knowledge base, together with his sense of humour, soon made him a respected colleague-with-a-mission.

The policy scene

In January 1995, the idea of an (inter-university) Research Institute for Psychology and Health (P&H) was implemented: P&H acquired its accreditation and was formally founded. Wolfgang Stroebe was appointed as scientific director. Two important policy processes served as backdrop for the establishment of P&H, one at the local and the other at the national level.

Locally, the Utrecht Faculty Board had already advocated the position to locate a substantial part of its psychology research in the health area. This policy underscored—albeit in very loose terms—a joint health-related research focus for the various psychology departments. However, that advocated common focus was not substantively specified, let alone how to implement it. Initially, though, that policy could be seen as supporting Wolfgang's mandated efforts to alter the research scene for the psychology staff. However, at that time the propagated policy was not, or not wholeheartedly, accepted by the staff. On various grounds, some researchers had difficulties in endorsing the idea of a health focus, given their past research records. And there was also the feeling that this joint focus was unilaterally, and thus unacceptably, put forward by the board. Furthermore, there were doubts among staff members as to the extent to which the concept—once implemented—would affect the work conditions and their research prospects. At the national level, the Ministry of Education had presented an incisive policy that requested universities to develop inter-university programmes for collaborative innovative research and advanced training. At each participating university, a proposed joint project had to be assessed as to quality, scope, and viability. Thereafter, on a national scale, the collaborative venture could go for its final test: "accreditation status", with funding prerogatives and scientific stature as important outcomes.

Obviously, the procedures in such a context drew Wolfgang into politically inspired activities, like scrutinising and contacting potential project partners, negotiating about the relevance of research inputs in the joint venture, bargaining for future administrative positions.

Indeed, stemming from those two policy processes, Wolfgang's work received some "directive guidelines". As a matter of fact, it turned out to be an involving context—an arena with arguing, discussing, quarrelling, negotiating, innovative thinking. Moreover, he had to manage this in a (for him) then foreign country, within an unfamiliar university setting, with a different funding regime, and with many other unknown features. Fortunately, he had an excellent administrative staff—competent, dedicated, and creative. But, understandably, he went through intense processes: he became puzzled, frustrated, amused, curious, inquisitive, and interested—i.e., a range of ingredients conducive to a more steady state of giving and receiving understanding and acceptance in the new entourage.

And—in passing, yet important—he was quick to start learning and speaking Dutch and it went very well indeed. His dark-sounding accent, reminiscent of the warm sound of a Schubert Lieder singer, became appreciated. The typical "Stroebe accent", either in Dutch or English, worked remarkably well.

Profiling the research institute

Developing a programme for research and training, embedding it in a newly designed infrastructure, and positioning this configuration in a broader scientific and political context: those are the essential aspects of implementing a concept such as P&H. How to understand this comprehensive process?

To simplify, it can be understood from at least two theoretical viewpoints. The first can be labelled as "new system creation", a perspective dating back as far as Howard Perlmutter's Tavistock Pamphlet from 1965. The second represents the knowledge base of "innovation and implementation theory", as inspired by group dynamics and organisation psychology. From the first perspective, the making of P&H would be seen basically as a design and construction process, hence the term "social architecture". It has socio-technological overtones, and examines the flow of (planned) activities leading—in identifiable stages—to an intended outcome.

In the second perspective, the emergence of P&H would be viewed in terms of the dynamics that lie behind the discernable, concrete implementation activities, on an individual as well as on an organisational level.

This last perspective offers two foci relevant for understanding the emergence of the new institute. The first focus is on the "organisational issues" that typically emerge within social units engaged in the implementation of a complex innovative idea—for example, the issue of defining the boundaries of P&H-to-be, and consequently the (re)articulation of the new substance for research and training. The other focus is on the emerging concerns (preoccupations) of individual staff members; i.e., personal concerns that gradually unfold when involved in an implementation effort—for example, the emerging concern over whether a person's professional competence will become fully accepted and acknowledged in the new programme, or a growing concern of individual members as to their expenditure of effort and commitment to a proposed research focus.

These notions help to chart the dynamics among people engaged in building up a new programme and institute. They serve to identify and address the emerging (organisational) issues and concomitant (individual) concerns, particularly in the formative stages of the enterprise. For example, staff members, steered by Wolfgang, attended an intense process of rendering the new system an identifiable domain with a specific mission—the issues of articulation and boundary definition (What's P&H all about? What do we stand for? What makes it special?). Also, early on, staff members became deeply concerned about the extent to which the arrival of P&H would affect their previous achievements and their future professional identity. Typical of this concern were the nagging questions centring around "membership", with identity-inclusion overtones (Is it worth my while investing in this new P&H venture? Would I qualify for membership, and at what price, given my research credentials?).

In particular, in attending to the issue of "boundary definition", Wolfgang showed a certain strictness that some initially felt as close to uncompromising. That perception particularly came up in situations where he, in turn, felt it necessary to defend and protect the intellectual integrity of programme and institute. He then showed a "friendly tenacity". But there were also the numerous situations in which concern-driven problems became settled by his pragmatic flexibility, intuition, and sense of humour. However, solid discussion was needed to win him over, notably when—in his view—a matter really mattered. Whatever the outcome, he stayed loyal.

An academic presentation mode

There were various options or vehicles to address the articulation issue. Here, one vehicle deserves mention: the so-called P&H Lecture Series. These lectures soon became a standard feature of the intellectual life of P&H. That certainly also applies to the international study conferences at Rolduc and the one-shot seminars. At regular intervals, renowned scholars were invited for scientific presentations under the auspices of P&H. Undoubtedly, this series and the conferences contributed to furthering the scientific articulation of the P&H domain.

How could that have happened? First, over time and taken together, the lectures presented an "orchestrated range" of research themes, a chosen number of substantive topics that, in effect, helped to delineate the domain. That is, the invited speakers put their themes on the P&H agenda, thus reinforcing existing items and underscoring potential new ones. Second, the Lecture Series (and specifically the international conferences) enabled P&H to enlarge and improve its network with renowned researchers, who in turn could lend their weight to the growing stature of P&H.

Wolfgang's efforts and insistence on high-quality standards made the series and the conferences a great success. They became a powerful vehicle for articulating the domain, in addition to an important concept paper written early on in the process. Wolfgang's use of theoretical presentations and study conferences, in effect, suggested an "academic presentation mode", a mode that implied public debate and explicit linkage to the external research worlds of relevance to P&H's developing identity.

This "academic mode" characterised Wolfgang Stroebe's determination to enhance conceptual cohesion among colleagues and to achieve high standards and stature for the new venture.

Lizet Hoekert
Office Manager Research Institute for Psychology & Health, Utrecht University, The Netherlands

Wolfgang came to the Netherlands in 1992. He had not originally planned to move countries at all, but he let himself be persuaded. In an interview, he said: "In Germany, I knew precisely on what topics I would have to lecture right up until the day of my retirement and I even knew exactly where that would take place." So he left all that certainty and security behind him, to move to unpredictability in Utrecht, bringing his wife and daughter with him. He adjusted remarkably quickly to the completely different situation at Utrecht University and a new life in the Netherlands.

The Minister of Education had that year (1992) decided that research in specific areas should be packaged nationally, into research schools. In doing this, the minister hoped to increase efficiency and make research more competitive on an international level. Soon after Wolfgang's arrival in the Netherlands, the first tentative discussions took place about this development. Wolfgang was seen as the potential scientific director of the Research Institute for Psychology and Health to be instigated by the Royal Dutch Academy of Arts and Sciences (KNAW).

Wolfgang held his inaugural speech on 29 May 1994. Not long before this, he had developed heart problems and undergone a bypass operation. Two weeks after the operation he began to work on his inaugural speech. Wolfgang would have to stand for a whole hour, which appeared almost impossible, but it worked. The subject of his lecture was "The illusion of group effectiveness" (just at the time when researchers were being placed in groups in the sub-areas within the research schools!).

Writing the mission for the Research Institute was an extremely difficult task. Many drafts of the proposal were discussed by those involved, under the guiding influence of Rein van der Vegt. Wolfgang's focus was on the goals and objectives of the Research Institute. There was a lot to discuss: The place of fundamental research, titles of the sub-areas, key members or no key members, key publications or no key publications, the sensitive issue of relationships with the Faculty of Medicine, criteria for membership, and so on. All these discussions gave Wolfgang the opportunity to get to know not only his Utrecht colleagues but also many others across the country. Many evaluations took place on an internal level, until finally, having received a positive judgement from the board of directors of Utrecht University, it was forwarded to the KNAW on 24 January 1995. On 7 March 1995 a special meeting was held in de Hartenark in Bilthoven to celebrate the foundation of the institute: 71 members were present. The group photo made on that occasion will be preserved with great care.

In the spring of 1995 a delegation was called to the KNAW to answer critical questions concerning the weak representation in the institute on the part of the Faculty of Medicine and the overlap with other research institutes. These were tough meetings, following which the only optimistic person appeared to be the Rector, Prof. J. A. van Ginkel, who had accompanied Professors Bensing, Maes, and Stroebe, who represented the institute.

However, to everyone's delight, the institute was accredited by the KNAW on 21 June 1995. The Research Institute for Psychology & Health, known to all as "P&H", was born. Wolfgang put heart and soul into his function as scientific director for the following 5 years. Following the difficult realisation/ birth of P&H, Wolfgang's next task was to ensure that the rules and regulations of P&H were obeyed. Long-standing regulations had to change, such as those between PhD student and promoter. Also at this time there was expansion: Increasingly, other groups at other institutions joined the institute. P&H commenced with 61 members and 40 PhD students, covering three universities (Leiden, Tilburg, and Utrecht). After 5 years these numbers reached 102 and 71 respectively, covering eight universities and one national institute.

The early success of the meeting at de Hartenark was so great that it was decided to organise—in November 1995—the First Dutch Conference on Psychology and Health, in a beautiful old monastery in the south of the Netherlands, in a village called Rolduc. There were 200 participants from all over the world. Invited addresses were given by Professors Andrew Steptoe, Stanislav V. Kasl, Susan Folkman, and Howard Leventhal. In fact, Wolfgang (together with his colleagues, assistant director Dr Henk Schut and treasurer Dr Frank Jan van Dijk) organised two Rolduc conferences, in 1995 and 1998, putting enormous energy and enthusiasm into the preparations for each of these meetings. Keynote speakers were chosen with great care, and Wolfgang's reputation as a host spread rapidly. After the success of the first Rolduc meeting, he decided to invite the members of the Scientific Advice Committee to attend the second conference, so that they could gain an impression of the spirit of P&H and start their site visit at the conference, which they then continued in Utrecht. Both conferences received exceptionally high evaluations—except, notably, for one feature, the freezing cold in the corridors of the monastery. Since then, other conferences have regularly taken place, such that the Sixth Conference on Psychology and Health will be held in May 2006. Each time, the conference has followed the format laid down in the first conference in 1995, and each time, the evaluations have been remarkably positive.

The first 5 years of the institute's existence were undoubtedly the most difficult and arduous. At that time, major decisions had to be made, and strategies/policies established, with which Wolfgang's successor, Prof. Wilmar Schaufeli, could then proceed. Wolfgang resigned on the occasion of the re-accreditation by the KNAW in June 2000. Wilmar had the challenging task of retaining the excellent reputation of P&H. Wilmar wrote in 2000, in the annual report of the institute, that Wolfgang and Henk Schut, together with Frank Jan van Dijk, had formed the institute into the shape and form that it had taken by 2000: a vibrant, internationally oriented, high-quality research institute that offers a greatly appreciated training facility for young scientists who are interested in psychological health research. P&H is much indebted to Wolfgang.

A quite different characteristic should not go unmentioned: Wolfgang's hospitality is unbeatable. As all who know him also realise, gastronomy is close to Wolfgang's heart, even appearing in his metaphors describing work-related matters. In the foreword to the 1996 annual report, in writing about his P&H staff, Wolfgang noted: "However, as every cook knows, even the best ingredients are not guarantees for success." Thus, one always had to wait to see whether the cook was in good or poor form on any particular day. So, much care was always taken, for example, in choosing a restaurant for the scientific advisory committee to dine, or for guest professors who came to present lectures or give workshops. Likewise, minute attention was paid to placement of guests at table, on larger occasions. We repeatedly pencilled in names on small-scale table images, only to rub them out and re-place them somewhere more suitable. Similarly, around the preparations for the cere-monies surrounding the award of Honorary Doctorate to Professor Susan Folkman, Wolfgang showed enormous care and meticulous attention to detail. No one in our Faculty comes anywhere near to this level of perfection on such matters.

I have very much appreciated working with Wolfgang, particularly his warm-heartedness, the care and concern that he always showed with respect to any P&H activity, the fact that, even when he was no longer my boss, he would drop by my office or stop in the corridor to chat, and his sense of humour. So I will miss him. A time will come to an end that cannot in any sense be brought back—indeed, it would be hopeless to try.

Author index

Subject index

Note: Page numbers in *italics* refer to figures; those in **bold** refer to tables.